Hangman's Call:

The Executions and Lynchings of Coos County, Oregon 1854 -1925

By Andie E. Jensen

Cover photo: Sheriff W.W. Gage – *Courtesy of Denise Sproed Merritt*

LAWMAN PUBLISHING
1381 Central Avenue, Coos Bay, Oregon 97420
Lawman_Publishing@verizon.net

ISBN: 978-0-9819363-1-4

Printed by Wegferds Printing & Publications | North Bend, Oregon
Indexing by Katherine Hodgin - Apropos Indexes | Coos Bay, Oregon
Cover Concept - Karen Wegfahrt

Printed in the U.S.A.

CONTENTS

FIGURES

FOREWARD

Over coffee in the Empire district of Coos Bay, I chatted recently with Andie Jensen about his book on ultimate justice on Oregon's coastal frontier. The courthouse, jail and sometimes the scaffold were only a few blocks from our table at Java Jones Coffeehouse.

Perched on a bluff overlooking the bay and the business district on wharves below, the county buildings were in the residential section of Empire City, the first settlement in Coos County. As you'll read in this landmark book, one Native American and three white men were tried and hung for murder in Empire. In 1896, after the mammoth steam-powered sawmill had closed permanently and the population of the town had dwindled from 600 to less than 200, voters decided to move the county seat to Coquille.

Andie moved to Coos Bay from Northern California in August of 2007 after nearly 20 years' experience in law enforcement. As a police officer, he had investigated many homicide cases. After graduating in 1975 from the Law Enforcement Academy at Butte Community College in Oroville, he joined the Glenn County Constables Office for the Orland Judicial District as a deputy constable. Next he was hired by the Biggs Police Department as a patrolman and finally by the Willits Police Department as a police officer. He worked there 16 years serving as a crime scene investigator, field-training officer and as member of the Mendocino County-Wide Narcotics Task Force. Promoting to the position of sergeant, Andie was in charge of patrol shifts, the training of new and experienced officers, and administrative functions of the department. In 1994, he received a medical retirement.

While in law enforcement, Andie wrote crime-related articles for local newspapers, the *California Narcotic Officer* and the *PORAC Law Enforcement News*, published by the Peace Officers Research Association of California. He plans to write more books on law enforcement in Southwestern Oregon and his next book will cover the history of the Empire, Marshfield, and Eastside Police Departments. Impressed by his meticulous research, I am amazed on how much Andie has learned about our history in such a short time. I highly recommend his book, *Hangman's Call: The Executions and Lynchings of Coos County Oregon (1854-1925).*

Frank Walsh
Empire Historian

PREFACE

Research of existing documentation of historical events can greatly help to dispel existing myths, misconceptions, and even prior published stories full of inaccurate accounts of these historical events. Perhaps the mere factual recording of events can help a community understand and recover from a perceived "black eye" held by the community for events which occurred in their past. This is part of the reason Hangman's Call: The Executions and Lynchings of Coos County Oregon (1854-1925) was written. Furthermore, it is important to understand surrounding events that helped mold the course of actions leading to the historical accounts of the hangings, which occurred. Perhaps we can even give a moment of pause to acknowledge the victims of these violent crimes, which follow.

The reporting of the first hangings occurring in the county we must face the question of legality. Were those hanged victims of the "Lynch Law" of the time? Perpetrated by a Vigilance Committee, or were they hanged in an attempt to adhere to the judicial system of the American society of the time? Existing evidence does not provide a solid conclusion. Only speculation based on various confirmed historical facts, coupled with statements of the time can lead to a plausible conclusion. However, your determination will rest upon your interpretations of the facts presented and how you perceive crime and punishment.

Additionally, throughout the history of our society we are often times drawn to the darker, more sinister side of humanity. We are driven to see, yet we are appalled by the carnage we find occurring around us. We want to know how and why the tragedy of murder is a never-ending part of humanity and continues within a civilized modern society. We struggle with the polarizing religious precepts of "an eye of an eye" and "thou shalt not kill." We want justice, yet struggle with the appropriate form of punishment.

Whether their fate was calculated and planned or an act of irrational passion spurred in the heat of the moment, it is important to provide acknowledgement of those who were needlessly slain. As much as possible information has been included about the slain victims. I question, why we know more about a killer than their victim? Thus, it is paramount to remember those victims overlooked and often times forgotten as well as the lives of those affected and shattered beyond the immediate victim and perpetrator. Family members on both sides take a toll based on the actions of one or more individuals. Even the communities, the social fabric, share the loss. For years after many, suffer from the actions of those committing crime against humankind and society. Therefore, it is the memory of these victims that we must remember and show compassion in rendering our decisions of innocence, guilt, and even punishment.

The documentation of these hangings was gathered from a review of court files, other noted writings, and the medium of newspapers published at the time of each murder. By proving the unedited and full news accounts of the time, you are afforded the opportunity to experience the various reporting and writing styles of the day. Furthermore, with supporting documents you will be able to seek out the kernels of truth layered within the testimony of the witnesses and other facts that may be incorporated within the events. Thus, to a certain extent the information will allow you to become an investigator of truth to determine if you, based on the information supplied, render the same fate to the perpetrator. Furthermore, this writing provides the laws in effect for the State of Oregon regarding murder in the first degree and a brief introduction to hangings, inclusive of the methods and medical processes to the body.

Finally, human nature is such that we relish the opportunity to sharply examine what others do, especially in matters of crime and punishment. We incorporate what we know based upon our education, life experiences, social psyche, and much more to render our decisions. Thus, the opinions regarding the validity of capital punishment, as an effective deterrent to crime, as a justified and effective method of punishment, rests solely with you the reader. This text was not written as a commentary on capital punishment, only as an accurate historical account of the executions and lynchings of Coos County Oregon. The stance of capital punishment rests within the hearts and minds of each individual and is very much like crime itself - a battle that will never be won.

Now presented are seven incidents of hangings which occurred within Coos County Oregon, one convicted murderer who cheated the hangman's noose having died in jail prior to his walk to the gallows, and three convicted murderers who were executed for the county at the state penitentiary in Salem. Some hangings were legal and some were not.

ACKNOWLEDGMENTS

Undertaking a project of this nature could not have been accomplished without the involvement of many people. Together they share a dedication and passion to preserve the history, along with striving to provide a truthful reflection of our great State of Oregon; the County of Coos; and each municipality and community, past and present. Each person has garnered expertise in specific areas of the county history, which have helped tremendously to present a complete picture within these snapshots of time relating to the executions and lynchings of Coos County Oregon between 1854 and 1925.

I thank the following for their assistance:

Alda Hofferber; Alonzo Tucker Playwright and Historian
Andy Jackson; Sheriff, Coos County Sheriff's Office
Becky Soules; Coordinator of Volunteer Activities at the Marshfield Pioneer Cemetery
Boyd Stone; Coos County Historian
Christine Zanni; Clerk, Coos County Sheriff's Office
Dolores Knight; Chief Reference Librarian Coos Bay Public Library and the Entire Library Staff
Denise Sproed Merritt, Great-great granddaughter of Sheriff William Washington Gage
Frank Walsh; Empire City Historian
Gregory W. Rieskamp; Information Support Manager, Oregon Department of Corrections
Hannah Contino; Front Desk Assistant, Coos Historical & Maritime Museum
Judy Knox; Executive Director, Bandon Historical Society Museum
Marilee Miller, Coos County Historian
Nancy Barkwell; Records Clerk, Coos County Courts
Robyn Greenlund; Coos County Historian
Susan Zick, Great-granddaughter of L.W. and Jessie Peare
Terri L. Turi; Coos County Clerk, and her entire staff

To those who I may have forgotten, past Historians and preservers of the truth, I give thanks.

The history of Coos County is not limited to just crime and punishment. To explore the rich history of Coos County the following museums eagerly await those with a desire to learn more. Many fine exhibits are located within each museum. Staff members and volunteers are eager to serve. More information can be obtained from their websites.

Bandon Historical Society Museum: www.bandonhisotoricalmuseum.org
Coos Art Museum: www.coosart.org
Coos County Fairgrounds Museum: fgm.sworegon.org
Coos Historical & Maritime Museum: www.cooshistory.org
Coquille Valley Museum: www.coquillevalley.org

Those without websites include the Coos County Logging Museum, Myrtle Point and Marshfield Sun Printing, Coos Bay. More information about these museums can be accessed from the Oregon Coast portion of the Oregon Museum Association website at www.oregonmuseums.org

One of the greatest historical treasures of Coos County is the museum of the Coos, Lower Umpqua & Siuslaw Indians located at 1245 Fulton Avenue, Coos Bay. At the museum, we are taken back in time to witness the pristine land and culture, which existed for centuries before the colonization of the Euro-American settlers. We can explore and marvel how the Native American were bonded with Mother Nature through the artifacts and we can cherish the language using a kiosk. A small sampling of the culture can be obtained through the Tribes website at www.ctclusi.org.

A donation of $1 from the sale of each book will be applied to benefit the Hollering Place project and to provide historical or informational displays there and at other sites of historical significance throughout the Empire District of Coos Bay on the Southern Oregon coast. The Hollering Place project is part of a downtown revitalization plan encompassing the pier and old town Empire which was the first seat of Coos County and site of the original Native American villages of the Waikdee, Hanistitch, Intesitch, and Walitch which were all located along the shore of the present day Empire. For more information about the Hollering Place and Empire, please visit www.thehholleringplace.com

CHAPTER 1

THE POLITICS OF HANGING

Hangings have existed for centuries as a legal, non-legal, and self-imposed form of punishment. America, having derived its judicial system from England, adopted hanging as the form of capital punishment for the United States. Thus, during Oregon's Territorial Government and subsequent Statehood, up to 1931, executions were exclusively performed by hanging. In the early years, responsibility of executions rested with local county jurisdictions and the actual task relegated to the elected sheriff. During the time of hangings some considered the hanging as an "art" whereas, others considered it a social event where the whole community could gather to witness the execution.

With the passage of time, others considered hanging grossly inhuman due to botched executions consisting of slow strangulations or decapitations occurring throughout the country. Additionally, it was alleged by some, that as the nation developed and grew the moral and social fabric became more "civilized" in their view of crime and punishment. This view of capital punishment was seen during America's Progressive Era period of reform beginning in the 1890's continued through the 1920's. It was during this period many changes in the social fabric of the nation occurred. The period, characterized, in part, by an ideology in the belief of humankind's ability to improve the conditions of life coupled with an obligation to intervene in social affairs.

It was during this Era of social reform that Oregon Democratic Governor Oswald West served the state. Taking office in 1911, West became the fourteenth governor of Oregon and sought only one term. However, during his term women's suffrage, various workers rights laws and prohibition all came into effect. West was also anti-capital punishment. In the Governors Inaugural Message to the Twenty-Sixth Legislative Assembly Regular Session of 1911 West had the following to say about capital punishment:

> Capital punishment should be abolished, in my opinion, in this State. The system of paying for a life with a life is, in my belief, merely a relic of that ancient and barbarous doctrine of "an eye for an eye and a tooth for a tooth."
>
> It is a fact, undisputed by the judicial history of this or any other State that the average jury shies at a verdict involving the sacrifice of human life. Murder, from the very nature of the crime, must be proven, to a great or less degree, by circumstantial evidence, and the average man, sitting as a juror, hesitates before casting his vote to deprive a fellow being, no matter how degraded his condition, of his life. The result of this is the hung jury, the failure to convict, and oftentimes, the cheating of justice, all of which means lessened safety to society in general and an increased drain upon the purses of the taxpayers of the State.
>
> The report of the Superintendent of the Penitentiary records 18 cases of capital punishment in the last seven and one-half years, the greatest number ever executed in this State during a similar period. This, in my opinion, bears out the argument that the desperate criminal, relying on the reluctance of the average juror and the caution of the court, in the imposition of the capital sentence, is more willing to take a gambler's chance with death for the furtherance of his criminal object, than he would be to face the greater certainty of a life spent behind the bars.
>
> Believing as I do, I therefore recommend to you, gentlemen, that you take steps to do away with capital punishment in this State. But in this connection I desire to urge that special and particular attention be paid to the restriction of the pardoning power for such cases. I hold that a sentence to life imprisonment for murder should mean what it says, unless post-trial evidence should bring to light some glaring in justice or very potent reason for change, and I contend that the substitution of life imprisonment for capital punishment should carry with it such safeguards as would insure in all cases that full justice be satisfied.
>
> Men sentenced to the penitentiary are, under the present system, delivered at the prison gates by the sheriff of the county in which conviction was had. This is a wasteful, extravagant, and unscientific method and should be discontinued in the interest of economy and for the benefit of the taxpayers of the State. I suggest, therefore, that provision be made for the transportation of convicts from their place of conviction to the penitentiary by prison guards. This system has been found to be most satisfactory in the

> transportation of the insane, and after several years of trial by the asylum management has been found to be more economical and more desirable in many ways than the old method.[1]

Despite Governor West's strong opposition to capital punishment nine Oregon convicted murderers met their fate at the state gallows during his term of office. One of those men was Coos county convicted murderer Frank Garrison, who on December 13, 1912 was executed by hanging along with three other convicted murderers.

After Garrison's execution, there was a seesaw affect as to the will of the citizens of Oregon regarding the laws relating to capital punishment. It was during this period of flux that two additional Coos county convicted murderers were executed at the state gallows on behalf of the county. Those two men, L.W. Peare and Arthur Covell were executed on May 22, 1925. For Coos County, hanging, as a form of punishment ended with these two executions. In fact, the hangings of 1925 were the last anyone from Coos county was executed.

For the State of Oregon, between 1904 and 1914, 24 men were executed by hanging at the State Penitentiary in Salem. November 5, 1920, marked the first hanging since the re-enactment of the death penalty. Fifteen additional hangings followed with the last occurring on October 30, 1931.[2] The total number of hangings prior to 1903 remained in the records of each county. However, according to the website, *Before the Needle,* Oregon executed 102 men by hanging, 12 of which were Native American.[3] Neither "Indian Pete" nor his associates were on that list. Carl Albrecht was also missing from this list. With this in mind, the actual number of hangings may remain unknown.

CHAPTER 2

LAW OF THE LAND

Within the Territory and later the State of Oregon, between 1854 and 1903, the authority to carry out executions was vested solely to the county sheriff. *The Revised Statutes of the Territory of Oregon*, passed January 31, 1854, dictated the authority of hanging as the punishment for murder in the first degree. Additionally, the statutes provided the procedure in which the executions were to be conducted.

Below are the appropriate sections of the Statute, which apply to murder in the first degree, and the execution of punishment for said murder conviction.

> **Chapter III OFFENCES AGAINST LIVES AND PERSONS OF INDIVIDUALS**
> **Section 1** As to what constitutes murder in the first degree;
> If any person shall purposely, and of deliberate and premeditated malice, or in the perpetration, or attempt to perpetrate any rape, arson, robbery or burglary, kill another, every such person shall be deemed guilty of murder in the first degree, and upon conviction thereof, shall suffer death.
>
> **CHAPTER XXXIII JUDGEMENT IN CRIMINAL CASES, AND THE EXECUTION THEROF**
> **Section 7** Death warrant, how signed and attested: what to contain;
> When judgment of death is rendered, a warrant, signed by the judge, and attested by the clerk under the seal of the court, shall be drawn and delivered to the sheriff; it shall state the conviction and judgment, and appoint a day in which the judgment shall be executed, which shall not be less than thirty days nor more than sixty days from the time of judgment.
>
> **Section 8** Punishment of death, how and by whom inflicted;
> The mode of inflicting punishment of death in all cases under this act, shall be by hanging by the neck until the person be dead; and the sheriff, and in the case of his death, inability, or absence, the coroner of the county in which sentence of death shall have been pronounced, by virtue of this act, shall the executioner; except in cases where a change of venue has been taken, in which case, the prisoner shall be sent back and executed in the county in which the prosecution originated.
>
> **Section 9** Sheriff's warrant, &c., where to be filed, clerk to subjoin abstract, &c;
> The sheriff shall return and file with the clerk the warrant, with a statement of his doings thereon, and the clerk shall subjoin a brief abstract of such statement to the record of conviction and sentence.

Prior to Oregon's Statehood on February 14, 1859, Matthew Deady served as an associate judge of the Territorial Supreme Court from 1853 to 1859. After which Deady was appointed to serve as a U.S. District Judge for the District of Oregon. In 1862, Deady received the appointment of code commissioner whereupon he prepared the Code of Civil Procedure, an Incorporation Act, Code of Criminal Procedure, Penal Code, and Justice's Code, all of which were adopted in 1864. Deady was later asked to publish all the laws and codes in force in Oregon, which became the General Laws of Oregon. Deady's work was compiled and annotated in 1866. The laws regarding first-degree murder remained the same, inclusive of the punishment.

In an effort to shield the public from the execution, the Oregon State Legislature passed a statutory law in 1874. The law, required executions to occur within the enclosure of the jail or jail yard and in the presence of twelve bona fide electors of the county who were selected by the county sheriff.[4] However, in Coos County the enclosure of the jail yard did not conceal the execution from the public.

Within the time of 1854 and 1903, four men were sentenced to execution by hanging via a jury trial within Coos County. Three were executed at the gallows located at the county courthouse in Empire City and one cheated the hangman's noose by dying in jail while awaiting his execution. Additionally there were four or five hangings of Native Americans within Coos County. One Native known only as "Indian Pete," was executed in Empire City at what has been historically referred to as the "hanging tree." According to research it is not know if the execution of "Indian Pete" was legal or not. However, the remaining three or four Native American hangings were probably not legal executions by the standards of statutory laws. Depending on the versions reported two or three Natives were hanged in Randolph, and one or two were hanged in Port Orford during the time it was part of Coos County.

In 1903 the Oregon Legislature, in order to restrict public attendance at executions, amended the law to require executions be carried out at the Oregon State Penitentiary in Salem. Oregon voters, in 1914, by way of a constitutional amendment, repealed the death penalty with 50.04 percent of the vote. The amendment became Article I, 36 of the Oregon Constitution. The issue of capital punishment was not yet moot in the State of Oregon. In 1920, the voters of Oregon restored the death penalty by repealing Article I, 36 whereupon Article I, 37-38 was approved. The move to restore capital punishment was carried by 56 percent of the voter. With capital punishment, back hanging was still the method to be used. At the penitentiary three convicted murders where executed for the County of Coos. One was executed in 1915 whereas the other two men were executed in 1925.

However, there was another law of the land, which extended outside the judicial system. Operating outside the statutory laws, Vigilance Committees began to immerge during the 19th century in the United States. Consisting of a group of private citizens who organized themselves for self-protection the Vigilance Committees were established in areas where there was no local law enforcement, or where the local government was ineffectual, corrupt, or unpopular. The groups, despite generally held opinions, were not mobs of unorganized individuals bent on revenge of the moment, but usually well organized, with charters defining their purposes and official membership lists. Some were public; however, many were secret. In the newly settled areas, vigilance committees provided security and in the west, as governmental jurisdiction achieved the degree that courts could dispense justice, the citizens abandoned the committees.[5]

The use of a Vigilance Committee may have been a part of "justice" during the formative years of Coos County by playing a role in the hanging of the Native Americans. Printed in the August 16, 1887 issue of the *Coquille City Herald* a lengthy article titled: **Lynch Law** addressed the use of the Lynch Law and Vigilance Committees. Included in the articles were the following statements:

> The Vigilance Committee was, indeed, part and parcel of the progress of the Pacific States and Territories and, while there can be no doubt that it often led to great abuses, it is not less certain that it was a heroic remedy for a far more wasting disease. ... The Vigilance Committee purged the community of its worst elements, and when law and order had been restored it passed out of sight.

The Lynch Law discussed in the article was not isolated to Oregon. Lynch Law was prevalent throughout the Nation for many years to follow. Lynch Law, defined by the *Virginia Lancet*, "as known by that appellation, had its origin in 1780 in a combination of citizens of Pittsylvania County, Virginia, entered into for the purpose of suppressing a trained band of horsethieves and counterfeiters whose well concocted schemes had bidden defiance to the ordinary laws of the land, and whose success encouraged and emboldened them in their outrages upon the community. Col. Wm. Lynch drafted the constitution for this combination of citizens, and hence 'Lynch Law' has ever since been the name given to the summary infliction of punishment by private and unauthorized citizens."[6] Another version of the term Lynch Law originated during the American Revolution when Charles Lynch, a Virginia justice of the peace, ordered extralegal punishment for Tory acts.[7]

The Archives at Tuskegee Institute, February 1979, reported state-by-state statistics regarding documented cases of lynching. The report indicated, for the state of Oregon, there were 20 whites lynched and one African American lynched.[8] No records are known documenting the number of Native American's who were executed under the justification of the "Lynch Law" or by acts of out-and-out lynching. The Tuskegee Institute opened July 4, 1881 in Tuskegee, Alabama as initially a school for training teacher. The school was devoted to educating the illiterate freed slaves of the civil War. Today the institute, a private school, attained University status in 1985, thus evolving to Tuskegee University.

In conjunction with the hangings of the Native Americans, another dark moment of Coos county history involved the lynching, by an unruly mob, in 1902 within the city of Marshfield.

CHAPTER 3

A BRIEF EDUCATION OF HANGING

To better understand hanging as a method of execution some basic information is provided. Methods, tools of the trade, and results are briefly presented.

How is that Done? - Methods of Hanging

The Short drop: Up to the 1850's, most hangings were carried out with little or no drop. Often the distance was just one to two feet such as being hanged from a tree after being released off the back of a cart, ladder, or horse. This normally resulted in death by either strangulation or Carotid or Vagal reflex. Thus, pressure on the Carotid artery and or Vagal nerve which causes very rapid unconsciousness and cardiac arrest.

The Standard drop: A standard drop of around four to five feet, which was used in many hangings during the later part of the 19th century and into the early 20th century. A drop of this distance was rarely sufficient to break the prisoner's neck. Hence, the prisoner died by strangulation. In many cases, the prisoner would be knocked unconscious by the force of the drop and the impact of the knot against the side of the neck.

The Long drop: This form of hanging was copied from England and used in the 20th century by some states. The procedure involved dropping the prisoner an exact measured length that was calculated according to their weight and could be modified to take into account the prisoner's physique. Thus, the force of the drop, combined with the position of the knot below their left ear, was designed to break the prisoner's neck causing instant unconsciousness, followed by rapid death. Even a "Table of Drops" was developed and published in a manual by the United States Army. The prisoner is weighed prior to execution and their weight in pounds, less an allowance of 14 pounds for the head, divided into 1020 to arrive at a drop in feet. It takes between half and three quarters of a second for the prisoner to reach the bottom of the drop, after the trap is sprung.

The Sudden suspension: Instead of the conventional gallows that dropped the prisoner through a trap door, some states used a method where weights connected to the rope jerked the prisoner upwards when the weights were released by the hangman. From 1894, it had been operated by buckshot, which was released by the weight of the prisoner standing on the trap. The shot ran down a chute until there was sufficient weight of shot to trigger the mechanism which then released the weight and shot the prisoner six feet into the air.

Tools of the Trade

The Gallows: Many different patterns of gallows have been used over the last 400 years. In some cases, they were built specially for one execution and never used again. This was the case for the three judicial executions, which occurred in Empire City. A tree was the earliest form of gallows, with a prisoner being either hauled up manually by the hangman or turned off from a ladder, horse or the back of a cart.

In many states, the gallows consisted of two stout uprights about 18-20 feet high joined at the top by a beam, often cross-braced to them. At about 10 feet from the ground was the platform, reached by steps and with the trap set into the middle of it. Single leaf traps were the most common and were released by a variety of mechanisms, usually operated by a lever on the top of the platform or by cords. Normally there was a catch to stop the trap door bouncing back and hitting the prisoner. In some cases, sand bags were connected to the door for this purpose.

The Noose: The coiled noose was used in most states up to abolition of hanging. Normally formed from Manila hemp rope the noose consisted of 5 to 13 coils. These coils slid down the rope delivering a heavy blow to the side of the neck, hopefully rendering the prisoner unconscious.

The modern noose is prepared in accordance with a procedure laid down in the United States Army Manual. The noose was formed from 30 feet of 3/4" to 1" diameter rope which was boiled to take out stretch and any tendency to coil. The rope was formed into six coils and then waxed, soaped or greased to ensure that the knot slides easily. The knot was placed beneath the prisoner's left ear with the noose drawn tight. It was realized that it was necessary to take out the stretch from the rope to prevent the prisoner bouncing up again in the trap, as often happened in earlier times. In some states, this was done by dropping a bag of sand of approximately the same weight as the prisoner and leaving, it suspended for some hours prior to the execution.

The Hood: It became common practice in later times to hood the prisoner on the gallows. The hood was either white, or more commonly black. During the 19th and 20th centuries the hood served to prevent the prisoner from seeing the hangman pulling the lever and moving at the crucial moment. In addition, the hood was used to prevent the witnesses from seeing the prisoner's face afterwards. The prisoners face tended not to be a pretty sight especially if the person died by strangulation. Some states used a long hood, which extended well down onto the prisoner's chest while others used a short one, which just covered the face. It was normal to put the noose on after the hood so that the material of the hood reduced rope burn.

What the Doctor Says - The Medical effects of hanging

The cause of death in hanging depends on the conditions related to the event. Typically, the hanging will cause one or more of the following medical conditions:

Closure of the carotid arteries causing cerebral ischemia: Compromise of the cerebral blood flow would occur by obstruction of the carotid arteries, even though the obstruction required far more force than the obstruction of jugular veins. Only seven foot-pounds of pressure would be enough to constrict the carotid arteries to the point of rapid unconsciousness. When death occurred through carotid artery obstruction or cervical fracture, the face would typically be pale in color and not show petechiae. Many reports and pictures exist of actual short-drop hangings, which seem to show the person died quickly, whereas others indicated a slow and agonizing death by strangulation. When cerebral circulation was severely compromised by any mechanism, arterial or venous, death results within four or more minutes from cerebral hypoxia, although the heart continued to beat for some period after the brain could no longer be resuscitated.

Closure of the jugular veins: In the absence of fracture and dislocation, occlusion of blood vessels became the major cause of death, rather than asphyxiation. Obstruction of venous drainage of the brain via occlusion of the internal jugular veins lead to cerebral edema and then cerebral ischemia. The face would typically become engorged and cyanotic, the turning blue through lack of oxygen. There would be classic sign of strangulation; petechiae, little blood marks on the face and in the eyes from burst blood capillaries. The tongue may have protruded. Induced carotid reflex, which reduced heartbeat when the pressure in the carotid arteries was high, caused cardiac arrest. Death also resulted from sudden stoppage of the heart due to pressure on the carotid arteries, which could cause a lethal carotid sinus reflex, or from vagal reflex, which caused unconsciousness quickly. This form of hanging was typical in suicides and quite normal for the inquest to find the victim having died from heart failure rather than strangulation.

Breaking the neck causing traumatic spinal cord injury: When released from a relatively high distance ones death was usually caused by the severing of the spinal cord. Severing was normally located between C1 and C2. The act may have been functional decapitation. High cervical fractures frequently occurred during judicial hangings. In fact the C1-C2 fracture has been called the "Hangman's fracture" in medicine, even when it occurred in other circumstances. Usually, accidental C1-C2 fracture victims did not immediately become unconscious; instead, death occurs after some minutes, due to strangulation. Another process that has been suggested is carotid sinus reflex death. By this theory, the mechanical stimulation of the carotid sinus in the neck induced terminal cardiac arrest.

Closure of the airway: Hanging with no or insufficient drop typically produced death by strangulation due to the weight of the person's body pulling down on the noose, thereby causing a tightening and constriction of the trachea and applied pressure to the large blood vessels in the neck. The condemned person usually struggled for some time after suspension, resulting from the physical pain caused by the noose. It could have taken up to three minutes for the person to lapse into unconsciousness in this form of hanging. Arteries go outside the fourth vertebrae instead of inside it, which subjects them to blockage if the pressure on the neck was high enough. Usually about 40 to 50 pounds for a normal person could cause the loss of consciousness in less than 15 seconds.

The Need to See - How the executed person is viewed

During suspension, once the prisoner lapsed into unconsciousness, rippling movements of the body and limbs may have occurred for a period. The rippling movement was usually attributed to nervous and muscular reflexes. The face could have become engorged and cyanosed; the process of turning blue through a lack of oxygen, and the tongue may protrude.

There is a popular myth about sexual stimulation of hanged men, because of the apparent erection some exhibited. This death erection effect was attributed to gravity causing the blood to settle in the legs and lower torso, thereby engorging the penis.

When is the executed person dead?

The time of death in such cases is a matter of convention. In judicial hangings, death was pronounced at the time of cardiac arrest, occurring at times from several minutes up to 15 minutes or longer after hanging. Whole body death resulted usually within less than 20 minutes. In Britain, it was normal to leave the body suspended for an hour to ensure death. Some witnesses have stated that upon the jerk of the rope and the snapping of the neck the person was dead.

The executed person after death

After death, the body typically showed marks of suspension including bruising and rope marks on the neck. Moreover, sphincters will relax simultaneously which caused urine and feces to be voided. In some cases, traces of semen have been noted due to the ejaculation while hanging. This form of asphyxia death is known, medically as anoxia, as the brain becomes starved of oxygen.

CHAPTER 4

THE EXECUTION SETTING OF EMPIRE CITY

The only remaining tangible piece of history for the original setting of the courthouse and jail is, in fact, the county jail. No longer used to incarcerate prisoners, along with those awaiting their execution, the old jail house was relocated and transformed into a family residence located on the south side of Lattin Avenue just off the Cape Arago Highway in Empire. Driving by the residence no one would suspect the rich crime related history this residence once contained.

Located within the *Journal of the County Court of Coose County - Board of Commissioners Coose County 1854 - 1859*[A] the records revealed the county did not have a jail until after July 13, 1859. During the meeting, Sheriff John McNamara was directed to "procure and fix up a building suitable for jail not to exceed $100." It is not known for sure where the building was located as some researchers believe the building was located on the mudflats where the rented court house was suppose to have been located. The March 1982 Coos County Historical Society Newsletter reported the courthouse was a log-slab cabin, which also housed the first jail.

A description of the jail was provided in *Coos County Courthouse 100 Years 1896 - 1996.*[9] The building, constructed in 1857, measured eighteen by twenty-four foot, and was a wood framed building. The walls, one foot thick, consisting of two layers of one by six inch planks laid side by side with the outside covered in rustic.[B] The jail and cell floor was constructed of a double thickness of half-inch plank with scantling between the two planks. Entering through the door, located in the center, was a three-foot six-inch wide corridor running the entire width of the building. The two front windows were six feet from the ground, which were protected by soft metal bars. The jail initially housed two wood cells constructed in the same manner as the outer walls. However, it was recorded that the left cells had two iron doors whereas the right cell had one iron door. Each cell had two twelve by eighteen inch windows about six feet from the ground secured with grated iron bars, a bed, a stove, and water closet which consisted of a hole that opened into a plain vault beneath the floor. Since there was, no ventilation for the water closet the stench became unbearable especially when the stove was used for heat.[10]

On October 30, 1894, the Coquille Valley Herald reported:

> The county jail at Empire City is now enclosed with a fence 12 feet high. This will shut off outside interference with the birds within, and make their security more probable.

It was not until March 1895 that the jail contained steel cells for housing the prisoners.

Figure 1: Coos County Jail, Empire City

Figure 2: Empire City Fort

[A] In the early years of the county the name was spelled Coose; however, it is not exactly known why the name was changed to Coos nor the exact year the "e" was dropped. Initially, entries were entered with both spellings, depending on who made the entries.

[B] Made of roughly dressed limbs or roots of trees.

In 1872, the first county owned courthouse was erected at a cost of $4,000. Located next to the courthouse was the residence of Judge Isaiah Hacker.[11] The county jail was placed on the north side of the courthouse.[12]

The site of the courthouse was originally reported to have been a crude fort. The unnamed fort consisted of a blockhouse, which was built within a stockade and a guardhouse. The stockade was reported to have been 50 by 100 feet and the blockhouse, 40 by 40 feet and built of hewn logs. The size of the guardhouse was unknown.[13] The fort was nothing resembling the forts thought of in the plains of America. The Fall-Winter 1997 issue of the Coos County Historical Society Newsletter provided the following insight about the fort:

> Conflict between Euroamericans and Indians in southwestern Oregon intensified by the early 1850s. As gold miners and homesteaders clashed with indigenous peoples in the Rogue River country, Coos settlers feared local uprisings. Expecting the Coos and Coquille tribes to join in the hostilities, they built a fort in 1854 in Empire City (now the Empire District of Coos Bay.) In addition, men from Port Orford arrived and organized "Captain Harris' Coos County Volunteers."
>
> Captain Harris donated land specifically to build the blockhouse. Under the Donation Land Act, he had claimed 1/2 section on the east side of lower Coos Bay. Filed in October 1853 at the government land office in Oregon City, #37 was the first land claim in Coos County.
>
> The men felled trees and placed the 15' long timbers upright in a 100' x 100' trench. Inside the stockade, a two-story blockhouse measured 30' x 30'. Its entrance faced east. A guardhouse was manned 24 hours a day. Settlers stored provisions and cattle feed in the 8' high first story. The 10' high second story had one large room which projected beyond the lower floor by about 5'. Round openings in walls provided observation
>
> During the day women and children were permitted to remain in their homes; everyone took shelter in the fort at night. They used a ladder to reach the second story. It was drawn up at night.
>
> In the summer of 1856, Oregon's territorial governor discharged the Coos County volunteers when it became apparent that the local Indians were not going to war. Furthermore, by 1856 virtually all coastal and interior Indians had been removed to reservations. The Coos were relocated to the Umpqua Sub-Agency at the mouth of the Umpqua River, about 20 miles north of Coos Bay.
>
> The fort served as a livery stable for a number of years before being razed in the early 1870s.

Since the Court Journal records of the first jail in 1859, it could be assumed the fort may have served as the first jail which housed "Indian Pete" as well as the location of his execution.

Figure 3: View from the bay of the Court House and Jail (located left of Court House) Coos County Historical and Maritime Museum, CHMM 967-126G

CHAPTER 5

POWER OF THE PRESS

A LOOK AT THE LOCAL NEWPAPERS OF THE TIME

Newspapers of Coos County have evolved through many changes over the years. Some have joined the pages of the past, others have merged with other newspapers, and others have endured and are still in publication to this day. Each newspaper provided a different glimpse of historical context with a splash of political insight. Thus, each possessed their own unique flavor of reporting which is why it was important to include whole articles in reporting the history of the hangings. As with an eyewitness, newspapers were subject to erroneous reporting of names and supporting facts. Thus, one must balance the facts based upon other newspaper sources and court documents when available. Furthermore, the newspaper has always possessed the power to form and shape public opinion involving the events of our daily lives. Many events of our history have been shaped by the media playing a key role to mold the perceptions of the citizenry. The media has always held the power to garner sympathy or to convict someone in the court of public opinion. Within *A Century of Coos and Curry,* J.E. Norton wrote:

> "PAPERS OF THE PERIOD covering the 1870's and through the 1890's were usually edited by men whose main object was a medium for the expression of ideas and opinions, and they had opinions and expressed them freely. In many cases, the effect this might have on the financial success of the enterprise made little difference to the editor. Politics was the issue upon which many papers and their editors starved, bled, and died."[14]

With this in mind a snippet of history of each newspaper resourced is presented.

Bandon Recorder: The first newspaper of Bandon, the *Bandon Recorder,* was owned by P.O. Chilstrom and J.M. Upton. First published November 10, 1996 the newspaper endured several changes in ownership with the *Bandon Recorder* ending publications on June 27, 1916.

Coos Bay Harbor: Established in 1905 by C.M. Sain and C.H. Keith the Harbor was the Republican newspaper for North Bend. Two years later the paper was sold. One of the buyers, Edgar McDaniel, served as editor and publisher until 1945 when he was forced to sell due to declining health.

Coos Bay News: Coos County's first weekly newspaper, published Wednesdays, provided early Oregon history and folklore along with the reporting of national and local news. Beginning in 1873 the newspaper was originally located in Empire City and relocated to Marshfield in 1885. The first publisher and owner was Thomas G. Owen. Owen, before relocating to Coos County served in the Confederate Missouri Cavalry from 1861 to 1865 In April of 1873. Owen was appointed Sheriff where he served until July 1874. Owen later became a lawyer. Jacob M. Siglin was the first editor. Siglin was a popular orator and attorney. Siglin's brother Zachery was the first Marshal of Marshfield, constable and later sheriff of Coos County. In 1877, Owen sold the newspaper to G.A. "Gus" Bennett who carried the banner of the Democratic Party and ran the paper until 1922 when it was destroyed by fire.

Coos Bay Times: With a desire for a stronger newspaper in the Bay area, several businessmen organized the Coos Bay Publishing Company in 1906. With a board of directors an editor and manager was hired. Within a year, Michael C. Maloney was hired as editor and his brother Dan E. was city editor and later manager. Michael was considered a forceful writer having worked as an editorial writer for the New York Word and Chicago Tribune. Maloney was so forceful he faced several lawsuits for libel.

Coquille City Herald: The first newspaper of the Coquille Valley was edited and published by its owner John A. Dean on a weekly basis. Initially an independent paper the Herald aligned with the growing Peoples Party; however, returned as an independent paper. In 1881, Dean was joined by his brother D.F. Dean. Then in 1890, John Dean sold his interest to J.S. McEwen who was a long-time printer and editor. In 1892, McEwen was elected represented the county in the state Legislature. With McEwen on board the paper aligned with the Populist Party and ran as an extremely patriotic newspaper. In 1901, McEwen sold out leaving D.F. Dean the sole owner until 1912. Dean sold the Herald to Lew A. Cates who in turn sold the Herald to H.W. Young in 1914. Young, owner of the Coquille Valley Sentinel merged the Herald with the Sentinel in 1917.

Coquille Valley Sentinel: Orvil Dodge began the Sentinel in 1905 as an independent newspaper. As owner, Dodge served as the editor and publisher until 1909 when he sold the paper to J.C. Savage. Savage in turn sold half interest of the Sentinel to Lew A. Cates in 1913. The history of the Sentinel continues to this day.

Marshfield Sun: Owned and operated by Jesse Luse. The Sun operated under his control from 1891 until his death in 1944. Aligned with the People's Party, Luse maintained a strong political tone in his paper. Luse was not afraid to report about the cities vice district, KKK activities, or the deeds of the prominent citizenry. The Sun building, a historic landmark, is now a summertime museum operated by William and Margret Luse, the son and daughter of Jesse.

Marshfield Weekly Coast Mail: Beginning 1878 the Coast Mail, located in Marshfield, was a weekly newspaper published on Saturdays, by a man named Webster. In 1879, Isaiah Hacker became a co-owner. Hacker was a political machine serving two terms as sheriff, State Legislator, Coos County Superintendent of Schools, Judge, City Recorder in Marshfield, Collector of Customs at the Port of Coos Bay, and again served as sheriff. Hacker also established an impressive business career. Freeman Lockhart was also a part of the Coast Mail. Lockhart was also a political machine having served as Justice of the Peace in Empire, County School Superintendent, County Clerk, and State Legislator. In 1884 John, A. Gray, an attorney and public orator, became editor until his death1896. Two more editors followed until the paper was sold to the Coos Bay Publishing Company in 1906.

Myrtle Point Enterprise: First published by W.C. Conner on November 16, 1895. The paper was popular and flourished with a philosophy of progressive and independent reporting to rival any publication in the state. In December 1917, the name was changed to the Southern Coos County American then changed to the Myrtle Point Herald on March 3, 1928. The Myrtle Point Enterprise is another paper with a long history, which continues to this day.

Western World: Established in Bandon in 1912 as an independent newspaper the World continues to this day.

CHAPTER 6

IN THE EYE OF THE BEHOLDER

THE ROLE OF A WITNESS

It is extremely important for people to remember that one of the greatest elements of recording history is that of the witness to an event. To determine the validity of what has been seen and recorded each statement must be thoroughly understood and even scrutinized. The different perspectives that come into play are paramount to establish truthfulness. Thus, we have to identify many factors to help establish the credibility of a witness. Even determining the motive of a statement is fundamental in establishing credibility.

Thus, we know from the world of law enforcement witness testimony, even at its best, is flawed by human perceptions and bias. The formation of a memory can be affected by environmental conditions such as temperature, color, lighting, sound and much more. Where one stands, an individuals attention span, the elements present affect the witness to be drawn their perception of an event.

Educators know people learn in different ways. There are those who are visual learners who retain more by seeing, others are auditory the keen listeners, some are tactic those who have to touch to learn, whereas others are more complex who readily use combinations of methods to learning. Thus, and individual can readily train their mind for what the eye will be led to see or even what we want to see and record in our brain. It is even supported gender plays a significant role in determining learning styles.

Filtering through all these layers can be the investigators worst nightmare, yet more often their best friend. The skilled and professional investigator realizes the witness can be lead down a specific path one wants them to go. Therefore, the witness must provide the truth, as they have seen it, quickly before outside influences take hold to alter their perception of the truth. Like the tools of artist, each witness begins to provide different stokes which begin to take shape on the canvass of an event the completion of which provides a work of completed art. With the portrait complete, the full truthfulness should be in hand.

However, statement must be obtained with lightning speed before the mind begins to wonder. The passage of time can greatly affect memory and the telling of a story. An investigator dealing with delayed witness reports knows the work of art so precious to preserve can inadvertently become an indiscernible abstract extending far beyond comprehension. Remember being in the classroom and telling a secret? At the end of the day how did the story change, what did it become?

Today we are ever faced with psychological analysis of our cognitive abilities regarding witness testimony. We have seen cases of memory implanting, brainwashing, and testimony under physical and mental duress. Have you ever talked someone in to remembering something you know very well they did not participate in? I have even said I remember what I was doing when John F. Kennedy was assassinated, but that has now almost been 45 years ago. Are my memories true? In my mind they are. Are they based in fact, that is subjective.

With all theses factors in mind the journey of crime and punishment via hangings of Coos County begins.

CHAPTER 7

THE CASE OF THE NATIVE AMERICANS

The first hangings in Coos County were those of several Native Americans for the deaths of two white men. Since these murders occurred during the infancy and formative period of structured government within Coos County, there is no formal governmental documentation of the crime. Therefore, there is no positive recordation of the crime and punishment other than that of the eyewitnesses. Thus, the telling of this story is based on reporting of several individuals at different intervals in time recalling of the events. With these facts established, were these hangings acts of a Vigilance Committee or a result of pure unruly mob Lynch Law justice?

Case Synopsis: The year 1854, two miners, only known as Venerable[C] and Burton,[D] were murdered while traveling a waterway by canoe during a mining excursion. The crime was committed by several Native Americans. It is unknown which tribe the Natives involved in the murders were from. Three different tribes were alleged to have committed the crime. The Coos Bay Indians, Nasomah, and the Upper Coquille Chocre la dunne.[15] Only one name was known, "Indian Pete" who was tried, convicted, and executed in Empire City. Two or three accomplices were executed in Randolph and one or two in Port Orford during the time in which Port Orford was part of Coos County.

The Motive: Theft and/or revenge. The motive of theft could be supported by the fact that property of the victim was found in the possession of "Indian Pete." The act based on revenge, and most likely motive, stems from a dawn raid of the native settlements of the Nasomah, or Lower Coquille Indians on January 28, 1854. Splitting into three different groups, White settlers took up positions opposite the Mae'ch-tchae dun (located at the present-day town of Bandon), K'ama'c dun, and Ni-les dun Indian villages. As dawn broke, the white men, by pre-arranged signal, set fire to the cedar-plank houses of the Nasomahs who were asleep inside. The flames quickly spread, engulfing the bark roofs and plank rafters of the houses, consuming their stored food supplies prepared for the winter. Once awake some Natives tried to extinguish the flames while others made their escape. Under the command of their three self-styled officers William Packwood, George Abbott, and A.F. Soapy shooting of the Nasomah people began as they emerged from their burning homes. Once the massacre was complete, at least fifteen Nasomah men and three women were killed.[16] The Whites reported to Indian Affairs, fifteen were killed which included one woman and two other wounded.[17] What is known is there was never any prosecution of those responsible for the murders of the Nasomah people killed without provocation.

The Witnesses: There are several witnesses to actual events. Others are reported afterward through their historical research of the time. The youngest witness to the execution of "Indian Pete" was Russell C. Dement at the age of six years. Dement resided with his parents in Empire City where his father was a blacksmith. A.H. Hinch was seventeen and a miner in Randolph when he and a friend recovered the bodies of Burton and Venerable; Hinch at that time was a miner and later a businessman, rancher and convicted murderer. Daniel Giles was an eighteen years old miner in Randolph when the murders occurred. Giles became a well-established figure in the history of Coos County and as a businessman. Ester Lockhart, witnessed the execution of "Indian Pete," was twenty-nine years old and would become the first teacher of the area. Andrew G. "Glenn" Aiken, age seventeen would become sheriff serving from 1876 to 1879. Orvil Dodge was a local historian who wrote and published the first history of Coos County.

The last witness testimony comes from the Native American telling of the events. Coquelle Thompson told of the events in the 1930's which were translated to English. Thompson also provided some insight into the culture of the Native American handling of killing another within their customs. Additional information was obtained from Coquelle Thompson's life story written by Lionel Youst and William R. Seaburg. Born in 1849, Coquelle Thompson

[C] Depending on the account the name was spelled Venerable, Venerbal or Venable.

[D] Dodge, in his writings, comments about Elija Burton, in 1853, traveling with Daniel Giles purchasing a yoke of oxen along with several other men. This was the only entry and there are several ancestry records for Elijah Burton with no location of death within the same age range as the other young miners.

became a farmer, hunting and fishing guide, and even rose to the rank of captain within the tribal police.

The Crime and Punishment: The first report presented is that of A.H. Hinch who detailed the death of two men and the attempted capture of the suspects. Hinch's story, reported in the following articles from the *Coos Bay News* newspaper, headlined on December 24, 1912: **Killed by the Indians.**

> In looking over some old papers the other day, we ran across an account of the murder of two white men by Indians on the Coquille in 1854. The account was written by the late A.H. Hinch, of South Slough,[E] who gave it to us one day in Marshfield early in the '80's. He spells the names of the men as Venerable and Burton. They had been working on the beach at Randolph with Hinch and Jake Evans, and left the camp in August 1854, to go up the Coquille river on a prospecting trip. They were killed by the Indians at Dead Man's slough, so called on account of the tragedy; but later changed to Iowa slough. Hinch was a young fellow of 19 or 20 at the time, and Evans was probably a year or two older. The story, as written by Hinch, will prove interesting not only to the old timers but to the new comers as well, and we will take pleasure in publishing it in the near future.

Headline of the *Coos Bay News* December 31, 1912: **Pioneer Days. — Two of the White Men who Were Killed by Hostile Coquille Indians.**

> (The following account of the murder of two white men by Indians on the Coquille in 1854 was written by the late A. H. Hinch, who gave it to us in Marshfield early in the '80's. The Jake Evans mentioned, who was Hinch's partner in black sand mining on the Randolph beach, was murdered a few months ago at South slough. At the time of the occurrence, Hinch and Evans were only boys aged 17 years. They were raised in Kentucky and crossed the plains with a wagon train seeking adventure in this portion of the then unknown West. We have re-written the story, using as nearly as possible Hinch's own words. He promised to add another chapter, telling what finally became of the Indians who did the killing, but we never received it.)
>
> Venerbal and Burton were two of the early settlers of Coos County who were murdered by Indians on the Coquille river in 1854. They left Jake Evans and my camp at the Randolph beach mines about the middle of August and went to the Coquille river, near the Hamblock place. There they dug and burned out a canoe, big enough to carry them and provisions and started up the river with the intention of prospecting one of the tributaries for gold. They only took a small supply of provisions, as they expected to be gone about a week or ten days.
>
> The Indians of the Coquille were always hostile to the whites and would commit crimes whenever they could find an opportunity. They always kept spies out for that purpose; nevertheless the prospectors would take chances and venture out in the mountains to hunt for gold.
>
> The boys proceeded up the river until they got as far as what was after wards called Dead Man slough. (Now called Iowa slough.) They met a canoe loaded with Indians coming out of the slough, and there were Indians on both banks of the slough. The Indian attacked them at once, shooting arrow at them. Venerbal was killed instantly and the canoe in which were their rifles and ammunition was upset. Burton got to shore and made a hard fight before they killed him, as one of the Indians confessed afterwards.
>
> A few weeks after the boys had left our camp, Jake Evans and myself concluded that they would have returned if something had not happened to them, so we decided to start out and try and hunt them up. There were no settlers' any where along the Coquille river except at the mouth, where Uncle Tom Lowe and James Sanders kept a ferry. We made our way up the river as far as the middle fork, hunting and keeping a sharp lookout for signs. On our way up we saw no sign anywhere of the boys, so we turned back and when we reached Cedar Point we met two Indians in a canoe. There was a little sand bar at the Point, which was a nice place to land, so we ran our canoe ashore. The Indians also landed at the sand bar, and we made signs and talked with them as well as we could, trying to find out if they had seen any white men in a canoe. They made signs that they had not. When we were ready to continue our journey down the river, one of the Indians made signs that he wanted to come with us in our canoe. I told him that he could come, but I suspected treachery, and we watched him closely. We placed him in the center of the dugout, so that if anything went wrong we could stand a better show to defend ourselves. We had not gone far before he strung up his bow and made an attempt to shoot me. I was in the bow of

[E] A slough is a body of water such as an inlet or tributary that is out of the main current of a larger body.

the canoe, Jake in the stern. Jake noticed his motion with his bow and told me to look out. I turned on him, made him lay his bow down and told him to take my paddle and go to work, He at first refused, but I raised my tomahawk, which made him change his mind. I was standing over him with the tomahawk in my hand, when Jake, who was watching the shore carefully, sung out; 'Look at the Indians on the banks!' There must have been 50 or more among the trees, armed with bows and arrows, and they also had a couple of guns.

When they noticed that we had discovered them, they came out and made signs for us to come ashore, at the same time talking in their own language to the Indian in the canoe with us. We kept our canoe under full headway, although the Indian with us made several attempts to stop. I stood with my tomahawk over his head, and the Indians on the bank saw that if they shot at us it was sure death to the Indian in the canoe. We got away all right. Neither of us had a gun or pistol with us, the only weapons we had to defend ourselves with were knives and tomahawks.

On our way down the river we met John Craden and a man named Elk Davis. We told them about our trouble, but they only laughed and said we were scared. When we got down as far as the mouth of Beaver slough, we let the Indian out on the bank and continued on down the river. We had only got about half a mile when we noticed some buzzards and ravens sitting on a pile of drift wood. Having a curiosity, as boys will, to see what these birds were doing there, we ran our canoe alongside of the drift and the first thing we saw was Venerable's head and shoulders. We identified him by a silk handkerchief that he had borrowed from Jake to wear around his neck on leaving our camp. He had been shot in the back of the neck with a bullet from a gun of some kind, and the buzzards had been eating the flesh around the bullet hole. *(missing text)* way safely to the mouth of the river.

The game night, two men named Santagram and Billy Burrows, an old trapper and pioneer of Oregon, were coming down the river and they ran their canoe ashore at the place after wards owned by Mr. Lowe and called Myrtle Grove. Their canoe ran up on something they thought was drift wood but on investigating they found it was the body of a white man. It was dark and they could not tell who it was. There was a rope made of grass around the body, and with this rope they anchored the body to a stake and came on down to the mouth of the river. When we met them and they told Jake and me about it. We were satisfied that it was the body of Burton, so the same night we went up the river and found it as they had stated, and it proved to be Burton's body. We had the two bodies on our hands then, and both of us being boys hardly 17 years old we didn't know what was the proper thing to do. Finally we concluded to take the bodies up the river to the old scow landing at John Hamblock's.

We left the bodies in the canoe and went up to Randolph and informed the miners that we had found Venerbal and Burton, and told them all the circumstances. The miners helped to bring the bodies to Randolph, where they appointed a coroner, selected a jury and held an inquest, after which the bodies were buried. Venerbal had $42 in his pockets, but Burton had no money. Burton's body was horribly mutilated.

The murders caused great excitement among the miners. It was their rule to protect each other, and the penalty for stealing or murdering by whites or Indians was death. All such cases were closely investigated, and if the miners were satisfied that a crime had been committed no pains were spared to bring the guilty parties to justice. The coroner's jury brought in a verdict that Venerbal and Burton had been killed by Indians, and immediately afterwards a volunteer company was raised and set out to find the murderers. The company consisted of 50 men. Of this number 31 started up the Coquille river and 29 went down to the mouth. I was in the company that went up the river. Our captain was a lawyer—a tall, slim fellow who bad brought a stovepipe hat with him to the diggings, and for this reason he was known as "Stovepipe." We made our way up to the mouth of Dead Man's slough where we separated. Twenty- six went on up the river, and Stovepipe, Ike Mocketlee, Frank Daniels, Bill Copely and myself went as far as the Isthmus. On our way we captured an Indian, who confessed that he helped to murder the boys and said he could show us where the Indians did the work. We tied him and placed him in the canoe and went back to the mouth of Dead Man's slough. He made signs that the boys were killed up the slough and that we would find their canoe hauled out on the bank. We left Copely to guard the prisoner and we started up the slough two on each side. We had not gone far before we found the canoe. We were standing talking when an arrow passed close to me and struck Stovepipe in the forehead. The blood from the wound flowed into his eyes, blinding him. Immediately afterwards we heard Copely holler and two of us ran towards the place where we had left him guarding the Indian. We met him half way, as white as a sheet and pretty badly scared. When he rested a little he told us that the prisoner had succeeded in freeing himself from the ropes which bound him and that at the same time two more Indians had suddenly appeared. One of them jumped into the bow of the canoe and fired at Copely, the ball making a flesh wound between the thumb and forefinger of his left hand. Copely drew his revolver and shot the Indian, killing him instantly, the body falling into the slough. The prisoner picked up a paddle and struck at Copely, but he warded of the blow and shot the Indian twice in the breast. The Indian jumped overboard and swam ashore, and while he was climbing up the bank Copely shot him twice in the back; nevertheless with four bullet wounds in him he ran about 100 yards to the river, jumped in and swam to the opposite side, making his escape.

By this time Stovepipe and his comrade had joined us and we got into our canoe and started up the river. We fell in with our company a little later on, and on our way up the river we captured 16 Indians. That night we placed them in an old Indian hut and three men of the company were put on guard. About midnight, when everybody was asleep but the guards, the Indians made a rush and escaped from the hut, taking one of the guards with them. The noise woke the members of the company who commenced shooting at everything they thought was an Indian, which resulted in the killing of one little boy about 12 years old, all the rest making their escape. So our hunt for the murderers proved a complete failure. We had lost our prisoners and our captain, Stovepipe, was suffering from a severe wound in his head. (The Indian who led the attack when the boys were murdered was afterwards captured and was hanged at Empire, but that is another story. — Ed. News.)

After this story was published, a sequel, to pick up where Hinch left off was written by A.G. Aiken. Aiken's story was printed January 14, 1913 by the *Coos Bay News*. Headline: **Pioneer Days — Sequel to the Story Published Lately, Concerning an Early-Day Tragedy.**

I was much interested in reading the account in the NEWS of the murder of the two young men, Venerbal and Burton on the Coquille by the Indians in the summer of August written by the late A. H. Hinch, who took a prominent part in bringing the murderers to justice. Hinch's story concludes when the Indians, which were captured by "Stovepipe" and his company of miner; from the Randolph beach mines, escaped at night from the Indian hut when they had been placed under guard. I will endeavor to enlighten your readers regarding the final termination of the affair.

I did not arrive here until October 1854, but my brother James Aiken came here in February of that year, and I got the information from him.—When day light arrived the next morning, after the escape of the Indians, Stovepipe and his men took the trail and succeeded in re-arresting nearly all of the Indians. They took them to the Randolph beach mines (Whiskey Run) where a jury was sworn in and a judge appointed. The trial resulted in three of the Indians being found guilty of participating in the murder of the boys, and they were promptly hanged at Randolph in the presence of the miners and a number of Indians who lived in the vicinity. One of the Indians who was tried for assisting in the murder was known as "Pete." He was cleared at the trial by two white men who swore that Pete had been engaged by them on the Isthmus as a guide to the Coquille country. They camped the night, of the murder at the head of Beaver slough. When they rolled into their blankets Pete was asleep in the brush near by, and when they woke up in the morning he was still there consequently they argued that he could not have taken part in the murder.

While Hinch states that the boys were killed at Dead Man's slough, we always understood that the killing took place at the mouth of Beaver slough, and Pete's confession afterward; would seem to settle the question without doubt. You must remember that the Coquille was a practically unknown country at that time. With the river bottoms covered with a dense growth of myrtle, maple and underbrush, and with numerous sloughs and creeks entering the river, it is not unreasonable to suppose that a mistake could be made in the location of a particular slough or creek.

While helping to round up the Indians in the Coquille country early in 1856, we captured Pete and his squaw at Burton Prairie. (This prairie was named after Burton who was one of the boys killed by the Indians, who had squatted there in 1853, but afterwards went down to the Randolph mines.) Pete seemed under the impression that we knew that he was implicated in the murder of the boys and he finally confessed. The confession was drawn from him by the late F.G. Lockhart after we had brought Pete to Empire. We decided to hang him. When the rope was around his neck, Mr. Lockhart spoke to him in Chinook, telling him that he would never go to the happy hunting grounds unless he told the truth concerning the murder of the boys, etc. Pete's confession, made in Chinook jargon was to the following effect; "There were two white men whose names I do not know. They were carrying goods across the Isthmus from the head of Isthmus slough to the head of Beaver slough. They hired me to take the goods down the slough to the Coquille river. On the night of the killing, the white men and myself camped at the head of Beaver slough. The white men were very tired and slept sound. I made my bed in the brush, and when they were asleep I got up, took my canoe and went down to the mouth of the slough and helped the other Indians to kill the two men. I killed one of them myself."

However, even before his response to the Hinch article, Aiken's story of the incident was printed twenty-three months earlier in the *Coos Bay Times*. This first telling of the story is slightly different in details. This first account does support the statement of another witness to the actual execution, Mrs. Ether Lockhart.

The article headlined: **55 Years Ago On Coos Bay — A.G. Aiken Recalls Thrilling Experiences With the Indians in Southwestern Oregon in Early days**, was printed on February 1, 1911.

The following account of the rather thrilling experiences of the early settlers of Coos Bay and Southern Oregon was written for the Times by A. G. Aiken one of Coos county's earliest pioneers and who was himself a participant in the events of which he writes. Mr. Aiken has promised some further chronicles of those early times which will prove interesting reading to the present residents. People today think they are isolated and suffer inconveniences but those tales of the hardships of the pioneers and perils of the pioneers stand out in sharp contrast with the blessings of civilization enjoyed now.

The *Times* would be pleased to hear from others of the pioneers who have interesting stories of early day struggles and experiences in the farthest frontier.

The following is Mr. Aiken's story: Just 55 years ago this month, or to be exact, on February 22, 1856, a number of whites settlers, 18 or 20, were killed at the mouth of Rogue river. The news reached Coos Bay a few days later. Capt. W. H. Harris, a Mexican war veteran, wanted some of us boys to go with him and help the Rogue river residents. We went as far as Port Orford. They had formed a camp of Minute Men at that place, under command of John Creyton. We started back next morning and organized a company, forty-three all told, elected W. H. Harris captain, built a fort at Empire City, where the old Court House now stands. We then held a council with the Indians. There were five chiefs present. We wanted to know if they were going to fight, or be peaceable. They said they did not want to fight but if they did not the Rogue and Coquille River Indians would come and kill them. We told them if they would come and camp on the little flat below Empire and let us know when any strange Indians came in among them and any fighting was to he done to let us know and we would help them and furnish them flour and meat. This they agreed to do and kept their word.

S. S. Man was appointed quartermaster. He employed Snil Dement and Jack Pense to kill elk and Patrick Flanagan had a pack train and he packed flour from the Umpqua. So the Indians had plenty of meat and flour. We then started out to find some renegade Indians that we knew to be bad. One Indian, Pete was not to be found. We went to Coos City where Judge Watson lives now, took an Indian trail to Burton Prairie, almost parallel with the Coos Bay wagon road. We arrived at Burton Prairie as wet as rats, each man carrying a pair of blankets and 10 days grub. The next day I killed my first deer. That was a feast for the boys. Some of the boys went up the North Fork of the Coquille above Burton Prairie and found fresh signs of Indians. The next morning we took up the trail of the Indians and trailed them into the head of Catching Slough, found where they had a canoe cached and had gone. We then made haste to Empire City and next day had Pete in the guard house. We tried him, mostly on Indian evidence, found him guilty and sentenced him to be hung.

We got a small fir about 8 or 10 inches at the butt end — trimmed it tip and put it in the forks of a wild Cherry tree. It was fixed something like the old fashioned well sweeps. We pulled down the top end and made it fast; tied the Indian to the top end; gave him about 6 ft. of rope. F. G. Lockhart was master of ceremonies. He told Pete if he had anything to say to do so and "delate Tva-wa" that is, tell the truth. Pete then asked to see Tyee Jim who was the first chief of the Coos Bay Indians. Jim was called. Jim said "Mica wake tickey wa-wa copa oak-oak cultis siwash," meaning "I don't want to talk to that bad Indian." Then, Mr. Lockhart told Pete to tell us all about the killing of the two men at the mouth of Beaver Slough,

Venerable and Burton. Mr. Lockhart impressed it on his mind if he told the truth that he would be all right in the next world and if he lied "Sahhalle Tyle hihue sulla" meaning God would be very angry with him. Pete then told how he had helped to kill the white men at the mouth of Beaver slough.

An unusual incident of the hanging of Indian Pete was that it was witnessed by a large number of other Indians and for several days following they practiced the new method of execution on their dogs. They fastened trees as we had done, tied the dogs to them and then cut the rope. Dogs could be seen hanging in all directions. Whether they did it in imitation of the white man's way or whether they wanted to send some dogs to the happy hunting grounds with Indian Pete we never learned.

Pete said: "I was helping two men to move some goods from the head of Isthmus slough to the mouth of beaver slough. They were camping their goods on their backs across the Isthmus to Coaledo and I was taking them down the Beaver slough in my canoe. The night of the killing, the men were tired. After supper they made their bed and went to sleep. I made my bed on the other side of the fire from them, when I was satisfied they were asleep I got up and went down to my canoe; got in and paddled down to the mouth of Beaver slough and helped to kill the two men. I killed one of the men myself. We threw the bodies into the river." One body was found below Beaver slough, the other was found at the mouth of Dead Man's slough, now called Iowa slough.

Three Indians were hung at old Randolph for the crime which Pete confessed Pete would have been hung then but those white men that Pete was working for, swore that Pete was with them the night of the murder. This crime was committed in 1854 and Pete was hung in 1856, before the war.

About one month later I helped hang Pete's brother on Battle Rock at Port Orford. Enos, a Canadian half breed was hung later on Battle Rock. He was executed for taking arms against the settlers and fighting with the Rogue river Indians.

Next is the account as told by Daniel Giles. First published in the *Myrtle Point Herald* the article was reprinted in the *Coos Bay Harbor* on April 4, 1935. Headline: **Daniel Giles at Randolph Buys Mining Claim and Part in Mill.**

Some time in January there came to our house a young Indian boy about 17 years of age and I noticed that he had lost one of his eyes. It had been knocked out some way, for the ball had been broken and the eye run out, so I inquired of him the best I could how he lost his eye. He said the Indians had put it out and that made the cause more interesting to me. By further inquiry I learned that he was an Umpqua Indian and was a prisoner of war among the Coquille Indians and that he tried to run away once and the Indians had caught him and put out one of his eyes and told him if he ever tried to run away again that they would kill him. He was very anxious to get back to his own people and asked me if I would take him back to the Umpqua valley when I went out there.

I told all my partners what I had learned from the Indian and what he wanted and asked them to let me keep him there with us until we could either take or send him to his people. My partners consented to my keeping him and he soon made himself very useful by getting wood and water and by doing chores around the house generally. A few days after the Indian boy was adopted into our family, one evening a man came to Randolph from the mouth of the Coquille river that the Indians had shot arrows at the ferryman and were in their war paint and singing their war songs.

He was sure they would kill the ferryman before morning if the men did not go to his rescue so there was a company of 25 or 30 men armed and on the march in a very short time. They went to the Indian town and surrounded it on three sides; the river was on the other side. Then they waited until daylight and when the first Indian made his appearance the whites commenced shooting and if it had been for the river I do not think there would have been one Indian man get away from that town alive. Some jumped into the river and by diving and swimming got away and some got away in canoes but as it was there were 15 Indian men and two squaws killed and some wounded that got away and the Indians did not try to fight at all. All they tried to do was to get away, so of course there was none of the white men hurt.

This, however, caused the Indians to seek revenge and was the cause of the death of several white men afterwards.

Sometime about the first of March in '54 the dead bodies of two men were found floating in the Coquille river near the mouth of a slough which afterwards we found were the bodies of men by the name of Venerable and Burton. These were two young men who were traveling down the river in a canoe by themselves as we afterward learned from the Indian who was living with us, and met some Indian canoes. One of the Indian canoes contained three large, strong Indians. They paddled their canoe along the side of the white men's canoe in a friendly way and then turned their canoe over and while the men were in the water the Indians knocked them in the head with clubs and drowned them. Then they weighted and sank them in the river and hid their canoe up a slough where they thought it would not be found. But as the old saying is, murder will be found out, so this hiding failed. The bodies got loose from their fastening and rose to the top and were found by some men who were coming down the river. The bodies were buried in a little knoll in the edge of old Randolph on the beach. I saw them both buried.

A few days before these bodies were found there was an Indian from the mouth of the Coquille river spent several hours talking to our pet Indian trying to get him to go back to the Indians but he would not as he was afraid they would kill him. After the dead men were found and buried a few days the same Indian came back again and tried to coax our Indian away and told him what Indians had killed those men and how they had done it. A few days after this he told me all about (it) and told me that he knew three of the Indians that had done the killing and they lived over on Coos Bay so I told my partners about it. They told some of the leading men in the town and two of them came and got me to make arrangements for our Indian to go with them to the bay and while the went to Empire City to stay all night for him to go to the Indian town on a visit.

That evening one of them with some white men who lived at Empire City would visit the Indian camp and the pet Indian was, by some sign agreed upon, to point out the Indians that had done the murder and then they were to go away and the next morning just before the day he was to slip out and meet the men near the Indian camp and show them where the Indians they wanted were sleeping. Then he was to go to Empire City and stay there until they got there with the Indians and then they would give him his breakfast. All hands would then come back to Randolph and try the Indians and if found guilty they would hang them. Their plans worked like a charm and they got the two Indians and our pet Indian back to Randolph the next day.

As we had no county organized at that time and the people had to make law to suit all occasions, they called the miners together and as the Indians soon acknowledged their guilt they were soon hanging upon the limbs of a tree in the edge of town.

The next eyewitness testimony regarding the hanging of "Indian Pete" was from Ester Lockhart, a resident of Empire City during the course of events. Mrs. Lockhart was among the first three White women to settle in the county and she started the first school. The book, *Destination, West!* chronicled Lockhart's life history and provided her account of the hangings.[18] The other source in text form was from the writing of Orvil Dodge who came to Empire City in 1863. During his life Dodge served as a photographer, attorney, newspaperman, and local historian. In 1998, Dodge published, *Pioneer History of Coos and Curry Counties, Or.* which was the first published history of the county. In the recording of their accounts Dodge reported three Native Americans committed the murders of Burton and Venerable whereas Lockhart recorded six. Both agreed as to the motive and the statement of the first "brave" native who was hanged in Randolph. With Dodge's and Lockhart's background in place the case is presented from their prospective.

In 1854 two young men named Burton and Venable, gold prospectors in the region, were traveling down the Coquille River by canoe. The two men heard a shot from the river bank from six Indians in two canoes. The Indians paddled out their canoes and seemed friendly; however, once they reached Burton and Venable the Indians overturned the canoe. Once in the water Burton and Venable began to struggle and were beaten in the head with the boat paddles soon dying of their injuries. To conceal their crime the Indians weighed the bodies down with stones where they sank to the rivers bottom. In time the bodies rose to the surface and were discovered by some of the settlers in a stream which became known as Dead Man's Slough near Randolph. Thought to be too gruesome of a name it was changed to Iowa Slough. The crime was solved when a sixteen year old Umpqua boy, who had been captured and tortured by the Coquille Tribe, was befriended by Daniel Giles who was about the same age. Loyal to Giles the young native learned the identity of the six murders who spoke freely of their crime in front of the boy. Once the identities were known the native boy provided the names to Giles.

According to Lockhart, acting on the information provided, the settlers found two of the natives in Randolph.

Whereas Dodge recorded; "the young Indian (Umpqua informant) was taken to Empire City where the guilty Indians were believed to be, and by signs made known two of them to the miners who were determined that justice should be mooted out. This was successfully accomplished at the large rancherie south of Empire City.

The plan adopted was an ingenious one, and worked to a charm without betraying the young Indians treachery to the tribe. They all returned to Randolph with the two Indian prisoners. The miners were called together, and were about to form a jury, but the prisoners acknowledged their guilt and they were soon hanged upon a tree at the suburbs of the town."

The confession consisted of one of the natives boasted of his crime claiming he was glad he killed and if he could he would kill again asserting the white settlers killed many of the natives without cause; hence, his crime was based upon revenge. The native made very eloquent speech stating the white people were interlopers, who had no right to come into this country and take the red men's land and turn them out.

The following is a quote from his speech:

> "The Great Spirit sent the Indians here long ago to have all this land for their own. The elk, the deer, the fish, the fowl, all were for the Indians alone. The white man has no right to any of these things. He has his lands, his homes. The Indians did not disturb them. I have done the white people all the harm I could. If I had many men, I would do more. I am not afraid to die. I am a warrior and a warrior knows no fear. I die, but I go to the happy hunting grounds of my father and my father's fathers, and from there my spirit will urge the Indians to exterminate every white man that comes into their country."

He remained unrepentant and stoic to the end. However, the other native, as reported by Lockhart, to be a coward and died like a whining dog. Whereas Dodge described him as, "crying like a child, begging for his life." According to Lockhart, soon thereafter two more of the murders were apprehended and hanged at Port Orford by a committee of angry and outraged settlers. Port Orford was part of Coos County at this time. Curry County did not form from Coos County until 1855.

Both Dodge and Lockhart agreed as to the next course of events. Not long after this several natives came to Empire City, which was not unusual in itself; however, it was noticed that some of the blankets bore the large initials of one of the deceased. Since the natives could not read they were oblivious to the damming evidence before the settlers. The native that carried the blankets were arrested, tried by a jury, convicted, and sentenced to be hanged. It was noted that the evidence brought before the court was furnished by the natives themselves.

Lockhart described the hanging as; "on the day of execution a gallows was erected from a long, slender fir pole fixed into the crotch of a big wild cherry tree. Freeman Goodwin Lockhart, husband of Ester Lockhart, served as the "master of ceremonies" for the execution. Speaking with the native known as "Indian Pete," Lockhart told him to confess this crime and "dirate wa-wa," tell the truth. Lockhart impressed to "Indian Pete" that if he confessed and told the exact truth he would go to the happy hunting ground. However, if he lied, "Sa-ha-le ty-ee hyas solleks" meaning, "God would be very angry with him." There was no mention in the story if Pete confessed to his participation in the murder or not.

Dodge described the event this way; "The sentence was death, by hanging. Some one conceived a novel plan to perform the execution, and consequently a long pole was placed in the crotch of a tree, with the small end as a fulcrum. The rope was adjusted to the short end of the pole and the large end being raised by the crowd of men the Indian was jerked into the happy hunting ground in the twinkling of an eye."

Lockhart recorded after the execution an unusual situation connected to Pete's execution occurred a day or two after the hanging. Natives in and around the settlement began hanging their dogs exactly as Pete was hanged. It was never learned why the canines were sacrificed; however, it was thought the act may have been done to provide Pete with company for his long and distant journey. Another thought was that by sacrificing their beloved pets the natives would be immune from the fate of Pete. However, Dodge recorded this unusual event as; "It is said that the natives preserved that rude gallows and hung their worthless curs on it afterwards."

The final white eye witness recorded was from the youngest witness, age six, who was the last to record his recall of the hanging. November 17, 1928 *The Sun* headlined: **COOS COUNTY'S FIRST LEGAL EXECUTION — R.C. Dement, Pioneer '53 Relates Early-day Event**

> In his 81st year and quite vigorous in mind and body, Russell C. Dement, of Myrtle Point, is the earliest

white pioneer of Coos county of this day. He was six years of age, when he came in October 1853. There were seven in the party and they all came here from Jacksonville, Oregon. The party was assisted in from Scottsburg by ox team driven by Curtis Noble.

It was our good fortune to meet Mr. Dement, though briefly, in Myrtle Point the other day, when in a cursory way he related a few early-day events well try to repeat. Coming from this source, you are assured that they are first-hand, and from the only living one that can furnish you with the same. Many people are imbued with the idea of the hostility of the Indians to the whites, particularly those who came in later years. True, they showed their savage blood in some localities, but the Coos Indians were an exception to the rule. They were very docile. To the south, in Curry County, the tribes were warlike. Mr. Dement said that he had often wondered how the Indians had survived, for when he came there was no food, and not even a domestic hoof, but the natives seemed well fed. In those days the streams were stocked with fish, deer and elk were plentiful, and there was also our standby of today — clams — and on these the Natives fed and flourished. In 1855-56 there was a general outbreak among the Indians on the coast, but the Coos tribe maintained their equilibrium. It was during this period that the Fort, or blockhouses, was erected at Empire City, and about a thousand Indians were rounded up and sent to the Siletz reservation.

While the Indians of Coos always retained their tranquility, when the natives went on the warpath with other localities, the only act of violence was committed at Iowa slough, on the Coquille, near the present site of Riverton. Here one white man bit the dirt, was killed by two Indians, known or assigned as "Indian Pete" and "Pete's Brother." Later they were tried and convicted on evidence furnished by their tribesmen, there being no whites in that section at the time of the murder. "Indian Pete" was hung at Empire City, and later "Pete's Brother" paid the penalty with his life at Port Orford.

I witnessed the execution at Empire City. It was a gruesome sight that still lingers in my memory, said Mr. Dement. Primitive as it was, it was effective in dispatching life. There was no such thing as a gallows. A secluded spot, then in a region of brush, was sought. A small sapling was cut down, limbed, and then placed in the forks of a larger tree. The butt end was secured to the ground, then a rope was thrown over the protruding top, which was hauled down to a point near the earth and made fast. Up to this point the executioner, George L. Wix,[F] led "Indian Pete," placed the noose around the murderer's neck, the bite being made fast to the small end of the bowed tree, the rope that held the tree was cut and up went the murderer into the air. It was all over, and scarcely a sign of a struggle.

The testimony of facts have been thus far have been presented from prospective of the white settlers. Now the Native American perspective is presented from Coquelle Thompson. Coquelle Thompson provided a series of interviews conducted in the 1930's to linguist Melville Jacobs and some of his associates. During the interviews Coquelle Thompson spoke of the murder case. Within the interview there were several words that were in the language of the Miluk (Lower Coquille)/Hanis Coos River and Coos Bay)/Upper Coquille phonology.[G] A translation of these words were not available from the Coquille Tribe Library, therefore they are omitted for easier reading. This is the story from the Native American perspective of Coquelle Thompson:

Finally two or three white men came down from head of Coquille. Not fight men, just pack. So my father take them mouth of river to Lane. A kind of Indian Chief Lane[H] Indian Chief at .... He got those men. Some damn fools want to kill those white men. That Chief don't know. That Chief let them go Fort Orford. He went up river. After they gone, maybe one hour. Those people get ready to go kill three whites they got in boat. They going to drown them. So right in middle river, they trip boat over. One white man swims just like fish, other two, they drowned. Killed trying to grab boat. They hit on head. That man run Port Orford. Reported Indians kill two white man. Lots soldier's there, all ready for war. They come over Mountain from ... on Rogue River to head of Coquille River. Coquille people all hid out. Very few stay in town. When soldiers come, don't kill, but gather up. Get all together. They got Chief, ..., they don't get my father. Can't find him. Soldiers put them all in big log house. Just full prisoners. Now they come back, report of killing. Oh mad, raise dickens. "Who done it?" Men had reported, "we stay man named Lane, ..." Four, five soldiers

[F] There was a George L. Wicks who was listed in the Muster roll of Captain W. H. Harris, Coos County Volunteers, which called into the service of the Coos territory of Oregon from March 20 to June 12, 1856. The 1880 U.S. Census listed Wicks as a native of New York and his age as 60. There are no known records for the last name of Wix in Oregon during the time period.

[G] Phonology is the branch of linguistics concerned with the analysis of sound systems as they function in languages.

[H] Chief Lane was chief of the Lower Coquille Miluk Tribe.

go see him, tell him, "you give me two men who kill white men (in jargon) and we don't bother nobody." Lane said, "if any my people do that, I willing to turn over to you." He inquire his people who took them across. Find out. Don't say nothing Lane said. Those soldiers got two, third got away. They told soldiers look for that kind man. Soldiers hunt, hunt. They come .... These people cook. Cook for soldiers. Must be in May. They feed them good. They tell people don't run away, don't run away, people might shoot you if you run away. When they go out to toilet. Soldier have to go with them. Those soldiers unknown to officers. Tell Indians they all be hanged tomorrow. People tell Chief. They watch close two or three guards with guns up guard all night. Men change every two or three hours. Keep doing that. They were scared. Don't realize they could report. Just lay on ground in that barn. Chief ... say, "you fellows dig." They had taken knives and all away, but some had knives!! When dark, no light, soldiers front. Those fellows dug, dug, pretty near daylight. They tried it. One man went through. They just picked up men. "You folks get ready now." Two or three soldier men right in door in front. Now they all get ready. They go out that hole. That man who dug, he had humpback. He couldn't go through. He had to give up any how. One man had asked to go to toilet. Soldiers took him outdoors. That's when get out hole. When half gone, they find out Chief, and all the bigger fellows were gone. They no where to go. They ran away and go home in night time. When man at toilet must be get done, brave man inside grabbed two guns right under each arm. Guns go off. He push guns and soldiers back. Men rushed out front. They all run, but old humpback and two, three old fellows, they don't go. It got to late. Those soldiers only shot one boy running. They shot him. They had got him way up above. He coming along road, not knowing they rounding up people. He didn't see all soldiers coming. He just come along. Pretty soon they all surrounded him. He stand there, look, look, he wouldn't give up his knife. Pretty soon, Captain got mad. He had all soldiers aim at him. He won't scare, he stand there. He went soldiers two, three each side, two, three front, two, three behind. They try to take knife away, he just hit around from over across. Old Ty Jackson already there across river. They see him. ... his Indian name. He was .... They see soldiers fooling around with him. Finally they got in boat, just stretch on water and go cross. He won't give up knife. Come right in door. Soldiers first bunch, try to get that knife. He just hit back. Chief ... say, "you sit down over there." ... ask, "what is it? They try to take my knife away?" "Well," Chief say, "give up, I'm here now. No use to try to fight here now." (They figured they were there because they just going kill them. They didn't know it was to find out who had killed the 2 white men). Chief say, "you give up that knife now." He won't hand it to them, he just sling it down on ground for them. He brave man. He came in that barn now. He said, "I won't stay here. I'm going to go, I don't care how many guns they got. I know what I going to do." Chief say, "oh don't say that. I'm here now. Maybe they ain't going kill me." That was night. They dug. He grab guns. Now all jump and run. They get out. How soldiers take time, maybe two, three minutes. So all up, grab guns, but its dark. Only three or four people left. Only four of them there. Got blankets covered up, dig grave. They buried him. Next day they take three old fellows and that humpback, put rope round their necks, scare them. Want to make them tell who killed those white men. Well, they don't know they from up the river and the white men were killed by mouth of the river people. They scare. At last rope around one old man. That white sailboat just stretch waves out on water and cruise(?) with it. They said to old man, "you know who killed those men." He said in Coquille, ... Mouth of Coquille River people. So they understand. They make him sit down. He had heard about it, but he couldn't talk white talk or jargon. Now those people who had run away last night. They all down mouth Coquille. They said got guns. They want to get those soldiers that kill that Indian boy. (Meanwhile the soldiers already had got as prisoners those two men who killed the white man. Lane had turned them over.) Soldiers said captain said, "I see Chief. You fellows be still. Now it get settled." Later on they give blankets. Captain ordered don't bother any Indian that belong Coquille. That was May. (That same summer, later they brought them all up here. They{re} soldiers come get us all. Take us Port Orford). Those two Indian men had to be hanged right there. Mouth river. They saw those men get hung. Some interpreted when soldiers Chief talk. They made them stand up on big barrel. Chief (or Liecht) speak a little while. He say, "you people know now. That's the way it goes. Our law. When white people kill each other, we hang them. You people don't know. You kill innocent people. Now you know." This first time ever see anybody hang. That's white man's law. They try to get in that way. Tell them all about it. They promised to pay ... for boy killed. They hang both of them there. Now all done, everything quiet. They didn't get that third one. Well, soldiers say, "let him go. He come 'round sometime. We get him." They don't know who, Ha! Ha! They can't get him.

> They went Fort Orford. About time they make treaty (1855). (I was six or seven. I can 'member little. We traveling.) They make treaty, Coquille city. They fix it for that boy get killed. White man say, "we make mistake." They issue white blanket, red blanket, white blanket. They make satisfied Coquille Tribe so they have to forget its trouble. Of course, they don't want to fight. But white people afraid they turn loose on them. So they issue. Chief say, "no, no more trouble." After treaty, Chief all signed there. … and others all gave Indian name. They don't want to move, but at last, pretty near July, they gave up. Chief say, "we stay here, maybe white people bother us, we kill white people, be nothing but trouble. We have to go where they tell us. Then government take care of us." They have to leave skins, canoes. My father say he have to leave two good canoes from Tillamook. Some canoes from California.

Coquelle Thompson also provided some insight into the Indian views of killing and retribution:

> Now if I kill somebody's boy, when it's all settled, that old woman like to see what kind of man kill her boy. So they bring that old man and woman to me. I shake hands with both of them. They pray for me. Rub all over my legs and chest and head and say, "I wish you long life, because my heart is clear and good for you. You pay my people enough money. I hope something help you. I wish sickness go way. I wish good clothes for you." They pray like that for you because you paid a lot of money. Medicine Doctor ate just like everyone else. Never eat their dream power. An old man at lower farm dreamed eels. He never ate them. He was a Doctor. He dream eels among other things. A Doctor would have two or three wives and one is a Doctor. I have to treat her good. She would be more important than head wife. A Doctor would fish just like all people. Chief didn't fish. People give him lots. His three or four wives cut the fish and dried them good. Chief didn't hunt either. Might go to hunting camp, but he'd stay in camp. Chief wouldn't fight but would send word to other Chief to meet him in middle, and they'd fight each other. He only fought another Chief. If he want to fight, he has to send word to other Chief. If that other Chief don't come, he don't have to fight. They all come together. If anybody get chance, they kill that other Chief, but his people watch him pretty close. If a Chief got killed then they have to stop. They have to pay a lot of money for him. Pay lots more for him than for any one else if they kill him. They paid equally for a man or a woman who was killed.

From the published biography of Coquelle Thompson we learn more. February 1854, during a heavy snow storm, three white men stayed with his family as them three men asked for help since they were without food and starving. There were two young natives in the camp who wanted to kill the whites, which was forbidden by Coquelle's father, who was the chief. After eating the men unpacked and gave Coquille's father a heavy wool shirt. After the snow was gone the men paid Coquille's father with two blankets and three twenty dollar gold pieces. Coquelle Thompson's father supplied the men with three young men to serve as guides to take them to the mouth of the river by boat.[19]

From the writings of Youst and Seaburg, 1942 Coquelle Thompson provided a version in this way:

> "The natives were to take the whites quickly and not to talk to any Indians along the way as his father was fearful the whites would be killed by the 'Coquille villagers.' The whites were not to even be seen by those at the Miluk village located on the north side of the river. The men were to travel the south side of the river and go immediately to Port Ordford."

Youst and Seaburg believed this story related to the death of two white men known as Venable and Burton who where discovered in March 1854.[20] Youst and Seaburg further wrote:

> In Coquelle's narrative of the incident there are three white men, coinciding with his story of the three white men who had stayed with his father. He said, "One of the white men swam just like a fish." He escaped, but "the other two were drowned, killed." One of Coquelle's storytelling techniques was to add a detail to make the event more vivid: "The men tried to grab on to the edge of the boat but were hit on the head." When word of the killings got to the whites, Oh, they were mad! They raised the dickens, "Who did it?" "At last," Coquelle said, they put the rope around an old man, they said to him, "Do you know who killed those men?" He said in Jargon, "Coquille sal djik sawa (mouth-of-the-Coquille River people)."
>
> Meanwhile, two Indians who were thought to have been among those responsible for the murders were apprehended and brought to Randolph for quick, vigilante justice. Coquelle told about it: "Those two Indian men had to be hanged right there at the mouth of the river. They saw the men hanged. Someone

> interpreted when the soldier's chief talked. He stood up on a big barrel. The chief or lieutenant spoke a little while." He said, "You people know now. That's the way it goes, our law when white people kill each other, we hang them. You people didn't know; you killed innocent people. Now you know. This was the first time the Indians ever see anyone hang. That's white man's law." Of course, in the Indian narratives no distinction is made between the vigilante mobs and the military: they are all called "soldiers." It was a vigilante mob that executed the two men, but Coquelle probably understood the justice of it in terms of blood payment. The Indians of the Coquille River valley would have had no trouble understanding the concept of blood payment. They used it themselves; it was only the method, the execution by hanging that was novel to them. Coquelle's people would more likely have carried out a sneak raid on the offending village in the very early morning hours before daylight.[21]

There were no accounts of the hanging in Empire City nor in Port Orford in Coquille Thompson's biography.

The newspaper and text accounts presented have revealed how fragile the kernels of historical truths are. The statements demonstrate the reality of how ones perceptions, bias, and perhaps even age and gender alter the presentation of events. Case in point, one cannot even pinpoint the year the murder and hangings occurred. A timeline provided by Giles, shows the crime occurred January 1854; Coquelle Thompson stated the crime occurred between February and March 1854; Hinch placed the crime in August 1854 and the statement of Dement indicated a period between 1855 and 1856. Statements regarding a trial were also in dispute. Mrs. Lockhart said there was a trial and her husband served as "master of ceremonies" for the execution. Mrs. Lockhart's viewpoint was supported by Aiken during his first statement to the press. However, Aiken stated "Indian Pete" was adjudicated of any wrongdoing during a trial in Randolph where two Native American's were convicted and executed. Whereas, others claim those hanged in Randolph were victims of mob rule, possessing a mentality based on Lynch Law or a Vigilance Committee. This view was seen in the statement of Giles. Thus, one can see how facts are altered by various impressions in the reporting of an event.

It appears the crime, and punishment most likely occurred in 1854, the same period in which the birth of county government was evolving. Coose County was created by the Territorial Legislative assembly on December 22, 1853. Prior to the formation of Coose County, matters of judicial acts, as established by the Territorial Legislation, were relegated to the United States District Courts. The District Courts maintained original jurisdiction in all felony and misdemeanor cases punishable by penitentiary sentence. No District Court cases were located regarding the crime of murder in 1854.

The establishment of the county judicial system, recorded within the *Journal of the County Court of Coose County,* revealed the first meeting organizing the County of Coose was held on April 3, 1854, in Empire City. Three judicial districts were formed and judges were appointed. The Coose Precinct with Judges William H. Harris, Z. Setz, and Curtis Noble. The Randolph Precinct with Judges B.J. Burnes, Sutherland and Joseph Unthank. The Port Orford Precinct with Judges Randolph Tichner, F.N. Smith and William Tichner.

With a judicial system and law enforcement in place by April 1854 to whom do you give credence? Remember, both Dodge and Lockhart were in agreement "Indian Pete" was given and jury trial prior to his execution in Empire City. However, Aiken reported "Indian Pete" was adjudicated of any wrongdoing at the trial help in Randolph and was executed in Empire City in 1856. Giles indicated the actions of the settlers may have been based on the Lynch Law mentality, as Giles implied, no county government existed at the time of the executions.

To further complicate the situation, the *Journal of the County Court of Coose County* revealed there was a jury trial in October 1854; however, the defendant(s) were not revealed. On October 5, 1854, a roster for jurors was listed in the Journal. October 8, 1854 there is mention of Deputy Sheriff H.H. Briggs, the examination of Dr. Hubbard, and the appointment of F.G. Lockhart as Justice of Peace for the Coose Bay District in Empire City. The journal listed the authorization to pay Lockhart $12.50. Furthermore, on October 27, 1854 the county authorized the payment to the jurors for three days of service. Could this record have related to a trial for "Indian Pete"? Additionally, there was no prosecution of any one named "Indian Pete" in the Territorial courts within Coose County nor are there any records for a trial in Randolph. Court records were examined until 1860 and nothing was revealed for any murder trials where Native Americans were prosecuted within Coose County.

Probably due to the remoteness of the county very little was reported in the *Oregonian* and *Statesman* newspapers of the time. Examination of both newspapers revealed nothing regarding the murders or any trials occurring in the newly formed Coose County.

Even though the execution tree of "Indian Pete" has long disappeared the "hanging tree" is an important part of the history of the Empire community. To add another twist to the case even the type of tree Pete was hanged from is in dispute. The tree was recorded as a wild cherry tree by Mrs. Lockhart and Mr. Aiken. However, the writing on the back of the original photograph of the Gilman execution described the "hanging tree" as, "a big spruce tree in the Court House yard" and others have commented that it was a Myrtle. One may ask how the tree was in the courthouse yard, but Mr. Aiken supplied the answer to that question when he stated "Indian Pete" was executed at the fort which stood at the location of the courthouse.

The mystery was finally solved on February 9, 1940 when the *Southwestern Oregon News* February 9, 1940

> HANGING TREE IS FELLED BY WIND
>
> EMPIRE, Feb. 7. — Coos county's historic old "hanging tree," a large spruce that stood in the yard of the first county court-house at Empire, is no more. Rotted by years of exposure the large tree fell during recent storms and now is lying along the line of the old courthouse foundation on the bluff overlooking government deck.
>
> The stump is three feet in diameter . According to unofficial reports, the tree actually was used for the hanging of several persons convicted of murder in the early days of Coos county. One victim of the noose on this tree is said to have been an Indian, named Pete.

The first sheriff of Coos County, J.H. Foster, a physician, was appointed pursuant Oregon Territorial House Bill number 66 on January 19, 1854. Foster only served until July1, 1854 when Charles Haskell was elected sheriff. Early entries in the Journal regarding the sheriff's office only revealed Deputy Sheriff Haskell being authorized $78.00 on the date of June 16, 1854.

In remembrance of all the victims to this event in history one cannot forget an associated victim to the murder case; the tragic death of an innocent native boy who lost his life during the first attempt to apprehend the murderers of Burton and Venerable. Additionally, the remembrance of all the Native Americans who where killed in the raid which may have triggered the murders of Burton and Venerable.

NATIVE AMERICAN BURIAL PRACTICES

For the local Native Americans the topic of burials is not one openly discussed due to the sacredness of the act. Published in the January 1901 *Marshfield Sun Special Edition* a perspective of Native American burials was described:

> When one of the community begins to show signs of dissolution (which is usually hastened by the sweating or the sanitary process to which the sick are submitted, the whole tribe commences a terrible outcry, which generally lasts through the dying agony of the sufferer. The body is then stretched upon the ground and sprinkled with sand and the ashes of sea-weed or kelp. The legs are forcibly doubled up toward the head, and the ankles tied as closely as the rigidity of the corpses will permit, to the neck. The relatives of the deceased shave their heads and placed the hair upon the body – thus rolled in a heap together with some shells and nutritive roots for the dead to subsist upon. The body is then lowered into the grave, which is made of a length to accommodate the dimunition of size to which the defunct has been submitted. The earth being thrown in, the whole tribe jump alternately upon it until the ground becomes quite solid. The baskets, clothing, spears and all personal property is formed into a heap, packed upon the grave, and covered securely with sticks and stones. With a chief, the ceremonies are more impressive and lengthy.

CHAPTER 8

THE CASE OF SEVIER LEWIS

Case Synopsis: The crime of murder was perpetrated at the farm of Hiram Hamilton Lewis, located in an unincorporated farming area of Coquille City in May 1876. The victim, Zachariah "Zack" Lewis, was working in the fields when he was approached, shot and killed by his older half-brother, Sevier Lewis.

The Motive: Sevier claimed there were unwanted advances toward his daughter, Sylvia, by his half-brother Zack. There was a darker, more sinister motive of Sevier's attempted concealment of alleged molestation of his daughter. It was alleged Sevier impregnated his daughter during an incestuous relationship.

The Lewis Family: Hiram Hamilton Lewis, born January 26, 1802 in Gallatin Co, Kentucky, fathered nine children from two of his three wives.[22] At the time of the tragedy Hiram Lewis was the county republican nominee for the state legislature in the pending election. However, the events of the murder ended his political aspirations. After the murder of his son, Hiram Lewis relocated to Lane County and died there January 19, 1879.

Sevier Lewis was the third child born from his father's first marriage. Born November 21, 1825 in Marion County Indiana, Sevier married his wife Elizabeth in Sonoma, California on March 8, 1854. They had seven children the last of which was born sometime between 1875 and 1878 in Oregon, most possibly in Lane County.[23] Depending on the resources examined Sevier's wife Elizabeth relocated to Lane County and remarried in 1882. The Lewis' second child was their eldest daughter, Sylvia Jane, born June 1, 1857 in Windsor, California. Sylvia married in September 1880 in Smithfield, located in Lane County, Oregon. Sylvia and her husband raised five children with the first recorded birth a set of twins born June 26, 1882.[24]

Zachariah "Zack" Lewis, born 1851 in Annally, Sonoma County, California, was the first born child from Hiram's second marriage. In Zack's short life he was never married.[25]

It is unknown exactly when the Lewis family arrived in Coos County. According to the 1870 U.S. Census the Lewis' resided in Smithfield, of the Richardson Precinct, Lane County. At the time of the 1870 Census Zachariah was residing in Russian River, Sonoma County, California.

The crime and Punishment: Orvil Dodge, in his *Pioneer History of Coos and Curry Counties, Or.* wrote the following about the candidacy of Hiram Lewis:

> "Lewis, an upright citizen living about, one mile and a half below Coquille City, was nominated by the republicans that spring for representative. There was one opposition to him in his own party in convention, nothing personal, however, but on account of his extreme age, he being more than seventy years. Time went on until about two weeks before the election, the whole community was horrified to hear that Severe Lewis, son of the nominee, had shot and killed his half-brother, Zachariah Lewis, on his father's ranch. The cause of the murder was jealousy. Severe Lewis had a wife and family of boys and girls, the oldest girl just budding into womanhood. Zack was a single man some 25 years of age. He had been paying his respects to the girl (his niece) until quite an intimacy existed between the two. Her father thought things was going a little too far, and warned his brother Zack (as he formally called) to desist coming on the place or having anything further to do with the girl, but it seemed the warning availed nothing. One morning, about the 15th of May, 1876, Severe, being enraged at his brother, shouldered his gun and went to his father's house, about one mile away, walked up within a few feet of his brother, who was plowing in the field, and shot him dead. Severe fled the country, and avoided the officers for some two years, and was finally captured on Puget Sound, brought back, convicted, and hung in Empire City — the first white man that ever paid the death penalty in Coos County. This happened only two weeks before the June election, in 1876. Col. R. H. Rosh, the democratic candidate for representative, had an easy victory to attain the office. The old gentleman and lady Lewis, father and mother, only survived a short time, and died with broken hearts."[26]

A darker more sinister version of the motive behind the crime has also been recorded. According to the other version Zack was taken into confidence by his nice, who stated she had been forced to have sex with her father and was going to have a child by him. Zack went to his half-brother Sevier telling him to stop or he would reveal the incident to the whole family. Zack then helped his niece move in with her grandparents in order to escape her father. Zack told Sevier if tried to retrieve his daughter, Zack would kill him.

May 31, 1876 the *Coos Bay Times* reported:

> A most shocking and cold-blooded murder was committed on Monday this week at the farm of H. H. Lewis near Coquille City in this county. Zachariah Lewis being shot and killed by his half brother Sevier Lewis. It appears that Savier Lewis, who has a family, had some difficulty with his younger brother, the nature of which is not known to the public; and last Monday after noon he deliberately loaded his pistol and yager,[1] and called upon his son, a lad about fifteen year of age, to accompany him, with the remark that they "might see some game before they returned;" proceeded to where Zachariah was plowing on his father's farm and shot him three times killing him almost instantly. After accomplishing his fiendish purpose he took to the woods carrying with him two pistols and his yager. As he has neither blankets nor provision with him, it is thought that he will not be able to evade the officers who are in pursuit of him. The boy who appears to have had no knowledge of his father's murderous purpose, is in custody. The barbarity of this deed is augmented by the fact that it was committed in the presence of the aged father of murderer and his victim. This assassin has been but a short time a resident of this county, and formerly resided in the interior of the State. — *Record.*

Jay Tuttle, Coos County Sheriff, apparently deputized Chris Dryden to apprehend Lewis for the murder. Dryden was unsuccessful in his attempt to capture Lewis which was reflected in the following letter to the Editor published by the *Coos Bay Times* on May 31, 1876:

> COQUILLE CITY, MAY 26th, 1876. *Editor News:*
>
> The republican candidate for sheriff was deputized to arrest the murderer of young Lewis last week. How diligently he performed his duty may be inferred from the fact it took him 24 hours to get to Coquille City (probably electioneering along the route) and after taking a nap, he leisurely, went back through the woods, without making even a pretence of a search for the murderer. What kind of a Sheriff will Chris make? How many thieves and culprits will he rush after in this enthusiastic manner, after he is elected. We want a Sheriff with some 'rustle' to him. Let no guilty man escape.
>
> Yours Respectfully, COQUILLE

December 19, 1877 the *Coos Bay News* printed the following two articles regarding the capture of Lewis:

> Sevier Lewis indicted for the murder of his brother by shooting him while plowing in the field near Coquille City about a year ago has been identified and arrested in Washington Territory and is now in jail awaiting a requisition from the Governor of Oregon. The murder as we now understand it is one of the most cold-blooded deliberate murders of which we have ever heard.

The second article headlined: **Murder and Incest**

> Last evening, says the Seattle *Dispatch* of the 10th inst., a stranger calling himself Harmon stepped into the bar room of the American House, and after glancing around cautiously for a moment engaged in conversation with those present. Something in the stranger's manner at once attracted the attention of a young man named Perkins, who, after eyeing the new comer a moment, called Mr. Haley, one of the proprietors of the house, aside and remarked that he thought he recognized in the stranger a murderer named Lewis. He stated that two years ago Lewis, then residing at Coos Bay, Oregon had seduced his own daughter, and on being charged with the crime by his brother, murdered the latter and then fled. A large reward was soon offered for his arrest, but no trace of him could be discovered. Haley and Perkins observed Harmon closely, and soon he went out. They followed him to the Vanity Fair saloon, where Haley engaged in conversation with him, and the three seated themselves at a table and drank some beer. After a few moments passed in this manner, Harmon went out with the remark that he was going to his lodging. The other two followed in the distance and saw him enter the Oriental Hotel. Giving him time

[1] A yager is a sharp hand hoe.

> to retire they entered and learned that he had gone to his room. One of the men then stepped across the street to the residence of Sheriff Wycoff and the other remained on guard. When the sheriff arrived the three men entered the room where Harmon was, and as they approached the bedside Haley held a lamp up and saw a large knife lying on the pillow; this he picked up and threw on the table. Mr. Wycoff then told the man to get out of bed and dress, which he did, at the same time showing considerable alarm, and asked under what law he was taken. When the handcuffs were being put on he resisted. He was taken to the county jail and while the sheriff was unlocking the door Haley held up the lantern and said, "Mr. Lewis do you recognize me?" The prisoner replied, "No." The light was then thrown on Perkins' face and as the prisoner looked at him he made a quick movement to one side as if to avoid notice. He was then asked if he recognized Perkins, and he replied, "No," but his looks seemed to betray him. When committed to jail he appeared very uneasy and asked for an attorney; on being told that an attorney could do him no good; that he must remain to be identified, he trembled visibly. Today, his manner is very nervous, so much as to be the occasion of remark.
>
> Lewis (as there seems to be no doubt but this is his name) came here from Lewis county, Washington Territory and said he was going to Skagit to locate a home. He told a man traveling with him that he had been charged with a crime in Oregon, but there was no truth in the charge. A letter was found on his person from a man supposed to be his son, the letter addressing him as "Cousin Harmon." Another letter from a wig maker was found with him; it seems that he had sent the money for a wig, with directions how to send it. From those and other papers found on his person there is but little doubt that the man calling himself Harmon is Lewis the murderer. He will remain in jail here until officers come for his removal to Oregon, there to be tried for his crimes.

January 2, 1878 the *Coos Bay News* reported:

> We interviewed Sevier Lewis in the county jail last week. His appearance certainly would not indicate a man who would commit a deliberate murder. All he asks, he says, is that the public do not pre-judge his cases before his defense is heard, which is always a reasonable request.

The court file for the case did not include any witness statements or testimony of the trial. What was revealed from the file. Coos County District Attorney C.W. Fitch brought evidence to the Coos County Grand Jury on May 27, 1876. The Grand Jury issued an indictment charging Sevier Lewis with the May 22, 1876, murder of Zachariah Lewis by shooting him with a pistol once in the stomach and once in the left side. The jury trial began on May 27, 1878 and the guilty verdict for the indictment of murder was signed by jury foreman Isaiah H. Atkinson on June 13, 1878.

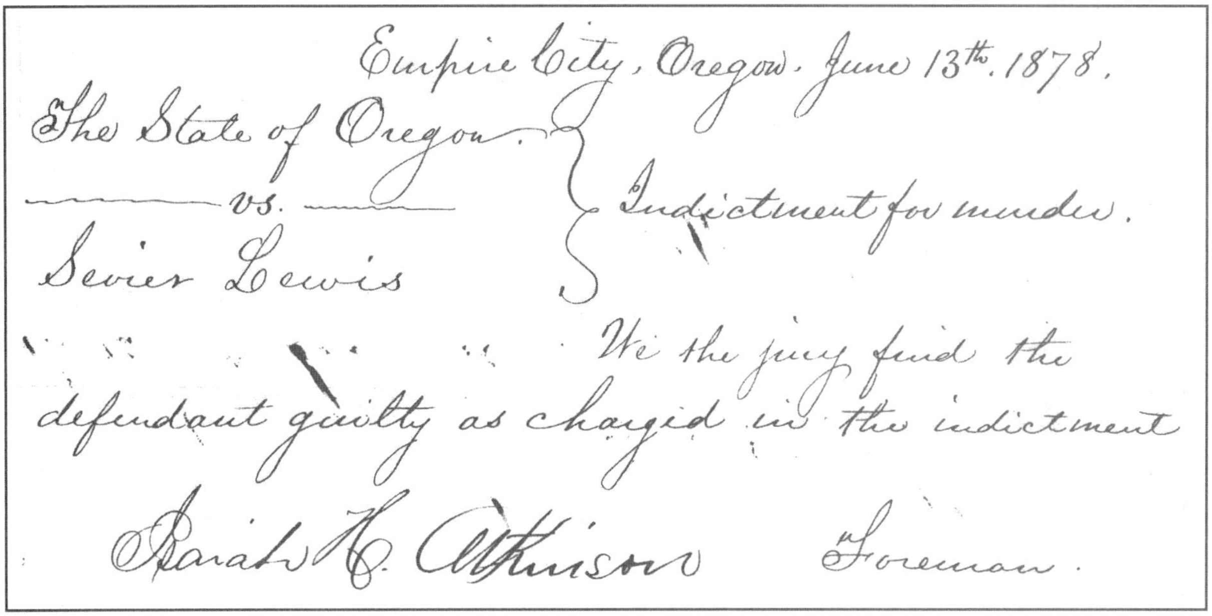

Empire City, Oregon. June 13th. 1878.

The State of Oregon vs. Sevier Lewis } Indictment for murder.

We the jury find the defendant guilty as charged in the indictment

Isaiah H. Atkinson Foreman.

Figure 4: Jury's Verdict for Sevier Lewis

On the 13th day of June, Judge J.F. Watson sentenced Lewis to be hanged by the neck until he is dead on August 9, 1878, and additionally charged Lewis $830.10 for court costs.

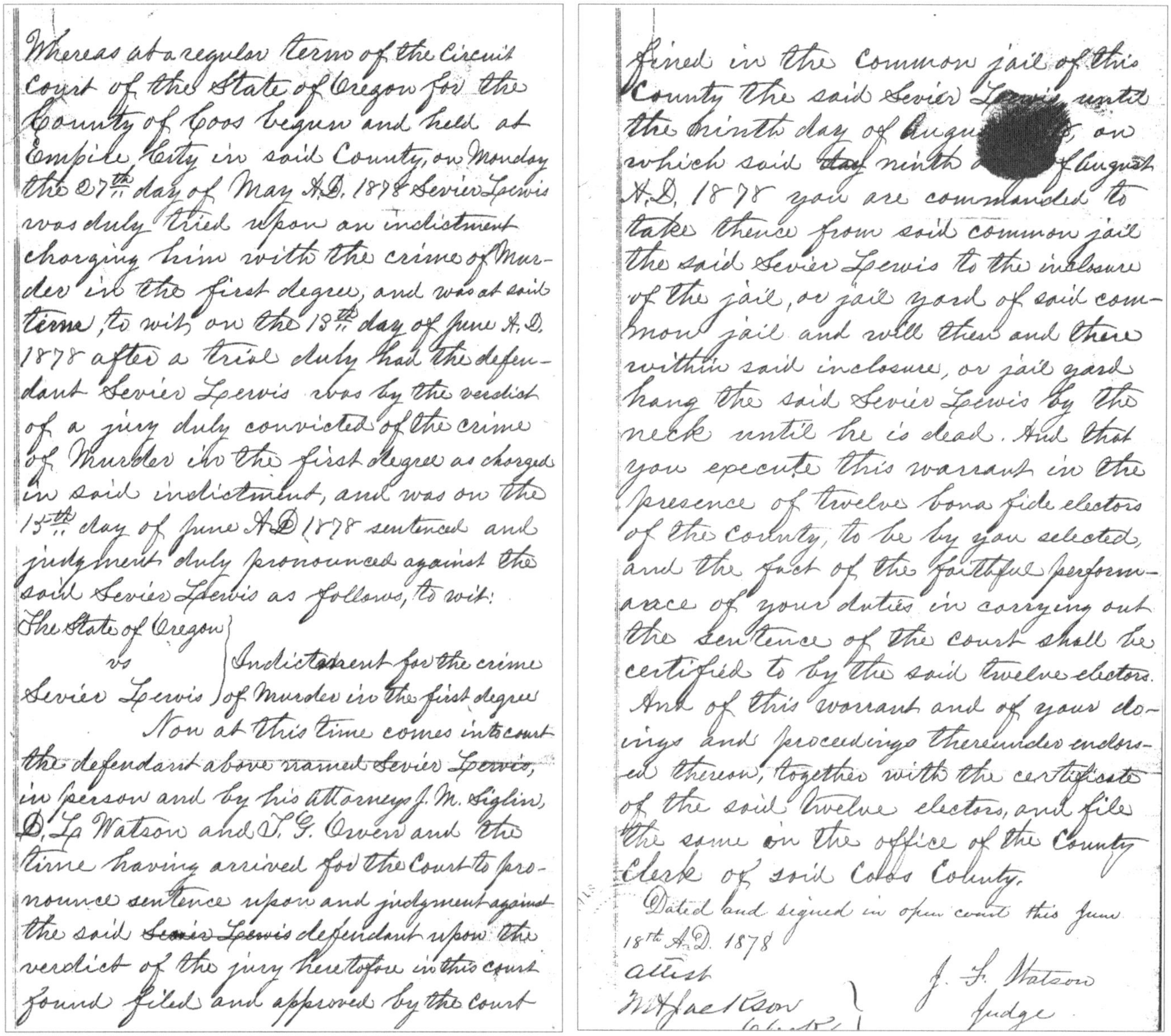

Whereas at a regular term of the Circuit Court of the State of Oregon for the County of Coos begun and held at Empire City in said County, on Monday the 27th day of May A.D. 1878 Sevier Lewis was duly tried upon an indictment charging him with the crime of Murder in the first degree, and was at said term, to wit, on the 13th day of June A.D. 1878 after a trial duly had the defendant Sevier Lewis was by the verdict of a jury duly convicted of the crime of Murder in the first degree as charged in said indictment, and was on the 15th day of June A.D. 1878 sentenced and judgment duly pronounced against the said Sevier Lewis as follows, to wit:

The State of Oregon vs Sevier Lewis } Indictment for the crime of Murder in the first degree

Now at this time comes into court the defendant above named Sevier Lewis, in person and by his attorneys J. M. Siglin, D. L. Watson and T. G. Owen and the time having arrived for the Court to pronounce sentence upon and judgment against the said ~~Sevier~~ Lewis defendant upon the verdict of the jury heretofore in this court found filed and approved by the court

fined in the common jail of this County the said Sevier Lewis until the ninth day of Augu[illegible], on which said ~~day~~ ninth [illegible] of August A.D. 1878 you are commanded to take thence from said common jail the said Sevier Lewis to the inclosure of the jail, or jail yard of said common jail and will then and there within said inclosure, or jail yard hang the said Sevier Lewis by the neck until he is dead. And that you execute this warrant in the presence of twelve bona fide electors of the county, to be by you selected, and the fact of the faithful performance of your duties in carrying out the sentence of the court shall be certified to by the said twelve electors. And of this warrant and of your doings and proceedings thereunder endorsed thereon, together with the certificate of the said twelve electors, and file the same in the office of the County Clerk of said Coos County.

Dated and signed in open court this June 18th A.D. 1878

attest W H Jackson Clerk

J. F. Watson Judge

Figure 5: Sevier Lewis' Death Warrant

The defense lawyers, J.M. Siglin, David L. Watson and T.G. Owen, applied for a stay of execution for the purpose of an appeal to the Supreme Court with Governor T.F. Chadwick until Judge Watson could return to Coos County and rule of their appeal. Governor Chadwick signed an order directing the warrant of execution from the 9th to the 13th of August 1878 at which time to proceed according to the law.

June 29, 1878 the *Coos Bay Times* reported:

> Sevier Lewis was convicted of murder last week at Empire and sentenced to be hanged on the 9th day of August, at Empire City. This will be the first execution ever had in Coos County. Lewis killed his half brother about a year and a half ago while he was plowing in the field, shooting him three times and once after he was down. The case was so aggravated that his lawyers had no hopes of his acquittal, but made a strong effort to have the degree reduced so as to result in imprisonment instead of hanging.

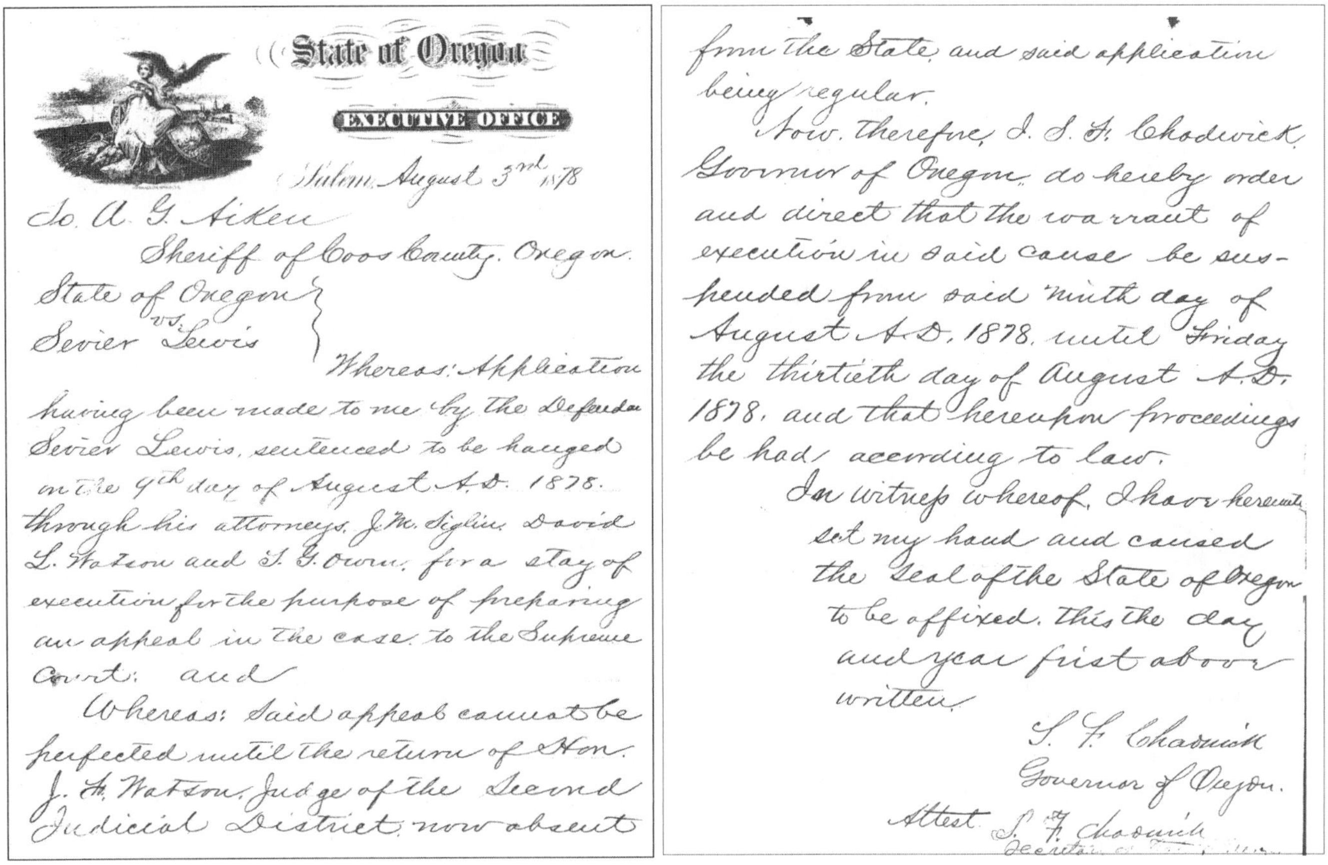

State of Oregon
EXECUTIVE OFFICE

Salem, August 3rd 1878

To A. G. Aiken
Sheriff of Coos County, Oregon.

State of Oregon
vs.
Sevier Lewis

Whereas: Application having been made to me by the Defendant Sevier Lewis, sentenced to be hanged on the 9th day of August A.D. 1878, through his attorneys, J. M. Siglin, David L. Watson and T. G. Owen, for a stay of execution for the purpose of preparing an appeal in the case to the Supreme Court; and

Whereas: Said appeal cannot be perfected until the return of Hon. J. H. Watson, Judge of the Second Judicial District, now absent from the State, and said application being regular.

Now, therefore, I, S. F. Chadwick, Governor of Oregon, do hereby order and direct that the warrant of execution in said cause be suspended from said ninth day of August A.D. 1878, until Friday the thirtieth day of August A.D. 1878, and that hereupon proceedings be had according to law.

In witness whereof, I have hereunto set my hand and caused the Seal of the State of Oregon to be affixed, this the day and year first above written.

S. F. Chadwick
Governor of Oregon.

Attest. S. F. Chadwick

Figure 6: Stay of Execution for Sevier Lewis

The original newspaper article of the *Coos Bay Times*, published September 4, 1878, providing the details of the execution has been lost to history. However, in a weekly column titled: "Early Day" a subsequent column was printed on September 5, 1911 by the *Coos Bay News:*

> (There is a two-column article on the execution of Sevier Lewis, in which his speech on the gallows is given. The execution took place in the court house yard at Empire, which was the county seat at that time. A. G. Aiken, at present a resident of Marshfield, was sheriff, and Harry McIntoch was deputy. We clip the following from the article in question)
>
> "All I have to say is I quietly submit; but justice or law do not require it. It has not been established, I have not been allowed to establish it myself. They have prejudiced the minds of men to not look at it in the light way. I do not care for dying. I care more for my children. I say that, right here on the gallows. There is a spirit in me that cannot give way. I want you all to know that I am going to die feeling honest, I do not care how much prejudice that there is, just enquire into it, and you will learn a great deal, you will learn that I am an honest man, (looking over the crowd.) I don't see any face in the crowd that I know; I have just looked all over it. I know there is no crowd that knew me would stand there and see my life taken away in this way. No Sir; there is prejudice in it. The lawyers and Judge did not know the facts or it would be different. I wish I was a speaker, so I could talk to you for a few minutes, I never spoke in my life.
>
> I would be willing to die if I knew my family were all right. If they were in good hands. They are in the hands of them that started this trouble and ruined my daughter. Gentlemen you are a good looking crowd. I am very sorry that you all don't know the truth, know all about it. I am very sorry you are not so you could know all about this trouble, you would act different. There are lots of you here that are good men, I know, at the same time I am satisfied and I feel;" (here the prisoner commenced talking in an undertone to the sheriff) after which he was quietly placed on the trap, and his feet tied; when the sheriff placed the black cap over his face he said "Oh hell, don't haul that over my face."
>
> At 3:50 the sheriff bid him good bye, the trap sprung and Lewis fell six feet through space, his neck

was broken he died without a quiver. Drs. Golden and Steele pronounced him dead in about ten minutes after be dropped; but he was practically dead the instant he fell.

Lewis was 53 years of age, but in appearance not exceeding 46; he was an American by birth, and in religion a compromise between an infidel and a spiritualist, but without any defined faith. He was about 5 ft. 10 inches high, weight about 175 lbs., a man of average intelligence but limited education, not a man whose appearance would indicate a criminal. The crime which culminated in his death on the gallows, if true as generally understood, are too horrible to relate. Several years ago his father and a number of brothers and a brother-in-law settled on the Coquille, very little being known of the family until two years ago, H.H. Lewis, the father to Sevier, was nominated by the Republicans to represent this county in the Legislature. The next occurrence of note was the report that Sevier Lewis went to the field where Z.T. Lewis his half brother was plowing, and shot him dead in the furrows, and then made his escape. The county Court offered a reward of $300 for his arrest, and nearly a year ago he was arrested in Washington Territory. It appears that there had been family troubles dating back many years, many dark pages remain unwritten, but the immediate cause of the trouble is over a daughter of Sevier Lewis's who is said to be the mother of a child by her own father, and it appears that Z. T. Lewis took an active part in taking this girl from her father's to her grand-father's as it is claimed, to get her out of her father's control, but as Sevier claimed for a different purpose. The cases of both are appealed to a court competent to decide justice between them.

On September 6, 1878 the *Corvallis Gazette* headlined: **EXECUTION OF SEVIER LEWIS** — On last Friday the incestuous father and fratricidal murderer above named, expisted his crimes at Coos Bay. The following particulars are from a special telegram to the Roseburg Independent, dated Empire City, Aug. 30, 1878:

Figure 7: Coos County Sheriff Andrew Glenn Aiken

The day opened here cool and pleasant. Long before the time of execution people from different portions of the county flocked into the city with the hope of witnessing the execution, and it was not long before it appeared that Empire City was enjoying a popular holiday, so unusually large was the crowd.

Before the condemned was brought there were wagers offered and taken as to how Sevier would conduct himself upon the scaffold, and many thought he would show the white feather just before he was launched into eternity.

There was an almost general feeling against the prisoner. It was regarded by all good citizens that the man who would outrage the person of his own daughter and then shoot and murder his own brother who was endeavoring to protect his outraged niece, deserved hanging at least since it was the worst penalty prescribed by law.

The execution took place at 3 o'clock. There were at least two hundred people present. Contrary to the general expectations Lewis showed great firmness, and met death as bravely as could have any man. There was no trembling of his body, and when, making his speech, which required at least fifteen minutes time, showed not the weakness that would have been expected in one facing certain death. In his speech he denied many things proven in his trial and even went so far as to deny that he had ever outraged the person of his daughter. He admitted the killing of his own brother, but claimed it was done to preserve her honor. He declared that emphatically the murder was not premeditated, and therefore he was not treated justly when he was hanged, and that he never thought of shooting until his brother appeared before him. Every care had been taken by the sheriff of this county to have the execution pass off without a mishap. The drop was sprung at the proper moment, and that moment Sevier Lewis' soul passed into eternity. His neck was broken by the fall, and he died without a struggle.

The general feeling here is, that in the death of Lewis the ends of justice have been served. One, perhaps, out of a hundred regret his punishment, but not one look upon it as undeserved.

The death struggle was short. Immediately after the heart ceased to beat the body was put in a coffin and hurried to the grave prepared for it.

According to the court expenditures Lewis was prescribed $21.00 worth of beer by an unnamed doctor during his incarceration. For the burial of Sevier the county paid; $5.00 to W. Rosskamh for the clearing of brush and grave digging, $10.00 to F. Mark for the coffin, and R.W. Getty received $8.00 for the burial with an additional $3.00 for the funeral. No records were found advising where the burial took place, nor even if the site was marked. The wood scaffold was erected by J. B. Gilbert who received $21.00 for materials and labor. The scaffold was erected within the jail yard as directed by Judge Watson in the Order of Execution. This afforded Lewis the opportunity to hear every rip of the saw and nail being driven as he awaiting his fate.

The true motive of the case will never be known. However, there may be a possible indicator to help determine if this was, in fact, a case of retaliation for unwanted advances toward his daughter Sylvia or was it an attempt to conceal a darker, more profane act of incest.

Recall that the ancestry records of Sylvia Lewis which indicated it was not until 1882 she bore children. An interesting observation regarding the youngest child of Sevier and Elizabeth provides further mystery to the case. Ancestry records indicated Lucy Lewis' exact year of birth as unknown; whereas, all the other Lewis children have their exact date of birth and birth place recorded. Depending on which source is examined the year of birth for Lucy ranged from 1875 to 1887. According to one file the only reference to a governmental document to establish a year of birth indicating the year as "1877/78" and her birth occurring in Lane County, Oregon.[27] The 1880 United States Federal Census for Richardson, District 64, Lane County, Oregon was the source given that the year of birth was 1877/78. This child, Lucy, raises the suspicion that the mother may have been in fact been Sylvia rather than Elizabeth in an effort to spare Lucy the truth of being conceived from an incest relationship. Fact or fiction we will never know for sure. The end result was the execution of Sevier Lewis, whose act of murder victimized more than just his half brother Zack.

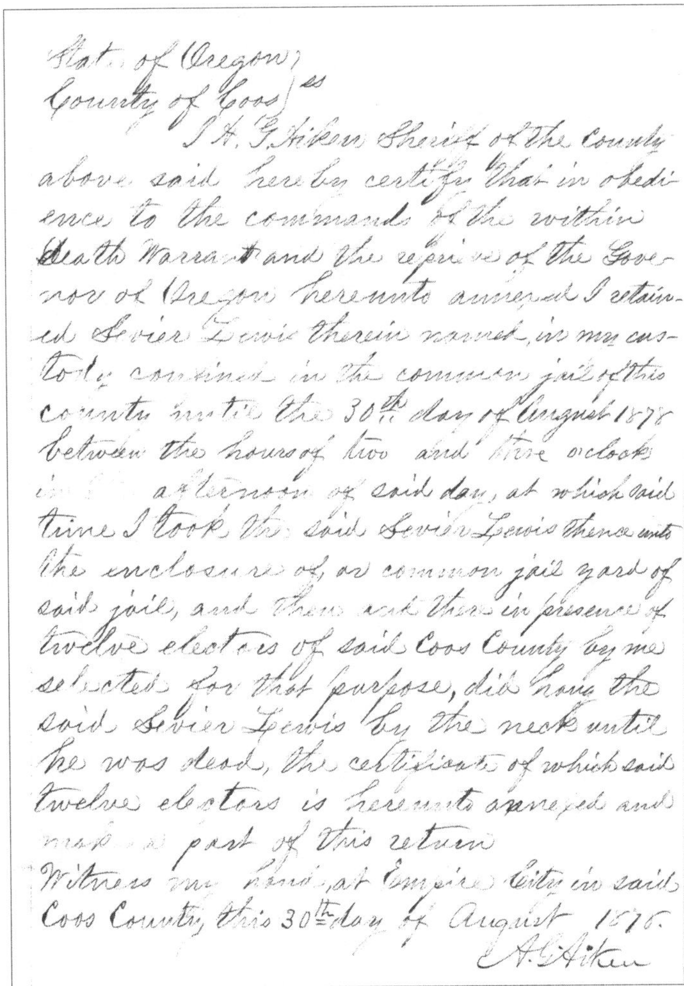

State of Oregon) ss
County of Coos)

I A. G. Aiken Sheriff of the County above said hereby certify that in obedience to the commands of the within Death Warrant and the reprieve of the Governor of Oregon hereunto annexed I retained Sevier Lewis therein named, in my custody confined in the common jail of this county until the 30th day of August 1878 between the hours of two and three oclock in the afternoon of said day, at which said time I took the said Sevier Lewis thence unto the enclosure of, or common jail yard of said jail, and then and there in presence of twelve electors of said Coos County by me selected for that purpose, did hang the said Sevier Lewis by the neck until he was dead, the certificate of which said twelve electors is hereunto annexed and made a part of this return

Witness my hand at Empire City in said Coos County, this 30th day of August 1878.

A. G. Aiken

Figure 8: Sheriff Aiken Statement of Execution

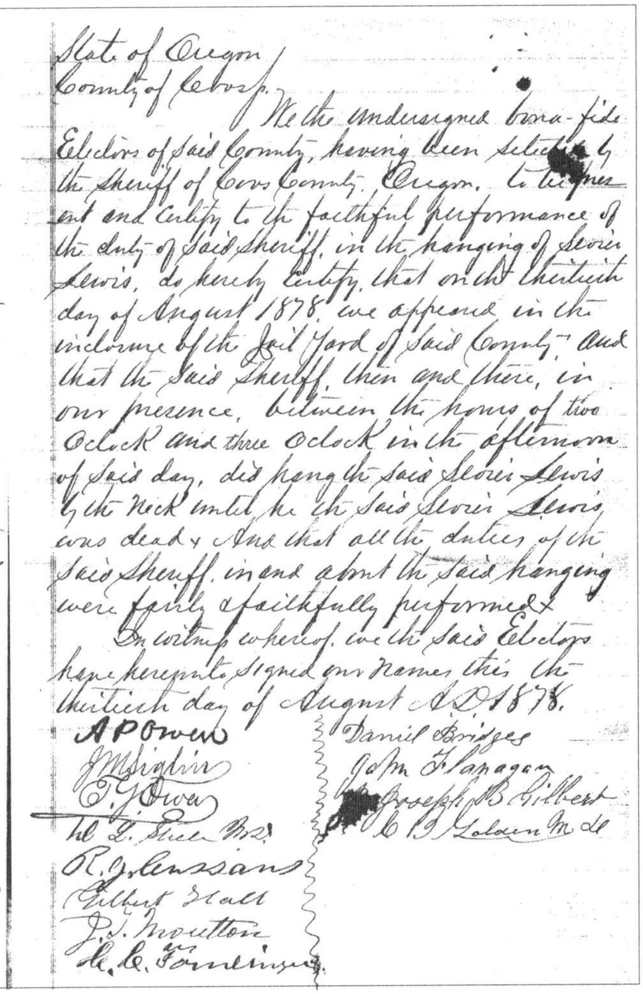

State of Oregon
County of Coos

We the undersigned bona-fide Electors of said County, having been selected by the Sheriff of Coos County, Oregon, to be present and certify to the faithful performance of the duty of said Sheriff, in the hanging of Sevier Lewis, do hereby certify, that on the thirtieth day of August 1878 we appeared in the inclosure of the Jail Yard of said County and that the said Sheriff then and there, in our presence, between the hours of two Oclock and three Oclock in the afternoon of said day, did hang the said Sevier Lewis by the Neck until he the said Sevier Lewis was dead & And that all the duties of the said Sheriff in and about the said hanging were fairly & faithfully performed &

In testimony whereof, we the said Electors have hereunto signed our names this the thirtieth day of August A.D. 1878.

A P Owen
J. M. Siglin
E. G. Owen
Gilbert Hall
J. J. Moulton
Daniel Bridges
John Flanagan
Joseph B. Gilbert

Figure 9: Witnesses Statements of Execution

CHAPTER 9

THE CASE OF JOHN F. GILMAN

Case Synopsis: John Gilman, a property owner, leased a portion of his property to Chris Eationhover, who was married with a five-year old son. Gilman asked the Eationhover family to leave; however, the Eationhover's would not relinquish the lease. Gilman initially attempted to poison the Eationhover's on an earlier occasion. After the poisoning attempt failed Gilman killed Elizabeth and her son William while Chris was away at work. Upon Chris Eationhover's return home he was attacked by Gilman and after a struggle managed to escape the fate of his wife and child.

The Motive: To forcibly remove the Eationhover family from the Gilman property.

The Parties: John F. Gilman, in the 1880 U.S. Census, listed his age as 52, occupation farmer, and place of birth was Indiana. His wife, Fidelia, listed her age as 53 and birthplace as Vermont. At the time of the Census the Gilman's had one nineteen year old daughter living with them. In 1886 Fidelia Gilman served as a mid-wife for the mother of Bonnie Sell.[28] The Gilman residence was an unpainted box-house, built of rough 1 by 12 inch board located on a small flat on the side of a hill.[29]

Chris Eationhover, in the 1880 U.S. Census, resided in Township 3, San Mateo, California. Eationhover listed his age as 28, indicating a birth year of 1852. His birthplace was listed as Prussia. Occupation at the time was that of a farm hand and he listed his marital status as single.[30] The only information for Elizabeth and William come from their burial records. Elizabeth Eationhover and her son William were buried in the Coquille Masonic Cemetery. Elizabeth Eationhover - Died July 15, 1889 age 21 years, 2 months, 21 days. For William, age 5 years, 5 months, 17 days.

At the time of the murder the Eationhover's were in a five-year lease of property from the Gilman's. The Eationhover house was located on the riverbank about 200 yards south of the Gilman residence.[31] Unable to bear the loss of his family Chris Eationhover committed suicide three years later on October 21, 1892 in Coquille City at the residence of E.S. Spurgeon. No burial records were located for Chris Eationhover.

According to Historian Boyd Stone, Fidelia Gilman went mad. Living with her daughter, Dora Miller, and granddaughter, Lela Miller, Gilman was known to have scrubbed the paint off the side of the house thinking she was scrubbing off blood.[32] The 1900 U.S. Census revealed Fidelia, at the age of 73, was living in the Norway Precinct.

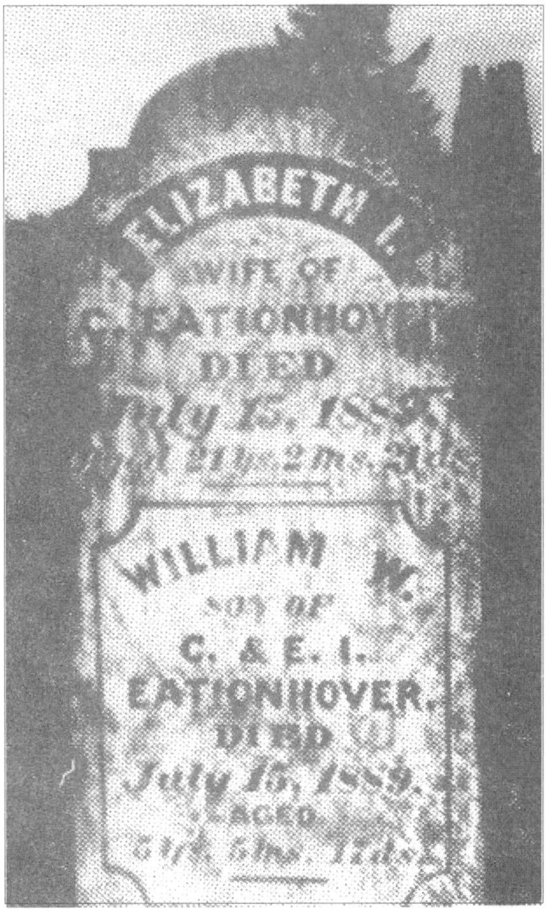

Figure 10:
In Memory of Elizabeth
and William Eationhover
Photo courtesy of Boyd Stone,
Coos County Historian

The Crime and Punishment: Dodge, in his *Pioneer History of Coos and Curry Counties, Or.* wrote the following account of the murders:

> The most fiendish plot to annihilate a whole family came near being consummated at John F. Gilman's place, two miles above Coquille City, July 13, 1889. Chris Eationhover had a five-years' lease on Gilman's place, and he and his family lived in a house back some forty rods from the Gilman residence. The family consisted of a wife and a boy five years old. Mr. Eationhover had been at work away from home for a week, and on arriving opposite his home he halooed for some one to come across with a boat. Mr. Gilman responded, and was unusually friendly, but when on the shore after crossing he struck him a fearful blow on the head, which felled him to the ground. Then a general fight ensued, but they were finally separated by Mrs. Gilman. Eationhover, who was badly injured, crossed the river to Mr. Tucker's and the alarm was given. Marshall Johnson, of Coquille City, and posse went up and arrested both Gilman and his wife. On being questioned, Gilman stated that Mrs. Eationhover and her boy had started up to meet her husband. Thinking that all was not right, the posse broke into Eationhover's house, but could not find the wife and child. A search was made, and soon their dead bodies were found, carefully covered with roots, dirt and moss a short distance from the house. The boy's body was under that of the mother. Mrs. Eationhover had been killed by a blow to the left side of the head with some blunt instrument, and the boy had been choked to death. Gilman was given a preliminary examination at Coquille City, and came near being mobbed hence he was taken to the county jail.
>
> John F. Gilman pleaded guilty and was sentenced to be hanged. The execution took place at Empire City, Friday - December 13, 1889. L. Harlocker was the sheriff. Mrs. Gilman was acquitted.
>
> This was not the first time that Gilman, had tried to destroy the Eationhover family. At one time, while the family was away, their bread was poisoned, but their lives were saved with sweet oil.

Contrary to the writings of Dodge, Gilman did not plead guilty to the charge of murder.

On July 17, 1889 the *Coos Bay News* headlined: **A Cold Blooded Murder.**

> News was received from Coquille City by wire on Sunday of a most horrible murder, which had been committed near that town, presumably on Friday morning. It seems that a family named Eatenhoover, consisting of husband, wife, and boy aged 6 years, had rented the farm belonging to John Gillman, about a year ago, for a period of five years. They built a house about 100 yards distant from the one occupied by Gillman and wife, with whom, it is said, they were not on the best of terms, owing to some little trouble growing out of a trivial affair about adopting a child. Eatenhoover was working on Heickendorff's place, a few miles distant, on the opposite side of the river, at the time of the murder, and was totally unconscious of the horrible deed which bereft him of his wife and child. He started for home Saturday evening, intending to spend Sunday with his family, and on arriving at the river bank, called to Gillman to bring a skiff and ferry him across, which was done. After landing, Gillman picked up a club, made from the butt end of an oar, and when asked by Eatenhoover what he intended to do with it, made some evasive answer. While on the way to the house, which is a narrow trail, Gillman slipped up behind his intended victim, and struck him a heavy blow on the head, felling him to the ground. Eatenhoover regained his feet and started to run, but tripped and fell, and Gillman then jumped on him and commenced jabbing him in the neck with a pocket knife. It seems the fiend had two knives in his pocket, one of which was a good one; but fortunately for Eatenhoover, he drew the knife with the broken blade in his excitement, which is the only reason that another victim has not been added to the list. Eatenhoover finally made his escape, and got to Coquille City, where he told his story, and a party of men immediately started for the scene. On arriving at the house, no trace of the woman and child could be found. The table was set as if fur breakfast, and the little boy's plate had some food on it. A close search being instituted, some blood stains were found, and the fact that murder had been committed became painfully apparent.
>
> The party scattered in all directions to find, if possible, the remains, and succeeded in discovering them buried in one grave in a gulch, a short distance from the house. They were taken to Coquille City, where a post mortem examination was held, and the fact was developed that the unfortunate victims had been strangled to death. Gillman was arrested and confined in jail.

As the facts became known the most intense excitement prevailed. Groups of men were discussing the horrible details on every corner, and the popular feeling was in favor of lynching. There were a few, however, who believed in letting the law take its course, and they were successful in the end.

Gillman confessed the murders; told how he had struck the woman with a hoe, knocking her down; that the little boy became frightened and ran away; that he overtook him and choked the poor little fellow and carried him back to where the mother was lying unconscious, but still alive. He choked her also, and hastily digging a grave under the butt end of a fallen tree, he threw the bodies in and covered them up. Another grave was found a little higher up the gulch, which, it is presumed, was intended for Eatenhoover when he should put in an appearance.

Sheriff Harlocker and Dave Hutcheson went over from the bay Sunday afternoon and took charge of the prisoner. They brought him here Monday, and in the afternoon took him to the county jail at Empire. He had been brought before Justice Simons at Coquille City, and was committed to jail, to appear at next session of circuit court. Mrs. Gillman is being held at Coquille City, as it is thought by many that she was connected in some manner with the crime. Gillman is about 60 years old, and has lived on the Coquille a long time. He was arrested a year ago on suspicion of having killed George Morras, whose body was found in the river; but the evidence was not deemed sufficient to hold him for trial and he was set at liberty. There were many who believed him guilty then, and their belief is strengthened by these later developments.

July 18, 1889 the *Plaindealer*, a Douglas County newspaper, headlined: **Murder at Coquille.**

Empire City, Or. July 15, Eastenhever, a tenant of John Gilman's on his farm, near Coquille City, returning from his week's work yesterday evening, was waylaid and attacked by John Gilman near his home; but succeeded in making his escape and gave alarm. A large party from Coquille City was immediately organized and returned to the farm, where they finally found to-day the bodies of Eastenhever's wife and child, who had been murdered and then buried near the house. A ready-made grave was also found for the husband. Gilman and his wife were arrested and the circumstances point conclusively to their guilt. Gilman wanted them to leave, which they refused to do until the lease had expired. There is great excitement here, and there are fears of lynching to-night.

July 24, 1889 the *Coos Bay News* reported:

The people here appreciate the account of the Eatenhover tragedy which appeared in last week's NEWS, as a temperate and accurate description. A gentleman in town says truly enough that it is "another Whitechapel affair," and likens John Gilman to "Jack the Ripper." It is regarded as significant that the culprit struck first at the woman. The slaying of the child and husband appear to have been secondary consideration. The motive for this frightful crime has not yet been stated, though Gilman has broadly hinted it. In the long run it is likely to be found that there is a certain bond of connection between the Morras mystery and the Eatenhover butchery. Mrs. Gilman appears to have played the part of lady Macbeth. She is cast in the same stern mould. If not before Mrs. Gilman was accessory after the fact.

There are no new developments in the murder case. Gilman and his wife are confined in jail at Empire, and the excitement having somewhat subsided, it is probable that the law will be allowed to take its course.

The court case file revealed that on October 9, 1889 John F. Gilman was indicted for the crime of murder and was arrested the same day by Sheriff Lintner Harlocker.

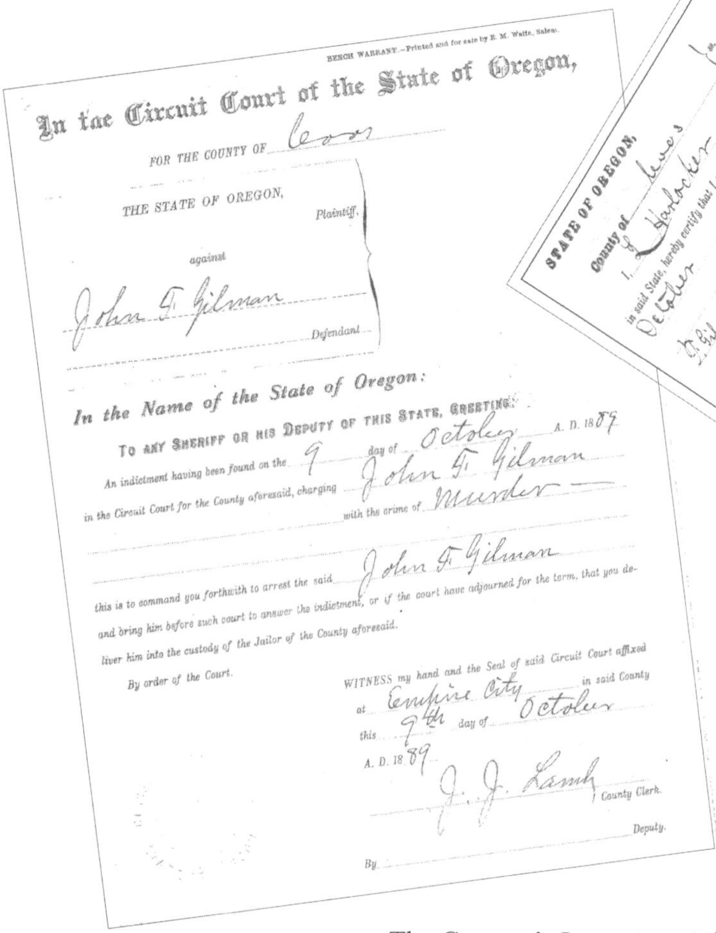
BENCH WARRANT.—Printed and for sale by E. M. Waite, Salem.

In the Circuit Court of the State of Oregon,

FOR THE COUNTY OF Coos

THE STATE OF OREGON, Plaintiff,

against

John F. Gilman Defendant.

In the Name of the State of Oregon:

TO ANY SHERIFF OR HIS DEPUTY OF THIS STATE, GREETING:

An indictment having been found on the 9 day of October A. D. 1889 in the Circuit Court for the County aforesaid, charging John F. Gilman with the crime of Murder

this is to command you forthwith to arrest the said John F. Gilman and bring him before such court to answer the indictment, or if the court have adjourned for the term, that you deliver him into the custody of the Jailor of the County aforesaid.

By order of the Court.

WITNESS my hand and the Seal of said Circuit Court affixed at Empire City in said County this 9th day of October A. D. 1889

J. J. Lamb County Clerk.

Deputy.

By

No. 1

In the Circuit Court, Of the State of Oregon, For the County of Coos

THE STATE OF OREGON, Plaintiff,

against

John F. Gilman Defendant

BENCH WARRANT.

Filed Oct 9th 1889

J. J. Lamb Clerk

STATE OF OREGON, County of Coos } ss.

I, Harlocker Sheriff of the County of Coos in said State, hereby certify that I executed the within writ on the Ninth day of October A. D. 1889, by arresting the said John F. Gilman in my county, and have the said John F. Gilman in my custody

Dated this 9th day of October 1889

Harlocker

Sheriff of Coos County Oregon

Figure 11: Bench Warrant for John F. Gilman

The Coroner's Inquest contained the testimony of two physicians who conducted the examinations of Elizabeth and William Eationhover. First is the testimony of Doctor J. D. Sponogle.

Dr. Sponogle being sworn deposed and says as follows

Q State your name age and occupation

A J D Sponogle age 44 years occupation Physician and Surgeon

Q How long have you been practicing as a Physician and Surgeon

A Twenty three years

Q Where do you reside

A In Coquille City Coos county Oregon

Q Did you as a physician examine the body of Mrs. Eationhover and son

A I did

Q What was your conclusion as the result of that examination

A Mrs. Eationhover came to her death by fracture of the second cervical vertebrae

Q What in your opinion was the cause of the fracture

A Was from a blow by some blunt instrument received on the left side of the face and head near the angle of the lower jaw.

Q What is the reason that the fracture of the second cervical vertebrae causes death

A It is from paralysis of the (unknown) nerve which has its origin below (*unknown word*) Joint

Q Were there any other marks of violence upon the body

A There were other marks upon the angle of the jaw on left side which resembled those made by scratching: There was no other marks or bruises on the body. Rigor Mortis not well marked

Q What marks of violence did you find upon the body of the son of Mrs. Eationhover and what was, in your opinion, the cause of death

A There was encircling his neck only the marks of a cord drawn tightly ante-mortem. There was also a dislocation of the two upper cervical vertebrae. The latter lesion was sufficient to produce instant death
Q Was there any other marks of violence upon the body
A There was no other marks of violence upon the body. Rigor mortis well marked.
Q What is you conclusion as to the cause of the death of Elizabeth Eationhover and her son Wm Eationhover.
A My conclusion is that their death was caused by the facts which I have stated and that they were murdered.

/s/ "JD Sponogle MD"

The next testimony in the Inquest was from Doctor S. L. Levere;

Dr. S.L. Levere being first duly sworn testifies as follows.

Q What is your name age and occupation.
A Name S.L. Levere, age 59, occupation Physician and Surgeon.
Q Were you called and present and did you assist in the examination of Elizabeth and Wm Eationhover her son
A I was and did so assist
Q Are you acquainted with the deceased and did you recognize the bodies as those of Mrs. Elizabeth Eationhover and her son
A Yes sir
Q State the result of your examination, what marks of violence you found upon the body of Elizabeth E. and what caused her death.
A I found upon examination the marks of a blow upon the left side of the head and neck. Made by some kind of heavy club with smooth surface. From which death producing dislocation of the upper vertebrae which blow caused her death.
Q Did you find any other marks of violence upon the body of the woman
A None at all
Q What was the result of your examination of the body of Wm Eationhover and her child
A In the examination of the child I found a work of a cord or small rope around his neck the not of it being in front by tightening of that rope or cord to a certain extent caused a dislocation of the upper and second vertebrae from which was the cause of the childs death.
Q Were there any other marks of violence upon the child
A None at all
Q What are your conclusions as to what was the cause of the death of Elizabeth and Wm Eationhover
A Everything in the examination were to show to me that they were murdered.

/s/ "S.L. Levere"

October 22, 1889 the *Coquille City Herald* reported two articles regarding the case.

The Gilman case is creating a great deal of excitement. Mrs. G. is out on bail of $3000 with W.A. Luse and Alex. Stauff on the bond. The motion for continuance was promptly denied and the case opened this (Monday) morning.

Headline: **TRIAL OF GILMAN. — Guilty of Murder in First Degree. — To be Hanged December 13, 1889.**

The trial of John F. Gilman for the murder of Mrs. Eationhover and five-year-old son was commenced last Tuesday morning before the circuit court. Forty-seven persons were examined before a jury was had. These consisted of B. A. Adams, B. F. Ross, T. A. Armfield, N. U. Martinson, George M. Sealy, C. E. Houser, H. W. Holverstott, G. W. Skaggs, Wm. Barkis, E. W. Guptill, S. J. Hulbert, James Masters.

On Friday, before, defendant had tried to get a continuance for reasons embodied in affidavits by himself as to his sanity; that he expected, to prove at next sitting of the court by Dr. Vance, Wm. P. Skelly and Laura Lawrence that his mind was unsound. The judge overruled the motion. There were a large number of witnesses examined, but as the testimony was so nearly alike, we give only that of some of the principal ones.

Testimony of Mr. Eationhover.

I am husband of the woman killed and father of the little boy. I came down the river from where I worked on foot, and got to river opposite Gilman's about 10 o'clock. I called out thinking wife would bring boat over, but Gilman answered and came over in boat. Gilman complained of being sick I offered to row the boat, but Gilman said he would paddle. He had a club in the boat and I asked him what it was for; he said to help him along. I fastened the boat when we landed and we went up the bank together. When we got in the corral Gilman struck me on one side of the head and almost knocked me down, and then another on the other side of the head, and then clinched, and both fell down and rolled over and I managed to getaway. I ran through the bars and he caught me. I broke away and went to house to get tool to defend myself, and he caught me and began stabbing. He tried to cut my throat. Pretty soon Mrs. Gilman came up. I broke loose and tried to run down the road, I stumbled and fell and he caught me again. We were down rolling 'round, and I got the knife away from him, and I finally got up and ran to the river. I made best licks and got into Gilman's boat and got across the river to Mr. Tucker's. Mr. Tucker helped me out and I was sick. When I was first struck on the head I cried "help, murder." The first I saw of my wife and child I found them, wife and child, buried near a tree, Sunday forenoon. Gilman was up where I was working on Thursday. I asked him how the folks were getting along, and told to tell them I would be home Saturday night. We had some little disputes with Gilman in regard to the berries and fruit on the farm. Gilman did not object to my staying on the place, but Mrs. Gilman did. My wife went with me when I left for work - part of the way — and took back the boat. I took the knife. I wrenched it out of his hand. My boy was five years old and could talk.

Cross Examination,

I was about four rods from Gilman's barn when first attacked. I had just got through the bars and he caught my clothes. I pulled away and he came through and caught me; I was reaching down under the house to get tools; he had hold of me and pulled me down. I was first attacked in the corral. I ran through the gate— he after me. We were walking side by side when he first struck, I could not tell what with. I clinched him and hallooed "murder." He pursued me up near the house and had the knife and cut me. Along the last of the light Mrs. Gilman came; I saw her have hold of Gilman's hand. I do not remember of telling Dr. Sponogle "that if Mrs. Gilman had not helped me I would have been killed." I have no financial interest in convicting Gilman. I have sued him for damages for the killing. Never had any particular trouble with him. He was always friendly after these quarrels. He had some petty quarrels with my wife; they always made up after them. I don't know any motive for killing. Heuekendorff's, where I worked, was five or six miles from Gilman's. He is a son-in-law of Gilman's. He had a club in the boat. I don't know why I asked him why he had the club. He threw that away before the difficulty commenced. It was about 30 yards from his house and a short distance from my house. It is a fact that prior to this time my family was poisoned. I don't know (missing) other enemies about the place. I had leased the place for four years. Mrs. Gilman once said she would see that we did leave. I received two blows; the first sounded as if it was a bottle. I thought it was a bottle but could not find any. It dazed me.

Testimony of H. B. Tucker,

I reside on the Coquille. I know John Gilman and Eationhover have known them about 18 months I live just across the river from them. On the night of the 13th of July, a neighbor said some one was crying "murder and help." I put on my boots and went out, I could hear talking. After I got to the river I could hear old lady Gilman talking loud; I could not hear what Gilman said, I saw wounded man in a boat. Mrs. Gilman said: "He's over;" and after a little she said, "John, you know you did it." Eationhover was cut in the throat and was bleeding and vomiting; he could not stand up; I had to pull him out of the boat. It was about 9 o'clock. It was not a very dark night I sent a runner down to Mr. Roy to ask for a doctor and officers. The light was burning, and as soon as the Gilman's got to the house they lowered the light. I saw Eationhover's boat on the other side of the river on Friday. There were no tracks leading to the boat. I saw Mrs. Eationhover and the boy on the Monday evening before; they were at my house. My house is about 500 yards from the Gilman house.

Testimony of Mrs. M. Willard,

I reside on the Coquille river; have lived there 16 years. I live on the opposite side of the river from the Gilman house. On Saturday, July l3th, me and boy started out to milk, and heard cries, "Oh, Oh, help." I thought first that it was on the landing. I ran up to Mr. Tucker's place and called them out; we could hear noise and cries, but could not make them out: then heard cow bells and trouble with the cattle, and then Mr. Tucker put boots on and I went home. I went back and found Eationhover prostrate on the ground, and I thought he was gasping his last. I could hear Gilman - sounded as if he was searching in the garden - and I heard Mrs. Gilman say: "I'll not tell unless I have to; but John, you know you did it." Eationhover was bleeding and could not stand without help. It was about 9 o'clock and was not very dark.

Cross Examination.

Mr. Tucker was with me all the time when I was on the bank of the river. I heard something splash in the water. Miss Mitchell and I thought it was coming over. It would be considerable satisfaction to see him hung. My feeling would not cause me to deviate from the truth.

Testimony of Mrs. J. Morgan.

Have lived on the Coquille about two years; have known John Gilman about nine years; know Eationhover and family; reside about 1 ½ miles from Eationhover place; I remember the trouble. Saw Mrs. Eationhover and boy on Thursday, 11th of July, they left about 4 o'clock p.m. Mrs. Eationhover and boy left; to go home. She said it was her intention to go up Saturday evening and bring Eationhover home. She said she was going up the river in a row boat.

Testimony of Joseph Johnson.

I have lived in Coquille City four years; am acquainted with parties to this case. I remember the trouble. I went up to the house of the defendant the night of the difficulty, with others, and found him at his house in bed with his clothes on. I asked Gilman what had become of Mrs. Eationhover and child, and he said he did not know unless they had gone up the river after Eationhover, as they had said they were going. He said he saw them Friday morning and they told him this. I took the defendant to Coquille that night. Sam Johnson, Devaul, and Boyrie were in the boat with me. Mrs. Eationhover and child were discovered Sunday morning about 9:30 o'clock. I saw the woman and child in one grave about 100 yards of Eationhover's home.

Testimony of S. P. C. Johnson.[J]

I live in Coquille City, and remember this difficulty. I went to Gilman's house on Saturday evening. I took my brother and others with me and found him in the house; he was lying in bed with his pants on. I opened the front door; they were lying on bed. I told them what I had come for and asked him about Mrs. Eationhover and boy. He said the last he knew she was going up the river for her husband, and that she might be at Mrs. Smith's. I think he said he saw her last on Thursday.

Testimony of John Baker.

Remember the difficulty; went up and helped arrest defendant. Evidence same as preceding witness as regards what defendant said about Mrs. Eationhover.

Testimony of David Hutcheson.[K]

Reside in Marshfield; remember the circumstance of this trouble; went over to Coquille City and came back with Gilman, Sheriff Harlocker and Dr. Cook. Gilman said he did not think there was any danger after passing China Camp creek. There were no threats to make him confess. Noticed his pants were stained, and asked him if it was blood on his pants; he said yes. Asked about blood in house. He said he killed them at the spring; he said he knocked her down and the boy ran away and he ran after him and choked him; he said he was a smart little fellow and might tell; he could talk and tell what be saw.

Cross Examination.

Saw Gilman the first time in jail; heard him make another confession. He was in jail and a crowd outside wanted him to own up; they said they had no objection to his coming over if he would tell all about it. Several told him to tell the whole thing. If he did not tell it all he was liable to be hung. There were about 100 men outside of the jail. He did not appear to be worried. I told him he had better tell. The old woman spoke up and said: "Yes, John, tell it all, you know you done it; and clear me." I went out and when I came back he was telling it again. Did not hear anybody tell him they would hang him. I said I was satisfied that you did the killing, and you killed Morras and he said; "Will admit I killed Morras, but will not admit this

[J] S.P.C. "Sam" Johnson was City Marshal of Coquille City and district constable granting him police powers to apprehend Gilman.

[K] David Hutcheson was the City Marshal of Marshfield as well being the district constable which would grant him law enforcement powers throughout the state.

killing." Bill Copely came in with a rope. Gilman was taken out of Coquille City in a wagon; we hurried out as fast as we could. Was not much afraid and don't think he was. The confession was made three or four miles out of Coquille City.

Joseph Johnson Recalled.

Gilman made a statement to me about the killing. Four of us were present. Asked him if he carried the woman away alone? He said "Yes, I did it, killed her in the gulch and killed the child to prevent its telling. The child ran toward the house and I caught it and choked it and broke its neck." He said he intended to murder Eationhover. Never intended he should reach the house. I did not hear any threats; did not see any rope until we were going out. It was not a rope to hang anyone, but was a little rope five or six feet long. Was friendly with Gilman until this happened. Tried to defend him.

H. B. Tucker Re-called.

Saw the defendant at Eationhover's house Friday evening before the trouble. Had been out to my chicken corral. Looked to see if the woman had come home, and saw him walking round the house with a tin bucket on his arm. I had seen him there frequently.

Sam Johnson Re-called.

There was a rope in jail when Gilman was there. It has been there a year, and is there yet. The wharf threatened to give way and I got it to tie up the wharf in high water. I bought it and put it there and it is there now. Heard no threats, and saw no rope then.

Testimony of Andrew Jackson.

Have lived on the bay 21 or 22 years; know Gilman; had a talk with him about this killing on Wednesday after he was put in jail. There was no threat of any kind. I went in there and said to him: "Old man you are in a pretty bad scrape." He started by saying that they were trying to get his property. I asked him if he was not sorry he killed the boy. He said he was sorry at first, but if he had it to do over again he would kill him. He said he strangled him with a string, and then put his head across his knee and broke his neck, and he showed me how he did it. Asked him if he killed George Morras, and he said "no." He asked me if I thought they would mob him? I told him I did not know.

Testimony of Capt. James Hill.

Reside on Coos bay; saw defendant in jail for first time. Had a conversation then with him. Samuel Davis and I went to see him. The old gentleman was looking through the wicket. He said he was feeling pretty sore; said that he had a fight with Eationhover; said he killed the woman, but wouldn't tell why but it would come out at the trial; said he attacked Eationhover because he said he would pitch into him. I said, "They will hang you as sure as God," and asked him if he had no remorse? He said it was hard to kill the boy; he was a pretty boy. Samuel Davis was there and heard it all. It was about a week after he was put in.

J. J. BAKER RE-CALLED.

I had a talk with Gilman the night he was arrested. He said "I hurt Eationhover; all that saved him was that I got hold of the wrong knife." I told him the people thought they both did the killing. He said: "I did the killing They can stretch my neck, but if they hang the old woman they will hang an innocent party."

SAM JOHNSON RE-CALLED.

Had a talk with Gilman on Monday after his arrest; took him up to the court, and he wanted Siglin for attorney, so the examination was put off. We went into the jail and his son said, "you had better have your preliminary examination and have it over." He said: "I actually killed the woman and child. I don't care about the woman, but the poor little child." On Sunday night my brother asked him if he slept soundly after killing that poor little boy, and he said, "Yes, why not?" I never saw anybody go in the jail with a rope, and never heard any threats in the jail against Gilman. The old man did not tell me at any time "for God's sake don't leave the door open."

TESTIMONY OF R. HOUGHTON.

Live at Norway; know the defendant, Gilman, 15 years. My place is about 3 ½ miles from his. Saw Gilman on the Friday preceding the trouble; he came out of the brush in the gulch and started up to the house. I was close to him; spoke to him and he nodded and passed on. I usually talked with him, but he did not want to talk. Saw the place of the grave, and told Cathcart when I saw him hunting, where I saw Gilman come out of the brush, and they went up there and found the bodies. Was there when the bodies were lifted out of the grave. Heard charges against Gilman a year ago that he killed George Morras.

TESTIMONY OF J. M. SIGLIN.

I had Eationhover's gun. Found it on the place. There is a log right by the county road; found the gun lying by the road by the log. I did not find it by chance. I had been informed that a gun had been hid, and the reason it had been hid. I had been informed that it had been hid about that place. The gun is in Anderson's stable, Received no information from Gilman. Albert Gilman and W. A. Luse were with me.

TESTIMONY OF MRS. COPLEY.

I helped to shroud Mrs. Eationhover. There was a bad cut on the back of head and near left temple; should judge her nose was broken; her arms were bruised; her left hip bruised; her right arm had finger prints on it; on the lower side of the right limb, near the body was a bad bruise.

After the witnesses were examined the charge was given and the jury retired. In twenty minutes they brought in a verdict as charged in the indictment—murder in the first degree—which is punishable by death by hanging. The judge read the verdict aloud and asked the jury if that was their verdict at which all bowed their heads and answered in the affirmative. His Honor then said that sentence would be passed at 4 p. m. the following day.

THE SENTENCE.

Promptly at 4 p.m. on Thursday the prisoner was brought into court the room being packed to its utmost capacity by citizens of the county. Addressing the doomed man, the judge rehearsed the case, how he had been accused, proven guilty, and condemned by twelve of his fellow citizens, etc. The prisoner being asked to stand up, the judge asked him if he knew any reason why sentence should not he passed, to which he answered in a voice audible only to those very near him and not at all so to this reporter. The judge stopped him and said, in substance: I have no patience with one who would commit such a dastardly crime that scarcely has a parallel in the annals of criminal courts. It is beyond human conception how one, possessed with even the commonest instincts, could commit so fiendish an act. You are condemned and despised by all good people, but it is useless to waste words on you. If the cries of that poor little, innocent boy to spare his mother could not arouse your sympathy, it isn't likely that any thing I might say could excite remorse.

Then the sentence of hanging, on Dec. 13th, — "Till you're dead and may God have mercy on your soul," at which the whole house save Gilman was deeply moved. He showed his accustomed stoicism.

Mrs. Gilman will have hearing at next term, it appearing from the testimony that she was cognizant of the facts. She is out on bail.

October 23, 1889 the *Coos Bay News* reported:

John F. Gilman, who murdered Mrs. Eationhover and little boy, near Coquille City on July 12th, was sentenced last Thursday to be hanged on December 13th, 1889. Mrs. Gilman, who was indicted for "aiding another who had committed a felony, with knowledge that he had commuted such felony, with intent that said person might escape arrest, trial and conviction therefore," is out on bail in the sum of $3,000, to appear at the May term of circuit court.

The Court journal revealed that both John and Fidilia Gilman were prosecuted at the Justice Court level. The cost of the trial for John Gilman was $65.45; which included seven special bailiffs and three special constables. The trial of Fidelia Gilman, who was acquitted, cost $13.

November 5, 1889 the *Coos Bay News* printed two articles regarding Gilman:

Gilman's attorney visited him on Sunday and informed him that a search of all the authorities would not reveal the shadow of a show for continuance or a new trial in his case; that he must made up his mind to pay the death penalty on Dec. 13, and tears came to the old man's eyes and he wept for the first since his incarceration. He is failing rapidly, it is said, and may not live till the day set for his execution. It is a sad, sad case all the way through.

John F. Gilman, is busily engaged writing a biography of his life. He protests his innocence of the murder of which he has been found guilty but Sheriff Harlocker will see that the law is carried out to the letter.

December 18, 1889 the *Coos Bay News* headlined: **EXECUTION OF GILMAN.** — He Walks on the Scaffold Without Assistance. — What he had to say Before he suffered for his Crimes.

On Friday last, Gilman, the murderer of Mrs. Eationhover and child, suffered the penalty of his crime at Empire City, several hundred people, witnessing the execution.

The details of the horrible crime were published at the time of its occurrence, and are yet fresh in the minds of the citizens of the county. It was the most deliberate and cold-blooded murder that ever disgraced the fair name of Coos county.

The double murder was committed on Friday, July 12th, 1889, but it was not until Sunday following that the facts were ascertained, the bodies found, and Gilman arrested. He had tried to kill Eationhover on Saturday evening, and came very near accomplishing his purpose; but Eationhover escaped and got to Coquille City, where a party was organized who proceeded to the Eationhover residence, which was close to Gilman's house, Eationhover having rented Gilman's farm, and both families were living close together. They found blood stains on the floor, and following up the clue they discovered the bodies of Mrs. Eationhover and child in a shallow grave in a gulch near by. Gilman was arrested and charged with having committed the crime. While in jail at Coquille City he confessed the killing; told how he struck the woman with a hoe and killed her in the gulch; how the poor little boy had run towards the house, and that he followed him and choked him and then broke his neck, giving us his reason for killing the child that he was a smart little fellow and might tell. Gilman narrowly escaped being lynched at Coquille City, but was finally safely jailed at Empire. He was tried at the October term of court, found guilty of murder in the first degree, and sentenced by Judge Bean to hang on December 13th. At his trial he stated that his mind had been affected for some time, caused by being struck on the head by a limb of a tree some years ago, and that at times he was not in his right mind.

Through the courtesy of Sheriff Harlocker and in company with Messrs. Siglin and Owen, attorneys for Gilman, and James Hill of the Mail, we were permitted to visit the condemned man in his cell, shortly before the execution. To inquiries if he wished to say anything for publication in regard to the crime, he said; "I was wild at spills; my wife often told me things I had done that I did not know of." Here he broke down and commenced crying, and through his sobs said "it is to bad, but I will try to go through," having reference to the approaching execution. Continuing he said: "If I had my rights and justice, in the way I was, I wouldn't hang. Mrs. Eationhover went to draw a pistol out of her pocket and said you —— —, then I struck her. I had gone to turn the cattle in, as it was getting late. I went through the gate and the woman followed me, and I struck her with a cane on the arm. I went wild then and remember nothing more — I was crazy. The blood spots found in and around the house were caused by a dog I had castrated that morning. I had always borne a good character up to this, and anyone can follow me up where I lived and prove what I say. If I had lived till the 24th of this month I would be 61 years old. I was born in Dearborn County, Indiana, and came to Scott's valley, Cal., in '56, where I lived 15 years. I have been in this county 18 years."

We asked him in regard to George Morras, who, it is generally believed, he had also killed. He was reminded of his fast approaching death, and his attorneys told him to speak out and tell the-truth about the matter. He most emphatically denied killing George Morras. Wiping the tears-from his eyes he said: "Why should I kill him? He was as good a friend as I ever had; it is wrong to accuse me of it. Everything bad that has been done on the river has been laid to me. I don't fear to die, but it is such a disgrace to my relatives. I was out of my mind if I committed these crimes." He broke down again here, and it was some little time before he could compose himself.

When asked if his wife knew anything about the murder of the woman and child, he said he was positive she knew nothing about it. "She was in bed after I got home; she would never do anything like that; she would talk plain, but there was no harm in her. She heard the fuss between me and the man; but saw or heard nothing of the other."

A little after one o'clock the sheriff stood on the scaffold and called the following names, who had been summoned as witnesses: Thos. Hirst, G.B. Sell, S. B. Cathcart, C. E. Edwards, J. P. Easter, J. A. Doake, D. H. Hutcheson, Abe Rose, T. W. Reinne, A. G. Aiken, Dr. Cook, John Flanagan. He then went to the jail, the door of which opened on the steps leading to the scaffold. Gilman was perfectly composed by this time, and heard the death warrant read without being visibly affected. His arms were tied above the elbows, and he walked on the scaffold without the least assistance, and without betraying the slightest emotion of fear. He stood on the trap and took a long look at the bay and surroundings, and turned his head towards the ocean, where the sun's rays were merrily dancing on the broad bosom of the Pacific, and then looking at the sea of upturned faces beneath him he said "farewell to all." There were on the scaffold, besides the sheriff, Attorneys Siglin and Owens, Atty. Hall, Dave Hutcheson, J. Hodson, and A. G. Aiken. After shaking hands with some of those on the scaffold, and while his legs were being tied, he said, "I recognize some of the people present, and I want to say good bye to all of them that will say good bye to me." At 1:16 ½ the black cap was put on; the noose was put around his neck and drawn taught, with the knot pressed close under the left ear. At 1:17 sheriff Harlocker sprung the trap, and the body dropped through to the space below, the feet being about six inches from the ground. There was not a quiver of any kind to show that he suffered the least pain. His neck was broken by the fall, and he died without a struggle. Drs. Cook, Leneave and Easter stood by the body till life was extinct. The pulse beat for a little over eleven minutes, and at 1:33 the rope was cut, and the body was lowered into the coffin by the two guards, Thos. Donnelly and J. F. Noyes. The remains looked perfectly natural as they lay in the coffin, the features showing no trace of the violent death he had died. A wagon was in waiting, and the body was hauled to the cemetery and buried.

There were some present that were under the impression that Gilman smiled at the crowd when he stood on the scaffold, but we think it is a mistake. We scanned him closely as we talked with him in the jail, and noticed, owing to the loss of upper teeth, that when his lips were compressed it looked as if he was smiling, when in fact such was not the case. We noticed the same look on his face when he was on the trap, and many erroneously considered it a smile. Shortly before the hour set for the execution, it looked as if the condemned man would break down altogether, and would have to be carried to the scaffold. He was offered liquor, but refused to touch it, saying he never drank anything. As the time approached, he regained his self control, and he faced death as calmly as though he meant it when he said, "I am not afraid to die."

Figure 12: Sheriff Lintner Harlocker

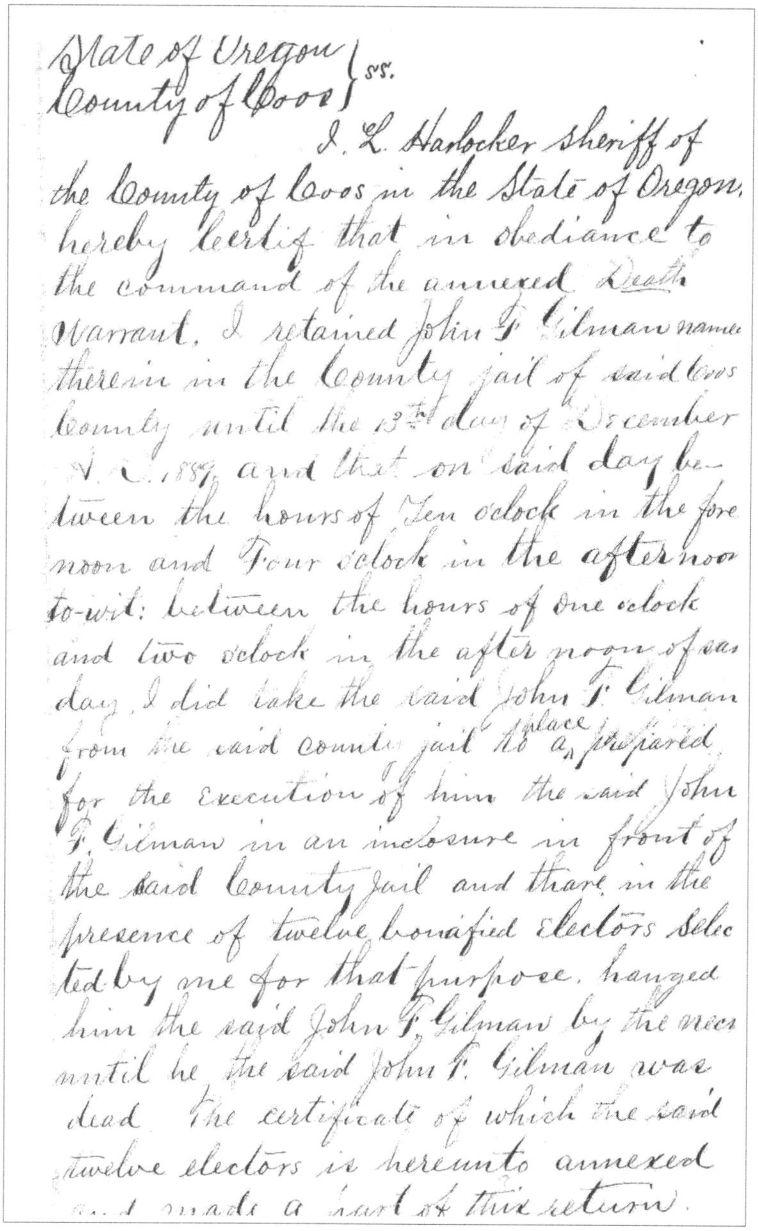

State of Oregon } ss.
County of Coos }
I. L. Harlocker sheriff of the County of Coos in the State of Oregon, hereby certify that in obediance to the command of the annexed Death Warrant, I retained John F. Gilman named therein in the County jail of said Coos County until the 13th day of December A. D. 1889 and that on said day between the hours of Ten oclock in the fore noon and Four oclock in the afternoon to-wit: between the hours of One oclock and two oclock in the after noon of said day, I did take the said John F. Gilman from the said county jail to a place prepared for the execution of him the said John F. Gilman in an inclosure in front of the said County Jail and there in the presence of twelve bonafied electors selected by me for that purpose, hanged him the said John F. Gilman by the neck until he the said John F. Gilman was dead. The certificate of which the said twelve electors is hereunto annexed and I made a part of this return.

Figure 13: Sheriff Harlocker Statement of Execution

Sheriff Harlocker performed his official duty in a manner to meet the approbation of all. The unpleasant task that devolved on him was faithfully executed, and was brought to a conclusion in a most creditable manner. The NEWS is under obligations to him for courtesies shown, which were duly appreciated.

December 19, 1889 The *Coast Mail* headlined: **UNDER THE GALLOWS, JOHN F. GILMAN PAYS THE PENALTY OF HIS BLOODY CRIMES.**

The details of Gilman's crime are yet fresh in the minds of the readers of the MAIL, which published a full account of his trial and sentence to death. The double murder was committed last July, when he killed Mrs. Eationhover and her little boy, a bright lad of six years and attempted to take the life of the husband and father.

He was sentenced by Judge R.S. Bean, and the date of his execution fixed at Friday, December 13th.

The fatal day dawned with a cloudless sky and the boats for Empire City were crowded with people on their way to witness the execution. At Empire City, the work of building the scaffold was in progress, and the resounding sound of the hammer upon the timbers in front of the jail must have made mournful music to the condemned man in his cell. During the forenoon multitudes visited the court-house yard and watched the progress of the preparations.

Shortly before 12 o'clock, James Hill, of the MAIL, in company with G.A. Bennett, of the News, and Gilman's attorneys visited the doomed man in his cell. He seemed to be broken down and yet struggled manfully to keep up and nerve himself to meet death. He was exhorted to tell the truth about the transaction, as there was no hope for him and he had but a few moments to live. He began weeping and bewailing his lot, and when his attorneys exhorted him to stand up and die like a man, he said through his tears: "I don' know whether I can, but I will try to go through." He declared that at the time of the killing Mrs. Eationhover started to draw a pistol out of her pocket and he struck her on the arm with a *(missing word).* "I went wild then and could remember nothing. I was crazy." he said: "If I had lived till the 24th of this month I would be 61 years old. I was born in Dearbon county, Indiana, and came to Scott's Valley, Cal., in 1856, where I lived fifteen years. I have been in this county nineteen years."

During the recital Gilman was seated on the bed, and was so broken down that Sheriff Harlocker thought it would be necessary to carry him to the scaffold. He proceeded further to emphatically deny the killing of George Morras and that his wife knew anything of the killing of Mrs. Eationhover and child.

Shortly after one o'clock Sheriff Harlocker ascended the steps of the scaffold and called the names of citizens who had been summoned to witness the execution, as follows:

Thomas Hirst,	G.B. Self,
S. B. Cathcart,	C. E. Edwards,
J. P. Easter,	J. A. Doake,
D. H. Hutcheson,	Abe Rose,
Thos. W. Reinne,	A. G. Aiken,
Dr. J. G. Cook,	John Flanagan

Gilman, at the near approach of death, seemed to gain control of his nerves, and heard the reading of the death warrant in his cell without a visible emotion. He was then brought from his cell dressed in a plain suit of clothes — the same he wore at his trial — and his arms were pinioned above the elbows. He mounted the steps of the scaffold with a firm tread, and stood on the fatal trap looking about with a sickly smile upon his wasted features. While his feet were being tied he made some common place remark about the number of people present, and said: — "I recognize some of the people present, and want to say good bye to all of those that will say good bye to me;" but when no one responded, as the sheriff pulled the black cap over his face, he said: "Nobody wants to say good bye to me."

The preparations being complete, at 1:17 o'clock p.m., Sheriff Harlocker sprang the trap, and the body fell to a distance of over six feet and swung half round, and without a movement of the muscles or a struggle of the slightest character, the soul of the murderer took its flight. Drs. Cook, Leneve and Easter stood by the body until the pulse ceased to beat, and in about eleven minutes pronounced life extinct. Thos. Donnelly and J. F. Noyes lowered the body into a plain coffin and the remains were taken to the cemetery and buried.

The unpleasant duty of Sheriff Harlocker was performed with a precision and carefulness characteristic of the man, and was well done.

There was no sympathy manifested for Gilman, and indeed could not well be, for the annals of crime furnish few instances of an cold-blooded and revolting homicides as the ones committed by this old man.

Figure 14: The Execution of John Gilman - Photo Courtesy of Coos County Sheriff Andy Jackson

Further review of the Court Journal revealed the following payment records regarding the Gilman execution; "Ordered that F. H. Nickenson be paid the sum of six dollars for assisting in quieting mob in the J.F. Gilman case." It is not known during what course of events a mob was quelled. For the cost of materials and building the execution scaffold, Ole Evenson received $38.00. The burial cost paid by the county amounted to $10.00 and another $7.50 for the burial lot was paid to John Flanagan.

Local Coquille lore claims the body of Gilman was claimed by family members. Buried on a knoll on the Gilman property, the gravesite was surrounded by a picket fence. The Gilman residence, vacant and alleged to be haunted, burned to the ground during a forest fire in 1936. The gravesite now sits under a house.[33]

During a search of records at the Coos Bay Library an undated and unknown source newspaper clipping was found. Headline: A TRY AT MURDER

> While George Sell lived at Rink Creek, John Gilman killed Gorge Morras. Thinking that Sell had witnessed the murder, Gilman planned to kill Sell also, but like most people … he failed to get everything done that he had planned. Gilman, however, made one try at Andy Anderson who was working in the fields. He heard a noise and turned around just in time to find Gilman slipping up behind him with a big club ready to strike him.
>
> Andy pulled his pistol and asked Gilman what he was doing. Gilman laughed and said, "I was just going to surprise you." and threw his club down and walked away.

The Court Journal entry for September 5, 1888 included payments for the George Morras Inquest. Included were witnesses John Gilman and C. Eationhover who each received $1.70 for their testimony. The search for the Coroner's

Inquest of George Morras was unsuccessful however; a newspaper account of the medical report was published in the August 29, 1888 issue of the *Coos Bay News*. The article records Morras as Morris. Headline: **Medical report upon the Case of George Morris**

I am legally qualified as Doctor in Medicine and Master in Surgery. After four years regular study in British schools, I began practice in 1872. I studied for, six months (1886-7) in Chicago, and hold a diploma from the Bennett College and Hospital, endorsed by the Illinois Board of Health. I possess an extra honorary diploma from Spain. My experience has been large and various, and I have held the position of Medical Officer to one of the largest dispensaries in London. I received instructions from Justice McDuffy to give evidence at inquest touching finding of body of Mr. George Morris in Coquille river, and, assisted by Dr, Leneve, I made a thorough post mortem examination. As seen before removal from the water, face and neck looked deeply congested, and arms and hands were brought up to the cheat. Corpse being laid out, signs of venous engorgement were very marked upon the front aspect from the chest upwards. From that point downward nothing calls for notice. Right side of head and face swollen, temple presenting a contusion caused by contact with some round or flat object before, or at instant of death. Eyeballs prominent, abrasions upon cheeks and nose. Arterial blood exuded from right nostril. Teeth clenched: on being separated blood exuded, but no frothy mucus.

At autopsy I carefully noted the site of the blow. The right temporal fossa was somewhat indented. There was no fracture, nor depression of bone, nor blood clot exhibited in the cranial cavity. The brain and its covering were rather pale. The cavity of the abdomen showed evidences of venous fulness, the liver being almost black from this cause. There was no rupture of any viscus.

In the cavity of the chest both lungs were highly congested; the air vesicles had abundance of air.

I discovered the essential cause of death in the right side of the heart, which was profoundly congested, and filled to over-distension with blood. The valves were frail, and the heart muscle generally of flabby texture.

In view of these results, and having heard evidence of witnesses, I submit that on the day in question, deceased, by physical strain in sculling a scow, incurred paralysis and overdistension of the right heart. Such a circumstance is not surprising on a hot day, with a man as appears from evidence not in good physical tone at the time. Blood stasis in the right heart would prevent aeration of either lung, and excite severe breast pang. The unfortunate gentleman appears to have cried aloud several times, and with teeth clenched and upper extremities brought to the chest for relief of agony, he reeled, fell, struck his head against side or end of scow, and rolled senseless into the stream. Doubtless nervous concussion, resulting from the injury, aided death.

I am satisfied that the fatal issue was brought about by heart failure, technically termed cardiac asphyxia. In this opinion Dr. Leneve concurs.

ANSWERS TO QUESTIONS PUT BY JURORS OR PERSONS INTERESTED.

The contusion of the head might have been received by contact with some hard object after the body had fallen heavily into the water, and before life was extinct. A blow from a sandbag or a flat piece of iron might have caused the contusion, while yet the man was on the scow. Serious concussion may arise from a hurt of the head resulting in death, post mortem examination of the brain yielding quite negative effects. A quarrel with some person may have practically the same effect on a flabby heart as overstrain in sculling. Pain is a common concomitant of heart disease. In angina pectoris there may be sharp paroxysmal neuralgia, and loud cries may be uttered just before death. A bursting aneurism will excite severe pain. I knew such a case, ending fatally in London. The heart of deceased must have been diseased for a considerable time, and much of the venous engorgement had been chronic in character.

W. K. VANCE, M. D., M. Ch.

Coquille City, August 24, 1888.

As is customary at inquests, and as our state as yet has no proper register of medical men, I beg to say that I have given my attention to pharmacy and practice of medicine for over 35 years. In 1846 and 1847 I studied in the Vermillion medical institute under the Illinois board; after which I studied medicine for three years with Dr. John Woods and other doctors. In 1851 I came to Oregon, and my work since then is well known to settlers. I quite agree with my friend Dr. Vance in his report. It is quite consistent with my experience and with precedents, that such an attack, accompanied by sharp pains, should overtake a man under the circumstances described. Moreover, I am aware that deceased has had a weak heart for years. The post mortem to my mind, beyond all question, reveals a definite cause of death from a doctor's point of view.

DR. S. L. LENEVE.

Also printed in the same issue:

Riverside people are concerned touching the disappearance of George Morris. It is probable he is drowned, and many friends are busied in dragging the river near his residence. His hat was found on a scow which he had been working on Monday, the 20th inst., the day of the disappearance. Mr. Morris bore an excellent character, and much sympathy is expressed for his family which has borne quite a succession of calamities.

LATER — The body was found somewhere in the vicinity of the scow. There was a bruise on the side of the head. A post mortem examination will be held.

September 5, 1888 the *Coos Bay News* reported:

The second autopsy on the body of Morras has been made be medical men instructed by relatives of the unfortunate deceased. This further examination verifies the very complete medical report of the case given to the public in last issue of the COOS BAY NEWS — a report, it may be added, universally accepted by our settlers.

The 1880 U.S. Census recorded George J. Morras was nineteen years old and born in Iowa. George Morras was buried at the Coquille Masonic Cemetery having lived from 1860 to 1888. At the time of his death Morras was engaged to John Gilman's stepdaughter.[34]

Was it a twist of fate that on October 21, 192, Chris Eationhover, like John Gilman, would die at the end of a rope? Tormented by the loss of his wife and child, Eationhover ended his suffering by hanging himself from a rafter of the home of E.S. Spurgeon in Coquille. Living with the Surgeon family, Eationhover believing he had nothing to live for scribed a note; "To Cecil: People talk too much. Can't come any more. Lay me by Libby and Willie. Settle bills and take what's left."

CHAPTER 10

THE CASE OF ASEPH H. HINCH

Case Synopsis: June 21, 1892 Andrew Wickman suffered a fatal gunshot wound from A.H. Hinch, on the South Slough. There was a quarrel over the use of a road used for logging. Wickman hauled logs and Hinch's son was using the same road to haul matchwood. Wickman drove the young Hinch away with a crowbar. The older, A.H. Hinch returned with a shotgun and opened fire on Wickman killing him instantly.

The Motive: It would appear the motive may have been a perception of Hinch defending his son for the alleged attack of Wickman with the crowbar.

The Parties: The victim, Andrew Wickman, was born July 16, 1848 and upon his death on June 21, 1892 left behind seven children and an invalid wife, Mary Elizabeth. The 1880 U.S. Census revealed that Wickman was a native of Finland and he was a resident of the South Slough Precinct at the time of the Census. With regard to the surviving Wickman family, the court journal recorded that an application for maintenance was received from Mrs. Wickman for herself, an invalid, and her seven children ages 17, 14, 7, 5, 4, 2 and six months. Due to the death of her husband the county authorized payment of $20 per month to support the Wickman family. Andrew Wickman was buried at the Marshfield I.O.O.F. cemetery. Mary Wickman was also buried at the I.O.O.F. cemetery in1927 at the age of 70.

Hinch, you may recall, was one of people who wrote about the murders of Burton and Venerable by the Native Americans. Hinch, reported to have been born about 1832 in Missouri,[35] moved to Coos County sometime prior to 1854. The 1860 U.S. Census, Randolph Precinct, list Hinch's first name as Athrof, age 27, being born in Missouri. Hinch became a miner, having discovered the black sand mine in 1866. He staked his claim and mined the black sand near Randolph. Hinch later traded the mine for a business in Marshfield and subsequently established a farm in South Slough. In the 1870 U.S. Census Hinch listed his name as A.H., 37 years old and born in Kentucky. Hinch, at that time, listed his occupation as a blacksmith. While residing in South slough Hinch committed the murder of Wickman.

Apparently this was not the first time Hinch was tried for murder. The District Court Journal recorded Hinch was indicted for first degree murder. On November 1, 1886 Hinch entered a plea of not guilty, requested a change of venue which was denied. A jury was impaneled which found Hinch not guilty.[36]

The Crime and Punishment: The newspaper account of the Wickman murder was first reported in the June 23, 1892 issue of the *Coast Mail* which does not appear in local archives. However, the article was reprinted in the March 30, 1939 issue of the *Coos Bay Harbor* as part of a weekly historical column authored by O.W. Briggs. Brigg's column, "Happenings of 47 years Ago" noted the past articles reported were from the collection of Mrs. Elizabeth Adams and Mrs. Mair Dano. If not for these three people this account of the Wickman murder would have been lost to time.

The Murder of A. Wikman

One of the historical tragedies of the county occurred on June 21, the murder of Andrew Wikman by A. H. Hinch, on a logging road near the head of South slough. The account printed in the Coast Mail occupied a column and a quarter and the gist was as follows:

Wikman owned the road and had, according to witnesses, given Hinch the right of hauling matchwood over it. It appeared that Hinch protested when Wikman hauled logs over the road, interfering with Hinch 's work. The coroner's jury, John Bear, Wm. Bettys, J. Davidson. Eugene Schetter, Chas. Jackson and Lee Minard made this finding: "We find that the person killed was Andrew Wikman at 10 o'clock today, or near about. And we further find that he came to his death by a gunshot wound in the right breast and was killed at the landing at his place on South slough, where he hauled logs. from evidence produced before us we are of the opinion that A. H. Hinch is the guilty party. We recommend that he be placed under arrest forthwith." Coroner was W. J. Butler.

Wikman was a Finn and an industrious man who had been a resident of the bay for 11 years, There were two children when the family arrived and five were born afterwards. The victim was 44 and bore a fine reputation as a man of character and not quarrelsome. Among witnesses who testified at the inquest which was hold at the scene were: John Larson, who found the body on the logging road a quarter of a mile from the landing. He knew of no trouble. He had delivered previously a note from Hinch to Wikman which said for Wikman to take his team off the road. John Hudson, a neighbor of Wikman, was informed of the shooting by Larsen. So was Charles Brown, another resident of the district. Dr. Tower said the bullet pierced the arch of the aorta and penetrated the right lung. Another note, or perhaps the one in question was described by Hilda Wikman, a daughter of the victim, who said: "Hinch wrote to papa that Milton says you are going to haul on the road today and he wrote 'if you haul logs on the road I can't haul matchwood, so now take your team off and save time and trouble." The girl knew nothing about any agreement between the two men about the use of the road. Hinch, in the Coast Mail article, was said to have killed an Indian woman previously and was a fugitive several years but finally brought to trial and was not convicted. Hinch was reported in the Mail to have surrendered to Sheriff Z. T. Siglin.

The report of the escape of Hinch also survived. The May 25, 1939 issue of the *Coos Bay Times,* Brigg's column "Happenings 47 Years Ago" published the article from the September 22, 1892 issue of the *Coast Mail*:

Hinch Escapes Jail

A. H. Hinch, who shot and killed Andrew Wikman on South slough on June 21, escaped jail at Empire in broad daylight and went into the woods south of the county seat. James Bohanan, deputy sheriff, that morning released Hinch from his cell to have access to the corridor and went to get a breakfast for the prisoner, and when he came back, Hinch was gone. It was found he had cut the bars with a saw probably made from a watch spring. He was seen by only one person, Mrs. John Lennon, while he was making his way to the Marshfield-Empire trail. Mrs. Lennon was well acquainted with the circumstances and knew Hinch. She went down town and informed the sheriff and deputy. Hinch came to the county in 1853 and has been resident in the lower bay to the date of his disappearance. He was a scout during the Indian war, and married an Indian woman.

Previously, Hinch had killed an Indian woman and escaped arrest, and trial, for three years mined at Randolph and made considerable money. He was arrested at Randolph three years after the first killing, but at his trial was released. He opened a business in Marshfield, ran behind and traded it to Andrew Nasburg for a Coos river ranch. Then the creditors took his farm away. Officers believed somebody was helping him to escape for one of his horses had been tied on the streets of Empire three days when he made his escape. Miss Georgina Cammann had seen the horse and took it to a barn that morning and fed it. Two men were arrested after the escape, under suspicion they had something to do with\the escape; Milton Hinch, a son, and J. K. Rines of South slough. Marshal Jack Farley made the arrests, but there was no evidence produced against young Hinch and he was released, while Rines' hearing was to take place later.

The murder was also documented by historian Orvil Dodge, author of *Pioneer History of Coos and Curry Counties, Or.* who wrote:

Andrew Wikman and A. H. Hinch, of South Slough, had a quarrel June 21, 1892, resulting in the latter shooting and killing the former. The quarrel was over the use of a road for logging purposes,

> Wikman hauling logs and Hinch's son using the same road to haul matchwood on. It is said Wikman drove Hinch away, with a crowbar. Hinch returned shortly after with a shot gun and opened fire on Wikman, killing him instantly. He was immediately arrested and, before his trial came off broke jail, but was captured again, convicted and sentenced to be hanged, but died in jail before the sentence went into execution.[37]

Dodge continued regarding the life of Hinch, even commenting about a prior allegation of murder at the hands of Hinch:

> Hinch was a pioneer of Coos Co. and in the early 50's was charged with the murder of an Indian woman on Isthmus slough. Nothing was done about it until after his discovery of the rich mines near Randolph in company with A. H. Thrift, then he was arrested and placed in jail. It was said that it was on account of his supposed wealth that the officers of the law arrested him and provided a way for him to dispose of his money. The criminal escaped several times and Mr. Moody, the sheriff, had much difficulty in finding his man. Finally he was brought to trial but was acquitted. Hinch was a merchant at Marshfield in 1872, but subsequently traded that business to Andrew Nasburg for a farm on Coos River. Debts that he had contracted while in Marshfield in the mercantile business hung heavily over the farmer and after a year or two his creditors sold his farm and Hinch retired to a comparatively secluded life. Hinch was a pioneer, it is true, and deserves credit for energy and courage in the early struggles and he did much to develop the mineral resources; but his ungovernable temper was his ruin.

An interesting fact regarding Hinch; according to the September 24, 1879 issue of the *Coos Bay News*, Hinch was even corresponded with Thomas Edison about the possibility of Edison obtaining platinum from Coos county for his use in the electric light.

A little more about Hinch's history was documented in the November 16, 1913 issue of the *Coos Bay News* when reporting about the life of Alex Thrift. The article stated the following about Hinch:

> In 1866 he (Thrift) and A.H. Hinch located what was afterwards known as the Lane blacksand mine, on the original beach at Randolph, about three miles inland from the present ocean beach. At that time, Bill Hill, who was then deputy sheriff at Empire City, came to Randolph and arrested Hinch for killing an Indian woman. A special term of court was called to try the case, and Hinch was acquitted.

With regard to this first allegation of murder the District Court Journal, page 100, revealed Hinch was, in fact, indicted for first degree murder. Page 123, dated November 1, 1866 noted Hinch entered a plea of not guilty, his attorney requests a change of venue with that request being denied and a jury was impaneled. The jury finding was not guilty.

After the killing of Wickman a warrant of arrest was issued on June 21, 1892 by Isaiah Hacker, Justice of the Peace in Empire City. The warrant was served the same day by Sheriff Siglin. From the court file the trial began in short order. In the file was a subpoena for George Miller to appear June 24th to give testimony for the state. The list of people paid for their services at the trial were as follows; Justice Isaiah Hacker; Sheriff Z.T. Siglin; witnesses Herman Hanson, John M. Hinch, Charles Brown, John Anderson, John Larson, William Metcalf, George, Miller, Joel Patterson, Miss Wakeman, and John Bear. The cost to the county for the trial was $83.80. However, there was nothing in the court file indicting when the trial concluded or the conviction.

After Hinch's escape a warrant of arrest was issued during the October term of the court for the crime of murder. The warrant was issued October 5, 1892. The only information regarding the capture of Hinch was from a December 24, 1912 article in the *Coos Bay News* reporting an unrelated murder which also occurred on the South slough. John

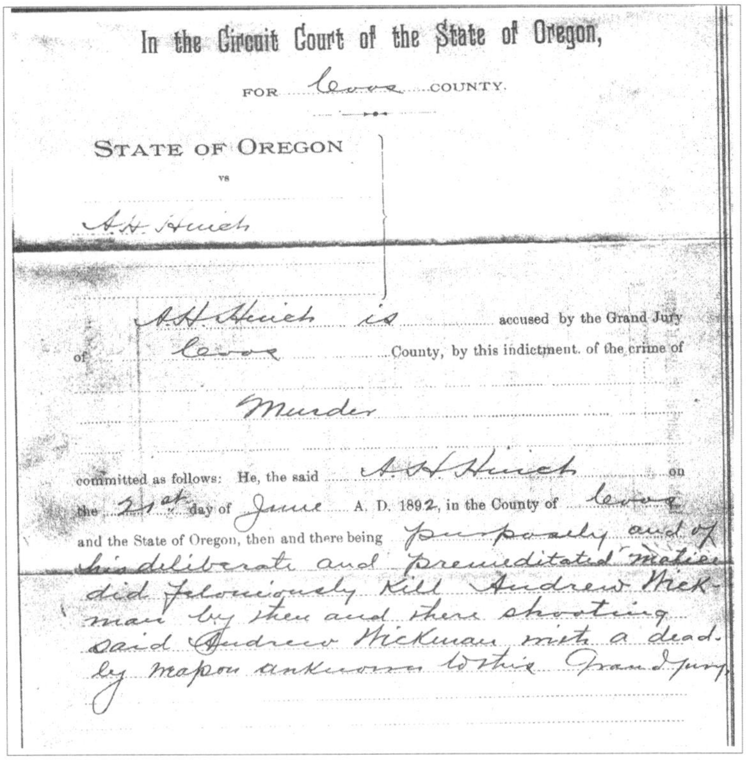

In the Circuit Court of the State of Oregon,

FOR Coos COUNTY.

STATE OF OREGON

vs

A.H. Hinch

A.H. Hinch is accused by the Grand Jury of Coos County, by this indictment, of the crime of

Murder

committed as follows: He, the said A.H. Hinch on the 21st day of June A. D. 1892, in the County of Coos and the State of Oregon, then and there being purposely and of his deliberate and premeditated malice did feloniously kill Andrew Wickman by then and there shooting said Andrew Wickman with a deadly weapon unknown to this Grand Jury

Figure 15: Hinch's Indictment for Murder

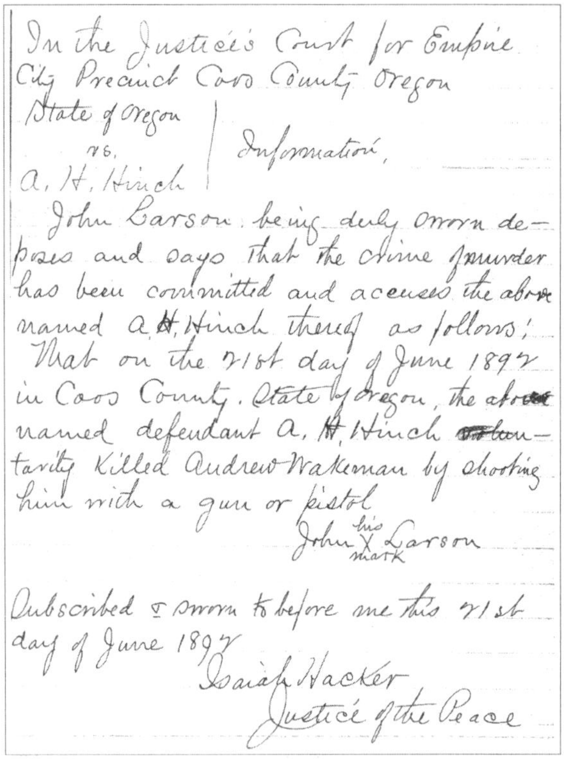

In the Justice's Court for Empire City Precinct Coos County Oregon

State of Oregon vs. A. H. Hinch — Information.

John Larson being duly sworn deposes and says that the crime of murder has been committed and accuses the above named A. H. Hinch thereof as follows: That on the 21st day of June 1892 in Coos County, State of Oregon, the above named defendant A. H. Hinch voluntarily killed Andrew Wakeman by shooting him with a gun or pistol

John his X mark Larson

Subscribed & sworn to before me this 21st day of June 1892

Isaiah Hacker
Justice of the Peace

Figure 16: A Witness Statement

Bear, referring to murders having occurred on the South slough, stated:

> The only man arrested and indicted for murder was A.H. Hinch, who killed a man named Wickman over a dispute about road building at South slough, a number of years ago, when R.M. Wieder was sheriff (1892-1894) Hinch escaped from jail at Empire and remained at large in the South slough vicinity until he was almost dead from consumption, when he surrendered to the authorities, dying a short time afterwards.

The court journal indicated there was trial in the case of the State versus Hinch on January 11, 1893. However, there is no indication if the case involved A.H. Hinch or another member of the Hinch family. Then on July 7, 1893 there is an entry regarding the payment to Dr. J.G. Cook in the amount of $18 for medical attention to A.H. Hinch. The next and last entry regarding A. H. Hinch was September 6, 1893 when the county ordered a $5.50 payment to C.A. Methin for assistance in the burial of A.H. Hinch.

Wednesday, August 2, 1893 the *Coos Bay News* headlined: **Death of A.H. Hinch**

> A dispatch was received from Empire, Tuesday morning, bringing the intelligence that A.H. Hinch, who killed Andrew Wikman at South slough last year, had died in the county jail of heart disease. He was an old pioneer, having come to the county in 1852, at which time he was 17 years of age, and took a conspicuous part in the Indian wars and the early settlement of Coos Bay. The old pioneers who know him in early days speak well of him, and recall many instances of kindness shown them by him.

On October 1, 1914 the *Coos Bay Harbor* printed an article regarding Edna Hinch, the daughter of A.H. Hinch. In the article was the following comment regarding her father's death:

> Her father was a white man and committed murder of Coos Bay. He fled to the woods and was found starving and died shortly afterward as a result of exposure.

CHAPTER 11

THE CASE OF CARL ALBRECHT

***Case Synopsis*:** Carl Albrecht was estranged from his wife, who days earlier sought a divorce of the grounds of cruelty, contacted her and after an unsuccessful bid to reconcile their differences Carl Albrecht shot his wife Hermanna, three times in the back on a public street in Marshfield. Albrecht attempted to flee whereupon he was apprehended after being shot by Marshfield Marshal Elrod.

***The Motive*:** Domestic rage over pending divorce and alcohol abuse by Carl Albrecht.

The Albrecht Family: Little is know about the Albrecht family. Newspaper accounts revealed more about the perpetrator, Carl than that of the victim only identified as Mrs. Albrecht. The identity of Mrs. Albrecht was located in the records for the Marshfield I.O.O.F. Cemetery.[L] Buried in Block 57, number 7 is Hermanna Susie Albrecht of Germany, who died at the age of 54 years. Her date of burial was February 20, 1896. However, according to the research of Marshfield Pioneer Cemetery Historian Becky Soules the remains of Hermanna Albrecht had been moved to an unknown location and there is no monument for her. What is known is Carl Albrecht was born in Germany on February 4, 1839 and married in 1866. Based on this information Carl Albrecht was fifty-seven years old when he executed his wife. The Albrecht's did have two children. Daughter Jennie later married Robert Krenger and son, Carl L., born in Germany in 1872. Carl L., a surveyor by trade, began working for the Mexican government in the Fall of 1895. He was totally unaware of his mothers murder and fathers execution until March of 1897. Carl L. Albrecht returned to Marshfield[38] and would later serve as a councilman for the city.[39]

The Crime and Punishment: February 25, 1896 the *Coquille City Herald* headlined: **The Late Marshfield Murder**

> One of the most deliberate and unprovoked murders ever committed in Coos county was that perpetrated by Carl Albrecht, who shot his wife down in cold blood on the streets of Marshfield, on Tuesday, Feb. 18th. Albrecht had gone from bad to worse with drink, until his abuses had become unbearable by his faithful wife, and she resolved to separate from him. Mrs. Albrecht was a hard-working woman, who had the respect of the entire community. Albrecht was in the habit of demanding her scant earnings and spending them in the saloons for drink. When Mrs. Albrecht actually left him and he saw that he must earn his own whiskey money he threatened to kill her. Seeing her on the street on that fatal Tuesday he followed her up, and engaged in an altercation with her. After talking in German for some little time he deliberately drew a pistol from his pocket and shot her to death. Having perpetrated his dastardly act, he undertook to make his escape by running down the Empire City road, but he was soon overtaken by City Marshal Elrod, who commanded him to put up his hands and surrender. He put up his left hand, but held his pistol in his right hand and prepared to use it on the marshal. Mr. Elrod, however, was too quick for him and fired first, disabling him. Two other shots were fired before the murderer was secured. Albrecht is now in jail in Empire and will in all probability, sooner or later, expiate his crime on the gallows.

February 26, 1896 the *Coos Bay News* headlined: **The Albrecht Murder** - Part of our last week's edition was run before the Albrecht tragedy occurred, and as the mention was made of the affair was not as complete as it would have been under different circumstances, we revert to it again.

> When Albrecht failed to affect a compromise with his wife, he determined to kill her, and procuring a revolver he went to their residence. About 3:45 p.m., he met the unfortunate woman on the street, opposite J.W. Cox's house. She was carrying a basket of washing at the time, and when he accosted her, she asked him to go away and leave her alone, turning her back to him at the same time. Witnesses to the tragedy say that the brute then shot her in the back, and that she fell to her knees, her body being supported by the clothes basket. While in this position he deliberately shot her twice more, and after walking a short

[L] The Marshfield Pioneer Cemetery was established in 1891 by the International Order of Oddfellows.

distance towards B street; fired two more shots, presumably to scare the witnesses, and to prevent an alarm being given. He went down Cedar street, loading his pistol as he hurried along, and had reached Webster's Point, on the road to Ferndale, when he was overtaken by marshal Elrod. Albrecht was then on the sandy beach, below the road and close to the plank walk leading to Ferndale. Dave Hutcheson, who was on his way to Ferndale at the time, was standing on the walk, and from him we learned how the arrest was accomplished. When the marshal ordered the murderer to throw up his hands, Albrecht threw up one hand, and pointed his revolver with the other. Elrod immediately shot at him, hitting him in the right shoulder. Albrecht seemed to be trying to get the plank walk between him and the marshal, and was also preparing to shoot. Two pistol shots then followed in quick succession, Elrod again hitting Albrecht, but the latter's shot went wild, and the marshal escaped without injury. Albrecht then surrendered, and was brought to town, where Dr. McCormac attended him. The bullet in his shoulder ranged downward, and probing for the ball proved ineffectual; as also did the attempt to locate the bullet which struck him in the hip and ranged upward. Both bullets are still in his body.

The coroner's jury returned a verdict of "willful and premeditated murder," and a hearing had before Justice Clinton resulted in the prisoner being held without bonds. He was taken to the county jail by Sheriff Gage, and if blood poisoning doesn't set in and his wounds prove fatal, he will get his just deserts by the due process of law.

The funeral of Mrs. Albrecht took place Thursday, from the residence of her son in-law, Robt. Krenger, where services were held by the Rev. W. Horsfall. There was a large attendance, and everyone had a kind word to say for deceased, whose industrious habits and many good qualities her numerous friends in the community.

In a separate article on February 26th the *Coos Bay News* wrote:

Albrecht, the murderer, seems to regret that the hanging can't take place right away, and it is the opinion of many that he will commit suicide if an opportunity presents itself. He concealed a case knife under his bed, Sunday, but it was found by the guard before the prisoner could use it. Others think he has no intention of committing suicide, but would have used the knife in an attempt to escape.

On April 22, 1896 the *Myrtle Point Enterprise* headlined: **A COOS COUNTY MURDER**

A terrible tragedy was enacted al Marshfield last Tuesday by C. Albrecht. For some time past he has been drinking to excess, and ill treatment of his wife caused her to institute proceedings for divorce. Albrecht has been trying to effect a compromise and failing to do so became desperate and waiting for a favorable opportunity shot and killed the unfortunate woman on the street near her residence, about 3:45 Tuesday afternoon. After committing the fearful crime Albrecht took the road for Empire; with Marshal Elrod close behind him. The marshal overtook him at Ferndale, and Albrecht showing a disposition to resist arrest, the marshal shot him twice, but unfortunately neither wound is liable to prove fatal. - *Coos Bay News*.

April 22, 1896 the *Coos Bay News* headlined: **Albrecht Escaped** - Albrecht, who murdered his wife at this place, escaped from the jail at Empire City, Sunday.

Our informant says that, the guard feeling indisposed, laid his tired form on the lap of the cell floor, became somnolent and took "forty winks." During the "forty winks" aforesaid, Albrecht left for the woods, but luckily, was intercepted by John Lennon and returned to jail. He was supplied with food, his pocket being full. Had he secured a weapon we might have had to chronicle another crime. When we state that the guard left all the doors open and lay down to sleep, comment is unnecessary.

A leather medal should be presented to those responsible for the retention of the prisoners in jail at Empire City, Coos county. Their inefficiency is remarkable.

April 29, 1896 the *Coos Bay News* reported:

Remarks have been circulated to the effect that Davis, the sleepy deputy sheriff, ought not be paid $166 for watching Albrecht. We differ. It is cheap when considered in the light of final and controvertible proof that a gang of bill stickers have but little time to devote to county matters. The court house will need a disinfectant on their departure for salt river; but, if they succeed in remaining, we may look for an epidemic of hog-cholera.

On May 6, 1896 *Coos Bay News* headlined: **The Albrecht Case** - The story went out that the guard fell asleep when Albrecht left; but the only authority for this story was the guard himself.

But this is good authority for some news venders - Herald. ED. NEWS: Jailer Davis who wrote the letter to the Herald last week has the unbluebing gall to request the county papers to publish his lame condo tiers.

The crime with which Albrecht is charged is horrible, and precludes the possibility of any sympathy being aroused in his behalf. The Herald is in eagerness to offer excuses for sheriff Gage, regardless of the maxims laid down as Christian tenets, to refrain from persecution, bestows another kick on the unfortunate man by saying that he alone is responsible for accusing Davis of being asleep. It is both false and cowardly. The county papers blinded by partiality which closed their column to such items of news as the escape of Albrecht, while open to insane and insignificant matters, will be marked in future. The Herald refrained from publishing the escape as news; but now it jumps into the ring in an attempt to exonerate the imbeciles who were responsible. I predict that, the partiality of the Herald in ignoring the escape, depriving its readers of a legitimate items of news, and its cowardly attack on a prisoner unable to defend himself, will be the means of estranging many who might have voted for Gage. Manly men despise any truculent efforts of that nature.

If A.H. Shroeder can obtain the votes on the Coquille commensurate with these which he will receive on Coos bay and its tributaries, it is a foregone conclusion that he will be the next sheriff of Coos county.

May 13, 1896 the *Coos Bay News* published the following two articles:

We hope that our remarks last week in reference to a cheese cage for the jail at Empire City will cause no undue excitement at the creameries. We feel confident that the voters will give us a new deal, next June, and rid the courthouse of that mucilage amalgam which now occupies it.

The examination of Albrecht failed to sustain the theory of insanity, which was his only chance and he was found guilty of murder in the first degree. Judge Fullerton sentenced him on Monday morning to be hanged by the neck until dead, on Friday, June 26th 1896.

July 1, 1896 the *Coos Bay News* headlined: **ALBRECHT HANGED**

He Pays the Penalty for the Murder of his Wife; Carl Albrecht, the murderer of his wife, paid the penalty for his crime on the gallows, at Empire on Friday. For about two weeks prior to the execution, the condemned man was frequently visited in his cell by Rev. Esbjorn, who enjoyed his fullest confidence, and whose kindly offices made an impression for the better on the prisoner. He frequently spoke of Mr. Esbjorn as his only and best friend, and on the day before the sentence of the law was carried out, recounted many of the incidents of his past life, seemingly not attempting to conceal any of the dark spots, but making full confession. In speaking of his wife, and when asked what lead him to commit the fearful crime, he said: "She wouldn't live with me; they wanted to take away my tools; I took to drinking hard, and my brain was not right when I killed her." Continuing, he said he intended to kill himself, but didn't get time to do so before being arrested. He frequently spoke to visitors of his intention to commit suicide, and made a feeble attempt to hang himself in his cell shortly after being incarcerated; but it was doubtful if he ever really seriously entertained the proposition. Those who knew him best say he was too cowardly to carry out his threats. Since Rev. Esbjorn commenced his visits, he talked no more of suicide, but said he would meet his fate according to the law. He frequently spoke of his wife to the minister; said he confessed that he was sorry for his crime, and added that, should he meet her in the unknown world, he would ask her forgiveness.

Through the courtesy of sheriff Gage, we were permitted to visit the prisoner in his cell, shortly before the execution. We watched him closely while the death warrant was being read and was surprised at the utter indifference he manifested. There, in the shadow of the gallows, with the officials present to carry the sentence of the law into effect; with the murmurs from the gathered crowd outside, who had come to see him die, he was solid as an image of stone; and even the dread words in the death warrant; "that you be hanged by the neck until dead" failed to make a muscle move in his face, nor drew forth a sigh from his impenetrable breast.

Was it courage, or bravado! Was it the action of a brave man who was not afraid to die! Hardly. It partook more of the vacant look of the ignorant, unlettered criminal; one who didn't seem to realize the his awful position, and acted more like one in a trance, that a human being posed of sensibilities and who was capable of comprehending the situation. When the reading of the warrant was finished, in answer to the question as to whether or not he wished to say anything for publication, he replied he had nothing to say. He looked weak and emaciated, the result of his would and attack of illness, and occasionally his hands trembled, but it was more from weakness than fear. He was brought on the scaffold at 9:44. A guard at each side holding his arms. The minister preceded him, and commenced reading from the German prayer book the "Liturgy for the Dying." Albrecht was standing on the trap when the minister began reading, and, taking off his hat, he maintained a respectful attitude until the close. The work of pinioning his arms and legs was then proceeded with, and in the meantime the minister read the following passages from scripture, which the condemned man repeated after him: "God be merciful to me a sinner; Lord remember me; Father into Thy hands do I commit my spirit; Lord Jesus receive my spirit." Shortly after he repeated the last passage, the black cap was pulled over his face. A.G. Aiken, who was formerly sheriff of the county, and who officiated previously on previous occasions, stepped up to the prisoner and adjusted the rope. The signal was then given, Sheriff Gage sprung the trap, and at 9:50 the murderer dropped through the platform to the space below. There was a convulsive twitching of the muscles of the arms and legs for a moment after the fatal drop, and then the body swung slowly from side to side, a grim spectacle to those who has silently watched the carrying out of the death sentence. Dr. Horsfall felt the pulse beats, and when 13 ½ minutes had elapsed he pronounced him dead. The body was lowered into the coffin shortly afterwards, and when the rope was removed the neck was found to be broken, and all indications point to the fact that death was instantaneous.

The crime for which Albrecht suffered is too well known here to need recounting at length. His wife, who was a hard working, industrious woman, and well thought of in the community, was about to procure a divorce from him on account of ill treatment. Albrecht secured a revolver, and made threats that if she attempted to carry out her intentions he would kill her. He followed her from place to place, where she was employed doing chores, and on the afternoon of February 18, 1896, met her on the street close to their residence. Language, used in a tone of voice that indicated they were quarreling, was heard by the neighbors. The unfortunate woman started to walk away from him, and the cowardly brute shot her in the back, and as she fell on her knees he shot her again, killing her instantly. He then ran up B street to Cedar, and was on the away to Ferndale when marshal Elrod overtook him. He resisted arrest, and was shot twice by the marshal before being taken into custody. At the may term of circuit court he was tried, convicted, and sentenced by Judge Fullerton to be hanged on Friday, June 26, 1896 between the hours of 8 and 10 o'clock a.m.

Carl Albrecht was born in a little village in the Herz mountains of Germany February 4, 1839. He learned the trade of shoemaking from his father and, being obliged to work on the farm in summer and his trade in winter, he had very little time for school. When twenty years old he left home for Bremen where he was married in 1866. In 1870, during the French-Prussian war, he enlisted in the 2nd Reserve that means to do duty in the interior and not on the field of battle. He came with his family to Coos bay on May 5, 1883, and resided here ever since.

Examination of the court records revealed a document titled, "Justice Court Bill of Costs." The courts for justice fees, constable fees, witness fees, interpreter's fees and deputy district attorney fee cost the county $20.55. Also located was the statement of execution of Sheriff Gage declaring the time of execution was 9:50 a.m. on June 26, 1896 within the enclosure of the jail yard.

Figure 17: Sheriff W.W. Gage - Photo Courtesy of Denise Sproed Merritt

[illegible] OREGON.

State of Oregon, Plaintiff, vs Carl Albrecht, Defendant. : Justice Court Bill of Costs.

JUSTICE FEES, H.I.CLINTON.

Verifying and filing Information,	.35	
Making certified copy of "	.45	
Issuing Subpoena,	.25	
Swearing three witnesses and Interpreter,	.40	
Making order to commit,	.50	
Making Commitment,	.50	
Giving and enterèng Judgment,	.50	
Two Docket entries,	.50	$3.45

CONSTABLE FEES, W.F.ELROD.

Arresting Criminal,	1.00	
Committing prisoner to jail,	.50	
Serving three subpeenas,	1.50	
Guarding prisoner,	2.00	
Attending Gustice Court,	.50	$5.50

[illegible]

[illegible]	[illegible]	
[illegible]		
[illegible]	[illegible]	$5.10

INTERPRETER'S FEES.

August Schmidt,	$1.50

DEPUTY DISTRICT ATTORNEY'S FEE?

J.S.Coke Jr.,	$5.00
Total,	$20.55

Figure 18: Albrecht Trial Expenditures

State of Oregon)
County of Coos) SS.

I, W.W.Gage, Sheriff of Coos County, Oregon, do hereby certify that I received the hereunto annexed death warrant on the 6th day of June, 1896, and that I did then and there endorse thereon the time of receiving the same.

I further certify that I executed [illegible] follows: That on the 26th day of June, A.D. 1896, the [illegible] being the fourth Friday in the said month of June, I did take the said Carl Albrecht, therein named, from the place of his confinement in the county jail to the place which I had caused to be prepared, in the jail yard of said county jail of said Coos County, in the state of Oregon, and that then and there, on said day, the 26th day of June, 1896, and between the hours of eight and ten o'clock in the forenoon of the said day, and to-wit: at the hour of nine o'clock and fifty minutes in the forenoon of the said day, in the manner provided by law, I did hang the said Carl Albrecht by the neck until he was dead. That the said execution took place within the enclosure of the jail yard where the defendant, the said Carl Albrecht, had been confined. That said execution took place in the presence of twelve bona fide electors of this said Coos county, Oregon, selected by me as such sheriff of said county, to-wit: A.G.Aiken, R.J.Cussans, J.T.Hall, Geo. S. Twambley, E.Lewin, S.C.Giles, Fred Garrison Richard Ayre, A.L.Johnson, B.D.Jones, R.D.Burgess and Joshua Nelson; and the fact of the faithful performance of me as such sheriff in carrying out the sentence of the said court as set forth in said hereunto annexed death warrant, has been duly certified to by the said twelve electors and filed in the office of the county clerk of said Coos County, Oregon. That I deemed it necessary and convenient to summon one good and competent physician to be present at the said execution and to examine the body of the said Carl Albrecht, and I did thereupon summon Doctor William Horsfall; and the said Doctor William Horsfall being present at said execution, did examine the body of the said Carl Albrecht after he, the said Carl Albrecht, had been hanged by the neck until he was dead, and the said Doctor William Horsfall did thereupon pronounce the said Carl Albrecht dead, and did so certify in writing, which said certificate is on file in this court and cause.

In Witness Whereof, I have hereunto set my hand this the 26th day of June, A.D., 1896, at three o'clock P.M.

W.W. Gage

Sheriff of Coos County, Oregon.

Figure 19: Sheriff Gage's Statement of Execution

In the Circuit Court of the State of Oregon for Coos County.

The State of Oregon,
Plaintiff.
vs.
Carl Albrecht,
Defendant.

State of Oregon)
) SS.
County of Coos)

We, the undersigned, A.G.Aiken, R.J.Cussans, J.T.Hall, Geo. S. Twambly, E.Lewin, S.C.Giles, Fred Garrison, Richard Ayre, A.L.Johnson, B.D.Jones, R.D.Burgess and Joshua Nelson twelve bona fide electors of the County of Coos in the state of Oregon, selected by the Sheriff of said Coos County, do hereby certify to the fact of the faithful performance of the said sheriff of said Coos County, Oregon, in carrying out the sentence of the above entitled court in the above entitled cause as follows:

That the said W.W.Gage, the duly elected, ~~and~~ qualified and acting sheriff of Coos County, Oregon, did, in our presence, on the 26th day of June, 1896, the same being the fourth Friday in the said month of June, take the said Carl Albrecht from the place of his confinement in the County Jail to the place prepared in the jail yard of said County Jail of said Coos County, Oregon, and that there between the hours of eight and ten o'clock in the forenoon of said day ~~in the manner provided by law~~ and to-wit: at the hour of 9:50 ~~00~~ o'clock in the forenoon of the said day, did cause the said Carl Albrecht to be hung by the neck until he was dead. That there was present at the said execution of the said Carl Albrecht one competent physician of said Coos County, to-wit: Doctor William Horsfall and the said Doctor William Horsfall did examine the body of the said Carl Albrecht after he, the said Carl Albrecht had been hung by the neck until he was dead, and the said Doctor William Horsfall did then and there pronounce the said Carl Albrecht dead; and did sign a certificate to that effect ~~..~~ said certificate is filed herewith.

Witness our hands this 26th day of June, 1896, at Em City, Coos County, Oregon.

1 A.G.Aiken
2 R.J.Cussans
3 J.T.Hall
4 Geo. S. Twambly
5 E. Lewin
6 S.C. Giles
7 Fred Garrison
8 Richard Ayre
9 A.L. Johnson
10 B.D. Jones
11 R.D. Burgess
12 J. Nelson

Figure 20: Witnesses Statement of Execution

CHAPTER 12

THE CASE OF FRANK GARRISON

***Case Synopsis*:** Roy Perkins, a former employee of Frank Garrison, was murdered by gunfire at the Eastside ferry building, moved, and dumped in the bay in an attempt to conceal the crime. The conviction of Garrison was based entirely on circumstantial evidence as there were no witnesses to the crime.

The Motive: Garrison claimed self preservation; however, it was believed Perkins was killed to keep him from filing a criminal complaint against Garrison.

The Parties: The only information regarding the victim, Roy Perkins is that he was buried at the Marshfield I.O.O.F. Cemetery on September 12, 1910. The only known information regarding the perpetrator, Frank Garrison comes from the newspaper accounts and the Record of Execution. Possessing a criminal record prior to committing the murder, Garrison, Oregon born, was 37 years old at the time of his execution.

The Crime and Punishment: September 5, 1910 the *Coos Bay Times* headlined: **BLOOD AND BULLETS FOUND IN EASTSIDE WAITING ROOM** — Believed That Roy Perkins Was Murdered in the Ferry Station. **BODY HAD BEEN DRAGGED TO WATER**. Search For Remains in Bay Will Probably Be Made By Officials.

> Discoveries made late this afternoon lead to the belief that beyond a doubt Roy Perkins was murdered in the waiting room of the wharf at Eastside. Indications of a man having been killed have been found. Blood stains are found on the floor and walls of the place and it is believed that Perkins was murdered there and dragged down to the end of the ferry slip and carried in a boat or towed from there and sunk in the bay.
>
> The discovery of the blood in the waiting room was made by Jack Flanagan and Alex Hall. The waiting is a small frame building next door to Flanagan's oil house It is seldom ever used excepting in rainy weather, so consequently the fact that a tragedy had taken place there was not noticed before. Flanagan happened to go into the waiting room to-day with Hall and saw the blood. A close examination showed that three bullets had been fired in the room and that a large amount of blood had been spilled.
>
> Marshal Carter[M] was notified and went to Eastside. Working on the theory that Garrison committed the murder, it is believed that he followed Perkins until the latter had reached the waiting room. The blood spots indicate that Perkins was laying down and was probably shot while in that position. The three bullets marks are plain and one of the bullets which had split was cut out of the wood by the marshal. Further examinations revealed the fact that the body had been dragged from the waiting room down the ferry slip to the water's edge. Here were found blood spots which indicated that the body had been laid down on the edge of the slip. Garrison is known to have stolen a row boat which was tied near the slip. One of the big rocks used as a weight at the side of the slip is missing and it is thought that this was used by Garrison as weight and that the body of Perkins was taken in a row boat or towed and dropped into the water.
>
> As it has been learned that Garrison landed at the stave mill and slept there all night it should not be a different matter to locate the body, as it probably some place between the ferry slip on Eastside and the stave mill on the Marshfield side of the bay.
>
> Marshal Carter notified Coroner Golden and also sent word to sheriff Gage, who has just returned to Coquille, and it is likely that the bay will be dragged at once.
>
> Garrison has not yet been told of the discovery that has been made. It is believed that when he is told that he will confess.
>
> **Search Kept Up**
>
> Mystery still surrounds the disappearance of Roy Perkins, and the officers are convinced that he has been murdered, but so far they have been unable to find any trace of his body. He left Sumner last Wednesday on foot for Marshfield and has never been seen since he passed the Black ranch three miles

[M] Carter would have served in his capacity as District Constable for this investigation. As Constable of District 2, Carter's jurisdiction included North Marshfield, South Marshfield, Coos City, Coos River, North Coos River, Sumner and Newport precincts.

from Sumner. Garrison was seen a few minutes behind him. Perkins left at Sumner all of his clothing and possessions and the officers point out that this, together with the fact that Perkins has never shown up in Marshfield, is enough to all that he is dead. In the minds of the officials, there is no doubt but that Perkins was murdered, but they are at a loss to where the body can be found.

After it was learned that Garrison stole a row boat and crossed the bay Wednesday evening and slept all night at the stave mill, leads one to the belief that possibly the body was dropped in the water. The search of the country between Sumner and Coos Bay is being kept up in the hopes that something may be found.

Garrison is still in the city prison. He was badly frightened for a time and said that if Perkins was found dead he had nothing to do with it but supposed he would be hanged anyway. He will not talk about the case now, but asks quite frequently if Perkins had been found dead. Some of the details of the stories he has told do not hang together very well and the officers think that he may confess if he is guilty.

About two months ago Garrison owed Perkins some money. Whether or not this had been paid is not known, but at any rate the two men had some trouble about the money. Perkins was working for Garrison digging clams and had about $100 coming to him for wages. The story told by an Eastside man is that about two months ago Perkins asked Garrison for his money and that Garrison became angry and pulled a gun on Perkins.

There is nothing for the officers to do but try to find the body of Perkins if he is dead. In the meantime, Garrison may confess or Perkins may turn up alive. It is not thought that the latter will happen as the officers think that Perkins would have heard of the arrest by this time if he was alive.

Only one small clue has been found that would lead to the belief that Garrison had been through the timber along the road. Near Ross Slough, about sixty feet in from the road, was found two slips of paper. They were evidently pages from an account book and on the pages were some accounts regarding clams. As Garrison was formerly a clam digger it is thought that the pages may have been from his account book. Graham, the taxidermist, says that the writing is that of Garrison.

On September 6, 1910 the *Coos Bay Times* headlined: **OFFICERS STILL SEARCHING FOR MISSING ROY PERKINS** — Are Convinced That Man Was Killed in Eastside Waiting Room. **THINKS THAT BODY IS IN THE WATER.** — Men Have Been Put to Working To-Day Dragging the Bay.

Nothing new has developed in the case of the missing Roy Perkins. Frank Garrison is held and is suspected by the officers as having killed him. The officers are working the theory that the blood stains in the Eastside ferry waiting room and on the Eastside wharf are indications that the man was killed there. The stains of course were not as fresh and bright when found yesterday as would have been the morning after the murder if such occurred there, but the officers explain that the reason the stains were not seen on the ferry landing before was due to the fact that there are always oil stains there and the blood spots were not noticed.

Sheriff Gage says that he did not look into the ferry station because he did not know there was such a place there he thought it was a part of the Flanagan oil house. He says that the ferry waiting room is seldom used in the summer time, and consequently the blood stains in the place were not seen until Monday, while the murder is supposed to have been committed Wednesday night or Thursday morning.

Faces Blood Stains.

This morning, Garrison the prisoner was taken by the Sheriff across the bay and into the waiting room, where the murder is thought by the officers to have been committed. The Sheriff says that Garrison did not act any different from the way he has been acting. The Sheriff says that Garrison is pretty well wilted but that be did not confess anything when confronted by the supposed scene of the alleged crime.

The officers will not allow anyone to see Garrison. He is still in the city jail. The Sheriff and marshal have been spending a good deal of time talking to him in hopes of getting something out of the man, but he has not told anything. According to the officers' statements they have not yet been able to get any confession from the man.

Must Find Body.

No formal charges of murder has been made against the man, as that of course cannot be done until the fact that a crime has been committed is established, and that cannot be done unless the body or some part of it has been unearthed. The man is being held as a suspect, but if necessary it is likely that some formal charge can be made against him in order to hold him. The officers say that Garrison stole a boat with which to cross the bay and he could be charged with larceny in order to hold him should Garrison make any attempt to be released or habeas corpus proceedings.

Collected Blood.

Sheriff Gage says that he has collected a sufficient amount of the blood on the floor of the waiting room to have it analyzed. Deputy district Attorney Liljeqvist wanted some of the blood, too, so the Sheriff says he has secured enough to take up to the attorney.

First to Find Blood.

Capt. Alex Hall of the Ferry Transit reports that the blood trace *(bottom of newspaper page was folded over and microfilm could not be read)* C. C. Going Sunday. Monday afternoon, Mr. Koontz told Capt. Hall, and the latter immediately called Marshal Carter who hastened to make an investigation of it.

Heard Shots.

Fred Bennett heard shots fired early Thursday morning about 2 o'clock. Night Policeman William Shupe[N] also heard the shots about the same hour on Thursday morning. He is quite certain about it and thinking that the shots came from the east side of the bay.

Examines Blood.

Dr. Mingus made an examination of the blood for the officers. He states that the blood is that of a mammal and that the blood corpsules were of the size of those in human blood, but he could not state positively that it was human blood for the reason that the corpsules of several other mammals are also of the same size as those of the human. The fact that the blood was dried made it more difficult for examination.

Made a Will.

J. E. Graham, who has been working on the case with the officers questioned Garrison for several hours. Mr. Graham says that Garrison fears that he is going to be mobbed and in his great fear that his end is near he wrote *(bottom of page illegible)*

September 7, 1910 the *Coos Bay Times* headlined: **REWARD OF $100 OFFERED FOR RECOVERY OF PERKINS' BODY** — County Court Takes Action in the Case of Alleged Murder. — **GARRISON HAS BEEN TAKEN TO COQUILLE.** — Bay Is Being Dragged But Nothing New in the Case. — REWARD $100. — The county court has authorized a reward of $100 for the recovery of the body of the missing Roy Perkins.

There is nothing new in the case of the disappearance of Roy Perkins today. The officers are doing all they can having the bay dragged in the hopes of finding the body. They are working on the theory that the body is in the water and several boats were at work today dragging the bay as thoroughly as possible.

The general opinion is that Perkins has been done away with. Frank Garrison, who is suspected by the officers of killing Perkins, was taken to the county jail at Coquille this morning and will he held in confinement there.

Garrison is evidently in a greatly disturbed mental condition. He has written several documents which might indicate that he was mentally unbalanced. One of these was a will which he wrote when he thought he would be mobbed. Another paper that he wrote to one of the officials indicates a greatly disturbed mental condition.

September 8, 1910 the *Coos Bay Times* headlined: **NO NEW DEVELOPMENTS IN PERKINS DISAPPEARANCE CASE** — The Body of Missing Man Has Not Yet Been Discovered. **GARRISON IS IN COQUILLE JAIL.** — Offer of Reward Starts Several Men to Join in the Search.

Nothing new has developed in the Roy Perkins case. This morning someone started a report that the body had been found, but it was without foundation. The search for the body in the bay is being kept up and the bay is being dragged all the time in the hopes of finding something.

The fact that the county has offered a reward of $100 for the recovery of the body stimulated some to go to the woods and make a search in the belief that possibly Perkins had been killed on the way in from Sumner. So far, however, nothing has been found of the body.

Garrison is in the county jail in Coquille, to which place he was taken yesterday in an automobile.

[N] Correct spelling is Shoupe. William Shoupe served as a Marshfield night officer from around 1909 to 1915.

Figure 21: Marshfield Marshal John W. "Jack" Carter

According to reports he has shown signs of not being entirely balanced mentally. Persons who have known him say that he was always a little strange in his actions. He is a native of Polk county and is the grandson of a preacher. Attorney Tom Hall knew of him in Polk county and says that Garrison always carried a gun with him and was said to have always slept with a gun beside him. It seems that he had a mania for carrying a gun of some kind with him at all times. It is thought that if he is guilty he will make some kind of confession before long.

On September 8, 1910 *The Sun* headlined: **Roy Perkins Missing — Frank Garrison Held as Suspect** Roy

Perkins is among the missing, and Frank Garrison is confined in the city jail awaiting developments.

Perkins was last seen on the county road by J.S. Masters, of Catching Slough Wednesday evening of last week, in the vicinity of the latter's farm. He supposedly was coming to Marshfield. Following him was Garrison. The latter spoke to Mr. Masters, requesting the use of his telephone, saying that he was going to town and wished to inform Paul Crooks as he had made arrangements to come to town with him the day following. As the Masters phone had been put out of commission by the dredger, Garrison was compelled to go the Black place to do his telephoning.

Perkins (missing word) and it is on the strength of this evidence supported by a statement made by the missing man to Judge Pennock, some months since, that he feared bodily harm at the hands of Garrison that the latter is being held. The statement to Pennock was made at a time when Perkins sought the Justice of the Peace's aid in collecting a bill alleged to have been due him from Garrison. Perkins' non-appearance in Marshfield, coupled with the report that his mission to this city was to secure a warrant for Garrison, led to the latter's arrest. He was taken into custody at his quarters to Jordan's Cove, Saturday morning. Immediately a search was started to find some trace of the missing Perkins. Automobile parties were organized, and the bush beat along the Sumner road where he was last seen. Numerous and bewildering reports of clues came in thick and fast enough to satisfy the gormand appetite of a sensation seeking public. The hounds owned by the suspect were turned loose on the trail; but without avail. Hope of a clue was about abandoned, when, directed as it were by some superhuman power, Alex Hall, of the ferry boat Transit, wandered into the waiting room, Monday, on Eastside, and there be found what the sleuths say to be unmistakable evidence of where the crime was committed. Seven bullet holes punctured the wall in a space the size of the palm of your hand; on the floor was a pool of blood; candle greece, donating the deed was executed in the dark hours of night, smeared the surroundings. There was mute evidence that some attempt

Figure 22: View of the Eastside Ferry Landing from Marshfield.

Coos Historical and Maritime Museum, CHMM 970-69b

was made, to cover up his track by wiping up the floor. Outside the waiting room was found traces of the blood and on the apron of the ferry was a blotch the size of a saddle blanket. What is still more strange the searching parties had traveled for days over this gang plank, looking for a dead man or some trace of evidence, but failed to observe this sign. Theory says that on this gang plank the missing Perkins was prepared for a watery grave, and as a rock is gone from that neighborhood, further weight is added to the theory. The mystery has brought to sight a score or more of detectives, experts have analyzed the blood, but, evidently cherishing some respect for their opinion, they are loathe to say whether the blood (missing) found in the Eastside waiting room is that of a human being, a Chinook salmon, red paint or crude oil. A specimen as seen under the microscope yesterday by the writer resembled by a one hundredth part that of human blood. A long shot, but apparently as close as the talent has come to solving the mystery.

In the mean time Garrison is being sweated. Only the officers know what he has to say, but it is believed that be claims to be innocent. An acquaintance, who has done business with Garrison for two years, asked the privilege of speaking to him yesterday in the presence of an officer but was denied.

Frank Garrison is well known in this city. For the past two years he has dug clams and disposed of them in Marshfield, and at one time the scene of his operations extended to Myrtle Point and Coquille, where, for a brief period, he maintained branch markets. Mentally he was not considered sound by his acquaintances. He was very fond of dogs and supported a good sized kennel. This caused him to be known by many as "Dog Frank." His habits were nocturnal and he invariably did most of his traveling by night. Perkins was formerly associated with him in his clam enterprise.

It is not our part to say whether this friendless man is guilty or not. We shall presume, with the law, that he is innocent, until be is proven guilty, and, granting that the surrounding circumstances seem suspicious they should not be used for advertising capital. Garrison, penniless as he is, is entitled to a hearing and subjected to the treatment or an American Citizen.

Since the above was in type the missing rock from the ferry slip has been found; dragging the bay has proved fruitless in bringing to light a corpse. Yesterday morning Garrison was whisked to Coquille in an automobile, train service presumably not being swift enough for his retainers, or more probably to the liking of the officials ideas of transportation. These proceedings may be heard from later through the county court, when the taxpayers are asked to square the uncalled for expenses. Garrison when he left was laboring under the hallucination that he was to be lynched and the third degree process, it is believed, if he is not found guilty of the alleged crime, will leave him a fit candidate for the lunatic asylum.

September 9, 1910 the *Coos Bay Times* headlined: **GARRISON HAS BAD RECORD** — Reports Received By Marshal Carter From Salem Are Not Favorable. — **FOUND HAT.** — A hat thought to belong to Perkins was found in the water near North Bend, it is reported this afternoon.

The officers are still having the bay dragged in the hopes of finding something of missing Roy Perkins. Nothing has developed in the case excepting the finding of some facts regarding Garrison, the man who is being held on suspicion. Marshal Carter has received from Salem some facts about Garrison and his photograph. His record is not a good one as will be seen by the facts, printed in the Salem papers reproduced below. Garrison's parents conducted a hotel at Roseburg. Marshal Carter and others here were acquainted with them. Garrison's grandfather was a preacher. The prisoner was a native of Polk county.

Record at Salem.

Garrison, who is under arrest and suspected of having done away with Roy Perkins, has not a very good record at Salem. The Statesman of that city says:

Frank Garrison, who is under arrest in Marshfield charged as a suspect and with having knowledge of how Roy Perkins came to his death is well known in Salem, having been one of the men who assaulted Sheriff John Knight in an attempt to make a jail break in 1895. Garrison, with Frank Brehm and a man named Combes, laid in wait for Sheriff Knight in the corridor of the jail and attacked him with a piece of oak firewood. They were unsuccessful in their attempt to escape and two of the men were given 10 and 12 year sentences respectfully for assault upon Knight.

September 15, 1910 the *Coos Bay Times* headlined: **PERKINS' BODY IS BURIED** — No Inquest to Be Held As Evidence Goes Before Grand Jury.

The body of Roy Perkins, which was found in the bay yesterday was buried last night. An examination was made of the body and it revealed that Perkins had been shot through the heart, the bullet going clear through the body. Some papers were found on the body and there is enough to positively identify it beyond a doubt. The evidence against Frank Garrison is sufficient to show Perkins, and, in fact, the officers have Garrison's own admission that he killed Perkins.

There will probably be no inquest here by the Coroner as the Grand Jury is now in session and can take up the case at once. It is planned now for all of the witnesses who can tell anything of the case to go to Coquille tomorrow morning and appear before the Grand Jury.

September 20, 1910 the *Coos Bay News* headlined: **Indicted For Murder.**

The body of Roy Perkins, who was missing since the night of August 31st was found Wednesday morning, Sept. 14th, a short distance front the mouth of the Coos river channel, by D. M. Charleston, inspector for the government, who in company with Ralph Young was going up Coos river in a launch to the government dredge. A rock was tied around the neck and another was fastened to the right foot, but in each instance several feet of rope allowed the body to float some distance from the bottom, and the water being shoal, with an extremely low tide, made the discovery possible. The body was brought to town, and an examination by Dr. Golden, coroner, showed that the unfortunate man had been shot through the heart. The flesh on the face and head had been eaten off by crabs and fish, but the clothing and articles found in the pockets conclusively proved the identity of the remains. The grand jury at Coquille indicted Garrison for murder on Friday. He had made a few admissions while in jail at Marshfield to Marshal Carter, stating that only one shot was fired, and also that the body was weighted down by rock. He did not definitely state that he had killed Perkins, nor did he state that the killing was done in the waiting room at the Eastside ferry landing, but when charged with having committed the deed there he did not deny it.

On November 22, 1910 the *Coos Bay News* headlined: **Garrison Found Guilty**

The trial of Frank Garrison, charged with the murder of Roy Perkins, occupied the attention of circuit court last week, and was brought to a close Saturday night when the jury returned a verdict of murder in the first degree. An effort was made to prove Garrison insane, but the testimony wouldn't sustain it. There were no eye witnesses to the murder, but if ever circumstantial evidence could be said to be conclusive in establishing the guilt of the accused, coupled with his own admissions, there certainly was never a clearer case than against Garrison, The evidence showed that the murder was premeditated, and no other course was open to the jury. Roy Perkins, the victim, was a harm less, inoffensive man, who left his camp at Sumner, August 31st, to lodge a complaint with the authorities at Marshfield against Garrison, who had stolen some articles from Perkins' camp.

Garrison said he would follow him and kill him, which he undoubtedly did, and after shooting him tied rocks to the body and dumped it in the bay. It drifted to the edge of the Coos river flats, where it was discovered two weeks after the murder.

November 24, 1910 *The Sun* headlined: **Garrison to Hang For Murder of Perkins.**

Frank Garrison will meet death on the gallows to expiate the crime of taking the life of Roy Perkins, who was most foully murdered a short time ago and his remains deposited in the bay, but later accidentally recovered.

It required just one week of the circuit court's time, in which some 40 witnesses were examined to try Garrison. He was ably defended by Judge Sehlbrede and Attorneys R.O. Graves and J. T. Hall. District Attorney George M. Brown and his assistant L. J. Liljevquist appeared for the State.

It was one of the most expensive trials the taxpayers have been called upon to defray the expenses of in many years. Witnesses were brought here from Astoria and Salem. Dr. Temmasy examining physician, came from the latter place to testify for the State and Mrs. Gardiner, an aunt of Garrison, was brought in from Polk county by the defense.

Besides pleading not guilty an additional defense of insanity was set up by Garrison's attorneys.

The jury was just four hours before deciding on a verdict. It is understood that they took seven ballots before a decision was reached, the preceding counts standing 10 for murder in the first degree and 2 for murder in the second degree.

Council for defense, after the verdict was read, moved for a new trial, which was denied by the Court. Judge Coke later passed the death sentence upon Garrison, and allowed his attorneys 30 days in which to prepare their bill of exceptions on appeal.

Under the law all executions take place at Salem, to which point Garrison is being taken. The day on which Garrison will meet death will be set in the writ of execution.

It is not known whether Garrison's attorneys will continue the fight for their client on appeal or will treat the decision as final.

The personnel of the jury that found Garrison guilty was as follows;

J.H. Barklow, 46 years old, man of family, resident of Norway.
Walter Sabin, 27 years old, residence Bandon,
F. W, Redfield, 50 years old, resides with family at Marshfield.
L. E. Brown, 31 years old, formerly of Douglas county.
O. H. Southmaid, aged 65 years, has family residence Myrtle Point.
T. T. Land, 44 years old, hardware dealer of Coquille.
L.F. Heller, 36 years, lives with wife and family on Cherry Creek.
A. O. Hooton. old resident of Coos, lives at Bridge.
J. L. Crosby, 41 years old, man of family, resides at Gravel Ford.
John Peart, 87 years old, lives at Coquille.
Ola Lund, 44 years old, resides with family on farm near Coquille.
Geo. Folsom, 62 years, farmer, resides Myrtle Point.

On November 29, 1910 the *Coos Bay News* headlined: **Garrison's Statement.**

Frank Garrison made a so-called statement after being convicted of the murder of Roy Perkins, in which he scores Marshal Carter, of Marshfield, whom he accuses of using every questionable methods of forcing a confession from him. Garrison's story is decidedly fishy. The idea that while he — Garrison — was in jail, in charge of the authorities and under their protection, that he was afraid one of the officers would kill him and throw him into the bay unless be confessed, is hardly worth consideration. To prove that the story was manufactured by Garrison, we were permitted by Marshal Carter to read a letter addressed to "Mr. Dr. Straw Mayor" by Garrison on the night of the day he was taken across the bay to the ferry landing to view the blood in the waiting room where he had shot Perkins. This was on the 5th of September, and according to Garrison's statement after his conviction, this was the night that Marshal Carter threatened to kill him if he didn't confess. In his letter to Mayor Straw, which is in Garrison's own handwriting, he thanks the Mayor "for your interest in my welfare, but I will say I have no complaint to make of my treatment here." He makes no complaint of Marshal Carter; the only time that he mentions him in the letter is when he says that "Mr. Carter offered me all to eat he could; I could not eat all." He also says in the letter that "I will not be long on earth," and further on adds: "when I get a little mad I loose complete control of my actions." — A letter to a Coos county official from Garrison's mother says that his right name is Frank S. Kennedy. He was her son by her first husband. Her letter shows that she regards him as a natural born criminal, and she believes him guilty of numerous other crimes besides the killing of Perkins.

On November 12, 1912 the *Coos Bay News* headlined: **Garrison Will Hang.**

Governor West has announced that, he will abide by the verdict of the people on the subject of capital punishment, and as that verdict on election day was in favor of retaining the law and against an initiative bill to abolish it, the five murderers incarcerated in the penitentiary, and to whom reprieves were issued pending the vote on the measure, will hang on Friday, December 13, the date when all reprieves expire.

Among the murderers is Frank Garrison, of Coos Bay. He was tried in the circuit court at Coquille in November 1910, and the jury returned a verdict of murder in the first degree. At the trial an effort was made to prove Garrison insane, but the testimony wouldn't sustain it. There were no eye witnesses to the murder, but if ever circumstantial evidence could be said to conclusive in establishing the guilt of the accused coupled with his own admissions, there certainly was never a clearer case than that against Garrison. The evidence showed that the murder was premeditated, and no other course was open to the jury. Roy Perkins, the victim, was a harmless, inoffensive man, who left his camp at Sumner, August 31st, to lodge a complaint with the authorities at Marshfield against Garrison, who had stolen some articles from Perkins' camp. Garrison said he would follow him and kill him, which he undoubtedly did and after shooting him tied rocks to the body and dumped it in the bay. It drifted to the edge of the Coos river flats, where it was discovered two weeks after the murder.

December 10, 1912 the *Coos Bay Times* headlined: **GARRISON IN LAST APPEAL** — *Coos County Man Sentenced to Die Friday Protests His Innocence.*

The Portland Telegram in a series of interviews with the men in the Salem penitentiary who are to be hanged Friday for murder, quotes Frank Garrison of Coos county as follows:

"I am not guilty. I was forced to say I killed Perkins at the point of a pistol in the hands of J. W. Carter, the marshal of Marshfield," declared F.M. Garrison, when interviewed. Garrison has a long prison record behind him, and was insistent on reviewing his case and fully explaining it.

"My conscience is clear as any man's. Any man who believes in a hereafter is not afraid to die if his life has not been too bad. I have always believed in a hereafter — it is not a belief which has come to me since coming here. I have no bitterness against the people for voting against the abolishment of capital punishment. I hardly know whether capital punishment should be abolished or not, but do not believe in hanging on circumstantial evidence. I would prefer hanging to remaining inside these prison walls all my life. If certain affidavits I have sent for reach me in time I do not think I will hang; but if not then I may."

He seemed to think he had new evidence and took particular pains to argue his case to the newspapermen and regretted to have them depart. He commented that there was a general conspiracy on the part of Marshal Carter and a party by the name of J. E. Graham to convict him of the murder of Perkins. Garrison had two trials, and at last was given opportunity to plead guilty of murder in the second degree but declined and was convicted of murder in the first degree.

On Friday, December 13, 1912 the *Coos Bay Times* printed four front page articles regarding the execution of Frank Garrison.

Headline: **FOUR MEN HANGED TODAY AT OREGON STATE PRISON** - Frank Garrison, One of Men Who Died on Gallows, From Coos County, **PROTESTED INNOCENCE UNTIL THE VERY LAST** Others Made Admissions of Guilt of Crimes Elsewhere.

SALEM, Dec. 13. — Four condemned murderers, Noble Faulder, Frank Garrison, Mike Morgan and H.B. Roberts were executed at the state prison here today practically within one hour.

The men were hanged in pairs Garrison and Faulder were first summoned to the death chamber, preliminaries were soon completed.

Asked if they had any statement make, Faulder practically admit, his guilt, but Garrison protested his innocence of the crime for which he was executed. Both men got through the ordeal with *(missing text)* Faulder was cut down after *(missing text)* minutes, while it was two minutes later before the physicians pronounced Garrison dead.

Within half an hour after the first executions, Mike Morgan and E. Roberts, also condemned to today, were ordered from their cells, and. after they were given an opportunity to speak, the trap was sprung. Both men met death calmly. Roberts admitted his guilt. He contributed his crime to persisted "hounding" of officers of the law having served several prison terms, and his work on an emery wheel which he stated affected his mind. Morgan did not make a statement, but Rev. A. A. Moore had been his spiritual adviser stated that Morgan had told him he had killed John York, a rancher in self defense. Roberts was pronounced dead in 15 minutes and Morgan two minutes later.

Hanged at 11:30.

Garrison and Faulder were hanged at 11:28. Garrison was cut down at 11:56, two minutes after the fall of Faulder. Garrison died with a protestation of his innocence on his lips.

Faulder said: "You must get at the root. Hanging does not cure crime." About fifty witnessed the executions.

Second: **DEATH TALE OF GARRISON** — Coos County Man Hanged Today Says He Is Victim of RING of Grafters.

SALEM, Dec. 13. — Garrison, just before he was hanged today, declared that he was the victim to protect an alleged "ring of grafters" in Coos county and some county officials, one of whom he charged directly with perpetrating the murder for which he was executed.

Morgan's body was claimed by Father Moore. The other bodies will go to relatives or be buried in the Potter's field.

Third: **STORY ABOUT THE CRIMES** — Murders for Which Four Men Were Hanged in Salem Prison Today.

SALEM Ore., Dec. 13. —The men executed in the State penitentiary here today had been held for period varying from four to thirteen months, as a result of reprieves granted by Governor Oswald West, to enable the electorate of the state to decide whether it desired the abolishment of capital punishment, or whether it believed that the extreme punishment should continue to be the penalty for first degree murder in this state.

Shortly after the legal hanging of two murderers in the fall of 1911 Governor West issued a formal statement to the effect that because of his personal conviction that the hanging of murderers was useless, not another execution would take place in Oregon while he occupied the executive chair.

This pronouncement led to criticism that the power of pardon, conferred only for use in extremis to prevent miscarriage of justice, was being abused and that Governor West was subverting the authority conferred on him.

Almost at once the Governor declared that instead of commuting to life imprisonment the sentence of condemned murderers, to abolish capital punishment life imprisonment as he intended, he would appeal to the people and, pending the decision of the electorate would reprieve to December 13, such men as might be sentenced to be hanged.

Governor West, firm in his purpose, prepared and caused to be placed on the ballot at the November election an initiative act abolishing capital punishment and substituting life imprisonment for the crime of murder. The electorate, by over 20,000 majority, rejected the proposed change, and Governor West, as he had pledged he would, when his announcement or intention to reprieve murderers was made, at once ordered the executions for the date specified in the reprieves.

The death chamber in the penitentiary here is equipped to execute simultaneously two persons. This necessitates the designation of three periods, one in the early morning, when Noble Faulder was sent to the gallows, and the others later in the day, when the death penalty was inflicted on Kike Morgan, Frank Garrison, and H.E. Roberts.

The act for which Noble Faulder was hanged was for the slaying of Louis Gebhardt, August 6, 1911. Several days before the killing Faulder, a laborer, threatened to shoot anyone who poisoned his dog. Of this, Faulder accused Gebhardt, a camp cook, on the day of the murder.

The crime for which Mike Morgan met the death penalty was the murder of John Yorke, a rancher, July 13, 1911, near Yorke's ranch, under the name Hallie Wilkes, Morgan who had deserted from company "H" Fifteenth Infantry, U.S.A. at Fort Douglas Utah, had been given employment by Yorke. While his employer was asleep, Morgan beat him to death with a club, later throwing the body into Rogue River, after weighting it down with a log chain, Morgan was captured a few days later at Glendale, where he had spent the small sum of money secured by the sale of Yorke's team of horses. Afterwards Morgan confessed. His relatives reside at Mount Carmel, Ill., and Lowell, Ill.

The deed for which Frank Garrison was executed was the killing at Eastside, near Marshfield, September 1, 1912, of Roy Perkins. He was twice convicted of murder. Garrison shortly after his arrest was alleged by the authorities to have made a confession that he had killed Perkins and threw his body into Coos Bay. This confession, although later repudiated, was used as evidence in the first trial. On appeal to the Supreme Court the case was remanded for new trial on the ground that the confession was extorted and he was again tried and convicted.

The crime for which H. E. Roberts alias Jack Roberts, was hanged, was the killing of Don M, Stewart, who with George Hastings was shot to death while automobiling near Portland, March 29th last. The young men neither of whom had reached his majority, were members of a party of five who were ordered to halt by a highwayman. The driver of the car instead of complying with the demand, increased his speed. As the machine sped past the would-be robber fired four shots from an automatic shotgun. Stewart and Hastings were almost instantly killed and two other members of the party were slightly injured. Roberts was convicted and sentenced in August last, Roberts was an ex-convict.

Fourth: **FINAL STATEMENT MADE BY FRANK GARRISON TODAY** — Coos County Man Executed at Salem Prison Makes Sensational Charges.

SALEM, Dec. 13. — In a statement which he gave to the warden just before the noose was fastened about his neck, Frank Garrison declared that he was innocent, but that it would protect grafters and criminals. His statement follows: "To the citizens of the State of Oregon:

This is my last statement before execution and I wish to say that I am innocent of the crime of murder of any degree. Even though I have been convicted twice of murder in the first, degree, I am a victim of circumstantial evidence. Perjured evidence was used knowingly to prove the circumstances. Even though I die tomorrow, I am innocent, I wish to state that I am holding no ill feeling against anyone of the jury that tried the case. But I believe in placing the blame where it belongs, on the district attorney and his deputy who made knowingly use of perjured evidence to secure my conviction. On one occasion I called my attorney's, C. A. Sehlbrede's, attention to the perjured testimony of Mrs. Carl Smeadberg. Her evidence in the courts of record of the two trials will show beyond all doubt it was perjured at one trial or the other. Sehlbrede told me to shut up. No, my life must be taken. I know too much. Certain officers must he protected, one of the Coos county ring of grafters who sells to the human vultures protection to prey upon young innocent, girls who protects the white slavers, who protects prostitution and the degenerated human vulture who lives upon the earnings of prostitutes who protects the illegal sale of liquor in houses of prostitution, protects gambling when protection if paid for, who even protects murderers, too, who even stoops to stain their own hands in human blood in order to protect some of their gang from prosecution. My life must be taken to protect Marshal J. W. Carter, who committed the murder that I will be hanged for. Who was implicated in the murder of W. L. Joyner and Jacob Evans of South Slough? My execution tomorrow will be another murder to their many to protect vice and graft. Oh, how I would love to be called to prove the assertions before a court of justice where the court stands for justice and not for the protection of a gang of grafters and murderers, where the court is not one of such a gang as is the case in Coos county, Oregon"

"I love the law of our country. I respect it as long it is used for the protection of life and property, for which it is enacted. But I detest some of the practices to which it is put. Our chaplain one day gave the word "law" a definition and said if any one could give a better definition he would like to have them do so. Here is the way I define the word:

"Law" is a set of rules enacted and put on our statute books for the protection of life, property and society, that is for what it is intended. But that in practice it is frequently used for the protection of vice, white slavery, prostitution, gambling, vultures to prey upon the victims of young girls and all kinds of graft, and to virtues from the law."

(Signed by)

"FRANK S. GARRISON."

December 14, 1912 the *Coos Bay Times* headlined: **SAY GARRISON HAD CONFESSED** Rumor That Local Attorney Had Admissions from Man Executed.

The execution of Frank Garrison and the statement he issued yesterday at Salem have caused much comment around town. The prevailing opinion is that he was insane, as well as being a dangerous criminal.

Tom Hall, who with R. O. Graves and C. A. Sehlbrede, defended Garrison in his two trials here is reported to have had a confession from Garrison. However, Mr. Hall will not make any statement about Garrison's revelation to him until he has consulted Judge Coke as to the rights of attorneys making public their client's statement.

Marshal Carter feels indignant over the text of Garrison's statement. He aided greatly in ferreting out the murder of Roy Perkins and says that there was not a doubt in the world about Garrison's guilt. He says that Garrison was probably prompted to the attack on him in the statement by a desire to get revenge. Sometime back, Mr. Carter says, Garrison was bitter at J. B. Graham, the detective who worked on the case, Archie Phillips and Capt. Harris than he was at him (Carter) but Garrison evidently forgot them in making his bitter attack.

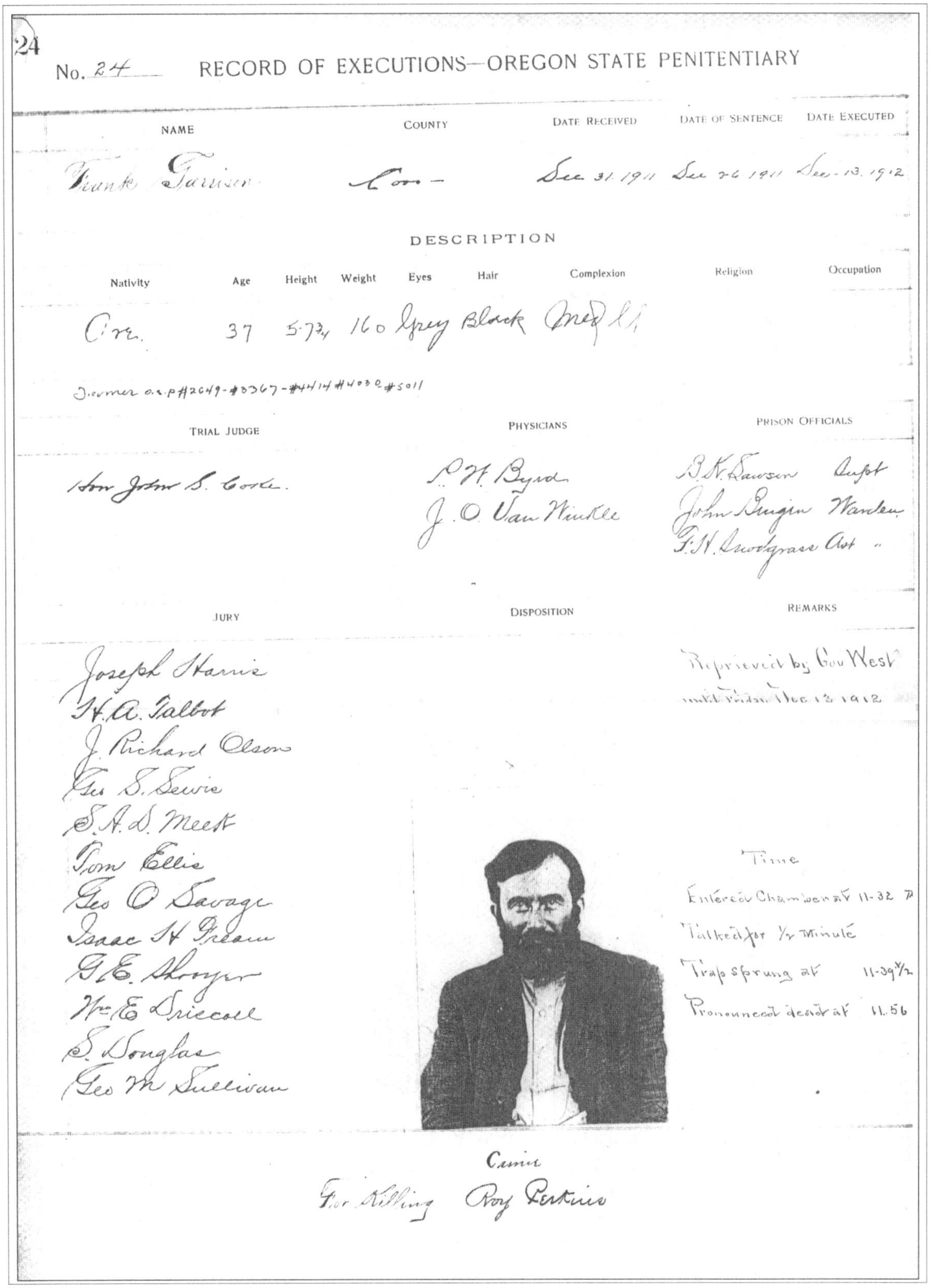

24

No. 24 RECORD OF EXECUTIONS—OREGON STATE PENITENTIARY

NAME	COUNTY	DATE RECEIVED	DATE OF SENTENCE	DATE EXECUTED
Frank Garrison	Coos	Dec 31. 1911	Dec 26 1911	Dec. 13. 1912

DESCRIPTION

Nativity	Age	Height	Weight	Eyes	Hair	Complexion	Religion	Occupation
Ore.	37	5-7¾	160	Grey	Black	Med		

Former O.S.P #2649-#3367-#4414 #4030 #5011

TRIAL JUDGE	PHYSICIANS	PRISON OFFICIALS
Hon John S. Coke	P. H. Byrd J. O. Van Winkle	B. K. Lawson Supt John Burgin Warden F. H. Snodgrass Ast "

JURY	DISPOSITION	REMARKS
Joseph Harris H. A. Talbot J. Richard Olson Geo S. Sewie S. A. D. Meek Tom Ellis Geo O Savage Isaac H Pream G. E. Shroyer Wm E Driscoll S. Douglas Geo M Sullivan		Reprieved by Gov West until Friday Dec 13 1912 Time Entered Chamber at 11-32 P Talked for ½ Minute Trap sprung at 11-39½ Pronounced dead at 11.56

Crime

For Killing Roy Perkins

Figure 23: Frank Garrison Record of Execution

Also printed was an article regarding Governor West's view of crime after the executions: **GOV. WEST SAYS LAX LAWS ARE BREEDING CRIMINALS** — Declares Weak Minded and Degenerates Are Allowed to Beget Weaklings. **MORE EFFORT MADE ABOUT LIVE STOCK** Urges Supporters of Hanging to Try and Aid in Removing Cause.

> PORTLAND, Dec. 14. — Following the execution of the four condemned men at Salem yesterday, Governor Oswald West today made the following statement: to the Associated Press: "This will not prevent crime. You must get at the root of the evil." These were the last words of one of the condemned men and they were to the point.
>
> I am not opposed to capital punishment as some think, because I am slopping over with sentiment, but because the practice seems to me to be entirely wrong and foolish. If we deliberately permit organized greed to breed, through the aid of poverty and vice, these criminals and degenerates, are we not in a way responsible for their acts? Is not the blood of their victims on our hands as well as that of the assassin? We spend much time and money educating the people how to select and breed and care for livestock. We impress upon them the fact that only through proper selection and care can desirable animals be produced. Yet we ignore these teachings in dealing with our low man for we only permit weak-minded and degenerate to mate and breed at will. We force their offspring to grow up in the midst of vice and awful poverty dwarfed morally, mentally and physically — and then hold up our hands in horror when, we hear of the commission of some awful crime.
>
> Let these who wish to prevent crime take time to look around and see the conditions under which some children are bred and obliged to grow up in. Let them lend a hand to those who are trying to remove some of the causes and they will do far more to prevent crime than by crying, "crucify him! crucify him!"

On December 17, 1912 the *Coos Bay Times* headlined: **FRANK GARRSION'S CONFESSION IS MADE PUBLIC BY TOM HALL** Attorney Says Murderer Admitted Crime in Detail to Him Soon After Killing. **CLAIMED HE THOUGHT PERKINS WOULD ATTACK** Refused to Make Admissions to the Jury as He Either Wanted to Go Free or Hang.

> Tom Hall today made a statement in which he states that Frank Garrison, who was executed at Salem last Friday for the murder of Roy Perkins and who went to the gallows with a protest of innocence on his lips, made a full confession to him of the murder.
>
> Hall states that when Marshal Carter and Sheriff Gage were "sweating" Garrison as the suspect, he accidentally encountered them at the Eastside ferry landing. The three were in the waiting room there when Mr. Hall dropped in. He immediately left, but Garrison sent one of the officers after him and called him back. Garrison set an appointment with Mr. Hall and a few hours later talked it over with him. The blood stains there still in the ferry waiting room.
>
> At this conference, Garrison told Hall the entire story of the crime. He said that he did not want to admit it, as he thought he could fix up a story that would acquit him. At any rate, he said he either wanted to go free or hang. Subsequently, Mr. Hall talked about the confession to Garrison and told him that if he would tell his story to the jury, he would be certain to escape the gallows. However, Garrison maintained his determination to either go free or to the gallows, but of course he confidently expected that he would go free.
>
> Even later when he was confined at Salem under the death sentence, he refused to let Mr. Hall try to get Governor West to commute the death sentence to life imprisonment by telling the story.
>
> The strange bravado spirit and deep-seated determination to get revenge that probably prompted Garrison to make the accusations against Marshal Carter and others something hard to comprehend. It was little short of the weird story of an insane man, but Garrison was not insane.
>
> Marshal Carter was highly elated today when he heard that Tom had given out Garrison's confession. While he felt confident no one who knew him would place any confidence in Garrison's wild attack, he was pleased to see that he was fully vindicated. He said that during his tenure of office since 1897, he had given his best and most conscientious efforts work and naturally in hunting down offenders like Garrison, he had to incurred their wrath. However, his record as an officer is such that attacks like Garrison's have no effect on him.

Mr. Hall's statement of Garrison's confession is as follows:

"As I promised you after having consulted a number of the members of the Coos County Bar association regarding the advisability of making a statement of the confession that Frank S. Garrison made to me about the killing of Roy Perkins, I will say that the following is substantially Garrison's statement to me: He was indebted to Roy Perkins and William Hower for labor which they had performed in digging clams and catching crabs, which he (Garrison) was selling at towns on Coos Bay and Coquille. His enterprise being a failure, and being unable to meet his obligations, he gave Perkins and Hower such goods and furniture he had in his possession in his cabin, with the understanding that they were to sell the same and give him credit on account. He stated that Perkins and Hower sold about twenty dollars worth and retained a sufficient amount to furnish a cabin near Sumner, where they engaged in peeling chittum bark, and gave him no credit thereof.

This made him angry, so he snatched his opportunity, and when Perkins brought his bark to Marshfield to market, he took, as he stated, such goods in Perkins' cabin as belonged to him and removed them to the boat landing on Catching Slough near Sumner, not expecting Perkins to return that day unexpectedly returned and found Garrison, at the landing with the goods. Perkins went to Sumner. Later he, Garrison, went to Sumner, where he met one of the Stutsman boys, who informed him that Perkins had started to Marshfield on foot to have him arrested for robbing his cabin. Garrison told me he then placed the goods on the boat which was between Sumner and Marshfield, with the understanding that the goods should be landed at the Marshfield dock. Then taking his dogs and gun he started on foot to try and overtake Perkins, and if possible prevail upon him (Perkins) not to have him arrested and try and adjust their difficulties without going into court. Enroute to Marshfield, he stopped at the home of Mrs. Smedburg and asked her if any one had passed. He was told that an old man had passed down the road a short time before. After getting some apples he (Garrison) continued on his way, arriving at the ferry slip at Eastside some time after dark. There he found Perkins. Perkins and he had a row and Garrison said that Perkins threatened to break his head with a stick, which he had in his hand and used for a walking stick. This row took place outside the waiting room, used in connection with the ferry. It being cold, both Perkins and Garrison went into the waiting room. Perkins laid down on a bench on the north side of the room and Garrison sat down on the opposite side with his gun across his knees. Several hours later Perkins made a. move which Garrison said startled him and fearing that Perkins intended to harm him, he shot Perkins, who died instantly. He then dragged the body down to the end of the ferry slip, where he procured two rocks from a box and made them fast with a rope to Perkins' neck and feet. He then took a skiff which was moored to the float adjoining the ferry slip, threw the body into the water, placed the rock that was attached to his neck in the boat and towed the body down the bay, to a place as he supposed, a short way below the mouth of Coos River, and sunk it. He then went across the Bay and slept the balance of the night in the Stave mill.

Garrison denied that he had any premeditated intention of killing Perkins and that he never robbed the body. He always maintained that Graham placed the stuff that was found under his cabin. I tried to get Garrison to make this statement in court at his trial but he said that he either wanted to go free or hang.

I make this statement for the reason that Garrison in his statement to the public just before his death, cast reflection on some of the witnesses and officers connected with his trial, which is absolutely untrue, and Garrison having been executed and no harm can be done by telling the facts that I believe the public should know."

CHAPTER 13

THE CASE OF LLEWELLYN WILSON "L.W." PEARE

Case Synopsis: During a severe drinking spree L.W. Peare murdered, by strangulation, his wife, Jessie, at their home. The next day Peare walked to the residence of their neighbor, Jim Culver, where Peare shot and killed him.

The Motive: No known motive for the murder of his wife, as Peare was so severely intoxicated according to his testimony he did not know why he killed her. Peare believed Culver was the root of Peare's problems which is why Peare committed that murder.

***The Parties*:** Nothing is known about the victim James R. Culver. Llewellyn Wilson "L.W." Peare was born June 6, 1856 in Leeds, Maine. Peare and his wife Jessie Clara, born in 1866 in the state of Washington, were married February 18, 1888 in Portland, Oregon.[39] They had two grown daughters at the time of the crime; Vestie Bushnell and Stella Shields. Jessie Peare was buried at the Catching Creek Cemetery.

Figure 24: L.W. Peare – *Coos Bay Times*, March 16, 1923

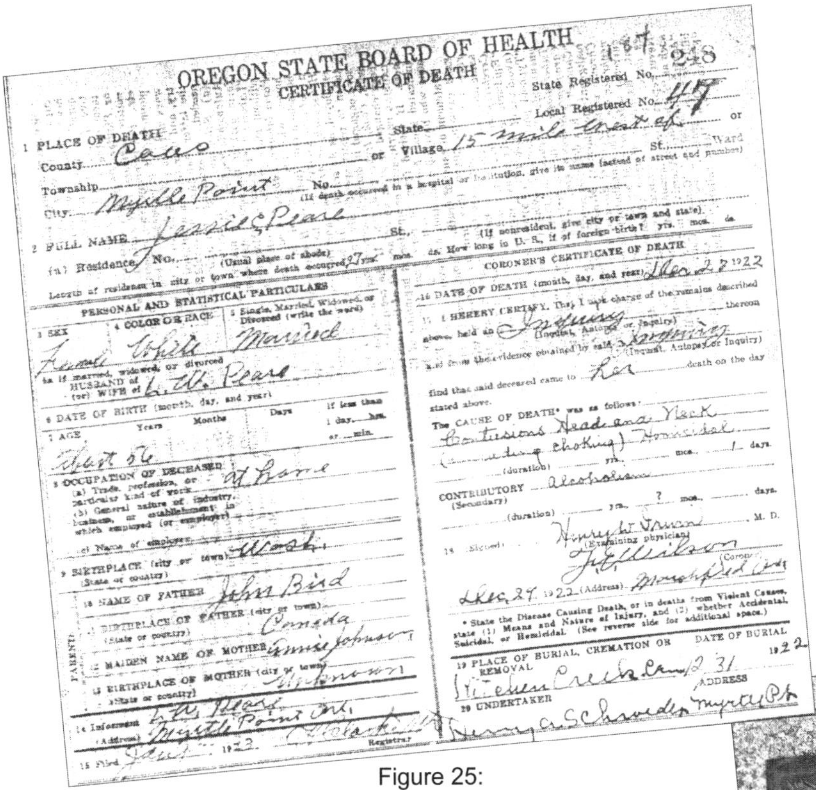

OREGON STATE BOARD OF HEALTH
CERTIFICATE OF DEATH
State Registered No. 218
Local Registered No. 47

1 PLACE OF DEATH
County Coos
Township
Village 15 mile west of
City Mystle Point

2 FULL NAME Jessie C. Peare

PERSONAL AND STATISTICAL PARTICULARS
3 SEX Female
4 COLOR OR RACE White
5 Single, Married, Widowed, or Divorced Married
HUSBAND of L. W. Peare
7 AGE about 56
8 OCCUPATION OF DECEASED At home
9 BIRTHPLACE Wash.
10 NAME OF FATHER John Bird
11 BIRTHPLACE OF FATHER Canada
12 MAIDEN NAME OF MOTHER Annie Johnson
13 BIRTHPLACE OF MOTHER Unknown
14 Informant L. W. Peare, Myrtle Point Ore.
15 Filed Jan. 1923

CORONER'S CERTIFICATE OF DEATH
16 DATE OF DEATH Dec. 27 1922
I HEREBY CERTIFY, That I took charge of the remains described above, held an Inquest thereon, and from the evidence obtained by said Inquest find that said deceased came to her death on the date stated above.
The CAUSE OF DEATH was as follows: Contusions Head and Neck (including choking) Homicidal
CONTRIBUTORY alcoholism
Signed J. E. Wilson, Coroner
Dec. 27, 1922 Marshfield Ore.
19 PLACE OF BURIAL, CREMATION OR REMOVAL Catchen Creek Cem. DATE OF BURIAL 12 31 1922
20 UNDERTAKER Henry A. Schroeder, Myrtle Pt.

Figure 25:
Jesse Peare
Certificate of Death

Figure 26: In Memory of Jessie Peare

The Crime and Punishment: December 29, 1922 the *Coos Bay Harbor* headlined: **L.A. PEARE CHOKES WIFE TO DEATH SHOOTS JIM CULVER AND THREATENS SAM STEVENS —RANCHER RESIDING IN SOUTHERN COOS HELD ON CHARGE OF DOUBLE MURDER** — Shot Neighbor Jim Culver, Then Returned Home choking His Wife to Death, Killed His Two Fine Dogs, and Started Out to Murder Others But Was Put Under Arrest.

Two are cold in death, while at least two others owe their lives to the ability of Sam Stevens to resist a man armed with a high powered rifle when on Thursday set out to "clean out" the entire neighborhood. L. A. Peare a rancher residing in southern Coos county, and an old settler, on Thursday morning went, to the home of his neighbor Jim Culver and murdered him in cold blood. He found Jim carrying in wood with which to cook a breakfast and shot him in the shoulder. He ran into the house Peare following close upon him, and after he had fallen on the front room floor fired another shot at very close range, tearing away a portion of the head and killing him instantly.

Peare then returned to his home, choked his wife to death, and left her body lying on the kitchen floor. He then shot his two dogs said to have been exceptionally well trained Shepherds.

He then went to the home of Sam Stevens where he made loud threats and said he was going to murder Stevens and Carl Bushnell. Stevens saw that the man intended carrying out his threats and grappled him, managing by hard work to prevent his shooting. He took the gun away and tied Peare with a rope so that he could not get away. Stevens then gave the alarm and sent word to Marshall Redell of Myrtle Point.

Confession Makes Plain Case.

Peare is said to have told the officers that he murdered Jim Culver and Mrs. Peare. He is quoted as saying he is "mighty proud of the job, intended killing Stevens and Bushnell, also his horses, and does not remember how he killed his wife. The cause is old trouble," he added.

Jim Culver and his brother Pete Culver resided on a 1400 acre ranch on the border of Coos and Curry county, and the house was located just over the line in Curry. They have resided there many years. They are cousins of Pete Anderson of this city. Mr. Anderson says he has not seen the boys for some time and knows nothing of the trouble if any existed between the men. The murdered man has a brother in the hardware business at Roseburg, another in the Coast Guard service at the Umpqua, and another near the home place.

Whiskey Probably the Cause.

Editor Bledsoe of the Myrtle Point American told the Harbor today that Peare had been drinking heavily and that he was known to have been under the influence of liquor when the deeds were committed. In fact officers who brought Peare to Coquille said that liquor was noticeable on his breath. Editor Bledsoe says that Peare has not been in Myrtle Point for some time, and the shooting came as a great surprise to the people of that city.

District Attorney Fisher is said to be filing a charge of murder against Peare today, and the confession together with the evidence obtained will surely mean an early ending for a man who let moonshine[o] get the best of him.

The bodies of Mrs. Peare and Mr. Culver are now in the morgue of Undertaker Schroeder at Myrtle Point.

On December 29, 1923 the *Coquille Valley Sentinel* headlined: **DOUBLE MURDER —** L.W. Peare Kills His Wife and Jas. Culver Near Curry County Line

The most brutal and totally uncalled double murder in the history of Coos county occurred Wednesday evening and Thursday morning about 18 miles southwest of Myrtle Point, beyond the head of Catching creek. The murderer was L.W. Peare, and the victims his own wife and Jas. Culver.

Peare had been crazy drunk every since Christmas on moonshine of his making;
and some time Thursday evening he choked and beat his wife to death and the next morning at daylight he went over to his neighbors home and killed him.

The revolting details of the dastardly crime are given by Deputy Sheriff Malehorn as told him by Peare, who seemed to be supremely happy that he had killed Culver. In fact Mr. Malehorn say that if Peare told

[o] Common slang term for home-distilled alcohol in places where production was illegal. The name was assumed to have been derived from the fact that moonshine producers and smugglers would often work at night; hence, under the light of the moon.

it once he told the story five hundred times before they arrived at the county jail here this morning at eight o'clock.

Peare, who has the reputation of being ugly and quarrelsome especially when drinking, had been quarreling and "bouting" with his wife Wednesday and along in the evening he choked her and beat her and pulled out great handfuls of her hair and suddenly she went limp and died "from fright," Peare said. He carried her into the bedroom and says he worked part of the night trying to bring her to consciousness, but with the whole house smeared with blood and two pillows soaked through with it, it would seem that a man even in his maniacal condition might known she was dead.

Throughout the night Peare kept drinking and in one of his frenzies shot and killed his two dogs and cat and shot the leg off a sewing machine. There was blood and brains scattered all over the house, but the latter must have been from the animals for there was no cut or bullet wound on Mrs. Peare body.

Just before daylight yesterday morning Peare started for Culver's home, three-quarters of a mile away and over the line in Curry county. He found the latter carrying in an armful of wood. He says, "I played it pretty slick;" I called "hello," snapped my fingers at the dog and followed him into the house for I had a pride against shooting a man in the back. As Culver dropped the wood and turned toward Peare, the latter shot him with his 30-30, the bullet entering the middle of his body and coming out his back. Culver started for him and Peare he hit him a blow on the nose, and beat around the head until Culver dropped. Peare says he was trying to tell him all the time why he was killing him. After he fell, Culver spit, and his murderer thought if he could spit he wasn't dead so he fired again, this time blowing the whole right side of his head off, and then to make sure that he was dead picked up some of the brains and rubbed. them between his fingers.

Starting back for home, he passed Sam Stevens to whom he told what he had done. Stevens didn't believe it, but he took Peare to his own cabin and made him some coffee. The latter continued to drink from his bottle but soon fell asleep in the warm room. Stevens then tied him in bed and went down to Joe Knight's who telephoned to Marshal Redell at Myrtle Point.

The latter phoned to the sheriff's office but both officers were out so he got Coroner Wilson on the phone and he went right over to Myrtle Point and with Redell up to get the bodies.

About seven o'clock last evening Sheriff Ellingsen and Deputy Malehorn left here. From Joe Knight's place they had one horse to carry them up the steep mountain road through the mud and rain, and took turns riding it. Arriving at Stevens' place they found Peare had freed himself from the ropes but had made no attempt to escape.

In telling the story of the double homicide, he compared himself to a boy with a pair of new red-top boots, tickled to death that he had killed Culver. He was 63 years of age, owns 400 acres of land on the headwaters of catching creek, and had lived there for 27 years. His wife was ten years his junior. They have two daughters - Mrs. Stella Shields, of Bancroft, and Mrs. Carl Bushnell, who lives of catching creek.

His other victim was about 55 or 56 years of age unmarried, and lived alone.

There is nothing in Peare's talk to suggest that he had killed the two for one reason. He did not like Culver, says he wasn't a white man, and after he killed his wife in his drunk-crazed condition, and knew he was in for it, he thought he would get even with Culver and send him to eternity, too.

Coroner Wilson found that Mrs. Peare's body was full of moonshine, but whether she had drunk it or Peare had poured it into her in his efforts at resuscitation is not known.

When shown the bodies of his victims at Myrtle Point this morning the murderer began to shake life a leaf, and had lost all bravery and cheerfulness he exhibited out in the hills. He was beginning to sober a little by the time the officers landed him in jail this morning.

District Attorney Fisher came over from the Bay this morning and Peare made a complete statement to him, although it was not so jubilantly told as it was last night. He is beginning to realize the enormity of his offense and is scared now.

Mr. Fisher went before Justice Stanley later and swore out a complaint, charging first degree murder.

January 5, 1923 the *Coquille Valley Sentinel* headlined: **MAY NOT BE TRIED** — Murderer Peare in Very Poor Health — May Cheat Gallows

L.W. Peare, self-confessed murderer of his wife and of Jas. Culver, up on the headwaters of Catching creek last week, was taken before Justice J. J. Stanley here Tuesday morning for a hearing. He waived examination and was held to the grand jury, which meets next month, without bail.

There is practically nothing to add to the story the Sentinel published last week of the double murder, but the report in the Bay and Portland papers that Peare endeavored to also kill Sam Stevens, Catching creek rancher, is incorrect. As Peare returned home from his murderous trip to Culver's cabin he saw Stevens at his barn and called to him. The latter has feared Peare when drinking, and so when he went up to the road to see what was wanted he placed himself in a position at the bend of the crooked road, where he would be face to face with Peare as soon as they met. Just before the murderer reached the bend he slipped and sat down and called to ask where Stevens was. The latter answered and Peare got up and as soon as he caught sight of Stevens he began to tell him that he had killed his wife and Culver. Stevens would not believe it at first, but Peare kept repeating in a high and hysterical tone of voice that he had done so. As he stood swaying in the road, with his rifle in front of him in both hands, the muzzle stopped for a second against Stevens' abdomen. Quick as thought the latter grabbed the muzzle with one hand, the stock with the other, and with a twist, took it away from Peare and threw it down the hill.

Peare went with Stevens to the latter's house and after he had fallen asleep Stevens tied him in bed in order to hold him until the officers' arrival, but he had gotten loose by the time they came that night.

Peare is extremely nervous and weak, and the officers seems to think he may not survive until his trial. He was taken to the Ralph Nosler's barbershop on Tuesday for a shave and a hair cut, which caused one wag to start the story that he had seen Ralph Nosler shaving a man with a safety razor, after looking up all his unusual in the rear room.

On January 12, 1923 the *Coquille Valley Sentinel* headlined: **Peare's Health is Better**

L.W. Pearce, in jail for murdering his wife and Jas. Culver, is regaining his normal condition, although still somewhat shaky as the result of his debauch and from the realization of his terrible crimes. He eats and sleeps well now and seems to be in better spirits.

He has given Attorney C.F. McKnight power of attorney to sell his personal effects and take entire charge of his defense.

March 9, 1923 the *Coquille Valley Sentinel* headlined: **Peare Trial Starts Monday**

The trial of L.W. Peare for murdering his wife and Jas. Culver last December is scheduled to start in Circuit court here next Monday. It is the only criminal case ready for trial.

That it is going to be hard fought is evidenced by the fact that both the state and defense asked the court to permit them to introduce ten additional witnesses to the five allowed by law. The request was granted.

It is reported that Geo. Neuner, of Roseburg, will assist District Attorney Fisher in the prosecution. C.F. McKnight and John D. Goss have been retained for the defense. It is said that the defense will be insanity.

Also printed in the March 9th issue: **Mere manslaughter**

Editor Sentinel: — The Sentinel and other papers always speak of L.W. Peare of "Catching Creek." He never lived on Catching Creek; he lived on the Floras Creeks hills, miles from Catching Creek. We should take off our hats to the jurymen who indicted him for manslaughter. After a man has abused his wife for forty years and then chokes her to death that is manslaughter. Is it any wonder the women are getting divorces from their men? — Subscriber.

March 12, 1923 the *Coos Bay Times* headlined: **INSANITY WILL BE THE DEFENSE OF L.W. PEARE** Faces Charge of First Degree Murder for Killing of James Culver, Neighbor — **IS ALSO INDICTED FOR THE MURDER OF HIS WIFE** George Neuner of Roseburg Assisting Ben Fisher in Prosecution of Rancher **WILL BE HARD FOUGHT** C. F. McKnight and John D. Goss Are Defending — Dr. Williamson, Insanity Expert from Portland. Is a Witness

COQUILLE, Ore., March 12. — The trial or L. W. Peare, Catching creek rancher, on a charge of first degree murder started in the circuit court before Judge John C. Kendall today. It is the first jury criminal case tried before the judge since he assumed office, so he starts out with a first degree murder case. Insanity is evidently to be the defense.

Murdered Two

Peare is the old man who lived for some years past on Flores creek near the Curry county line. For a week following Christmas he was on a spree, keeping drunk on moonshine of his own manufacture. His wife had also been drinking and they quarreled, it was said because she refused to testify in a law suit which Peare intended bringing against his son-in-law.

Peare choked his wife to death then killed his dogs and cats and armed with a rifle and carrying a bottle of moonshine, went to the home of James Culver, a neighbor and killed him also. He started for another neighbor's house but by the latter was captured.

Peare was indicted for second degree murder for the killing of his wife and first degree murder for the killing of Culver. It is the first degree murder charge on which Peare is now being tried.

Insanity Claimed

Insanity is to the defense, it is understood. C. F. McKnight is Peare's attorney and associated with him in the defense in John D. Goss.

Dr. Williamson, an insanity expert of Portland, is here as a witness.

Peare has not been well since confined in the county jail and is rather shaky and shows signs of age and illness.

Neuner Assisting

District Attorney Ben S. Fisher is being assisted in the prosecution by George Neuner, district attorney of Douglas county, who is engaged by relatives of Culver to help prosecute.

The case it is expected will be a hard fought one. Judge Kendall did not anticipate calling a special venire until the regular panel had been exhausted. It was anticipated that a jury would not be secured until tonight or tomorrow. It will probably require four or five days to get through with the case.

On March 16, the *Coos Bay Harbor* headlined: **MURDER WRITES WILL FOLLOWING CHOKING TO DEATH OF HIS WIFE** — L.W. Peare of Southern Coos County, Being Tried at Coquille This Week Before Judge Kendall, Defendant Claims Insanity.

One of the sensations brought out in the trial of L. W. Peare at Coquille yesterday was caused when Coroner Fred Wilson produced a hurriedly scribbled and is without doubt the hand work of the defendant. The will was found on the table by the Coroner and the Sheriff when Peare was arrested. It has since been held secretly pending the trial.

Peare is on trial for his life, charged for the murder of his wife, an act that is the most fiendish of any ever committed in this or any other county in Oregon. According to best evidence them an actually choked the woman to death. Also for shooting and instantly killing Jim Culver, a neighbor, whom he blamed for trouble alleged to exist in the family. He then set out to kill others, but met defeat in his purpose when Sam Stevens over powered him and took the rifle away from him.

Copy of the Will.

This is the will which L. W. Peare left on his table in. his home, after the murder of his wife: "Joe Knight is to have the land, Lloyd Ely is to have the cattle, Carl Bushnell and Jim Culver are the cause of this.

L. W. PEARE

Vestie is to have Five dollars.

Stella is to have 5 dollars.

L. W. PEARE."

The trial is making good progress, the prosecution having completed its work, and the evidence for the defense is being taken. It is believed that the trial will end Monday or Tuesday.

March 16, 1923 the *Coquille Valley Sentinel* headlined: **TELLS AT LAST** — Peare Makes an Unexpected Disclosure This Morning

From 11 o'clock for three-fourth of an hour this morning the defendant L. W. Peare was being cross-examined by state's attorney Neuner, of Douglas county, and Peare during this time came across with an entirely unexpected feature of the case an one of which there had not been heretofore the slightest intimation. Mr. Peare had been before examined by his own attorneys, and it was during his cross-examination by District Attorney Neuner, of Douglas county, for the state that he disclose conditions that had existed in his home before the killing of his wife which would, if anything could, explain his homicidal frenzy and the butchering of his wife and James Culver.

What Peare said about his moonshine, his still[P] and his sprees would fill several columns of the Sentinel and just at the hour of going to press we can touch but very few points before getting to the astonishing developments that came before he left the stand.

He told about a quarrel with his wife three years ago in which ho nearly killed her. "We sat up all night," said her. "She had been drinking and so had I." They had been drinking mash and "drank all night long."

At this time they had a quarrel and he nearly killed her. It seems that for a while he thought she was dead; and they were so thoroughly scared by what happened.

"Why did you again make moonshine after it made so much trouble when you thought you had killed your wife," he was asked.

"I didn't make any more moonshine for a long time," was the answer. "I agreed that I wouldn't drink any more until she told me that I could."

After some time had passed his wife seems to have felt the old appetite come back and "she told me if I would be careful she would let me." So she helped him make it and "we had a nice time with moonshine, drinking it and enjoyed ourselves."

When the two quart limit law applied to booze bought in this state, he used to bring it home—as much as four quarts at a time; and they would make a night of it, saving a little to drink before breakfast in the morning.

Asked about his still he said he had had it fifteen or sixteen years. Being pressed to tell what date he got it, he blurted out the reply:

"Ask A.J. Sherwood, he could tell."

Later he said the still had been given him with a wagon load of apples, and he pounded up the apples with a maul and made a drink that he seemed to think was excellent, though he didn't mention ever having heard of "Apple Jack."[Q]

"How often did you have a spree in the last three years?" was the next question.

"I put everything out of the way, didn't keep it in the house at all."

Of this time he also testified that his wife was using the copper part of the still as a wash boiler.

"How many more than the two times you have told about did you get on a spree in the last three years?" was another question. "Can't think of but one." "Only once so drunk that you did anything unusual."

"Go back a few years longer and I could think of all kinds of sprees. Four quarts didn't last long. I didn't go on any serious sprees with it."

"During: the time did you ever drink enough to be sick?"

He said he did and was sometimes sick three or four days.

Asked about Bushnell and trouble about Culver's cutting hay and if he knew what year that was, he answered:

"I'll have to think a minute, I had, all those things down."

He told about having nightmare when he was sick and digressed in the narrative to tell about "a fellaw up in jail last night talking in his sleep." He also said, "I had nightmares when I wasn't sick. I have more the older I grow — idiotic stuff, Can't realize they are not true when I wake up."

"When a boy I dreamed of falling — it was a horrible sensation — and just as I struck, woke up."

Asked about the testimony of the witnesses Stephen and others about the day the killings occurred and whether their testimony was not substantially correct he said, "Yes, with a few exception."

Asked about his allusion to relationship between his wife and Jim Culver he said he "told it to very few people; if I had talked about her I wouldn't have lived with her."

He said the relationship "had been going on for some time. After I commenced forming that opinion I became more and more sure."

Urged to tell what he saw between them he said:

"I didn't see very much."

[P] A still is a device for the distilling of alcohol (moonshine) in which the substance is vaporized by heat and then cooled to condense the vapor.

[Q] Applejack was a strong alcoholic beverage produced from apples having originated from the American colonial period. Made by concentrating hard cider, either by the traditional method of freeze distillation or by true evaporative distillation. The term applejack was derived from "jacking" a term for freeze distillation.

"First Culver used to come to my house sometimes three or four times a week. After that written notice he never came. I didn't form all this conclusion until the last year."

It had been in his mind "eight or ten years, perhaps longer than that."

"What was the first time you called your wife's attention to it?"

"Didn't for a long time. It grew thicker as the years went on. The last time he talked with my wife was right in my presence. In the eight, years they had met hundreds of times. My wife sometimes went over to his house. She went over there to get him to come when I was sick."

"You and your wife were dear to each other?" was another question.

"Sometimes and sometimes not so much," was the answer.

"Did you tell any one what you thought was the relationship between your wife and Culver?"

"I didn't, I wouldn't go about the country and talk about my wife and still live with her."

"I can't remember about the talk I had with Fisher. I will accept what he says about it as the truth. Ask him."

District Attorney Fisher, Coroner Wilson and a stenographer, he said, were present when Fisher advised him of his rights not to testify against himself.

It seemed that when Fisher asked about having any trouble with Culver and his wife he said, "No," and talked about trouble with the stock.

He added this rather significant statement, "I wouldn't have said anything about Culver and my wife now except for the advice of my attorneys."

"Who was the first you ever mentioned it to?"

"I don't remember about telling anyone." He "told it to his attorneys."

He "didn't want to tell about it but they told him to tell the truth. That's the only time I ever had any serious trouble."

He had before detailed being struck in the head and knocked senseless by the limb of a fir tree, but didn't know how long it was before he recovered consciousness. He had never had a doctor in his life when he was sick.

Before leaving the stand he went over to the jury box and let every juror who wished to put his hand on his head about three inches back from the center of his forehead and feel of his skull where the fir limb struck him.

It took all day Monday and Tuesday and until afternoon Wednesday to secure a jury to try L.W. Peare on the charge of first degree murder in killing James Culver. One panel after another was exhausted before 12 men satisfactory to both the prosecution and defense could be secured and 93 veniremen were catechised before that result was accomplished.

For the first time in the ten years the writer has lived in Coos county there is a murder trial where the penalty if the defendant is found guilt; will be death, as it is also the first time since capital punishment came back by the vote of the people that the death penalty has been invoked in this county.

The following are the jurymen before whom this case is being tried:

Ralph D. Moore, Bandon, lumberman.
P. J. Rooney, Marshfield, machinist
Albert Bezosky, Gravel Ford, farmer.
E. H. Harnden, Coquille, farmer.
Hugh J. Lawhome, McKinley, logger.
Paul E. Beuer, Myrtle Point, shoe maker.
W. L. Finnie, North Bend, merchant.
Roy A. Mercer, Mars Wild, restaurant man.
Richard A. Felter, Bandon, dairyman.
P. J. Devereux, Bandon., dairymen.
L. L. Sumerlin, McKinley, farmer.
A. E. Glossop, Marshfield, barber.

Attorney Neuner made the opening statement for the prosecution.

Besides the defendant the other witnesses for the state were examined in the following order: Sam Stephens, O. J. Hamburg, Elmer Stanford Robert L. Hildebrand, Ed Ellingsen, F. E. Wilson, Sam Malehorn, Mrs. Bushnell, daughter of the defendant.

Besides the defendant, the witnesses called for the defense, of whom the first had taken the stand just before dinner are Ray Dement, Taylor Dement, H. W. Pike, Sam Malehorn Harvey P. Smith, and J. L. Knight.

This noon the Sentinel asked Attorney C. F. McKnight how long it would take to finish the trial of Peare. He thought that perhaps the defense's witnesses might all be examined this afternoon; but that it might take most of the day, tomorrow to hear the two distinguished specialists it nervous diseases, who will be called to the stand last, Mr. William House of Portland, for the state and Doctor W. T. Williamson, who has two sanitariums in Portland, for the defense. Both are being called to give opinions all over the country and Dr. Williamson has just returned from Chicago.

So he hardly thought the case would go to the jury before Monday.

The next article headlined: **PICKING JURORS** — A Topsy Turvy Case That verses the Usual Rules of Selection

The writer spent a couple of hours in court; Tuesday afternoon very interestingly in listening to the examination of men summoned in the special venires called for the trial of L.W. Peare for the murder of James Culver. The jury box was full when we went in, but although six or eight men were examined "touching their qualifications" for service on the jury while we were there it still lacked one when court adjourned that evening, No sooner had a juror been accepted than the defense made a preemptory challenge of some one that had already been "passed for cause" and the net result of the two hours work was two more jurymen seated — perhaps temporarily — one of them being our friend, J. E. Montgomery, of Marshfield, former superintendent of the Coos and Curry Telephone company and an experienced newspaper man, (Mr. Montgomery afterward fell by the wayside under a preemptory challenge.)

The defendant was, of course, the center of interest, though, he listened to the proceeding with apparent stolidity and if he realized the gravity of his position and the fate that might await him at the hands of the jury which was being impaneled, he did not manifest it. He is apparently about sixty years of age, though his dark brown hair is not even tinged with gray and he is growing bald at the crown. However, he has an entirely grey moustache and his rugged face at least looks careworn. There was nothing "horny handed" about him, but the fingers that so recently handled a rifle with such deadly effect looked soft and white as those of a dry goods clerk.

His attorneys are John D. Goss, one of the leaders of the Marshfield bar and C. P. McKnight, who is perhaps Coos county's best known criminal lawyer, whom every one who attended the successive Harold Howell trials here three or four years ago, will remember. His associate counsel in one of those trials was John C. Kendall, who is now the presiding judge.

Harking back to those Harold Howell trials now the thought obtrudes this his defense, like Peare's now, ought to have been insanity rather than an alibi, for the passing years only serve to reinforce the conviction that those trials resulted in a miscarriage of justice.

District Attorney Ben S. Fisher represents the state in the pending case, and associated with him is District Attorney George E. Neuner Jr., of the Douglas county district, who has been retained by the murdered man's friends to assist in the prosecution. So the stage is set for a battle of the giants here this week.

Between the attorneys of the state, and intently watching every move in the case, sat Peter Culver, a brother of the murdered man, who will leave no stone unturned to see that Peare gets his desserts. Another brother, George Culver, of Roseburg, came in Wednesday to be present at the trial.

From the very start on Monday this murder has been developing exceptional, we may even say unique features. Indeed, to the Sentinel man it seemed a topsy turvy one.

There are to be no surprises in this case. The defense begins by placing its lone trump card on the table face up, admitting without question that Peare shot James Culver to death and announcing that it claims that he was insane when he did it. It follows that the burden of proof is shifted from the prosecution to the defense, the presumption of law being not only that every man is innocent until he is proper, guilty, but also that every man is sane until he is proven insane. Beyond this the state is not slow to claim, even before the trial has begun that the "reasonable-doubt" proposition enters into the case in what is to us an entirely novel way — that if the testimony as to the mental condition of the defendant leaves in the mind of any juror the least doubt as to the mental status of the accused, that doubt must be resolved, not in his favor, as would be any doubt about his committing the murder, but on the contrary it favor of the state;

that is, unless the defense, with the burden of proof upon it, fails to satisfy every juror that the defendant was crazy, when he committed the act, he must find him guilty of murder in the first degree as charged in the indictment. This is why we call this a topsy turvy case. There is no presumption of innocence after the defendant acknowledges that he committed the crime, but a presumption of guilt which can only be overcome by positive proof that he was in a condition of moral irresponsibility.

The defense even goes farther that this, according to the theory developed in their examination of talesmen. It not only admits the killing but hypothetically assumes that Peare was crazy drunk when he fired the fatal shot, which, of course, would be no defense at all. So it comes to this that he must be shown to be crazy in more than one way at the same time or there will be no ground on which to base a verdict of not guilty.

Even this is not all. Peare's attorneys seemed willing to admit that the state of mind in which he was at the time he killed Culver was due in some degree to his long continued excessive use of intoxicating liquor and that the quality of the moonshine produced by his own still may also have had the effect to derange his mind. His advancing age as well as his extreme dissipation are, it seems to be another reason why the jurors are to be asked to pronounce him not guilty of the crime of murder.

These theories bring to mind the celebrated case of Harry Thaw, the feeble-minded millionaire, who killed Sanford White, and who was sentenced to an insane asylum instead of the electric chair.

The *Sentinel* is far from expressing any opinion as to how far or in what way Peare was insane though it has no doubt that his attorneys are right in practically admitting that he was crazy drunk at the time and it feels that it will be to the credit of human nature if the "experts" who are to testify in that behalf can convince the jury that he was irresponsible.

So far we have given some idea of how this case was presented by the attorneys who have the burden of proof on their hands, in their examination of prospective jurymen. But the questions were by no means confined to the insanity feature of the case. In not less than two instances in the two hours, the jurors under examination had stated that they had a very positive opinion formed from reading or conversation with people who were informed about the case and that it would be very difficult for them to disregard those prejudiced opinions in considering the evidence placed before them. And then after Judge Kendall had directed that such a juror should be accepted, and the counsel for the defense had taken an exception, when the state's attorneys came to question the juror, they drew from him the fact that he was conscientiously opposed to capital punishment and could not pronounce a man guilty where the punishment for his offense might be death. Of course, then there was an objection from that side and the juror was immediately excused. Jap Yoakam was one of these men and the other was from the Bay. Of course, a man who had very strong feelings of that sort found it easy to evade jury duty, and the last vote on capital punishment in this State shows that a very large percentage of the electors feel that way, and the field from which qualified jurors can be secured is thus greatly restricted.

The most positive statement made by any juror as to opinions that would disqualify him for service on the jury on account of prejudice were made by our old friend, L. J. Roberts, who was for years editor of the Myrtle Point Enterprise. He intimated to us afterwards that his opinion was not entirely based on what he had heard about the facts in the ease since the killing.

Of course, there were the usual stock questions put to all those jurymen examined in addition to the novel ones we have indicated above. They were asked whether they knew anything about the case or had read anything about it in the newspapers; and the manner in which the last question was put seemed to convey the impression that in some way it was discreditable to pay enough attention to newspaper stories to base an opinion on what they said, although that is what every one of us is doing dozens of times every day on all sorts of subjects. And there is never anyone to object to any sort of question to a juryman as "leading."

Another line of questioning was whether it would tend to bias the juryman against the defendant. If during the trial it should develop that he was not only accused of killing Culver but that he had also been indicted for killing his wife. The demand seemed to be for jurymen who would consider the alleged offense in the Culver case on its own merits and would not consider another killing the defendant is charged with having committed on the same day in that connection.

On March 16, 1923 the *Coos Bay Times* reported several articles regarding the trial. The first headlined: **SLAYER TELLS HIS STORY OF KILLING CULVER** — L. W. Peare on the Witness Stand Today Gives All Details of the Murder **COULD NOT REMEMBER OF KILLING HIS WIFE** Says He Had Been Drinking Moonshine and that His Mind Was Blank on Many Points **BELIEVED NOT JUSTIFIED** — Says He Knows Now He Had No Right to Shoot Culver but that He Felt Differently at the Time Of the Murder — **INSANITY EXPERT SAYS DEFENDANT WAS CRAZY** — Dr. Williamson, insanity expert of Portland, was put on the stand this afternoon and testified that Peare was insane. He said he might appear normal but that he suffered delusions and gave his opinion that the man was crazy when he committed the murders.

COQUILLE, Ore., March 16. — L.W. Peare this morning on the witness stand told the details of killing James Culver. This was after he had been on the stand all yesterday afternoon when he gave preliminary evidence of his life and actions leading up to the time of the murder.

There were occasions when Peare said his memory was not good. He did not remember anything about killing his wife. They had both, been drinking and he said moonshine made his mind a blank. He simply knew that something was the matter with her and that she was dead and he could not revive her.

On many other points he was not clear and in some respects he showed a remarkable memory for details. Yesterday he was a little nervous at times but this morning he was perfectly cool and composed. He spoke in a commonplace manner and could be heard all over the over the court room. He insisted on telling details of everything and was allowed to go ahead and give his story in his own way.

When Peare went on the stand this morning he was asked and told about the arrangement he had made with his son-in-law, Carl Bushnell. He said he had written down the details of the deal and intended to have it properly drawn up by a lawyer. Carl was to take charge of matters and he was to leave him property in consideration.

Peare said that the last work he did was to repair a saddle. This was before Christmas and he had been drinking a good deal at that time. He told of hearing his wife making a noise in another room. He thought she was laughing but went to see her and found her on the floor. He picked her up and put her on the bed and went to find whiskey. The witness said he and his wife always had a drink before meals. They had both been drinking a good deal. The witness went into a good deal of detail regarding the whiskey and of having bottles concealed.

The witness said he took a big drink and went to his wife and tried to give her a drink. He said he could not remember very well. He said he got into bed and tried to cuddle his wife but she was dead and was not breathing. He said he then decided to kill the cats and dogs. He got his 22-caliber gun. He said:

"As soon as I could see the sights I think I killed the cats first. Then I shot the little dog and then with a bigger gun I killed the big dog."

"I think the next thing I did was to scribble the note. I don't know why I did it but I guess I wanted people to see it."

"I decided then I would kill Jim Culver. An overwhelming impulse overcame me. I felt he had and Carl were the cause of my problems. I probably included Bowman too. I thought that Culver did a good deal against me and thought he intended to do more against me."

"Do you think," asked Attorney Goss, "that you had a right to kill Jim Culver?"

"I don't know but I suppose I did then. I don't think I had the right to kill anyone or that anybody has a right to kill anyone but I guess I didn't think that way at the time."

In answer to questions the witness said he had been told that Culver had intended renting an adjoining farm and would try to interfere with his range.

When asked if the other witnesses had told the facts about the case the witness said: "As near as know, I wouldn't feel safe in disputing anyone. I remember of going to Jim Culver. I think I told Mr. Fisher about as good a statement as I told anyone. I tried to tell him the truth. I cannot remember all I told him now but I think I told him most everything."

Telling of being at Culver's the witness said:

"I had my gun. The dogs a Culver's came up to me. I snapped my fingers at them. Culver went into the house and to the wood box and I shot him. He fell down. I stood there. I think he tried to raise up. I thought he was going to speak. He did not. I shot him in the face."

"They tell me about picking up this blood and stuff. What I think happened was that little white pieces of skull scattered around. I picked up some to see what I had done and what I hadn't. I put then down again. Mr. Wilson can tell better about that."

"I went out of the house at once and did not disturb anything. I then went and got the whiskey had left outside. I then took it in my head to see Joe Knight. I saw Sara Stevens. I had my gun and transferred it from one hand and waived to him that I wanted to see him."

The witness said he could not remember whether he told Steven what he had done but did remember that he asked Stevens to take a horse and go to Joe Knight and asked Stevens to give him some coffee. He said they went to Steven's house and was told to lay on the bed.

At this point the witness was not clear. He thought Stevens gave him some whisky and some coffee but could not remember. He said he had not had any dinner, breakfast or supper and remembered he wanted coffee and felt the need of it because he had been drinking moonshine.

"Why did you kill the dogs and cats?" asked the attorney.

"I realized only my wife and me knew the dogs and cats and I didn't want anybody to abuse them I knew I was going somewhere but I didn't know where."

"Why didn't you kill the rest of the animals?" asked the attorney.

"I had tame cattle but was not as attached to them as I was to the dogs and cats which were around the house. I was very much attached to the horse but I did not think of them. In fact I could have ridden one of the horses as well as hiking around on foot I remember after the officers came I thought of the horses being tied in the barn and I wanted Joe Knight to turn them out."

The attorney asked why the witness wanted to notify Joe Knight. Peare told of business deals in which Joe Knight had helped him, Knight gave him apples to make applejack and that the witness said was another reason he was friendly to Knight.

Peare also told of selling calves to Knight. The latter did not pay right away and Peare told him to keep the money and pay him with provisions and other things he needed. Peare said Knight thus handled money for him. Peare said for that reason he wanted Knight to sell his cattle after this happened.

The witness was asked if had any trouble with Mr. Hamburger. He said he had never had any words, drunk or sober with Hamburger.

Cross Examination

The court ordered five minutes recess, the prisoner had a smoke and then the witness was turned over to the prosecution. He was cross examined by Mr. Neuner. He was questioned about the road leading Stevens. The witness said he thought it was after dark when the officers took him from the Stevens house. Mr. Neuner asked Peare if he was familiar with the road.

"Oh yes," said Peare. "I have driven it night and day time, drunk and sober."

Peare said he thought his place was *(text missing)* Myrtle Point though some neighbors thought the distance as less. He guessed they stayed some time at Knight's as everyone was cold. He said he was more sober than he had been. The witness remembers seeing Ole Hamburger at Knight's, and of seeing Coroner Wilson, Deputy Malehorn, Sheriff Ellingsen and others.

The witness was asked what him of a bottle he took to Stevens house. The witness indicated a bottle, shown, in the court room and said he thought it was the one he had with him. He said he had seven bottles at, his house. In answer to questions he described his making moonshine. He used 50 pounds of corn and 35 pounds of sugar at a time. He usually drew off one bottle and then double distilled the rest. He would put more sugar in the mash and use it again.

When asked how many batches he had made during the year preceding the murder. He said, he made a batch a year ago Christmas and then did not make anymore until last Christmas.

The witness said there was quite a period between the Christmas season of the two years when he had no whiskey excepting that he had a drink at the Myrtle Point fair and I made some beer. He said after he made moonshine he took the filled bottles out of doors and hid them around under logs so if anyone came to arrest him or make trouble they would not be found.

When Mr. Neuner suggested that Peare made the moonshine for himself and not to sell the witness said:

"No, I never sold a bottle of whiskey in my life, neither commercial or moonshine. I never received one cent of value for anything of the kind in my life."

The witness was asked about his cats. He said he had two big ones and a kitten. He killed the big cats but took a snap shot at the kitten when it was running. It went under the house and he didn't know what became of it.

He said the last he remembered of eating was on Dec. 27. He was asked about the drinking. He said he drank on Christmas day and that his wife did also. He said she always drank with him. When asked if she got drunk he said:

"She did not get as bad as I did but she drank enough to feel it."

Asked about his dogs he said he was attached to them and had trained them. He said one was 10 or 11 years old and the other about 4 years old. He said he had the oldest dog when he owned sheep and when Culver had sheep. He said he had a dog which killed one of Culver's sheep but that he killed the dog and they did not have any personal trouble about it.

The witness said the only trouble he had with Culver was that he had told on the witness stand as far as he could remember but said his memory was not sufficiently good to remember what he told yesterday. Mr. Neuner asked Peare when he saw Culver outside the house why he did not shoot Culver then.

"I suppose it was because I did not want to shoot him in the back. I waited till he went in the house, dropped down the wood and turned around. I don't remember of saying anything about a cow. I don't think I said anything to Culver when I shot. I might have but I don't remember. He did not say anything at all to me. When I fired he fell face down. I think I told him to speak. After I shot him the second time he did not move. I don't think I was in Culver's home more than two minutes."

Peare was asked whether or not he closed the door when he went out. He said he was not sure. He reported that his memory was not very good.

When questioned closely about the drinking at the time of his wife's death he would not be certain. He said he could not be sure how many drinks he took but supposed he took one whenever he wanted one. He would not be definite about the hour of going to the Stevens' house but supposed it was in the forenoon. He said the clock was not wound at his house and he did not have the time of day.

Peare when cross examined said that he had a still for 15 or 16 years. "I think I had one that long. A.J. Sherwood will know."

Peare exhibited his hurt where he said he had been crushed by a tree some years ago and the members of the jury were given an opportunity to feel the bump.

Several witnesses were put on the stand to tell of Peare being ill.

The second headlined: **EVIDENCE FOR THE PROSECUTION ENDS — CASE IS RESTED AND TURNED OVER TO THE DEFENSE** — More Witnesses in Rebuttal Will Probably Be Introduced Later However

COQUILLE, Ore., March 16. — The evidence for the prosecution in the murder case of L. W. Peare was closed yesterday, after which the defense began the introduction of testimony. It appears quite likely that the taking of testimony will continue until Saturday night before it is completed.

Proud of Act

The prosecution yesterday afternoon put on the witness stand Deputy Sam Malehorn following the testimony of Sheriff Ellingsen. Malehorn told as had other witnesses about the statements of Peare shortly after he was arrested and later on. Among other things Malehorn told what Peare had to say regarding the killing of Culver. Malehorn asked him why he killed Culver. Peare said; "You have seen a boy with a new pair of red top boots. Well, you know how proud he was of them. I am just that proud of having killed Jim Culver."

The prosecution also put on the stand Vesta Bushnell, daughter of Peare. She testified to the hand writing of a note which was left, by Peare at the time of the murder when he evidently expected to kill himself. The paper indicated whom he wanted his property to go to and stated that Jim Culver was to blame for the whole trouble. The daughter testified that the handwriting was that of her father.

This closed the evidence for the state for the present. The prosecution will undoubtedly have evidence in rebuttal and yet has to put on the stand its expert as to the man's sanity.

Defense Opens

The defense in opening the case put several witnesses on the stand to testify regarding the business integrity of the defendant. They were Taylor Dement, H. W. Pike, Harry P. Smith and J.L. Knight. They all said that Peare was a man of reputation for honesty and would pay his just debts.

The next article headlined: **PEARE'S HANDS ALWAYS SHOWN — PRISONER ALWAYS KEEPS THEM BEFORE HIS FACE**

COQUILLE, Ore., March 16. — Hands, a pair of slim but broad hands, the knotted fingers of which quiver slightly, is the chief impression which one gathers of L. W. Peare, the old rancher on trial for first degree murder. The hands which he says have done hard work most of his life are now pale following his confinement in jail. They are slim and lifeless looking but they are always in evidence. All through the trial Peare folded and unfolded his hands in front of his face and while on the witness stand he continually kept his hands in front of his face.

The hands which choked his wife to death, the hands which pulled the trigger of the gun used to kill Jim Culver, are kept in front of the face of the accused man. The fingers that it is said he besmeared with the brain and blood of his victim he clasps and unclasps.

Once Attorney Goss told Peare to keep his hands from his face and the jury could hear better. Peare placed his bands in his lap but a few minutes later they were in front of his face nervously opening and closing.

Peare said that his hands have been used for hard work, very hard work, all his life, but as those white hands and long fingers opened and closed in front of the face of the confessed murderer, one is reminded of the choking, the shooting and the story of the dead man's brains and blood which has been told on the witness stand.

The last article headlined: **PEARE TELLS OF HIS TROUBLES - RECITES FEATURES OF HIS LIFE TO THE JURY** He Choked His Wife and Pulled Her Hair and He Killed Her

COQUILLE, Ore., March 16. — When L. W. Peare was put on the witness stand by the attorney's for the defense yesterday afternoon to tell his story, the court room was crowded. The evidence of the defendant was listened to with much interest.

Peare did not speak very loudly but he was easily heard by the jury and in fact although his voice was low all that he said could be heard at the back of the court room. It was after 2 p. m. when Peare was put on the stand and he was still testifying when court adjourned at 5 o'clock and the judge announced that the testimony would be continued this morning. Last evening Peare had not yet reached the point of telling of the murders. He was allowed to begin early in his life and recite a good many facts. He showed quite a remarkable memory for details of his early life and insisted on telling them. He answered questions put by Mr. Goss and all though he went into a good deal of detail which was not material he was not interrupted.

Once when he was describing some matter Mr. Neuner objected. He said that there was too much evidence which had no bearing on the case being given. Judge Kendall said he thought this was true and that the witness was telling a great deal that did not enter into the case. At that time he was describing his relations with some of the neighbors Mr. Goss said that the very reason that the facts were trivial made them important. He said he wished to show whether Peare had real grounds against his victims or whether the grounds for ill feelings were founded on trivial facts.

He said that it was evident the only way the witness could testify was to let him tell the story in his own way and this seemed to be recognized. Peare did tell his story in his own way and told everything that he wanted to tell.

Peare said that he came to the Floras creek many years ago and before that time lived at Vancouver, Wash. There was one time during the afternoon when Peare seemed to weary of the whole thing. His voice faltered and grew weak. He talked as a man far away. It appeared for a few moments that he might break down. He had been telling of his wife.

Finally he said:

"Oh well, this horrible thing has happened, and here I am and that is all there is to it."

"No it is not," said Mr. Goss. "We want you to go on and tell the jury of your relationships with these different people so they will know about this affair."

Peare had several favorite expressions. He usually referred to his wife as "the woman" in most every case when answering in the affirmative he began his statements with the expression "Oh yes," and when in the negative he always said "No, no."

When he referred to his wife there seemed to be quite an emotional feeling, and several times he expressed his liking for his wife.

On one occasion he said:

"She did a great many things that a woman ought not to have done. She did not always treat me right but at that I thought a great deal of her."

Another time he said:

"I would not have killed her for the world. If she had left me I would have gone plumb crazy. I would have given her anything I had if she had left me."

The strange feature of the evidence of Peare was that, he seemed to put great importance on very small matters. Once he said that there was something he would like to tell about his wife that he did not want to tell in the court room He was asked directly if there were any relations between his wife am Jim Culver and after much deliberation and after being asked a second time he finally with some effort said:

"Yes."

"What were these relations?" asked Mr. Goss.

"I will not tell it before all of these people. I will tell the court and the jury but I will not make the statement before all of these people unless forced to do so."

Mr. Goss told the witness that, it would scarcely be possible to clear the court room for the statement and urged the witness to say what he had to tell.

"Well, I will tell it if I have to but I hate to say it before all these people."

It was then that some spectacular revelation was expected and this is what the witness said:

"I had been told that Jim Culver had assaulted some women and want to say that if he had wanted to insult or assault my wife he had plenty of chances to do so. Why, he even at one time sat on a log and spit tobacco juice and boasted that if any married woman came to his house he could say what he wanted to her."

Peare seemed to put great stress on the fact that the opportunity for Culver to insult his wife existed. The matter of drinking whiskey was a subject which was drawn on by Attorney Goss from the witness in detail. Peare was asked to tell about his drinking in the earlier days and later since the state has been dry. Peare said that he has always drunk some. He said that he did not believe in a man spending his money for drink and deprive his family of what they needed, but that when be had bought provisions for his household if he had any money left over and felt that he could afford it he would buy a bottle of whisky for himself and sometimes he bought two.

He said that when he had real whisky he did not get drunk. At least he never intended to and never allowed himself to drink to the point that he could not attend to the job he had on hand.

But after the state went dry he resorted to moonshine. He said that he made some before the state went dry. A friend gave him a load of apples and with a copper still he made a drink and he thought he got some pretty good stuff.

Later after the state went dry Peare said that he made moonshine. He said he drank it and his wife did too. He said that while he could previously drink whisky, he could not handle the moonshine. He said that it made him sick at his stomach and when he got too much he said his mind went blank.

He told of one occasion when his mind went blank. This was in answer to a question as to whether or not he had ever had any trouble with his wife. The witness said:

"Yes I did. I thought I had killed her once. This was about three years ago. She wanted me to go. For some cows where about to have calves. I don't want to go. I found that she was right as we later found the cows with the calves. But I had been drinking a good deal and I did not think I could go for the cows. She made me start out and we got aways and I did not want to go any farther. I did not remember anything more until the morning and I found I had no wife at home. I thought then that I had killed her. I learned later that I had choked her a little and pulled her hair but had not materially hurt her."

"I searched about the next day for her and went to several places. Finally I met her and I told her that I if she came back and treated me all right we would get along. She wanted to leave me and I said that if she must go I could not help it but that I still thought that if she treated me better we would got along all right. I still thought a great deal of her although she had not been treating me right."

"I told her something I had heard about her and after that she treated me better."

Carl Bushnell is the son-in-law of Peare. The witness was asked to tell of his relations with Bushnell. The story was a long-drawn-out one. It seemed from the evidence that Bushnell had been doing Peare's mowing for him during haying season. There was one time when Bushnell did not come to do the mowing and Peare was sick. Peare felt that because Bushnell did not come he had turned him down and that his friendship had been lost. Peare told of his financial relations with Bushnell. He said that the latter owed him some money and that he had gone on a note for Bushnell for $100. He asked Bushnell for the money and asked him to relieve him of the surety on the note. Bushnell said that he would and never came to see him again.

When closely questioned Peare said that he thought Bushnell was turning him down and wanted to see him die when he failed to call upon him when he (Peare) was sick in bed.

The relationships with Culver were told by Peare. The only trouble he had with Culver in a business way was about a fence many years back. Culver had built a fence between the properties of the two men. Later on Peare wanted to build a fence and hook onto the fence built by Culver. Peare said that Culver wanted him to pay for an undivided one-half interest in a mile of fence and charged $80. Peare thought this was too much. Culver was willing to take cows in payment. Peare said that if he could put his price on the cows he was willing to pay the price asked for the fence. The witness said that Culver never came to take up this proposition. Later Peare said that Culver served papers on him about the fence. Peare consulted a lawyer and on his advice paid the $80 for the half interest in the fence. This seemed to be the only financial trouble between the two men. The only other trouble according to Peare's testimony was that Culver had the opportunity to insult Mrs. Peare if he wanted to do so. In ending his statement about his relations with Culver Peare said:

"I never in my life did anything to harm Jim Culver in any shape or manner."

Peare told of feeling sick at times. He went into details about on occasion some years back when he was hit on the head by a tree. He said that this injury at times hurt him. It made him have pains in his head. He described his sickness. He said there were times when he could not sleep for three days and three nights. He several times repeated this period of time. He said each time that it was three days and three nights that he could not sleep. He said when he was normal and working he had no difficulty about sleeping.

He told of times when he felt despair. He feared that he was going to break down in health and that his son-in-law had gone back on him and he had his wife to look after and did not know how they were going to get along.

Mr. Goss asked him why he should worry when he had a 400-acre farm. Peare said that he did not make any money. He said last year he made only $400 and that he had to pay taxes out of that and also had to pay out about half of the total sum. He said that he feared he would get down sick and not be able to make any hay and have to buy feed and that he could not keep up.

March 17, 1923 the *Coos Bay Times* headlined: **EXPERTS DIFFER IN OPINIONS OF PEARE'S SANITY** — Dr. Williamson Says He Is Insane and Dr. House Says Defendant Is Not Insane **INTERESTING TESTIMONY GIVEN BY PORTLAND MEN** — Jurymen Get the Views of the Alienists Who Were Called as Witnesses in Case — **DR. E. MINGUS TESTIFIES** — Marshfield Physician Says That Peare Is Not Crazy — Made Examination of Prisoner Since He Was Arrested

COQUILLE, Ore., March 17. — Interesting testimony was given by inanity experts in the trial of L. W. Peare in the circuit court yesterday afternoon. The Portland physicians differed as to their opinion of the sanity of Peare, the defendant who is charged with the murder of James Culver. Insanity is the defense which is being made.

Dr. Williamson of Portland, who as put on the stand by the defense says that Peare is crazy now and was at the time he killed Culver, while Dr. House, who went on the stand or the prosecution, says that Peare not insane.

Dr. Mingus Testifies

Dr. E. Mingus of Marshfield says at Peare is not insane. Dr. Mingus examined Peare on December 30 and once since in the county jail. A legal point was raised during the testimony of Dr. Mingus and the jury was excluded while the point was discussed. It was held that Peare had not been told of his rights regarding the making of a physical examination after his arrest. The court held that Peare had been told his rights and held that the testimony of Dr. Mingus, who examined him, was admissible and the jury was allowed to return to the court room and hear the testimony of Dr. Mingus, who said Peare was not crazy.

Prominent Doctors

The Portland alienists took directly opposite views on a number of points. They are both physicals who have served as doctors in asylums and they both now conduct sanitariums of their own in Portland, for the special treatment of nervous diseases. Dr. Williamson surprised those in the court room when he said that he was 72 years of age. He has gray hair but is wonderfully well preserved and those who had seen him did not think that he was 72. If he had said he was fifteen or twenty years younger the statement would have been accepted.

Both of the physicians showed their knowledge and study of insanity cases and it was clear that the authorities on the subject. They were both cross examined but their opinions were fixed as to their views regarding the defendants condition. Neither of the doctors attempted to deal in technicalities which would not be understood but both gave their evidence in as plain words as possible and explained Peare's condition as near as they could in terms which could be understood by the jury.

Declared Insane

Dr. Williamson said that Peare was insane now and was insane at the time of the murder and had suffered from a form of insanity for probably twelve or thirteen years. He said that Peare's case was incurable. He said he appeared normal but that he suffered delusions and when normal might at any time do an insane act. The witness cited the cases of a judge he knew. He said the judge appeared to be a perfectly normal person but at one time stopped the trial of a case and ordered the bailiff to take up the boards of the floor in the court room to find out who the people were under the floor. He imagined that he hear people talking under the floor. This was a case of the same kind of insanity as Peare suffered, he said.

Had Delusions

Dr. Williamson said that one outward sign of Peare's insanity was the fact that he showed no emotion regarding his wife while on the stand and spoke of the killing of the cats and dogs. He said Peare had delusions and spoke of the delusions that there existed improper relations between Mrs. Peare and Culver which turned out to be nothing.

Dr. Williamson also spoke of Peare having had dreams which he described.

About the Dreams

Dr. House took an opposite view on these points. He said that the bad dreams Peare told about were not signs of insanity. He said that after eating a ham sandwich or a Welch rabbit before going to bed he had just as bad dreams and recently when he had a fever of 103 he had dreams which were terror; compared to those Peare described. He said the dreams might happen to anyone who was suffering any bodily disorder.

Did Show Emotion

Dr. House insisted that Peare did show emotion. He said he showed emotion when he referred to his wife and declared that he would have collapsed if he had stayed on the witness stand ten minutes longer the first afternoon the defendant testified.

As to the delusions of Peare regarding his wife and Culver, the doctor admitted that the grounds for suspicion were trivial but said that this did not indicate insanity, as many husbands were jealous or suspicious of their wives on just as slight grounds as those of Peare.

Killing the dogs and cats, Dr. House, said was not a sign of insanity. He said anyone who was fond of pets and felt that they would not remain to care for them might kill the pets rather than leave them to the danger of abuse by someone else.

Drunk but Sane

Dr. House said that Peare was probably very drunk when he killed his wife. The witness said he thought probably Peare did not remember killing his wife but this was not because he was insane but because he was drunk. The witness said that while Peare was very likely drunk when he killed Culver, he was not crazy and that he decided to kill him and followed out that decision and went to Culver's home and killed him. The doctor was asked if it was not impossible for a drunken man to follow out a set idea. The doctor said a drunken man would often follow out one idea for twenty-four hours. He made a distinction between a man being drunk and being insane.

Both Dr. Williamson and Dr. House left for Portland last night.

Made Will in Note

There was a good deal of interest attached to the alleged will left by Peare. After he killed his wife he scribbled on a pad at his house his directions as to what he wanted done with his property. It was a wandering sort of statement but the substance was that he wanted Joe Knight to have his ranch, wanted his cattle to go to some other friend, desired $5 given to his daughter Mrs. Bushnell, and everything else was to go to Joe Knight. The statement was rather difficult to make out and was not entirely clear.

On March 20, 1923 the *Coos Bay Times* headlined: **JURY DECIDES PEARE MUST PAY DEATH PENALTY** — Verdict Returned at 7:30 p. m Yesterday Finds Defendant Guilty as Charged **SLAYER OF JIM CULVER DISPLAYING NO EMOTION** — Jurors Out Two Hours and Fifteen Minutes But Spent Some Time Eating Supper — **MOTION FOR NEW TR1AL** — Court Give the Defense Attorney Thirty Days in Which to Prepare the Formal Motion — Exceptions to Instructions

COQUILLE, Ore., March 20. — L .W. Peare is guilty of first degree murder and must be handed for the murder of his neighbor Jim Culver. This was the decision of the jurors who heard the case which has been in progress for a week.

The case went to the jury at 5:15 p. m. yesterday and the verdict was returned at 7:30 p. m. The jurors occupied some of the two hours and fifteen minutes eating supper so the actual time in the jury room reaching a decision was not long.

Peare showed no signs of emotion when the verdict of the jury was read in court.

No Recommendation

The jury had been instructed by the court that it could find a verdict of guilty as charged which meant that Peare was guilty of first degree murder and must he hanged. It was also instructed that should the jurors see fit they could find the defendant guilty of first degree murder and recommend life imprisonment as the punishment.

No recommendation was made by the jury. The verdict, was simply that Peare was guilty as charged.

Agreed Quickly

Three ballots were taken. After the jurors retired the first ballot indicated that all thought him guilty of murder in the first degree. Then another ballot was taken to determine the punishment. Nine were for hanging and three for life imprisonment. Two of those who were for a penitentiary sentence changed over with the majority who were for hanging. The jurors then ate supper and on returning to the jury room a vote was taken and it was unanimous for finding the defendant guilty of first murder as charged and allowing the punishment of hanging.

Motion for New Trial

C.F. McKnight for the defense made a motion for a new trial and he was given thirty days by Judge Kendall in which to file his formal motion. Whether or not the cases will be appealed if the motion for a new trial is overruled, the defense attorneys said, would not be determined until they had gone over the records.

After the reading of the instructions by the court yesterday afternoon Mr. Goss for the defense took exception to a number of the instructions. Other exceptions were recorded throughout the trial.

Neuner's Argument

The court room was crowded yesterday afternoon. The final argument for the state, was made by George Neuner, district attorney of Douglas county, who made a very impressive speech.

Mr. Neuner challenged the position taken by the defense and said that Peare was either guilty of first murder or nothing at all and asked for a verdict of guilty as charged or no punishment for the crime.

First in Many Years

Following the arguments the court read the instructions and the jury retired.

The Peare case is the first in Coos county which resulted in a conviction for first degree murder and infliction of the death penalty since the trial of Frank Garrison about eleven years ago when he was found guilty of killing Roy Perkins and was finally hanged after two trials in the circuit court of Coos county.

The Instructions

It required about three-quarters of an hour for Judge Kendall to read his instructions to the jury. The jury was charged regarding the question of sanity and much of the instructions dealt with this feature in detail.

The question of sanity was seemed up with the instruction that the whole matter hinged on whether or not that the jury believed that the defendant at the time of the murder knew the difference between right and wrong.

Judge Kendall explained that if the jury found the defendant guilty as charged, which was first degree murder, the crime would be punished by hanging but that the jury could recommend life imprisonment as a punishment for first degree murder.

The court gave the jury six forms of verdict, either of which could be returned.

They were as follows:

Guilty of first degree murder as charged

Guilty of first degree murder will recommendation for life imprisonment.

Guilty of second degree murder.

Guilty of manslaughter.

Not guilty on grounds of insanity.

Not guilty.

The bailiff, J. D. Davis, was sworn in especially as officer in charge of the jury. It was 5:15 p. m. when the case was finished and the jury retired. The verdict was returned at 7:30 p. m.

Judge Kendall had arranged to remain in Coquille all night to be ready for call in case the jury was late in returning a verdict.

Susan Zick, great-granddaughter of L.W. and Jessie Peare and granddaughter of Vestie Bushnell stated that the daughter mentioned above was Stella Shields and she spent most of her life in the state hospital, rest homes or in care centers. What first caused her problems was catching her husband with another woman, after which he hung himself in the barn where Stella found him which resulted in a nervous breakdown.

April 20, 1923 the *Coquille Valley Sentinel* headlined: **PEARE TO HANG** — Sentenced by Judge Kendall This Morning — June 2 The Date

At 10:00 a.m. this morning Judge John C. Kendall pronounced sentence on L.W. Peare, convicted last month of murder in the first degree, ordering him "hanged by the neck until dead," and without any appeal for divine mercy. The date of execution was set for June 2 at the penitentiary, and the sheriff instructed to remove him to Salem within 20 days from this date.

Peare was utterly unmoved, and walked a firm step to the point where he received the sentence. When asked if he could give any good reason why sentence should not be pronounced, he mumbled something, which those at the rear could not catch, but he did not show the slightest feeling or any interest in the proceedings whatever aside from looking the judge squarely in the eye.

His attorney immediately served notice of appeal to the supreme court and asked a stay of execution pending a decision.

Last Tuesday Judge Kendall denied the motion for a new trial and announced that sentence would be pronounced Friday morning.

The crime for which Peare was sentenced is well known to the Sentinel readers, it being the cold-blooded murder of Jas. Culver on the 27th of last December in the south end of the county and over the divide beyond Catching Creek.

The indictment on the charge of second degree murder - the choking to death of his wife - was not pressed in the Circuit Court; the prosecution of the first degree charge being successful.

On May 4, 1923 the *Coquille Valley Sentinel* headlined: **CUT HIS THROAT** — L.W. Peare Attempts to Cheat the Gallows in Jail Here Tuesday

L.W. Peare, Floras creek murder, and sentenced to be hung on the second of June, attempted to commit suicide Tuesday afternoon about one o'clock by cutting his throat with a safety razor blade. One of the prisoners heard him gasping as he slashed away, trying to reach the juglar vein and gave the alarm.

Mrs. Price, who boards the prisoners, called Deputy Sheriff Malehorn at home and he came in from his home on the highway in about two minutes.

He found Peare with his head over the toilet, but too exhausted from the loss of blood to hack any longer.

He had cut deep gashes on both sides of his neck, from just below the ears to the chin, almost deep

> as the width of two fingers, but without severing the jugular.
>
> Dr. Richmond was called and within fifteen minutes from the time of Peare's attempt, the doctor was stopping the flow of blood.
>
> He appears to be getting along all right and will probably recover, but he is seeing things. He told Jailer Kern that there was a rope slowly descending from the ceiling and he was frightened. Kern showed him it was only a crack between the iron plates. He then insisted that the chain which supports the window sash was lowering.
>
> The full horror of the double crime he committed and the realization of the penalty he will have to pay are doubtless preying on his mind to such a extent that he can really see the rope with a noose around it descending toward his head.

Peare, at the age of 67, along with Coos county sentenced murderer Arthur Covell, were hanged on May 22, 1925 at the gallows of the state penitentiary in Salem. Two articles relating to the executions of Pearce and Covell are located at the conclusion of the Covell case. Peare received the distinction of being the oldest person executed by hanging in the State or Oregon.

CHAPTER 14

THE CASE OF ARTHUR COVELL

Case Synopsis: Arthur Covell, an astrologist, who was paralyzed from the waist down due to an accident, resided with his brother Fred and his family at their deceased parents ranch south of Bandon. Not liking his sister-in-law, Ebba, he planned her murder according to a selected astrological date. The actual murder was committed on September 3, 1923 by Alton Covell, the stepson of the victim. Alton murdered his stepmother by suffocating her with an ammonia soaked rag. Alton's fourteen-year old sister, Lucile, was also aware of the murder plot and kept the younger three children in the yard while Alton committed his assigned task.

The Motive: Dislike of Mrs. Covell by her brother-in-law, Arthur. Arthur was quoted as saying; I had no use for her" and "She didn't fit into our family."[40]

The Covell Family: Doctor of Chiropractics, Fred Covell was the son of Charles E. and Isabelle who resided in DeKalb County Illinois where Charles served as a Private in the military. Having enlisted on August 1, 1861 Charles was mustered into "D" Company, Illinois 44th Infantry.[41] Fred Covell was born June 24, 1885. Charles and Isabelle had two other sons, Robert William, born June 17, 1897 and Arthur who was born December 14,1879. All three were born in Kansas. There was also a daughter, Bella; however, there is no information regarding her. It is not known when the Covell's moved to Bandon. Charles and Isabelle purchased a farm in the Two Mile Precinct south of Bandon. Charles died on March 22, 1911 and was buried in the Grand Army of the Republic (G.A.R.) cemetery in Bandon. Isabelle died September 16, 1921 and was buried next to her husband. [42]

Not much is known about Fred Covell. Prior to his marriage to Ebba, Fred Covell had been married three times. From these marriages he fathered two children. Alton, who was sixteen at the time of the crime, suffered from mild deafness in addition to being mentally challenged, often times referred to as feeble-minded. Lucile, aged fourteen was the younger sister of Alton. Lucile's mother died during Lucile's birth. At the time of the 1910 U.S. Census Fred Covell was employed at the Saint Helena Sanitarium, Hot Springs Township, Napa County, California. Employed as a nurse, Fred Covell listed his marital status as single.

Ebba Wiren-Covell was born February 14, 1892 in Astoria Oregon to Oscar and Caroline Wiren. Employed as a lighthouse keeper Captain Wiren moved his family to Bandon on March 11, 1903 where Ebba attended school. After graduating, Ebba completed a course in San Jose, California and became a school teacher. Ebba, first employed in Astoria, later returned to Bandon where she continued to teach.[43] According to the Coos County Polk's Directory of 1913[R] Ebba was a school teacher and resided with her parents at the Coquille lighthouse.

On September 12, 1917 Fred Covell entered into marriage with Ebba Catherine Wiren. The 1920 U.S. Census for the N.W. Bandon Precinct revealed the couple lived in Bandon where the residence served as the Chiropractic office. The couple had their first child, Gladys who was four months old at the time of the Census. Prior to Ebba's murder two sons followed the birth of Gladys, John and David.

Arthur Covell, according to the 1920 U.S. Census for the Two Mile Precinct resided as the head of household with his mother Isabelle, nephews Byron age 13, Alton B. age 12, and his sister Bella age 34. Arthur listed his occupation as Farmer. Arthur reported he was injured in an accident during the fall of 1920. The injury fractured some of the vertebrae, partially split his pelvis which strained his spinal cord leaving his nervous system deranged.[44] At the time of the murders Arthur was an astrologist.

Sometime after his mother's death Fred moved his family into his parent's house in the Two Mile Precinct. Since there was no mention of Lucile listed in either household in the 1920 Census it is not known when Lucile moved in nor when Byron moved out. After moving his family Dr. Fred Covell maintained his Chiropractic office in Bandon.

[R] Polk's Directory, founded by R.L. Polk and Company of Detroit, was first published in Coos County in 1904.

The obituary for Ebba Covell published in the September 6, 1923 issue of Bandon's newspaper the *Western World* included the following:

> Deceased was a woman of accomplishment and of splendid character. She was devoted to her home and children and as far as her friends knew was happy.
>
> Funeral services over the remains were held at the Ellingsen undertaking parlor this afternoon. Rev. A. W. Bell of the Episcopal church officiating. Burial was at the Bandon cemetery.
>
> The chapel was filled to overflowing with friends of the deceased and a beautiful floral offering paid tribute to her standing in the community.[45]

Ebba Covell was interred at the Averille Pioneer cemetery in Bandon. It is not known where exactly as there are no records of her location.[46] A search of the cemetery revealed no location as several monuments were missing.

Stars Spelled Her Death

MRS. EBBA COVELL, wife of Bandon chiropractor, who was murdered by her 16-year-old stepson because his uncle, Arthur Covell, crippled mystic and astromancer, "read in the stars" that September 3 was the date set by the planets for her to die.

Figure 27:
Ebba Covell -
Coos Bay Times,
October 17, 1923

The Crime and Punishment: September 6, 1923 the *Western World* reported:

Sept. 6, 1923 — The community is shocked and puzzled over the mysterious death of Mrs. Ebba Covell, wife of Dr. Fred Covell, local chiropractor, which occurred at the family home or Two Mile, about five miles south of Bandon, Monday morning. As the result of an investigation by a coroner's jury and further investigation by the sheriffs office conducted on Tuesday, the husband of the dead woman was placed under arrest Tuesday night, charged with murder, and is now being held in the county jail a Coquille.

Undertaker is Called

The first information received in town was when Undertaker Wm. Mavity was summoned to the Covell home to take charge of the body. This was early in the afternoon. Accompanied by his sister, Mrs. S. Mundy, he went to the scene and found the body laid out on the bed in a room adjoining the kitchen. He was informed that the body had been found lying on the kitchen floor but the cause of death was not known. He brought the body to the undertaking parlor and notified City Health Officer Dr. R.V. Leep of the circumstances.

Neck Dislocated

Deputy Coroner L.J. Radley summed a coroner's jury of the following men: O.A. Trowbridge, E.T. Wolverton, M.M. Young, N.E. Barklow, E.S. Tuttle and G.P. Hammans. Drs. Leep and Gale were instructed to hold an autopsy. It was found that the woman's neck was dislocated near the base of the brain; that she had a large bruise on the right side of her face and that she had numerous bruises on her body, indicating that she had been severely beaten. The heart was found to be normal and the stomach was sent out for a content analysis. The latter was done before it was found that the neck was dislocated.

The jury returned a verdict at about 8 o'clock Tuesday night which read as follows:

"We, the coroner's jury, sworn to inquire into the death of Mrs. Ebba Wiren Covell find the cause of death to be from a dislocated neck, cause of dislocation unknown to the jury."

Husband is Arrested

Deputy Sheriff S.A. Malehorn, assisted by Night Officer E.E. Oakes, went to the Covell home Tuesday afternoon to inquire into the situation. They found that Dr. Covell had gone to town to meet Capt. And Mrs. O. Wiren, parents of the woman, who were due to arrive on the Charm from Winchester Bay. They interviewed other members of the family and investigated the grounds, getting whatever information was obtainable.

Dr. Covell met the Charm with his automobile and took Mr. and Mrs. Wiren and the latter's son, Loyal, to his office, opposite Hotel Gallier, where he told them his version of the affair. The Wirens went to the hotel across the street and later Dr. Covell motored to the office of Justice of the Peace Radley to talk over rumors of foul play he said he had heard.

Accompanied by Deputy Malehorn and Officer Oakes he was taken to the morgue and shown the body with the dislocated neck and its bruises. He stated that he had no idea how the bruises came on the body and that he didn't know the neck was dislocated, neither could he account for the discoloration on the face. He admitted however that from all appearances his wife had been killed. He was returned to the office of Justice of the Peace Radley and a warrant was issued for his arrest on charges of murder.

Maintains Composure

All through the investigation, in fact from the time the body was taken into custody. Dr. Covell maintained his usual composure. Although wearing a worried look he showed no particular signs of emotion and talked freely. He is naturally of a cold disposition, although friendly and talkative. There was apparently little change in his attitude when the warrant of arrest was read. He was sitting with folded arms while the instrument was read by Mr. Radley and when the latter concluded, he nodded his head and said: "Well, well, so you think I'm a murderer, a felon; that I killed her."

He was informed that he could plead at once or first get the advice of an attorney as he wished and was also instructed about preliminary hearings. When asked if he wanted to plead he answered: "I've told you all I know about it I don't see that I have any plea to make."

What Family Says

According to statements made by the members of the Covell family the body of Mrs. Covell was first discovered by Alton, the 16-year-old son, at some time in the middle of the forenoon. Mrs. Covell was supposed to have been in the kitchen doing housework. Dr. Covell's brother, Arthur, who is an invalid suffering from a broken spinal column sustained in an accident three years ago, was lying on a mattress under a tree near the house. With him was his niece, Lucile, aged 14, who is a sister of Alton, children by Dr. Covell's previous marriage. She was taking care of the three small children. Alton was across the road a distance of several hundred yards looking after the cow. Alton came to the house to get a drink of water and on walking into the kitchen saw the body of his step-mother lying on the floor. He rushed out to tell the others and the sister, Lucile, went into the house. Arthur stated he thought perhaps she had fainted and yelled to the others to place cold towels on her face. Later he directed them to pick her up and carry her into the bedroom onto the bed. After doing this the boy went out to help the invalid uncle into the house. In the meantime, the girl tried to call Dr. Covell's office to notify him but could not get him. Shortly she tried again and could not get him. Then the uncle was helped to the phone and tried. He was successful. He said: "Come down at once, something dreadful has happened." Arthur stated that after one look at the woman he felt himself collapsing and asked to be taken upstairs to his bed. He said Dr. Covell arrived in about 20 or 25 minutes and worked over the body of his wife but finally gave it up.

Practically identical stories were told except as to variation in time. Although three of the grown people were but a short distance from the house none heard or saw anything that might explain the cause of the woman's death.

Dr. Covell stated that when he received the telephone message he rushed home as quickly as possible. He didn't know what had happened and thought perhaps one of the children had been injured or that a brush fire might have done some damage. His brother only stated that "something dreadful had happened." After working over the body, he said he thought perhaps she had fainted and in striking the floor bursted a blood vessel in the brain causing instant death. But he could not account for the discoloration on the face because the body was lying on its back and side and had apparently not struck on the face in falling.

The stories of the family were told before they knew that an autopsy had been conducted and the dislocation and the body bruises had been found. When informed of these facts they could offer no suggestion as how it might have happened, maintaining however that they had heard no disturbance or commotion of any kind in the house.

Lucile stated that her step-mother had started washing that morning but had stopped to press her dress so she could start school the following day when she (Lucile) left the house after being instructed to take the children out and take care of them. Later, she says, she and her brother finished the washing and hung it out.

The officers have information on the case that is not made public and it is likely that there will be additional developments within the next day or so.

Boy Also Taken

Dr. Covell was held in the local jail Tuesday night, and yesterday Sheriff Ellingsen, accompanied by Deputy Malehorn and Officer Oakes returned to the Covell home. They brought Arthur to the local hospital where he will be cared for until he can be removed to the county farm. Alton was taken to Coquille with his father and will be held in the county jail as a material witness. Lucile and the three little children were left with Mrs. Lockwood who will care for them until after the funeral. Mr. and Mrs. Wiren intend to take the three small children back with them to Winchester Bay. They are Gladys, aged five; John, three; David, 15 months.

Dr. Covell has been married three times. Mrs. Ebba Wiren Covell was his third wife. The first two are also dead. Two children from the first marriage, Lucile and Alton, have been residing with the family at Two Mile.

From the evidence at hand the officers working on the case are fully convinced that Mrs. Covell was killed and that the act was committed by someone within the family or at least that the members of the family have knowledge of the facts concerning the death and are keeping them secret. This is likewise the conclusion of all those interested in the case who have expressed themselves.

Photographs have been taken of the bruises and marks on the body of Mrs. Covell and will be used to prove that the woman had been violently treated before being killed. The latest tell-tale evidence consists of marks on the face showing bruises where a strong hand had grasped the face, covering the mouth and the tip of the nose. A bruised spot was found where every finger touched. The large bruise on the right side of the face was probably made by the palm of the hand. The theory is that this was done when the neck was forcibly dislocated by twisting the head.

Various articles of clothing have also been taken from the home by the officers. These it is said shed further light on the theory of the killing.

A point that disproves the family story is that the body when taken over by the undertaker was already becoming rigid. This does not take place until at least six hours after death, therefore does not coincide with the time that the body was found.

Attends Beach Picnic

The day prior to her death she with her husband and three children attended a picnic with a number of friends on the beach. The party was made up largely of members of the Seventh Day Adventist church of which Dr. Covell is a member and in the conduct of which he took a leading part in the local congregation.

Monday afternoon, the day of the death, Dr. Covell sent his son Alton to the home of Roy A. Giles informing him of the death of his wife and asking that he get in communication with Elder Rhodes of the Seventh Day Adventist church who lives at Sutherlin, and have him come to conduct the funeral.

Mr. Giles got the elder by telephone and the following day he and Mrs. Giles Went to the Covell home to extend their sympathy and offer assistance. Dr. Covell then told him the funeral would probably be held Wednesday, subject to the wishes of Mr. and Mrs. Wiren who would be consulted upon their arrival.[47]

September 6, 1923 the *Coos Bay Times* headlined: **DR. COVELL'S SON IS PLACED IN JAIL IN BANDON MURDER** – Sixteen-Year-Old Step-Son is Held for Investigation of Killing of Stepmother – **WOMAN'S BODY SAID TO BE BADLY BRUISED** – Sheriff's Force Find Indications of Brutal Attack Prior to Death – **STORIES ARE CONFUSED** – Crippled Brother of Accused Man Is Brought to County Infirmary – Investigation Continues Today

COQUILLE, Ore., Sept. 6. — Alton Covell, 16-year-old son of Dr. Covell of Bandon, who was arrested in connection with the murder of the latter's wife and step-mother of the boy, was taken into custody by Sheriff Ellingsen and Deputy Malehorn.

Father and son are now in the county jail and are held without bail pending a further investigation of the case.

Arthur Covell, an invalid brother of Dr. Covell, was brought to the county infirmary to be cared for.

Sheriff Ellingsen. Deputy Sheriff Malehorn and District Attorney Ben S. Fisher are making a thorough investigation of the case again today and expected to go to Bandon this afternoon to fill in the missing links in the chain of evidence which they are gathering.

Was Brutal Murder

"You can say that Mrs. Covell met her death in one of the most brutal murders" was the announcement of the sheriff's office today. The officers are rather reticent about the various evidence they have discovered until they piece in the missing links.

Mrs. Covell's body is said to have been found to be a mass of bruises, indicating a long, hard struggle prior to the blow which the sheriff's office believes dislocated her neck and caused her death. This blow was on herein, probably. Marks about her body indicate that she was also kicked.

Trouble in Family

As near as the officers can gather, there was considerable trouble in the Covell family.

Arthur Covell, the helplessly crippled brother, who sustained a broken back in an auto accident, told the officers that he did not like the dead woman and was rather emphatic about it.

He was reticent but said that Alton had come out in the yard where he (Arthur) was lying in the sun and told him that Ebba (Mrs. Covell) had met with an accident and was lying on the floor. He said he told Alton to bathe her wrists and temples with water and to get her on the bed. She was found lying on the kitchen floor, he said.

Later word was sent to Dr. Covell at Bandon and when he arrived at noon, he went direct to the bedroom and worked for an hour and a half trying to restore heart action, the officers were informed. When he could not, he came out and told Arthur that she was dead and then sent a message to her father, Capt. Wiren, at the Umpqua lighthouse.

Dr. Covell in talking with the officers said that he thought Mrs. Covell must have met her death from a fall.

Mrs. Covell, who was possibly 30 years old, was not a husky woman, although not frail. She weighed about 130 pounds and the officers believe that she put up a strong defense.

She was the mother of three small children, the eldest five and the youngest 16 months.

Besides her own three children, Dr. Covell's 16-year-old son and a l4-year-old daughter and his invalid brother Arthur resided with them. The place is about five miles south of Bandon and a quarter of a mile from the nearest house.

Alton Covell is six feet tall and weighs about 145 pounds. He has a habit of talking with his mouth tightly closed and is difficult to understand.

He has been rather backward in talking to the officers, they said.

Neighbors Not Notified

The officers in investigating the case found that the neighbors did not learn of Mrs. Covell's death until the report came back from Bandon.

Married Four Times

In talking with Dr. Covell, the officers started to query him on his past. They found that the dead woman was his fourth wife. One was divorced, one died of cancer and one died of childbirth, he told them. He could not tell the officers the maiden names of all of them.

On September 7, 1923 the *Coquille Valley Sentinel* headlined: **BANDON MURDER** – Dr. Fred Covell and son, Alton Accused of Killing Mrs. Covell Last Monday

Dr. Fred Covell, Bandon chiropractor, was placed under arrest here Tuesday evening following the verdict of the coroner's jury that Mrs. Covell who was found dead at their home, had suffered a dislocated neck and possibly other injuries, says a Bandon press dispatch dated Wednesday.

He is being held in the city jail without bail and will probably be taken to the county jail at Coquille.

The coroner's jury did not make an extended investigation, following the report of the physicians, as they felt that it could be better handled by the grand jury.

According to the evidence, Mrs. Covell was found dead on the porch of their home, five miles south of Bandon, by a 17-year-old son of Dr. Covell by a previous marriage. He is said to have found her about 9 o'clock in the morning.

Dr. Covell said that he received word that "something awful had happened at home" about noon and hastened there.

No physician was called and it was 3 o'clock before the undertaker was called.

Dr. Covell says that he is at a loss to explain it.

Mrs. Covell, who is a daughter of Capt. And Mrs. O. Wiren, formerly of Bandon but now of Gardiner, had been in excellent health. She was the third wife of Dr. Covell, his first two wives having died. His five children resided with them, as did an invalid brother, who is helpless as a result of a broken back sustained in an auto mishap.

Capt. And Mrs. Wiren and their son arrived here last evening from the Umpqua lighthouse, where he is now stationed.

Dr. Covell has been a practicing chiropractor here for about nine years.

Among others marks found on Mrs. Covell's body was a gash in her chin and a bruise on her forehead.

The story from a Bay paper hardly covers the story of this dastardly crime and there are many inaccuracies.

Dr. Covell and his sixteen year old son are now held in county jail and have been subjected to severe examination by the officers without breaking down. The officers are convinced that they know what happened.

The murdered woman was Dr. Covell's fourth wife. The first one was he divorced the second died at childbirth and the third died from cancer according to his story.

Mrs. Covell was discovered in the kitchen about eleven o'clock by her stepson, Alton, who says he carried her into the adjoining bedroom and placed her on the bed. He then attempted to call his father but it was not till one o'clock that the doctor's crippled brother got him on the phone and informed him that something "serious had happened." Their place is on Two Mile, south of Bandon.

The doctor took about 25 minutes to reach home, and then locked himself in with the body for an hour, and it was not till three o'clock that he called the undertaker.

Dr. Covell's story is that he arose about six o'clock and that his wife got up between 6:30 and 7:00, cooked breakfast and fed the children. The doctor reached his office in Bandon about nine o'clock.

The boy's story is that about nine o'clock he carried his uncle down stairs and out into the yard and that he wasn't back in the house until eleven when he discovered the body. The two hours had been spent looking for and watering their cow which had broken through the fence.

The body of the murdered woman showed evidence of the most brutal treatment. There were two long gashes on her forehead, her face from the bridge of her nose both ways was black and blue down her cheeks and under her chin, and it looked as though she had received a severe blow on the chin. Her body around her hips and over her stomach was a mass of bruises with blood clots under the skin where she had been kicked or struck with great force. They were not long marks as would have been made by a club, but rather round as though inflicted by the toe of a shoe.

Her hair was twisted and torn. Besides this, the displacement of the vertebrae in her neck was sufficient to cause death, and the boy says her head fell back as though her neck was broken when he carried her into the bedroom.

The fourteen year old step-daughter says that she was out in the yard with the three children, the oldest one five, of the murdered women. She knew nothing of what had happened until her brother discovered the body.

One peculiar thing in connection with the murder is that notwithstanding all the marks on the body, the clothing was not disarranged nor dirty. Another thing is that the officers were unable to find any of the unfortunate woman's night gowns, except one which had never been worn.

The entire Covell family say that they saw no one around or near the house Monday morning. They also say that Mrs. Covell did not "fit" with the Covell family.

When Covell was taken to the morgue where his wife's body lay, he is reported to have laughed harshly.

The officers are proceeding along two lines in determining who was guilty of the crime. One is that the deed was committed before Covell left for town, in which case he probably is the murderer.

The other theory is that the murder occurred after he had gone and this would indicate that the 16-year old boy, Alton, was guilty of the atrocious crime.

There seems to be little doubt in the minds of the officers and of the people of Bandon that one or the other is guilty.

September 7, 1923 the *Coos Bay Harbor* headlined: **COVELL CASE YET PUZZLES OFFICERS** Bandon Murder of Last Monday Under Probe Dr. Covell and Son Alton Held in Jail.

There are few developments in the Bandon murder case, in which interest is expressed all over the county.

Mrs. Fred Covell, wife of a chiropractic doctor, at Bandon, was found dead last Monday at the home in the country, five miles from the city. Since then investigations have been made up to last night, to gather evidence for the preliminary hearing, which will probably be held not later than Monday.

The woman's body was bruised in many places, as if she had fought for her life. Her neck was broken. The condition of Mrs. Covell's clothing indicated that it had been placed on her after she was killed, as it was not soiled as it would be had she been dressed when murdered.

Dr. Fred Covell, the husband, and Alton, his son, age 16, are in jail at Coquille, as suspects and held without bail. Neither will talk to the officers, excepting to deny any knowledge of the crime.

The evidence in the case, what there is to date, shows that the body was becoming rigid at noon on Monday and this would show, some say, that the murder had been committed early in the morning. The corpse was found by young Covell on the kitchen floor shortly before noon.

There was a rumor that the woman had been seen at noon by people passing that way, but it could not be true if Covell's account of the finding was accurate.

Dr. Covell was summoned as soon as the body was discovered. He said he had left home for his office about 8:30 in the morning, and claims that is an alibi for him.

There are three or four children in the family, and that the body was not discovered sooner or that none of the children, or crippled Arthur Covell who lived at the home had not heard the incidents of the murder or seen who had done the deed is a matter the officials cannot understand.

It is held that a chiropractor, having knowledge of the human anatomy could have dislocated the woman's neck without leaving any signs of a struggle, had he so intended. The officers, while holding Covell, are keeping their findings to themselves and what they have learned will probably not be divulged until the preliminary hearing is held.

On September 28, 1923 the *Coos Bay Harbor* headlined: **COVELL HELD FOR GRAND JURY ACTION** Bandon Chiropractor has Preliminary Hearing, Evidence Adduced at Session Not of Convincing Kind.

At Bandon yesterday, Dr. Fred Covell was bound over to the October grand jury in the sum of $10,000 bail. The preliminary hearing was held before Justice Radley.

Alton Covell, the man's son, who was held jointly at first, was not bound over for the murder of Mrs. Fred Covell.

Some new evidence came out at the hearing. It was stated that the death of Mrs. Covell was not caused by a broken neck, experts having examined the corpse and decided that while there was evidence of disturbance in the vertebrae in the neck, the bones were not disjointed.

It was also shown that Mrs. Covell had eaten breakfast on the day of her death. There had been a theory among the officers that she had been murdered on the night of September second, which was Sunday, but finding of undigested food in the stomach proved that she had eaten that morning.

Until yesterday it was not generally known that the county had engaged a detective to ferret out what was possible to learn about the case and get it into condition for the hearing.

District Attorney Ben S. Fisher said that, while there was little evidence that the prosecution wanted to divulge at the preliminary hearing and all that they expected to gain at this gathering was to have one or probably both suspected men bound over to the grand jury, which meets late in October this would give the prosecution an opportunity of securing other leads which might, in the end, result in placing the blame for the murder where it belongs.

Luke S. May, held to be the best criminologist in the northwest, is the detective who has been running down what clews were possible to establish, but it was admitted that his success was not very great.

May is president of the Realare International Detective Agency, of Seattle, and also president of the Northwest Association of Sheriffs and Police. His experience is almost unlimited and he is considered a very capable man.

Officials of the county, on the arrest of Dr. Fred Covell and his son, Alton, realized that the circumstances of the murder of Mrs. Covell were such that it would require some very intelligent and constant work to ferret out the details of the affair, and so Dr. Covell and his son were held in jail without bond, during a time sufficient to give Detective May a chance to obtain incriminating evidence.

The defense, represented by Charles F. McKnight and Grant Colby, of Marshfield and Coquille, was in no hurry for the case to be called and the state had all the time it wanted.

Detective May, had worked on the case for something over two weeks, and made one trip to Portland during the time. Where Mr. May worked and the details of his activities were not made public, but it was known he put in considerable time in the hope and expectation that the daughter, Lucile, a girl of 14 years, knew something about the case that would shed some light on the murder.

According to statements made yesterday, the girl had not given the state any encouragement that she knows much about the case, yet the prosecution was still convinced that she was probably holding back something.

The history of the case is fresh, as the murder occurred on the morning of September third, Labor Day. Mrs. Covell was found dead on the floor of the kitchen at the family ranch home, five miles from Bandon. The body was discovered by the son, Alton, between ten and eleven o'clock. Dr. Covell, who is a chiropractor, was at the time in his office in Bandon. He was informed of the situation and went home, and worked for two hours on the hope of bringing Mrs. Covell back to life, it was reported at the time.

Sheriff Ellingsen and Deputy Sam Malehorn worked on the case for two days and then placed Dr. Covell and the son under arrest, and placed them in the county jail.

District Attorney Ben S. Fisher, also made several visits to the ranch home to investigate, but did not find anything worth while as evidence.

On arriving here Detective May was informed of the apparent difficulties he would encounter running down the criminal and admitting that the case was one which looked from the start, to be very mysterious.

Figure 28: Coos County Sheriff Edwin P. Ellingsen

Figure 29: Private Detective Luke S. May

October 12, 1923 the *Coos Bay Times* headlined: **ALTON COVELL, AGED 16, AND ARTHUR COVELL, HIS CRIPPLED UNCLE, INDICTED FOR MURDER** — Boy Admits That He Killed Mrs. Ebba Covell, Stepmother, by Administering Ammonia to Her Mouth and Nose but Says That Uncle Helped Him — **WILL BE HELD WITHOUT BAIL AS CHARGE IS FIRST DEGREE MURDER** — Youth Talks to Times Representative Today and Gives Details of the Killing at Bandon Which Had Been a Mystery Since It Occurred September 4 — **OLDER MAN INFLUENCES HIS YOUNGER RELATIVE**

Alton Covell, aged 16 years, and Arthur Covell, his uncle and a crippled astrologer who has confessed to planning many crimes, are both held on a charge of murder in the first degree for the killing of Mrs. Ebba Covell, wife of Dr. Fred Covell, at the home south of Bandon on September 4.

The accused youth this morning told a Times represent of the crime and of how Mrs. Covell was suffocated by applying ammonia poured on a rag and placed at her mouth and nose while she was in the kitchen of the home, but he says that the uncle helped him.

It appears that the elder man had a hypnotic influence on the youth, who declares that he did not want to do things which the uncle told him to do but that he always obeyed his commands.

"I could not kill anyone" was the boy's appeal this morning in almost childish tones, just after he admitted that his confession was true, "I did not do this alone, My uncle helped also."

Dr. Fred Covell, husband of the murdered woman, has been released from jail. The grand jury returned not a true bill at the same time that the indictments against the other two were returned.

Arthur Covell, the cripple, was brought today from the poor farm where he had been held. The boy has been in jail since he was arrested following the death of Mrs. Covell and today he is in his cell room with the knowledge that murder charge hangs over his head. Up until he confessed to the grand jury he denied knowledge of the murder.

The charge being first degree murder, it is not possible for the defendants to plead guilty, it is said, and a jury trial is necessary to determine what the punishment shall be. First degree murder can be punished by death or imprisonment in the penitentiary.

Although a defendant is only sixteen years of age, the law permits hanging one of that age of the jury sees fit.

Arthur Covell was brought by Sheriff Ellingsen and Deputy Malehorn from the poor farm this afternoon and is lodged in the county jail.

This is the second murder case in Coos county in the past few years. Harold Howell, aged 15, of Bandon, was tried three times on a charge of murdering Lilian Leuthold, but was acquitted after the third trial.

Alton Covell, aged sixteen years and the son of Dr. Fred Covell of Bandon, was indicted last night at 10 by the grand jury on charge of first degree murder for killing of Mrs. Ebba Covell, wife of the doctor. He admits the crime but says his uncle Arthur Covell, the cripple helped him.

The indictment charges that death was caused by suffocation with ammonia applied by the hands of Alton Covell. Arthur Covell was also indicted for first degree murder.

Not a true bill was returned in the case of Dr. Fred Covell, the dead woman's husband and he was releases from jail.

Boy Tells Story

The accused youth talked to a representative this morning at the county jail. He talked in low tones. He is slightly deaf but answered without hesitation.

"Yes, the story I told the other men about it is all true. I did kill but I had help. My uncle, Arthur Covell, helped me. He is a cripple but he can walk on crutches."

"The ammonia was put on a rag. It was all done in the kitchen. I had nothing very much against her but my uncle did not like her. She never went up stairs to wait on him and she fussed because he ate so much. We talked about killing her for quite a while and we had the ammonia for a month. We got it for that purpose."

Clears His Sister

"No my little sister, Lucile did not help any. She had nothing to do with it," the boys said. It is understood that the girl knew the night before of the plans to kill Mrs. Covell.

Showing some emotion the boys said:

"I could not kill anybody. I did not do it alone. My uncle helped me."

It is said that information learned was to the effect that the girl Lucile was supposed to have taken two smaller children to the home of a neighbor on the morning that Mrs. Covell was killed.

Appears Quiet

Alton Covell is only sixteen but is quite tall. He appears quiet and modest and up until he made the confessions to Sheriff Ellingsen and Deputy Malehorn and Luke S. May, the Seattle detective, which lead to his repeating the story to the grand jury, he had kept silent. None of the officers had been able to make him tell anything while he has been confined in jail but it was believed that he would finally come put with the truth.

Appears in Court

Last night after the indictment was returned the youth was awakened from bed and with some other prisoners was arraigned before Judge Kendall to answer the charge.

He appeared in the court room in his shirt sleeves, having been called out of bed. When asked if he wanted to wait to plead he said he did.

Followed Uncle's Will

When telling of the influence of his uncle upon him he said today:

"I was born in Washington but have lived in Bandon most of my life. My uncle raised me and my sister Lucile. We lived at our grandmother's house and after her death we lived with my father. I took care of my uncle all the time since he was hurt. When he would tell me to do things I did not want to sometimes but it seems like I always did what he told me to anyway."

Has Powerful Will

Arthur Covell, the uncle, is described as being a man of wonderful will power. He has eyes which will outlook most men and his wits were keen enough to outdo the officers for a time during their searching investigation. The cripple has been kept at the poor farm where he was taken after the tragedy and under guard.

Makes Statement

Dr. Covell after being released last night remained in jail until morning when he left. He said "I did not know who committed the murder. I am crushed. Excepting one who has been through same thing no one can realize awfulness of my position. I am glad that the mystery has been sifted to the bottom. Such a hideous crime must be punished whoever committed it. My grief is very great even though the accused is my son he must face justice. However as he is my son I will stay by him to the extent of seeing that he has a fair trial."

"I will remain in Coos count until the matter comes to some conclusion and then I will move from this section. It is all a terrible fair and I am glad that the mystery is to be solved. I can truly state that I knew nothing of how Mrs. Covell met her death and the result is all a surprise to me."

Laud Grand Jury

The murder of Mrs. Covell occurred on September 4, when she was found dead at her home. Officers have since been working on the case. The grand jury members also did some splendid work in the case as they went into it thoroughly and the result was the indictment of the guilty parties.

The witnesses before the grand jury were Dr. Covell, Alton Covell, Lucile Covell, Mrs. Wiren, a sister-in-law of the dead woman and several others. The grand jury last night went to the poor farm to get a personal statement from the cripple.

Account for Bruises

It is supposed that the bruises found on Mrs. Covell's body were caused by her struggles when ammonia was administered to her nose and it was learned that her death occurred in three minutes.

Confessed Crime Plan

Arthur Covell several days ago confessed that he had planned to carry out various crimes at Bandon including thefts and murder and that he intended to execute these through the help of others. It was after this confession that the statement came from Alton Covell.

October 12, 1923 the *Coquille Valley Sentinel* headlined: **MURDER MYSTERY IS SOLVED** Alton Covell Confesses Killing His Stepmother By Suffocating Her with Ammonia - His Uncle Was the Directing Head Who Planned the Method For Committing the Deed - For a Month the Entire Family Has Been Close Mouthed and Kept the Details of the Killing of Mrs. Covell Entirely to Themselves

Arthur Covell, crippled brother of Dr. Fred Covell, and Alton, the sixteen and a half year old son of Dr. Covell, have both confessed to their part in the murder of Mrs. Covell at the Covell ranch below Bandon on the morning of Sept. 2. Both of them were indicted by the grand jury, that for Arthur being one of the blind indictments returned by the grand jury last night.

Sheriff Ellingsen and Deputy Malehorn went out to the county farm this morning and brought the cripple in to the county jail. His confession was not made to the grand jury which went out to the infirmary yesterday, but was made to the superintendent, E. C. Church, last evening, after he learned that Alton had confessed to the murder. He then told Mr. Church that he, and he alone, was responsible for the dastardly crime. He did not deny that Alton had carried out the actual perpetration of the deed, but his was the master mind behind it, which planned and directed the feeble-minded youth's actions. He exonerates Dr. Fred Covell, who was released from jail today, from any previous knowledge of the crime, and the authorities have known absolutely that the doctor was in Bandon when the deed was committed.

For three or four days past a guard has been in constant attendance on Arthur Covell, at the county farm, for following his amazing story of criminal intentions, as given on page six of this issue, the officials have been certain that he would eventually come through.

No one has been allowed to see him, his mail has been censored, and every precaution against escape has been taken.

Just what took place at the time of the murder cannot be definitely stated now, but the confession secured from the thirteen year old girl by the grand jury, as to what she knew, and from Alton Covell as to his part in it, proved beyond doubt that Mrs. Covell was killed by the use of ammonia. A rag, soaked with the stuff, applied to her mouth and nostrils, caused her death within three minutes. The, bruises on her face were burns, and the bruises about her lips and arms may have been caused by her struggles to defend herself from the homicidal intent of her stepson, and may have been caused when the children dragged her in and put her on the bed.

To Dr. E. E. Mingus, of Marshfield, goes the credit for being the one to suggest that some death-producing fluid, or its fumes, were the cause of Mrs. Covell's death, after the doctors at Bandon had sworn that her neck was not broken and that they were unable to tell what did cause her death.

This put the authorities up against a hard proposition, for the cause of death must be stated in a prosecution for murder.

It was at this time, just after Dr. Covell's preliminary, that Luke S. May, of Seattle, was requested to come down here to investigate the case, and was given a contract with the county.

He worked zealously on the case, as did Messrs. Ellingsen and Malehorn of the sheriff's office, and District Attorney Fisher, and through their combined efforts the know-nothing attitude of the uncle and children was finally circumvented and the confessions secured.

The grand jury also made separate investigations of their own which resulted in some confessions.

The Covell family are peculiar in some ways, and for five weeks baffled every attempt to unlock their lips, even the five-year old daughter of the murdered woman refusing to tell what she knew, and it was only by leading up to it in other ways that a thing could be learned from her. She inadvertently let it out that Alton did not like her mother and quarreled with her.

At another time, when asked about her mamma, she said that "she was pretty, but she wasn't pretty when she died."

"How was that?" was the next question.

"She had blood all over her. Alton wiped it off," was her answer to the next query, "and threw the rag in the stove."

Thus, piece by piece, was the conspiracy of silence finally broken down and the whole story told. The newspapers have not been able to get all that story but enough is known to prove the statement that Arthur Covell possesses a diabolically cruel and inhuman mind, which planned the fiendish crime, and persuaded his nephew to commit it.

Dr. Covell, against whom no hint of participation or pre-knowledge now exists, has been freed by the grand jury. One statement made by him since his incarceration was, "I'm afraid I made an awful mistake keeping Alton out of the state institution," referring to his departure from Portland while the papers committing Alton to the feeble-minded asylum were in process of preparation. He is free of all suggestion of complicity, but what is worse, he knows that his own son is the guilty, and that his own brother is the fiend that he is.

Arthur Covell will be taken before Judge Kendall tomorrow for arraignment. His arrest was made on bench warrant issued by the grand jury.

Directly below was the following article headlined: **Like Rue Morgue Case.**

Luke S. May, the criminologist, who has been working on the Covell murder case for the past month, left last evening for his home in Seattle, after being in the county since Sunday on this trip. He took some of the evidence, to be produced at the trial, with him for further laboratory investigation. Before leaving the sheriff's office he stated to a Sentinel representative that when the case was brought to trial the details would provide as striking a story of criminal intent as any fiction ever written, not even excepting the Rue Morgue murders, or any other of Alexander Dumas' masterpieces.

Also headlined: Crimes He Contemplated Diabolical wholesale crimes including theft, arson and murder of men, women and children and the wiping out of whole families, were planned carefully and shrewdly by Arthur Covell, cripple brother of Dr. Fred Covell, of Bandon, held for murder of his wife, according to the confessions of Arthur Covell made at the county farm to L. S. May, the noted criminologist, of Seattle, says the Coos Bay Times.

May was employed by Coos county to work on the Covell murder case. He is president of the Revelare International Secret Service of Seattle. When Mrs. Eva Covell, wife of Dr. Covell of Bandon was found dead on the back porch of her residence on Sept. 4, it was discovered after the undertaker was called that she had been subjected to violence at the time of her death or shortly before. As the death appeared to be a mystery an inquest was held and it was deckled that Mrs. Covell had been murdered and her husband, Dr. Fred Covell and his son by another marriage, Alton Covell, aged sixteen, were both held to wait action of the grand jury in connection with the murder.

Arthur Covell is a brother of Dr. Fred Covell and made his home with the family. He is forty-eight years old and two years ago was crippled in an auto accident and cannot walk. We was taken to the poor farm and held as witness. District Attorney Fisher employed Mr. May to work on the case.

In the course of his investigations into the case May learned that Arthur, the cripple brother of the doctor, was an astrologist. Notes were found which indicated that he was using a cipher code of some kind and this led to a search which divulged the key book of the man's plans in crime.

Mr. May went to the county poor farm and had an interview with Covell.

May was reticent about discussing the affair Tuesday before leaving for Coquille where he is to appear before the grand jury but he admitted that Arthur Covell had made a confession to him. May says that in all his experience in criminal work, and he has had much to do with murder and mystery cases on this coast, he has never heard a more horrible confession of crimes planned.

Covell does not tell of anything he has done in the past but he admitted all the plans he had made for crimes to be carried out in Bandon. These crimes included wholesale theft of homes in Bandon, stealing of automobiles and the covering up of the thefts, the elimination of traces of crime by arson and of murder of men, women, and children. In two instances it was planned by the man to wipe out entire families in the course of carrying out his criminal intents.

Mr. May says that he never heard of crimes which were planned for execution and concealment more craftily than were those to which Covell confessed.

Covell is an astrologist and a mathematician. May says he is by no means a man of ordinary mind. He used the signs of the planets as a guide as to the times to carry out his crimes and the details of these contemplated crimes had been worked out to the finest point. May having secured Covell's notes and code book was enabled to approach him to advantage and secure a confession by mental process rather than by any third degree methods.

These confessions while secured in the course of the investigation of the murder of Mrs. Fred Covell have no direct connection with the death of the woman. Arthur Covell was at the Fred Covell home at the time of Mrs. Covell's death but he claimed to the officers that he was in the yard sunning himself and knew nothing o the case of her death.

The cripple is improving since he has been at the poor farm. His spine was injured in an auto accident and he has been unable to walk though he is strong in the arms. He has been getting better and it is not unlikely that he may under treatment be able to walk.

In order to bring about the prosecution of a case of murder in connection with the death of Mrs. Fred Covell it will be necessary to establish the cause of death. The Bandon physicians who examined the body were at the preliminary hearing unable to give any direct cause of death. This is a fact which must first be established in any murder case.

Mr. May did not have a chance to see the remains until ten days later when the body was disinterred. The tissues of the body were broken down and the first post mortems had destroyed the evidence which would lead to establishing the cause of death.

It is not unlikely that it may be impossible to establish the cause of Mrs. Covell's death in which event no one can be prosecuted but Mr. May has at least through the investigation learned of the plans of Arthur Covell to carry out, wholesale crimes in this county and these discoveries and the confessions will prevent his execution of a career of arson, theft and murder.

Covell intended to make use of other persons as confederates in carrying out his plans.

Arthur Covell has lived at Bandon for a number of years past. He met with the auto accident which caused him to be a cripple about two years ago, and since that time has resided with his brother, Dr. Covell. Previous to that time he resided on a ranch with his mother, who is now dead, and he raised Alton and Lucille Covell, two children of Dr. Covell by a former marriage. Dr. Covell was married three times before he wedded Miss Eva Wiren, daughter of O. Wiren, keeper of the lighthouse at Bandon for many years.

After Arthur became a cripple and took up his home with Dr. Covell, the two children he raised, Alton and Lucile, were also taken to the Dr. Covell home. Alton is 16 years old and is six feet tall and weights 160 pounds. He is slightly deaf. He is held to await the action of the grand jury along with his father. He has been writing poetry since he has been in jail, and letters he has sent out to relatives have been written in verse.

When the county secured Luke S. May to work on the Covell case, it got the services of one of the best detectives on the coast. Mr. May works along the most modern and scientific lines and has been connected with many big murder cases and other big mysteries. He is an expert on the different lines which are employed by criminals. His career as a detective is an interesting one but he says that the case of Arthur Covell is even to him a remarkable one.

Mr. May was unfortunate in being called in time to establish the cause of death of Mrs. Covell, which is a necessary step if anyone is to be prosecuted for her murder. The fact that he has discovered and thus checked the criminal plans which Arthur Covell admits he intended carrying out will probably save much distress which might been caused.

October 13, 1923 the *Coos Bay Times* printed three articles regarding the Covell case. Headline: **ARHTUR COVELL PLEADS GUILTY**

COQUILLE, Ore., Oct. 13. — Arthur Covell pleaded guilty to murder in the first degree in the circuit court here today. Judge Kendall did not accept the plea and will not take action until Monday as it may be determined that it is necessary to have a trial in a first degree murder case.

Alton Covell withheld his plea until Monday when he will be arraigned again. It is believed that he intends to stand trial.

Second: **PLANNED TO KILL PRESSEY FAMILY — ARTHUR COVELL HAD THEM LISTED IN CRIME SCHEMES** — Fact Is Told by Luke S. May In a Statement Given Out to Associated Press at Seattle **PRESSEY LIVES NEAR THE COVELL RESIDENCE**

The E. J. Pressey referred to in the following telegram is supposed to be R. M. Pressey, dairyman who lives south of Bandon, and who was a neighbor of the Covell family.

SEATTLE, Wash., Oct. 13. — Declaring he has turned over evidence to the Oregon authorities revealing a series of 12 planned killings, and a number of arson crimes said to have been contemplated by Arthur Covell, aged 46, noted astrologist and a cripple, who with his nephew, Alton Covell, aged 16; was indicted at Coquille yesterday for slaying Mrs. Fred Covell wife, of a Bandon chiropractor, Luke S. May, Seattle professional criminologist, who was called into the case, has returned to Seattle.

May says that after decoding a number of Covell's mysterious horoscopes he will submit to the Coos county authorities additional evidence that the crippled astrologist planned the murder of E. J. Pressey, wealthy Oregon dairyman, and his wife and three children, together with the burning of the bodies by firing the residence. Robbery was believed to be the motive for the crimes.

Third: **GRAND JURORS SAY THEY SOLVED COVELL MURDER** — Coos County Investigators Resent Claims Made by Detective Luke May **CONFESSIONS SECURED IN GRAND JURY ROOM** Solution Showed Different Theory Than Detective and Others Had Held **NEW STORIES ARE TOLD** Arthur Covell Makes Confession to Grand Jurors After Detective May had Left for Portland

Coos County grand jury members were both surprised and amused today by press dispatches in which Detective Luke May claimed the honors for the solution of the Covell, murder case at Bandon.

The grand jurors state that when they began the investigation of the Covell case Wednesday morning, Detective May, District Attorney Fisher and the others were completely at sea. They state that May's theory was that Dr. Covell was responsible.

Not until the grand jury had obtained the admissions from Alton Covell and his sister when they appeared as witnesses in the grand jury room was the real solution of the murder obtained.

They state that Detective May and the other officers did not know of the real nature of the crime and who was responsible until the grand jurors informed them.

Furthermore, they state that Detective May was unable to get any admissions about Mrs. Covell's death from Arthur Covell and not until after Detective May had left Coquille for Portland did the latter confess.

All the confessions were made direct to the grand jury, they state.

That Mrs. Covell was smothered with ammonia fumes and that Alton Covell did it was not revealed or indicated until the grand jury obtained the facts direct from the confessions, the grand jurors state.

Detective May is said to have been paid $100 per day and expenses for his work on the Covell case. Aside from his detective business, he has a school for sleuths on Puget Sound. While the grand jurors say that he is a fine fellow and clever and worked hard, they do not propose that he be given credit for something he did not do.

MAY INTERVIEWED

Luke S. May is interviewed at length in a Portland paper of last evening. Among other things the interview says:

The full extent of crimes by the astrologist will never be known until his records are fully deciphered by May, an expert at that work. He declared here that Covell admitted as much as he had deciphered, but would not tell more, nor would he reveal all the crimes he had been responsible for in the past.

Every Angle Reasoned

"He reasoned every angle to perfection," May said. "He had analyzed every possible thought that would come into the minds of investigators and then he had plotted to meet that thought and overcome it."

"He is a writer of horoscopes and a student of them. He had read the planets and his horoscopes and he had determined just when each of his victims would offer the least resistance to him and when his own person would have the most influence and power. When the signs and stars were more favorable for committing the crimes and covering them — then they would be committed."

"No business man ever had his plans more skillfully laid, or more carefully, than he," Mr. May said. "He knew the every cost and the every gain. Each dollar was accounted for, each moment — yes, almost every second — was to be carefully utilized."

"He so planned murders for money. There was no other motive. He had a motive planned for each crime that would divert suspicion to one innocent person."

Psycho-Analysis Used

"The boys were to be his tools. They were to be coached and carefully schooled for each crime."

"He wrote horoscopes for the Hollywood movies and for astrological schools in Boston, New York and other big cities. The Lewellyn George college of astrologers of Portland was included. He made good money from all of these for he is a master."

May declared that he was able to get at the solution of the murder of Mrs. Fred Covell only through chemical analysis. She was killed by the application of chemical to the nose.

The criminologist said he was able first to get into Arthur Covell's plans by the use of psycho-Analysis, by reasoning along with his reasoning, and thinking as he thought.

On October 15, 1923 the *Coos Bay Times* headlined: **ARTHUR COVELL IN DIARY TELLS BANDON PLOTS** — Confessed Slayer of Sister-in-Law Had Written Plans for Other Crimes **WELL KNOWN BANDON PEOLE LISTED TO DIE** — Proposed to Have Wills and Agreements Ready Where-by to Claim Property — **BOOK ACCIDENTALLY FOUND** — Kidnapping, Murder and Arson Some of the Wild Dreams of Cripple Who Spurred Nephew to Strangle Mrs. Covell

Bandon folks are in for a few thrills from chapters from the diary of Arthur Covell, confessed principal to the murder of his sister-in-law Mrs. Ebba Covell, near Bandon.

The book which was accidentally picked up and turned over to District Attorney Fisher and Sheriff Ellingsen furnished the basis for the "startling deductions, code cipher translations, psycho-analysis" etc. of Luke May, the Seattle detective and criminologist who claimed the honors of solving the mystery and who, the Coos county grand jury members say, simply "stole their thunder."

However Detective May got the book and is demonstrating his ability as a master press agent by giving out chapters of it at Seattle, Portland and elsewhere.

District Attorney Fisher and Sheriff Ellingsen have been carefully guarding this book as one of the secret surprises to be sprung in the Covell trials and Detective May has simply slipped one over on them.

The book was found by William B. Brummet of Bandon when he and others went over to the Covell place to get a box of stuff to send up to Arthur Covell at the Coos county farm. Brummet turned it over to the authorities.

Early last week, District Attorney Fisher turned it over to Detective May as a lead for the circumstantial chain. Immediately Mr. May gave out his sensational story of the "confessions of Arthur Covell."

Judge C. R, Wade, former Mayor Geo. P. Topping and other prominent Bandon people were slated as victims of the reign of crime that Covell had plotted, according to the entries in the book.

From the book, the first intimation that ammonia was used to strangle Mrs. Ebba Covell was gathered, and when this lead was sprung on Covell, he confessed the balance.

May Gives It Out

Although the Coos county officials have been carefully guarding the contents of this "diary of prospective crimes" as it might be called, Detective May is giving it out at Seattle. He left yesterday for the mountains to recuperate from his strenuous deductions here. However, the following details are given in a press dispatch regarding the Covell revelations.

Designs on Bandon Woman

"One of the papers I have revealed a carefully worked out plot to kidnap a young Bandon woman," detective May stated. The young woman was referred to in the paper as the "Doan girl" who is daughter of a prominent Bandon family of that name. After a new home was built the younger Covell was to have kidnapped the girl.

"A note was to have been previously prepared and left where the girl's parents would discover it."

Another paper disclosed detailed plans for the "accidental death" of J. Ira Sidwell, a Bandon business man. He was to have been found with his neck broken, apparently having fallen downstairs in his place of business. In an inside pocket of his coat was to have been found his will, leaving all or a portion of his property to Covell. This will, in the process of being written and nearly completed I have in my possession. It bears the date March 3, 1922, and reads:

Finger Points to Grave

"I, J. Ira Sidwell, being of sound mind, lately dreamed a dream and heard a voice very distinctly say to me, In three weeks! In three weeks! Then I saw a finger jointing to a grave. I somehow feel depressed over this dream and knowing that life is always uncertain, and we are often struck down without warning, I am mindful to put my affairs in order, prepared for whatever is near.

I wish to make these provisions with regard to the settlement of my estate.

First this present will, duly executed, according to law, revokes any and all other wills heretofore made by me.

Second, I desire to ease somewhat the burden of a young man whom I highly admire, and who is now handicapped for life by a serious misfortune. I refer to (the name is omitted) but I think that the person referred to is obviously Covell himself) of Bandon, Oregon, and my sympathy for him so great that I am cutting off all rights of my heirs as they can take care of themselves but Mr. __________ cannot.

Third, I hereby give and bequeath unto the said ________ absolutely everything I own

Pinned to the rough draft of the will was a slip of paper containing pencilled notes in Covell's handwriting and reading: Copy as it now is but with one-half interest as whole interest might make motive seem too plain."

Thrifts Marked for Death

The entire family of a man named Thrift at Bandon, May declared, was to have been wiped out by Covell when "the stars were right." Thrift according to the alleged plot, May stated, was to have been waylaid on his way from farm to town and killed. After dark Mrs. Thrift and her three children were to have been chloroformed in their home and the house burned, May said.

"At the proper time a pre-dated check would be found showing that Covell had purchased the Thrift property before the murders," May asserted.

"Another of the documents revealed to me a plot to kidnap and kill William B. Brummet a wealthy Bandon citizen, in 1924. Mr. and Mrs. E. A. Hartman, a neighbor named Lockwood, and a Mr. Squires were marked for killing. In working on the Covell case May had the body of Mrs. Fred Covell exhumed. At her death it was reported that her neck was broken. An examination after the exhuming of the body showed this was not true. May said for since burial a strange discoloration of the flesh about the nose and mouth had taken place. By a chemical analysis in a private laboratory," May said, "he discovered that the discoloration had been caused by ammonia and that death was caused by ammonia-soaked cloth applied to be nostrils."

October 16, 1923 the *Coos Bay Harbor* headlined: **LUCILLE COVELL WRITES TO JUDGE**

Peculiar Missive Attributed to Girl, Who Seemed Bluffing the County Officials into Wrong Conclusions.

The Covell case, still full of interest because of its peculiar angles, had nothing in it so far any more astonishing than an alleged letter written by Lucille Covell to a judge, supposed to be Judge Kendall. The letter is given to the press by Detective May, who worked on the case, Lucille Covell was confessedly outside the house, keeping the children away while the murder was committed.

"Looks to me you don't half know what you are doing. I could be a better justice of peace and officers than any of you people."

"Alton is innocent and you ought to know it."

"You set up there and let dad off on that amount of money so he can kill a dozen other wives."

"I would stake my life any time that Alton is innocent. Why don't you open your eyes and see things?"

"Then if you call my brother feeble minded, you are all feeble minded."

"He is hard of hearing and you have to explain things to him. You don't understand him. Dad has put all the blame on him. You don't understand that. If you don't see this in a different light I will take your job myself." Yours truly,

"LUCILLE COVELL."

On October 16, 1923 the *Coos Bay Times* printed five articles regarding the Covell case. The first headlined: **LUCILE COVELL, AGED 14 YEARS, ADMITS SHE KNEW OF MURDER PLAN FOR MONTHS BEFORE THE KILLING** – "I Knew They Were Planning to Kill Her but I Thought It Would Pass Over and Didn't Think Much About It," Child Says — **HER FATHER WOULD HURT UNCLE IF SHE TOLD HIM OF THE SCHEME TO MURDER** — Child Says She Did Not Tell the Truth to the Grand Jury When She Claimed She Did Not Know Until the Night Before — **SAYS THAT ALTON WAS PERSUADED TO COMMIT ACT**

All of the details of the murder of Mrs. Covell were told in a Times representative yesterday, by Lucile Covell, 14-year-old daughter of Dr. Covell, after she had posed for a photograph.

The child admits that she lied to the grand jury when she said she did not know of the details of the murder. She says she knew of the plans for a month ahead but did not think they would ever materialize and did not want to tell her father for fear that he might do harm to her uncle, Arthur Covell, the helpless cripple who had pleaded guilty to murder and who assumed all the responsibility for the crime.

Sorry It Happened

The little girl tells of the influence the uncle had over Alton, who actually killed Mrs. Covell. She stands up for her uncle and her brother however, with the statement that Alton was a fine boy and her uncle a fine man, She admits that she likes them both. She expresses regret that the killing occurred and says that Alton is sorry too but claims she did not realize what it meant.

The girl says she would not never have told anything if others had not told first. She seems to think that the confessions were first extracted from Alton and the uncle, while as a matter of fact she was the first to tell.

Never Knew Mother

Lucile is very large for her age. She has blonde hair, bobbed, is pretty and attractive in manner but would impress one as having the manner of a girl sixteen or seventeen years old. She says she never knew a mother as her mother died when she was born.

The child has told those about her that she does not want to see her father because she is ashamed to see him.

Her story is the only detailed recital of the murder which has been made public, outside of the facts learned from the witnesses before the grand jury.

Star Witness

The girl will be the star witness in the case of Alton Covell who yesterday pleaded not guilty to the charge of first degree murder and whose trial will be set at a later date to be decided upon by Judge Kendall after consultation of the lawyers. Grant Colby of Coquille will defend Alton Covell.

Lucile is in charge of Juvenile Officer A. T. Morrison and wife. While her manner is quite cheerful and pleasant she admits that the horrors of the murder return to her mind and that when she goes to a movie show she must direct her attention on the picture or the scene of the murder comes back before her eyes. She was told that likely she would be a witness in cases of her brother and her uncle.

Could Kill Silence

"I don't see why they should want me," she said. "They seem to know everything. No, I was not the first one to tell. By heck, I never would have told anything but they told me others had confessed and they told me they had my uncle's notes so I thought I might as well tell too. I told the grand jury that I did not know about the murder before hand but I did know. My uncle and Alton talked about it for a month and I knew it."

Feared for Uncle

When asked why she did not tell her father that murder was planned the girls said:

"I thought it would all pass over. I did not think they would ever really do it and of course I did not realize what it meant. I never saw but one dead person in my life. I saw a dead man once. Besides my dad has a very bad temper and I feared if I told him my uncle and Alton were planning to kill my stepmother my father would hurt my uncle."

It was suggested to her that her silence had caused her stepmother's death. She said:

"Well I thought they never would really do it. But it had to be done and my uncle wanted Alton to do it. Alton hasn't a bit of nerve. He is slow in some things but when you get something in his head once he knows it. He understands astrology. He went to a school of astrology in Portland. I know a little about it. The 'aspect' was right for September third they said to kill my step-mother. Alton will do anything for anyone he likes. He liked my uncle very much. My uncle is a fine man and Alton is a fine boy. He would not hurt anybody. He did not want to kill my step-mother but it just had to be done."

The child could not tell why the murder had to be committed. She seemed to accept that as a fact. She has said that the uncle told Alton he would do the killing himself if he could but being crippled was unable to do so and that it was up to Alton.

Alton Nice Boy

"I know Alton did not want to hurt anybody," the girl said. 'He is an awfully nice boy. He didn't want to do it from the first but he thought about it for a long time. Yes, we had the ammonia, for a month. Alton tells me everything he is going to do and everything he intends to do. The night before my stepmother was killed I knew what they were going to do. I was afraid to tell about it. I was not afraid of my uncle. I knew he would not do anything to me but I was afraid to tell my father.

Did Not See Killing

"The morning my stepmother was killed my uncle was in the yard. I was out of the house with the children. I did not see her killed. The children did not see it either and we were with my uncle. Alton killed her in the kitchen. I don't think I heard any screams but I heard a lot of noise like someone jumping around. Alton came out and told us what he had done."

"I went in and helped Alton pack her out of the kitchen and put her on the sofa. Alton was pretty badly excited. I telephoned my father but couldn't get him. My uncle telephoned my father and told him something terrible had happened and my father came. Alton went to the gate and met him."

"Alton was really sorry for what he had done." After it was over I was doing the washing and Alton said; "I am sorry I did it. I would not have done it for the world." I said; "I am sorry you did it too."

When asked if Alton had done any other deeds of crime at the instigation of his uncle the girls said:

Sometimes Stole

"No, he did not do anything very had. Yes, he stole some but not any more than most kids his age steal. The things he stole he took because it was something he wanted for himself."

The girl was asked if Alton set fire to the many houses which were burned at Bandon.

"Oh no!" she said. "He never set fire to any houses in Bandon. I am sure he never burned any houses for he would have told me if he did. I don't know why my uncle wanted to kill my stepmother. It had to be done. Uncle did not like her. She was quite a nice woman but they did not like each other. They never quarreled because they were never together. Alton took care of my uncle. I never would have told a word if the others had not told, I am sorry they did it but I thought it would all pass over. Alton and my uncle I like very much."

No Motive Given

The girl is perfectly composed and common place in her discussion of the murder excepting that she seems to have accepted as a fact that the stepmother had to be killed. She is not able to give any motive excepting that the cripple and Mrs. Covell did not like each other. She says Mrs. Covell did not ever see any of Arthur's notes that she knows of.

No Chance For Heaven

When some suggestion was made to the girl about doing wrong and going to heaven she said: "Oh, I never expect to go to heaven. I have told too many lies."

The girl admits freely that she lied to the grand jury about her lack of knowledge of the plans for the murder and now says that she knew for a month ahead that it was to take place.

Second: **MAY HAVE BEEN THE FIRE FIEND — BANDON PEOPLE WONDER IF COVELL BURNED HOUSES** — He Confessed Incendiarism as Part of his Plans—City Suffered Many Fires

For several years Bandon has had many fires of a mysterious origin and now people of that city are wondering whether or not Arthur Covell, the crippled astrologer and murder schemer, who pleaded guilty to the killing of Mrs. Covell had any thing to do with these fires.

In his confession he said that he had planned theft and murder and that he expected to cover up some of the crimes by burning down houses. Notes which the district attorney holds shows that fires were a part of the schemes.

Now some of the people are wondering whether Arthur Covell might not have had something to do with the burning of the residences in cases where the origin was a mystery and where it appeared quite evident that fires were of incendiary origin.

Covell confessed to having planned fires to cancel crimes he expected to perform in the future but did not confess anything as to his past acts expecting his part in the killing of Mrs. Covell.

At any rate many of the Bandon fire mysteries were never solved and Arthur Covell in addition to confessing that he was a thief and murderer has told that incendiarism was part of the plans in the horrible series of outrages he had in mind.

Third: **LOCAL WOMAN HAS MET COVELL — CRIPPLE FIEND NOT UNKNOWN TO SOME IN MARSHFIELD** — Had Called Upon Him to Read Their Horoscopes and Paid Fee of Five Dollars

Arthur Covell, archfiend, crippled astrologer, hypnotist, and confessed murderer, was not unknown to some Marshfield women. He would read one's horoscope and tell of the future and there are several women of this city which believe in that sort of thing and who had called upon Covell and had him read their future according to the planets, his way of telling what is to come to pass.

And in these cases the Marshfield women paid the fee he charged which is said to have been five dollars. Just how much he fattened his pocketbook through the superstitions of Marshfield women is not known but it is a fact that at least several women of this city had called upon the murderer to hear his version of their futures.

Fourth: **ARTHUR COVELL TRIAL IS SET NEXT FRIDAY** Crippled Confessed Murderer Is Carried into the Court Room This Morning **COURT ACCEPTS PLEA BUT ORDERS TRIAL** Says That the Gravity of the Case Is Such That an Open Trial Is Necessary **CLAUDE GILES TO DEFEND** Named by the Court and May Ask for a Postponement by Thursday Because He Is Not Familiar with the Case

COQUILLE, Ore., Oct. 16. — Arthur Covell, the cripple who takes the blame for the murder of Mrs. Fred Covell which was committed by his nephew, Alton, was arraigned in the circuit court, this morning. He was carried into the courtroom by Deputy Sheriff, Sam Malehorn and a trusty at the jail. Judge Kendall said: "You entered a plea of guilty to the charge of murder in the first degree last Saturday. The court now accepts that plea but owing to the gravity of your case the court deems that you should have an open and fair trial and the court will appoint an attorney for you if you have none."

Giles Is Named

Covell was asked if he wanted an attorney and if he had anyone in mind, and the prisoner said he would take an attorney but did not have anyone special in mind.

Judge Kendall said he would appoint Claude Giles to defend the cripple. The court added that Mr. Giles was president; of the Coos County Bar association and that it regarded him as an able lawyer. The judge said he would set the trial for next Friday morning and would empanel a jury.

May Ask a Delay

Mr. Giles said that he was not at all familiar with the case and that he might ask for a postponement of the trial in order that he could familiarize himself with the details, but if he asked for a postponement he would do so by Thursday morning.

Lucile Is Present

Lucile Covell was in the court room in charge of Mrs. A. T. Morrison, wife of the juvenile officer. Also with the girl were Mrs. Schallenbarger and daughter of Canary. Mrs. Schallenbarger is a sister of the dead mother of Lucile and Alton Covell.

As the prisoner was being carried from the court room Lucile grasped his hand as he passed.

Claims Arthur Covell Had Cryptic Code To Outline Plans For Many More Crimes

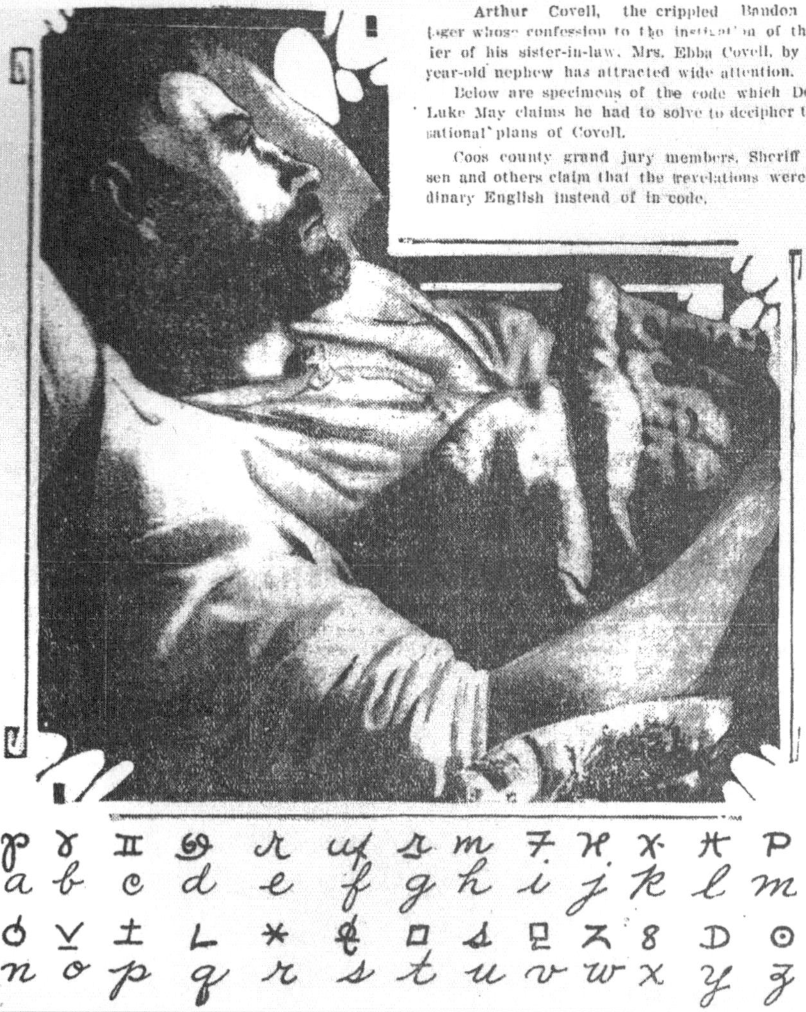

Arthur Covell, the crippled Bandon astrologer whose confession to the instigation of the murder of his sister-in-law, Mrs. Ebba Covell, by his 16-year-old nephew has attracted wide attention.

Below are specimens of the code which Detective Luke May claims he had to solve to decipher the sensational plans of Covell.

Coos county grand jury members, Sheriff Ellingsen and others claim that the revelations were in ordinary English instead of in code.

Figure 30: Arthur Covell - *Coos Bay Times,* October 17, 1923

The final article of the day headlined: **LINKS COVELL TO TAYLOR CASE — LUKE S. MAY THINKS HE MAY HAVE HAD CONNECTION** — Some of the Horoscopes Show That the Bandon Cripple Communicated with Hollywood

SEATTLE, Wash., Oct. 16. — Deciphering of numerous horoscopes seized from Arthur Covell, 46, the crippled astrologist who, with his nephew, Alton Covell, will be tried separately at Coquille for the killing of Mrs. Ebba Covell a month ago may reveal a strong clew to the slaying of William Desmond Taylor, film director; according to an announcement made by Luke S. May, criminologist who has been investigating the Covell Case.[S]

"I have a large number of these horoscopes in my possession and intend to make an immediate intensive search for a possible clue," May stated. "Most of the horoscopes in my possession were sent to members of the film colony in Hollywood. I am firmly convinced that there is a connection hidden under

[S] No records were found linking or even mentioning Covell with the Taylor murder. Taylor was murdered at his home in Los Angeles on February 2, 1922. On October 21, 1964 Margaret Gibson provided a dying confession to the murder of Taylor.

the three-cipher code of a few horoscopes."

May made definite charges that the astrologer's papers, which he brought back from Oregon, included deciphered plans for the sending of letters signed "K.K.K." In an alleged effort to further his schemes the kidnaping of the wife or a Bandon banker and later the killing of the banker after obtaining the ransom money, the alleged duplication of a slaying by ammonia and the building of a cafeteria to be furnished and operated from the furniture, produce and stock obtained from his intended victims.

Youth Confesses Killing

Alton Covell confessed to the charge that he had killed his step-mother after he received an opportunity to write it out, May asserted.

"The confession was written on the night of October 9 and I turned it over to the Grand jury on the afternoon of October 10." May said. The written confession, made public for the first time, follows:

"I want to start and lead a clean life and I want to he able to look back on everything I do and not be ashamed of anything I will do in the future. I don't know what made me do it. I don't understand why I done such a thing. I will see that it never happens again. I want to look back on a clear trail."

"I put the ammonia on the rag and Ebba was standing by the stove. I walked up to her from behind and on the right side. I put the rag over her nose with my right hand and held her arms with my left. I held it on her nose for about three minutes after I let her down on the floor. There was a little ammonia left in the bottle and I threw it down into the gulch."

Deed Reported to Uncle

"Then I went out and told my uncle that I had done it. Lucille (his sister) and my uncle (the astrologist) knew about the plan first. He told me to get the ammonia and how to use it."

"Before turning the confession over to the grand jury," May stated, "Arthur Covell was shown what, the nephew had written but declared. I might later. I'll have to think it over."

"According to facts that I have collected, the nephew purchased the ammonia one month before the death of Mrs. Covell to avoid suspicion. In other words, her death was set one month ahead."

"All of the data prepared by the astrologist were contained in envelopes marked on the outside lefthand corner, The Centenary Methodist Episcopal, Portland Area."

"In addition to the names of Mr. and Mrs. Thrift and their three children, Mr. Widwell, Walter Hartman and Mrs. K. A. Hartman, Mr. and Mrs. Lockwood and their daughter. Mr. Squires and Mr. Brummet, who I said Saturday were to have been killed, I believe I have positive evidence that the following would also have been slain:

Mr. and Mrs. Charles Richert; the entire Pressey family, who reside on a dairy farm; Mr. Johnson, a Bandon furniture dealer; Mr. and Mrs. Nordstrom, and their two children, who live on a farm; Clayton B. Zeok; George P. Topping, who was to have been the administrator of the alleged Zeek will; Martha E. Keck: Byron Enoch; William R. Brummet. who was a very good friend of the Covells; Elbert Dyer; Chris Rasmissen; Dr. Huston; Mr. Corson banker of Bandon, whose wife was to have been kidnaped and held for $5000 ransom; Mr. Sparks, store owner; C. W. Ward, and Mr. Belding, Bandon lawyer."

The Richerts and Hartmans were to have signed a will bequeathing their properties to Sidwell, who was to have been found later with his neck broken after a fall down his store steps.

Slaying Plan Deciphered

"I have deciphered two slaying plans and one robbery in which Byron Enoch, a nephew of Covell, and the son of William S. Brummet who was to have been killed, was to have been a lookout and taken a prominent part. Squires, Dyer and Rasmussen were to have been lured away on the prospect of finding oil and leaving a note to friends that they would not tell where they intended to find the oil. They were to have been killed according to my evidence, over Squires' store at Bandon. Dyer was to have been slain with ammonia if he failed to bring an automobile."

"After going through all the: data," May asserted, "I have evidence that Covell intended to purchase a cafeteria, outfit it with furniture obtained from his victim operate it with the stock taken from the farms of other victims am finance it with checks made out by some of the slain parties to G. L Miller & Co, for bonds which were to have been transferred to Covell."

October 17, 1923 the *Coos Bay Times* headlined: **SAYS COVELL SENT KRONEBERG NOTE — DETECTIVE MAY HAS NEW PHASE OF MURDER CASE** — Declares he has Deciphered More Horoscopes Indicating 26 Murder Plots

> SEATTLE, Wash., Oct. 17. — Criminologist May after deciphering further horoscopes of Arthur Covell, Bandon astrologer, said twenty-six deaths were planned when the individuals came under the planetary influences.
>
> May said the horoscopes showed Covell planned two bases of operation, Bandon and Hollywood, Calif. May said the disclosures indicated four juveniles were relied upon to execute "orders" received from the stars.
>
> May said the letter received by Mrs. Ottillie K. Kronenberg of Bandon, who manifested confidence in the innocence of Dr. Fred Covell when he was under suspicion of causing his wife's death, and signed "K K K" was sent by Arthur Covell. The letter threatening that she would be hanged to a tree if she discussed the Covell case again.

On October 18, 1923 the *Coos Bay Times* headlined: **MAY GIVES MORE OF COVELL PLANS**

> SEATTLE, Oct. I8. — Twenty-six residents of Bandon and vicinity were marked for death at the hands of Arthur Covell, crippled astrologer and confessed murderer, according to Luke S. May, professional criminologist, who today announced his results in deciphering the murder plot code of the Coquille prisoner.
>
> More additional names added to the long list previously announced were those of Mr. and Mrs. John A. Dickey of Bandon. Dickey is the owner of a general merchandise store. The plot which involved the Dickeys is similar to the other crimes planned by Covell, according to May. They were to be brought together and held while funds were obtained on a personal check. Then they were to be murdered.
>
> In each case Covell's plan was to obtain the money then kill his victims. The checks were to be sent to a bond firm for the purchase of bonds and these were to be delivered to Covell in various banks of the state of Oregon.
>
> Still another of the Covell family was involved in the astrologer's schemes by discoveries made by May last night. This is Byron Enoch, aged 19, a stepson of Fred Covell, who is serving as a sailor on the Mary E. Moore, which operates out of Bandon.
>
> Enoch was to be the principal in the blackmailing and murder of Roy B. Corson, cashier of the First National bank of Bandon, according to the deciphered plans. While the murder plans of the astrologer sound like the weird imaginings of a fictionist May says that they were set down with remarkable attention to detail and might easily have been consummated.

October 19, 1923 the *Coos Bay Times* headlined: **COVELL NOTES TELL ABOUT A DISAPEARANCE** Believed There Is Some Connection With Disappearance of San Diego Man — **NAME OF MAN HELD IS FOUND IN NOTES** — E. Drew Clark Was Suspected of Knowing Something — COVELL KNEW HIS NAME Recent Discovery May Lead to Further Connection of the Man Held for Murder with Case in California

> PORTLAND, Ore., Oct. 19. — It is learned here that notes of Arthur Covell, the cripple astrologer held for murder at Coquille, contains a name which may connect up with a famous case in San Diego.
>
> On Feb. 7 last Gorge E. Schick, a broker of San Diego, disappeared and was never found. E. Drew Clark, an astrologer of Portland, was held in connection with the disappearance. Now it has been found that in some of the notes of Arthur Covell appear the name of Clark which leads to the belief that possibly Covell has some connection with the disappearance case and that possibly Clark was in Oregon and met with Covell.

October 19, 1923 the *Coquille Valley Sentinel* headlined: **COVELL'S YOUTH** — H. C. Getz Knew Arthur Covell As a Boy in Portland 30 Years Ago

> With all the columns and columns; that have been printed about the Covell case, the stories given out by Luke S. May at Seattle, regarding the astrological intentions of Arthur Covell, and the statements by the chiropractors, Drs. C. R. Bloyd and Fred A. Covell, concerning the effect of the injury he received three years ago, which might have turned Arthur's trend of thought in a criminal direction, there has been nothing about the early youth of the man who May said was plotting the death of a score of Bandon

residents and the securing of wealth as a result.

Howard C. Getz, of this city, book keeper for E. E. Johnson in the mill office here, knew the Covell boys — Arthur and Fred — in Portland more than 30 years ago. Arthur at the time was about 13 or 14 years of age, a year or two older than Mr. Getz.

They were next door neighbors for nine months and attended the same school, and Mr. Getz, was very well acquainted with Arthur.

He says that at that time Arthur was just as different a boy from the man he is now as day is from night. Arthur was the constant companion of his mother, stayed out of school to help her when she was sick and cared for her very tenderly. She died about two years ago, a year after Arthur's accident. When a boy Arthur was kind to dumb animals, would pick up stray cats and dogs which had been injured and relieve their suffering.

He was always studious and took great delight in reading of and following scientific research; he was even then a student of hypnotism and astrology. In fact Mr. Getz says that from what he knew of him at the time he would not have been surprised had Arthur become a Dr. Steinmetz in the scientific world.

Moving from that neighborhood Mr. Getz lost track of the Covells until he came to Coquille some six or seven years ago and even after meeting him here a few years ago he saw nothing about him to indicate that he was destined to become one of the most notorious criminals of the north west. So it was with the greatest shock that he learned of Arthur's confession.

The above has not been written with any idea of arousing sympathy for Covell for he is responsible for the death of Mrs. Ebba Covell, and probably planned other murders, to be committed by his dues, but it helps substantiate the chiropractors' claim that the injury to his back and the pressure of bone splinters on his spinal cord had something to do with causing the development of his criminal proclivities.

Second: **DR. COVELL'S DAUGHTER TELLS OF MURDER**

The following story of the killing of her stepmother, Mrs. Ebba Covell, by Lucile Covell, the fourteen-year old daughter of Dr. Covell, the husband of the murdered woman, is the one she told a representative of the Coos Bay Times last Monday:

Lucile is very large for her age. She has blonde hair, bobbed, is pretty and attractive in manner but would impress one as having the manner of a girl sixteen or seventeen years old. She says she never knew a mother as her mother died when she was born.

The child has told those about her that she does not want to see her father because she is ashamed to see him.

Her story is the only detailed recital of the murder which has been made public, outside of the facts earned from the witnesses before the grand jury.

The girl will be the star witness in the case of Alton Covell who Monday pleaded not guilty to the charge of first degree murder and whose trial will be set at a date to be derided upon by Judge Kendall after consultation of the lawyers. Grant Colby, of Coquille, will defend Alton Covell.

Lucile is in charge of Juvenile Officer A. T. Morrison and wife. While her manner is quite cheerful and pleasant she admits that the horrors of the murder return to her mind and when she goes to a movie show she must direct her attention on the picture or the scene of the murder comes back before her eyes. She was told that likely she would be a witness in cases of her brother and her uncle.

"I don't see why they should want me," she said. "They seem to know everything. No, I was not the first one to tell. By heck, I never would have told anything but they told me the others had confessed and they showed me they had my uncle's notes, so I thought I might as well tell too. I told the grand jury that I did not know about the murder before hand but I did know. My uncle and Alton talked about it for a month and I knew it."

When asked why she did not tell her father that murder was planned the girl said:

"I thought it would all pass over. I did not think that they would ever really do it and, of course, I did not realize what it meant, I never saw but one dead person n my life. I saw a dead man once. Besides my father has a very bad temper and I feared if I told him my uncle and Alton were planning to kill my stepmother my father would hurt my uncle."

It was suggested to her that her silence had caused her stepmother's death, she said:

"Well I thought they never would really do it But it had to be done and uncle wanted Alton to do it. Alton hasn't a bit of nerve. He is slow in some things but when you get anything in his head once he knows it. He understands astrology. He went to a school of astrology in Portland. I know a little about it. The 'aspect' was right for September third they said to kill my stepmother. Alton will do anything for anyone he likes. He liked my uncle very much. My uncle is a fine man and Alton is a fine boy. He would not hurt anybody. He did not want kill my stepmother but it just had to be done."

The child could not tell why the murder had to be committed. She seemed to accept that as a fact. She said that the uncle told Alton he would do the killing himself if he could but being crippled was unable to do so and that it was up to Alton.

"I know Alton did not want to hurt anybody," the girl said. "He is an awfully nice boy. He didn't want to do it from the first but he thought about it for a long time. Yes, we had the ammonia for a month. Alton tells me everything he is going to do and everything he intends to do. The night before my stepmother was killed I knew what they were going to do. I was afraid tell about it. I was not afraid of my uncle. I knew he would not do anything to me but I was afraid tell my father."

"The morning my stepmother was killed my uncle was in the yard I was out of the house with the children. I did not see her killed. The children did not see it either and we were with my uncle. Alton killed her in the kitchen. I don't think I heard any screams but I heard a lot of noise like someone jumping around. Alton came out and told us what he had done."

"I went in and helped Alton pack her out of kitchen and put her on the sofa. Alton was pretty badly excited. I telephoned my father but I couldn't get him. My uncle telephoned my father and told him something terrible had happened and when my father came Alton went to the gate and met him."

"Alton was really sorry for what he had done." After it was over I was doing the washing and Alton said, "I am sorry I did it. I would not have it for the world." I said, "Yes I am sorry you did, too." When asked if Alton had done any other deeds of crime at the instigation of his uncle, the girl said:

"No, he did not do anything very bad. Yes, he stole some but not any more than most kids his age steal. The things he stole he took because it was something he wanted for himself."

The girl was asked if Alton set fire to the many houses which were burned at Bandon.

"Oh no!" she said, "He never set fire to any houses in Bandon. I am sure he never burned any houses for he would have told me if he did. I don't know why my uncle wanted to kill my stepmother. It had to be done. Uncle did not like her. She was quite a nice woman but they did not like each other. They never quarreled because they were never together. Alton took care of my uncle. I never would have told a word if the others had not told. I am sorry they did it but I thought it would all pass over. Alton and my uncle I like very much."

The girl is perfectly composed and common place in her discussion of the murder excepting that she seems to have accepted as a fact that the stepmother had to be killed. She is not able to give any motive excepting that the cripple and Mrs. Covell did not like each other. She says Mrs. Covell did not ever see any of Arthur's notes that she knows of.

When some suggestion was made to the girl about doing wrong and going to heaven she said: "Oh, I never expect to go to heaven. I have told too many lies."

The girl admits freely that she lied to the grand jury about her lack of knowledge of the plans for the murder and now says that she knew for a month ahead that it was to take place.

October 23, 1923 the *Coos Bay Times* headlined: **MAY STILL BUSY ON COVELL CASE**

Detective Luke May still insists that Arthur Covell's "book of revelations" was in code, and has given out a long story at Seattle to prove it, including also the code of letters and characters that stood for the letters of the alphabet. One revelation which May contends was in code was regarding the kidnaping of the little daughter of Mr. and Mrs. Roy Corson of Bandon. Concerning it the article says:

The Corson kidnaping plot was found in the astrologer's handwriting in double code, May said. Peggy the daughter according to the scheme, was to be seized first and a letter sent to the parents. This letter, prepared in advance, was found among Covell's documents, not coded, but in a sort of short hand.

Cryptic Message

It reads:

"Yr dau is be tak aw lo a dis p; f the co. If u ev wan lo so her al u mu do as we sa. No us to lo for yr da as u wi no fin he. Sh is sa & se & as to wh sli live ion li an than 30 d. he ar ou to. If wan yr da Pe ha ag do ex as we sa."

Usually, May said. Covell put his writings into this shorthand form then coded, making it unusually difficult to decipher. Apparently he had not finished with the Corson letter, which, fully expanded from the shorthand would read:

"Your daughter is to be taken away to a distant part of the country. If you ever want to see her at all, you must do as we say. No use to look for your daughter as you will not find her. She is safe and secure and as to whether she will live longer than thirty days, here are our terms. If you want your daughter Peggy back again, do exactly as we say."

Says Girl Is Bad

Concerning Lucille Covell. May has given out the following to a Seattle paper:

Letters from Lucille Covell to her crippled uncle, Arthur Covell were made public here yesterday by May revealing for the first time the loves and hates, the intrigues and the strange mental complex of the 14 years, a woman in stature, has ad- Covell murder case.

"This girl," said May; "a child in years, a woman in stature has admitted she knew of her uncle's scheme to have her stepmother suffocated with ammonia. She knew her brother, Alton, was to do the deed. Her letters now show what her attitude was when her own father was arrested for the crime and might have forfeited his life on the gallows had not the truth come out."

Calls Him "Sweetie"

When Lucille was in Bandon, the little Oregon sea coast town when the murder took place, and her uncle was in Portland, stopping with a woman astrologist, Mrs. C. E. Hecht, on March 19, months before the crime, the girl wrote-begging the uncle's pardon for a previous letter she had written him, "a snappy letter."

She addressed him as "Sweetie" and signed herself "Sis" his pet name for her. Her letter read in part:

My love affair is about the same. I haven't seen Harlan yet.

"Dad is having the house repaired and changed. What our dear mother liked and was happy with is not good enough for this High Horse. She is too toney. I wish I could come and see you, but the beautiful Mrs. High would not let me."

Despite her stepmother's wishes in the matter Lucille did go to Portland to visit her uncle. Her brother, too, was there. She stopped until she was taken back to Bandon, in the home of J.H. O'Malley between Portland and Vancouver, Wash., according to May.

Girl Admits Theft

"I asked her," May said, "where she obtained the money to make this trip. She admitted she had taken it from her stepmother's mother Mrs. Wiren."

Her next letter to the astrologer uncle contained the following:

"I wish you would send me a chart and tell me when I will ever be as pretty as some of these movie stars, and if I will ever be one."

"Dad said when you go to the hospital again he is going to have Alton come back and learn some Bible. (Hell.)"

Then, on September 3, came the killing of Mrs. Covell, the stepmother, with Lucille, according to the confession in the case, standing in the yard outside the house where the death struggle was taking place, guarding the smaller children until it was over. This is the letter received by the judge after her brother was arrested following the release of her father on bail:

"m writing you asking why don't you let Alton have a chance on that $10,000 bond like you did dad."

"Looks to me you don't know half what you are doing. I could be a better justice of peace and officers than any of you people."

"Alton is innocent and you ought to know it."

"You set up there and let Dad get off on that amount of money so he can kill a dozen other wives.

I would stake my life anytime that Alton is innocent. Why don't you open your eyes and see things?"

"I Will Take Your Job"

"Then you call my brother feeble-minded. If he is feeble-minded, you are all feeble-minded."

"He is hard of hearing and you have to explain things to him. You don't understand that. Dad has put all the blame on Alton. You don't understand that either. If you don't see this in a different light I will take your job myself."

Yours truly,
"Lucille Covell."

October 26, 1923 the Coquille *Valley Sentinel* headlined: **NO ONE DID IT ALL** — Luke S. May Gives Credit to All Connected with Covell Investigation

Seattle, Wash., Oct. 24, 1923.

Editor Sentinel: — I have just received a clipping from the *Coos Bay Times* of October 13th.

To make my position clear as to who should receive the credit for the solution of the Covell case, I will thank you to print the following statement.

For very obvious reasons I cannot at this time divulge certain interesting things about this case, which may come out at the proper time, and I would not make a statement of any kind at this time if this article did not directly damage my reputation by untrue allegations. Falsely alleging that I claimed sole credit for unraveling the case and on the other hand containing untrue statements about the manner in which the confessions were obtained from Alton Covell and the theories Coos County Officials and I held about Doctor Covell's guilt.

A statement, "that Alton Covell did not give me, personally, a complete written account of the murder, in the presence of Sheriff Ellingsen, several hours before he appeared before the Grand Jury," is also erroneous.

When Alton Covell made this confession I reported it to District Attorney Fisher direct. He then asked me to show it to the Grand Jury and I delivered it to them before Alton had ever appeared before that body.

No one person or separate group of persons should claim full credit for solving any case, and for any individual or separate group of individuals to claim the whole credit on this particular case would be childish, and statement by any person to the effect that "I have made such a claim," is grossly misinformed. In every instance, I have stated as I do now that the Grand Jury, the Sheriff's office, the District Attorney. Justice of Peace Radley and Doctor Mingus, were all necessary factors in the solution of this case. Contrary to published statement, "that the officials were entirely at sea," I want to state at this time that the whole affair worked out as foreseen by Sheriff Ellingsen, District Attorney Fisher, Sam Malehorn and myself, and our plans included the assistance of the Grand Jury.

When the Grand Jury convened Coos County was exceptionally fortunate in having the best Grand Jury it has ever been my pleasure to work with. They were not only men of intelligence but willing to work. We were particularly fortunate in the selection of Matt May as foreman. He deserves the whole-hearted appreciation of every loyal Coos County citizen, for his initiative and hard work not only in the Covell case but in the other matter handled by the Grand Jury. There was at all times the closest cooperation between Matt May, foreman of the Grand Jury, District Attorney Fisher, Sheriff Ellingsen, and myself. Every one connected with the case worked hard and unselfishly with no thought of individual credit. It was the most striking example of whole-hearted co-operation in my whole experience. If petty jealousies and selfish motives could be set aside in all other communities as completely as evidenced in this case, crime would be reduced to a minimum.

Regarding Arthur Covell's last confession, this was secured by the Grand Jury, but to eliminate the work done by the Sheriff, District Attorney and others, leading up to the final confession, and to give any one individual more credit than the others in this particular, would be like the man who comes along after a large building is almost completed, drives the last nail and then declares, "I built that house." The newspaper men played no small part, by keeping the fact secret that I was in Coos county making an investigation until the secret part of it was completed. This materially helped in the exoneration of Dr. Covell, because we were able to obtain full unbiased statements from people who would otherwise have kept still and I wish to thank you for your assistance in this regard. I have yet to find the newspaper who will break a confidence when the interests of justice are at stake, and he is requested to assist in his professional capacity.

This has certainly been demonstrated to be true in this case, for almost daily, men from the press interviewed me on the progress of the investigation and many of the theories advanced by them turned out to be true.

I will thank you to make this statement, for everyone who assisted deserves credit for assistance they rendered in clearing up what at first looked like a real mystery.

With kindest of personal regards and hoping to meet you again in the near future, I am

Sincerely yours,
"L.S. May"

On November 8, 1923 the *Coos Bay Times* headlined: **COVELL PRESENTS PATHETIC PICTURE — DEFENDANT IN MURDER TRIAL SHOWS PRISON PALLOR** — Jurymen Selected Are All of High Standing and of Substantial Positions

COQUILLE, Ore., Nov. 8. — When court adjourned yesterday for short recess there was a pathetic incident noticed but by few. It was a time when everyone went out into the corridors for a rest and a smoke. Judge, jurors, lawyers, court officials and all connected with the case went out of the court room — all but one. In the portion of the court room where the trial is conducted there was one man left alone because he could not move without assistance.

Arthur Covell, the defendant, a cripple who cannot walk, was stretched out on his cot, for that moment forgotten. No one was there to talk to him. He was absolutely alone in the room. From the skylight directly above his cot shone down the bright sunlight and intensified the helplessness of his condition. Like an injured man in a hospital his head was half buried in two pillows. A big pillow was laid over part of his body and on this he rests his hands.

Shows Prison Pallor

The beard he wears seems to make sharper the lines of his drawn face. His prison pallor makes his eyes which he sometimes turns toward some object or person in the court room, seem more piercing. His attire of rusty coat and faded overalls does not add to his appearance and the coarse socks which hang loosely above his shoe tops seem to cry out with the utter uselessness of his bony and wasted legs.

A position on his back with his face turned upward seems to be the most comfortable for the cripple, alleged schemer of murder and crime, and he seems to look out of the glass covered opening above him as though searching for the stars on which he depended to guide him in his great program of criminal acts, which his astrological notes are claimed to have shown.

Can See But Little

The defendant sees but few persons during the course of the trial. He can turn his head and get a partial view of the court room but such action is with much effort and evident pain. The front of the clerk's desk obstructs the view of the judge on the bench and his own attorney must be seated in a position facing the jury and witness stand and with his back to the defendant.

This is the human physical derelict whom the jurymen must say likewise a mental wreck and fit subject for an insane asylum, or much decide that he is guilty of murder in the first degree and must pay the penalty of death by hanging, although the defendant could not stand on his feet on the gallows.

Sentiment Barred

Jurymen and Jurywomen before they are accepted had to say that the condition of the cripple on the cot before them would not influence them or cause them to hesitate to return a verdict of hanging if guilt is proved. It is a requirement of the law that sentiment shall not sway a jury in decision and that the condition of a defendant does not lessen the magnitude of a crime if guilt is proved.

Miserable Appearance

When Covell is being carried into the court room from the county jail his appearance is even more miserable. A crumpled, helpless, useless remnant of physical humanity he is packed to and from the court room while justice is being worked out to decide what shall be his fate for the part he played in the murder of Mrs. Ebba Covell.

Whatever may be that fate Covell cannot complain of the conduct of his trial or the makeup of the jury. The case is being conducted with the utmost care and Judge Kendall has taken pains that every point in the examination of jurors be carried out according to law. The persons selected as members of the jury are all of high standing and of substantial position in the community. The lawyers and court officials congratulate themselves on the class of men and women who were with much ease chosen for the case.

Jurors Well Known

Covell, according to representation made, is penniless and it was necessary for the court to appoint a lawyer to defend him as he could not employ an attorney. The members of the jury who will decide the fate of this man of physical and financial poverty, represent a good deal of individual wealth and in some cases are representatives of the big interests of the community.

Mrs. Elisabeth Goss is the wife of John Goss, one of the prominent members of the legal profession. Mrs. Sloan is a well known Coquille woman. W. J. Conrad is a member of the firm of Adelsperger and Conrad, big timber owners and dealers. Lester Dement represents a prominent family of cattlemen and is engaged in logging operations. W. C. Swaine is logging superintendent for the Coos Bay Lumber company. O. W. Fensler is a well known merchant of Myrtle Point and John Kronholm is also a well known man of Coos Bay and represents the mercantile business. Thomas Manly and Richard Danielson are both ranchers of Bandon and men of good standing in the community where the defendant resided. A. Y. Myers also among those tentatively chosen is in the real estate and lumber business and C. A. Sanford represents the carpentry trade and resided in North Bend. So the members of the jury are reliable representatives of various walks of life and come from different sections of the county.

Mr. Danielson was the only one of the jurors who had any acquaintance with the Covell family. He stated that he knew Mrs. Covell, the murdered woman, and her husband, Dr. Fred Covell but was not acquainted with the defendant nor Alton Covell or the other children.

Allowed Newspapers

The question of newspaper publicity entered a good deal into the case. Judge Kendall said it would be impossible to get 12 competent persons who had not read of the case and all he asked was that those who had read the newspapers and formed an opinion be willing to set aside the opinion formed from the newspaper accounts and try the case entirely on the evidence presented in court. All of the jurors said they could without difficulty set aside what opinion they had formed from reading of the case.

Judge Kendall asked the jurors not to discuss the case with anyone but said he thought it was useless to ask them not to read the newspapers. He said he thought the newspapers would print only what occurred in the progress of the trial and that there could no harm come from the jurors reading the papers.

Worked Smoothly

That the jury was secured so easily was a matter of some surprise. It was feared that it would be necessary to spend much time and examine a large number of persons before a jury could be selected but the work progressed with much more speed than was anticipated. The jury could probably have been all closed before last night had not the regular panel been exhausted. The special venire was not to report until this morning

November 9, 1923 the *Coquille Valley Sentinel* headlined: **COVELL ON TRIAL** — Arthur Covell Case Started Yesterday Morning — Much Interest Manifested

At 10:15 yesterday morning two ladies and ten men had been accepted for jury duty in the case of the State of Oregon vs. Arthur Covell, indicted for first degree murder, and on trial for that crime.

The trial started Wednesday morning and the speed with which the jury was selected - six hours and ten minutes - is something new in a case of this prominence. The following is a list of those who will decide the fate Arthur Covell, when the attorneys have made their final arguments and Judge Kendall has given his instructions:

Lester T. Dement, banker, Myrtle Point.
Elizabeth H. Goss, housewife, Marshfield.
W.C. Swain, log superintendent, Powers.
Thos. Hanly, rancher, Bandon.
W.J. Conrad, timber operator, Marshfield.
John J. Kronholm, merchant, North Bend.
Clara B. Sloan, housewife, Coquille.
C.W. Fensler, merchant, Myrtle Point.
Richard Danielson, dairyman, Parkersburg.
A.Y. Meyers, coal operator, Marshfield.
Chester A. Sanford, carpenter, North Bend.
August J. Hoelling, hardware salesman, Marshfield.

In opening the case, District Attorney Ben S. Fisher told the court the known facts leading up to the murder and started what the state would attempt to prove by its witnesses. The story was practically the same as made public in the press at the time of the grand jury indictment.

Claud Giles, attorney for Covell, did not outline his plan of defense but left it to develop as the case progressed. He stated that the state would find it impossible to prove all the charges made.

The first witness called by the state was W.R. Mavity, Bandon undertaker, who told of the bruises on the body of Mrs. Fred Covell, and the particular marks on her face, which were first pink, then scarlet, then dark red.

He was followed by his sister, Mrs. Annie Mundy, who also viewed the body.

Dr. Leep, of Bandon, and Mingus, of Marshfield, testified as to the marks and bruises on the body, and the latter testified that in his opinion, Mrs. Covell came to her death from suffocation caused by a caustic alkali applied to her nose and mouth.

For two or three hours Dr. Fred Covell was on the stand yesterday afternoon and on cross examination was grilled by attorney Giles, whose questions indicating that he might be going to plead his clients innocence by charging with originating the crime.

The doctor was on the stand again this morning and was followed by his daughter, Lucille, who admitted that she knew a month before hand that her stepmother was going to be killed at eleven o'clock on the morning of Monday, Sept. 3. She also testified that she assisted Alton in carrying Mrs. Covell into the bedroom.

When R.A. Jeub, one of the grand jury which indicted Arthur Covell, was called to the stand about eleven o'clock Mr. Giles gave further indication of what his line of defense is to be when he objected to certain testimony - Arthur's written confession to the grand jury on the plea that it was made through fear. Not fear for his own life, but for the safety of Alton Covell, his nephew.

Mr. Jeub was questioned regarding the means of securing Covell's confession and the assertion was repeatedly made by Mr. Giles that Arthur knew that Alton and Lucille had confessed and his confession was induced through fear for them.

As this matter had a very important bearing on the case, Judge Kendall asked Mr. Giles to give authorities in support of his claim that the confession of Arthur should be not be considered because of his fear, and to give the attorney time to look them up, he adjourned court at 11:20 until 1:15 this afternoon.

As was the case yesterday the court was packed, every seat being taken, but the judge will not permit the aisles to be filled by people standing

During the long hours of the morning and afternoon judge Kendall ordered a recess of 15 minutes, the court room cleared and the windows thrown wide open for ventilation purposes.

Up to this noon's adjournment Arthur had not been on the stand in his own behalf, but Mr. Giles has announced that he would be called later.

Court officials are predicting the case will be given to the jury before tomorrow evening.

One of the exhibits introduced as evidence is the photograph of the dead woman, showing the nose, chin, check, part of the throat and spots on the eyebrow where the ammonia burned the flesh, giving it a leathery or bloody appearance. It is a very gruesome picture and almost anyone would know from looking at it that her death was not an accident.

November 9, 1923 the *Coos Bay Harbor* headlined: **COVELL MURDER TRIAL IN PROGRESS MAY FINISH LATE SATURDAY** — Two Women Chosen on the Jury, Probably Most Notable Case Ever Heard in Coos County, and is Attracting Nation-Wide Attention.

Arthur Covell went to trial Wednesday morning at Coquille for his participation in the murder of Mrs. Fred Covell, his brother's wife, at the family home on a ranch south of a Bandon last September third. The case has attracted unusual attention from all parts of the United States and because of the peculiar angles, is noted and being read with avidity everywhere the news dispatches are issued.

Covell was interested in astrology and according to records obtained by officers who visited the Covell home and secured papers, he had been doing a thriving business in casting horoscopes for more than a few prominent people along the Pacific coast, among them many in the Hollywood colony, all of whom were able to afford such amusements.

Covell was named accessory and the officers held that it was his influence which caused the death of the woman, through urgency upon his nephew, Alton, a large 15 year old youth, to put the woman out of the way. Both Arthur Covell confessed their parts in the murder, Alton saying that he held an ammonia-saturated rag to Mrs. Covell's nostrils and mouth until she succumbed.

Evidence of the truth of this statement was corroborated by discolorations which came out upon the woman's face following her death. It was said that parts of her face were black, a day or so after death.

Because of the expectation that selection of a jury might be a slow proceeding and that many would be rejected, Judge John C. Kendall ordered an unusual venire for the opening of the case, asking for 31 men and women to be on hand to possibly sit on the most famous case that has occurred in Coos county.

Those who were called for the first day included:

Fred McClellan, August Hoelling; John H. Stadden, Thos. Sumerlin, C. A. Lagerstrom, Elizabeth Adams, George Haines, Charles Kaiser, Ralph Thom, Charles Kennedy, Fred Lyster, Clara Krantz, John Luttrell, Roy Landrith, Herman Banks. Stella Bynon. John Beloni, Henry Hess, J. W. Asplund, Nels Austad, Frances Stack, George Slagle, Stella Denning, Lafe Compton, Alfred Rodine, F. L. Greenough, Howard Imhoff, Isabelle Tower.

Much surprise was occasioned at the county seat on Wednesday when fine and unexpected progress made in the selection of a jury for the Arthur Covell case and a temporary jury would have been chosen before the day was over, had it not been that the venire ran out and Judge Kendall had to adjourn court until the next day.

As it was, nine men and two women were sitting in the jury box when the recess was called at three o'clock.

Rapidity of progress was due in considerable part to a statement made by Judge Kendall in which he said that there was no reason as he viewed the situation that because people had read accounts of the Covell case that they might not be able to consider the evidence according to the testimony and eliminate from their minds any opinions they may have formed.

The accused crippled Arthur Covell was taken into the court room by men from the jail. He was carried on a cot, not being able to travel. The cot was set down in the vicinity of the desk of Miss Ines Bunch, the county clerk, and Covell's attorney, Claude Giles was sitting just in front, where he could consult the prisoner if he found it necessary.

Those who had been accepted temporarily when court adjourned on the first day included: Mayor Henry Schroeder, Myrtle Point, a furniture dealer; Lester Dement, rancher of the same city; Mrs. John D. Goss, Marshfield; Mrs. Clara B. Sloan, Coquille; W. C. Swain, logging superintendent for the Smith-Powers company, John Kronholm, North Bend, clothier; A. Y. Meyers, Marshfield, real estate; Richard Danielson, Bandon; C. W. Fensler, Myrtle Point, clothier; W. J. Conrad, Marshfield, mill and timber operator; Thos. Hanly, rancher on the Coquille river and Bandon port commissioner.

The questions asked by counsel for the defense during examination of the jurors indicated that the defense might possibly be on a different line than had generally been expected. Most people had been looking forward to a plea of insanity. Wednesday's questioning did not point that way.

Attorney Giles was insistent on prospective jurors answering two questions to his satisfaction; one of these referred to Covell being an astrologer and the jurors were asked if that fact could create any prejudice in their minds; the second question was whether the fact of Covell's having first pleaded guilty and later withdrawn the plea and pleaded not guilty would be considered as probably proving Covell's guilt; Attorney Giles also asked each juror if he or she were opposed to capital punishment.

District Attorney Ben S. Fisher is appearing in the case for the state and of course asked of all prospective jurors whether they are opposed to capital punishment and in particular if they would feel squeamish about hanging a guilty person if proven so, and was a cripple.

A number who were examined said they opposed capital punishment and of course were not accepted. Ellis Dement, of Myrtle Point, who was excused, had formed an opinion from newspaper accounts, which he thought was so deeply implanted that evidence would not change it. He was, of course, excused.

One man who was accepted, W. C. Swain, admitted having an opinion, but said that it was not impossible for his mind to be changed.

Covell was paler than when he first went to the county jail, if that were possible. He has been a sufferer for the past three years and naturally became sallow and showed the lack of outdoors life and exercise.

Covell's eyes are dark and keen, his beard which he wears in Van Dyke style is also black. He is wearing the same clothes he had when he was taken to jail. Because of his injuries the prisoner insists that no style be used in his dress and since the first, has been attired in overalls. His coat, one, which he wore while on the farm, where the murder of his sister-in-law occurred, is faded and his appearance in general is such as to cause pity from an unprejudiced spectator.

The prisoners in the jail had made his appearance as presentable as possible and it appeared that he had recently had his beard trimmed and cut down rather close.

The Covell trial got well under way by Thursday morning and the expected delay in getting started was not realized.

Judge Kendall, who is showing new ideas in affairs of court, was responsible for the speeding up of jury examinations and getting the case to trial. Judge Kendall several times interposed explanations, which hurried the proceedings. For instance, the counsel for the state and for the defense was not in the court room yesterday morning at the time court was to be called to order. Judge Kendall sent Bailiff Nosler out to round them up when they appeared, advised them that nine o'clock didn't mean ten.

In the instructions to the jurymen and jurywomen, Judge Kendall said that he did not feel it necessary to warn the jury against reading the newspaper, as often occurs in court trials.

He said he believed the jury, which had already been examined along the line of possibility, was capable of judging without considering anything that would appear in the papers. Judge Kendall believed that all that could be said pro or con, relative to the case had been exploited and all that remained would be evidence and the jurors would be hearing that before it would be printed in the papers.

District Attorney Fisher, on Thursday was able to make his opening statement by ten o'clock, for the 12 members of the jury had been chosen and the box was full. Mr. Fisher went over a review of the case from a time in last July, when Arthur Covell had returned from being treated in Portland and went to his brother's ranch below Bandon where he was to be kept by his brother Fred Covell and family until further arrangements.

"It was there," said the district attorney, "that Arthur Covell had time to ponder his designs upon his brother's wife."

It was possible, according to Mr. Fisher's argument, that the family jealously between the woman and the cripple was what started Arthur Covell's mind on the road to murderous intent. Arthur Covell, returning to Bandon, remained on the main floor of the home for a few days and was then moved to the second story because Mrs. Covell wanted him out of the way.

Mr. Fisher said that the state would show that Arthur Covell had a tremendous influence over Alton Covell, who is suspected to be the real murderer, and also over Lucille Covell, the girl of 14, whom he said was called into some of the plotting with the cripple and the brother Alton.

In this talk Mr. Fisher told of the purchase of ammonia at Bandon the agency which the plotters used in ridding the house of the presence of Mrs. Covell. The person who bought the ammonia was not named but it was either the boy Alton or the girl, Lucille, for they were the only ones in the plot, and the details of the affair were kept unbeknown to any but the trio.

Attorney Claud Giles brought out three particular interesting items in the address to the jury, on opening. Mr. Giles said they would have no experts to give testimony as they had no money to pay for such evidence; that Arthur Covell would be placed upon the stand in his own defense and that he would at that time make no statement relative to the line his defense of the prisoner would follow. That would develop with the evidence as the trial proceeded, Mr. Giles told the jury, and court.

Four or five witnesses were examined during the first day of trial, including Dr. R. V. Leep, Undertaker Mavity, a woman of Bandon and Dr. E. Mingus, of Marshfield.

Dr. Leep told of the many bruises upon the body and discoloration of the woman's face after death. It was not until Detective Luke May, came into the case a week later that Dr. Mingus was called in and this was at the time the body was exhumed. Dr. Mingus said on the stand that his opinion on seeing the face of the dead woman was that she had been burned by a caustic alkaloid and based his opinion upon the leathery appearance of her skin. All the doctors who gave testimony yesterday said that the bruises upon the body were not sufficient to have caused death.

The defendant was not expected to be called to the stand today, as it was thought the prosecution would last over until Saturday.

Attorney Giles said that many new angles would be brought out during the trial and there would be some surprising things disclosed. He also said that the state would be unable to prove many assertions, which has been made by the district attorney.

Chester Sanford, a carpenter of North Bend, and August Hoelling of Marshfield, clerk at the Ekblad Hardware store, were the two jurymen added on Thursday morning.

November 9, 1923 the *Coos Bay Times* reported the court appearances of Dr. Fred Covell and his daughter Lucile. First is the article of Fred Covell headlined: **DR. FRED COVELL TELLS HIS STORY — BROTHER OF DEFENDANT PUT ON WITNESS STAND** — Chiropractor Tells of First Knowledge of Wife's Death and How He Found Her.

COQUILLE, Ore., Nov. 9. — Dr. Fred Covell was called to the witness stand yesterday afternoon. He was asked all about his family and his home and the details of events leading up to the murder. In the course of remarks Dr. Covell said that he and his wife and three children lived on the lower floor of the house. Arthur and Alton slept in one bed upstairs and Lucile in another room upstairs. When Arthur returned home from Portland in July he was taken to the farm house. His bed was not ready so he was put on the sofa in the front room. Mrs. Covell objected to this because it occupied the front room and Arthur was moved upstairs.

The Sunday before the murder Dr. Covell and all members of the family went to the beach. Mrs. Covell was normal on that occasion but Alton was reticent. The doctor was asked if his wife was crying while on the picnic and the doctor said he thought not as he would have known it if she had been. He said she seemed to enjoy herself and have a very pleasant day.

Doctor Leaves Early

On the morning of the murder the doctor said he arose about 6 o'clock, his usual time. Two of the children played with their mother while she was still in bed. The doctor left the house about 8:30 for his office at Bandon. Mrs. Covell, as was her custom, with the baby went a short distance in the car with the doctor and then went back home. She was in a hurry because she intended to do the washing and was anxious to get Lucile's clothes ready for school. This was the last the doctor saw of her alive.

After he had been at the office and had telephoned once to his wife to ask her what she wanted him to bring home from town, he got a telephone call from Arthur saying something terrible had happened and for him to come home. He went at once. He first saw Alton, who looked very pale. Alton had one of the little children with him. The doctor asked him what was the matter. Alton did not answer, probably because he is a little deaf and had a bad cold and probably did not hear the question. Lucile then said that "mama was sick" and in the house. The doctor said that he found Mrs. Covell on the bed. He noticed the peculiar mark on her face but did not know what caused it. Mrs. Covell had at times suffered fainting spells and he thought possibly that she had died in a spell. He tried to revive her but without result and finally the body started to become rigid. The doctor said he know then that she was beyond recovery and he took the little children in to see her. He then told Gladys, the oldest of the three little children, that her mother was gone and they sat down and cried some.

Arthur Gives Sympathy

The doctor said he then went upstairs and saw Arthur. The latter said: "Fred, I am sorry for you that Ebba is gone. You have had more than your share of trouble and I feel very sorry for you."

Dr. Covell said that Arthur was very fond of Alton and Lucile but not so fond of the other children, as he had raised Alton and Lucile. The doctor said he had always tried to be a loyal brother to Arthur.

The doctor said he tried to get central on the telephone and finally got a message over the phone to the parents of his wife, Capt. and Mrs. Wiren, at Gardiner he also sent word to the undertaker. The latter arrived and expressed his sympathy and asked if Mrs. Covell had been sick long, and the doctor said she had not been ill at all lately that he knew of but told of the fainting spells.

Did Not Suspect Murder

The doctor told of some marks on his wife's body but said that he did not suspect anything wrong until the examination was made at the undertaking establishment. He said that the next day he did not go the undertaker's until late in the day because he had some visitors who had come to express sympathy. The officers told him they did not want to talk to him until 8 o'clock at night and he went at that time and was placed under arrest.

On the cross examination by Attorney Giles which was very close, the doctor explained why he did not go to town earlier the day after the murder. Mr. Giles asked if he was not afraid to be around Bandon and the witness said not. He had callers and wanted to receive their sympathies and therefore did not get away until late.

Is Cross Examined

"What did you go down town for?" asked Mr. Giles. "I went to see what they had learned."

"What you had learned? What the officers had learned in the investigation."

What made you think there would be an investigation? "Because of the mark on her face."

Then why did you not call the doctors or officers right away when you saw the mark on the face and knew that it would mean an investigation? "My heart was full. I was stunned by the death and did not think of it."

Mr. Giles then asked a question but there was an objection. Mr. Giles said; "I want the question answered because I wish to show the attitude of the witness. I want to show that his attitude was not regarding the defendant but that it was an attitude of protecting himself."

Objection Sustained

Mr. Fisher objected and said the matter was not one which should be discussed in the presence of the jury. The judge said such was the case and that any discussion on that point must be with the jury excluded.

Court then adjourned for the day to resume the cross examination of Dr. Covell this morning.

Regarding Arthur's condition in the course of his testimony Dr Covell said that Arthur during the last six months had changed some what in his humor and was easily upset by matters which ordinarily would not have bothered him.

Radley on Stand

At the afternoon session yesterday Justice Radley was called to the stand to tell of a conversation he had with members of the Covell family. He said that he told Lucile if she stuck by the story she told it would hang Alton Arthur Covell asked how they could do that and said that if they tried to hang Alton he would have something to say about it.

Undertaker Mavity was called to the stand again and asked about the clothing which was worn by Mrs. Covell. He said that she wore underwear of the union suit kind of medium weight, and when questioned closely said that the underclothes extended down to a point between the ankles and the knees.

Surroundings Examined

Attorney Giles asked some questions regarding the surroundings at the Covell home. Justice Radley was questioned regarding a gulch at the back of the house and the timber surrounding it. He said that while investigating at the premises he went through the brush for about 75 yards and struck a trail which led to the main road. He said it was possible for a person to go from the house that way but said he did not find any tracks when he made the examination, which was several days after the murder.

Deputy Sheriff Sam Malehorn testified about talking with Arthur Covell the first day he investigated the murder and then the day after. Arthur did not have much to say. Malehorn told him Dr. Covell had been arrested and told the cripple that he suspected him also of knowing something of the crime. Arthur then had nothing more to say, the deputy testified.

Relates Incident

Charles Rickert testified about an incident in 1920. He said the Covell family was residing in Bandon and Arthur Covell engaged him to take him to the Covell farm. On that occasion Arthur said he did not want to stay at the house in town because he did not like Mrs. Covell. On cross-examination the witness said that he never had any trouble with Arthur and knew him well and had found him easy to get along with.

The second article headlined: **LUCILLE COVELL TELLS COMPLETE STORY AT TRIAL** — Niece of Defendant Gives Clear Testimony of Mother's Murder. — **WITNESS PERFECTLY COOL AND CONTAINED** — Defense May Prove Arthur Covell Sacrificed Life for Children **TECHNICALITIES DISCUSSED** — Girl Makes Attractive Appearance on Stand — Smiles as She Tells Horrible Story of Crime — Testimony Clear

COQUILLE. Oregon, November 9. Lucile Covell, 14-year-old daughter of Dr. Fred Covell and niece of the defendant, was put on the witness stand this morning. She told her story of the crime and how she knew all about the plans for a month ahead and then after she helped Alton carry the dead body of the woman he had murdered from the kitchen to another part of the house, prepared a meal and she and Alton and the children ate lunch in the kitchen where the murder had occurred, while the body was in the front room.

While they were eating Dr. Covell, who had been called by Arthur, arrived at the house.

Witness Attractive

Lucile was attired in a tastefully made dress of silk pongee the same color as her flaxen hair, which is cut Dutch boy. She wore a string of pearl beads. The neck of her dress which was cut low, was faced with lace, and her clear complexion touched with color in the cheek showed brightly under the light of the court room. She appeared quit pretty and attractive, smiling; much of the time while she was testifying and was perfectly cool and self-contained. She answered the questions and did not seem at all excited at any time.

In the course of her testimony she said that she knew of the murder plans for a month ahead and that Alton had bought the ammonia a month before the killing. She said she did not tell because she never thought it would really take place.

Feared Her Father

The girl also said that she did not tell because her father had a bad temper and she feared that he might hurt her uncle. On the morning of the murder she took the children from the house at 11 o'clock am took them down in the gulch back of the house. Alton carried Arthur out of the house and put him in the yard and she went to where Arthur was seated. She heard scuffling in the house and later Alton came out. Later she went into the house and helped Alton carry the dead woman to another part of the house. She then prepared lunch for the children and she and Alton and the children ate lunch.

The witness said she tried to get her father on the telephone but failed and then Arthur got him on the phone and said something awful had happened and the doctor came home. Arthur was then taken upstairs. The girl said that throughout the day she was busy about the house doing the housework. Before Mrs. Covell was killed the girl and the others ate breakfast with her as usual.

Closely Cross-Examined

The girl was cross-examined closely by Attorney Giles. She insisted she feared what her father might do to her uncle if she told and that her father had a very bad temper.

When the girl was first put on the stand Attorney Giles objected to the state trying to prove the crimes through a co-conspirator. Mr. Giles then made his argument on the question of corpus delicti not being established. The court overruled the objection and Mr. Giles asked the exceptions to this ruling be put in the record.

No Corpus Delicti

When Lucile Covell was put on the stand Giles objected to using her to prove death. He claimed the corpus delicti had not been established.

Giles said that two doctors could not give the cause of death. The theory of only one doctor was that the woman was killed by ammonia and the same doctor said the lips were not burned and he said there was nothing to show that there was any ammonia in the lungs. Mr. Giles held that the state must show every allegation in the indictment and claimed that there had been no proof that Ebba Covell was killed by any particular means or any particular person. He held that there was nothing so far to show that Alton Covell had anything to do with the crime.

Proof Held Necessary

Giles held that the corpus delicti must be proved before there was any case and that it had not been proved. The attorney held that the case had not been proved there had been a crime committed. Mr. Giles held that the commission of a crime must be showed before a corpus delicti could be established.

Judge Kendall said he felt that there was evidence to establish a corpus delicti but as to whether there is sufficient evidence is a matter for the jury to determine. The objection was overruled and Mr. Giles asked that the records show exceptions to the line of defense and that the state admits the witness is a co-conspirator. Mr. Fisher said the state admitted nothing about the witness being a co-conspirator.

Church Testifies

Superintendent Church of the county poor farm was called to the stand. He told of talking with the cripple and said that the latter told him he wanted to take all the responsibility because he was to blame and that he did not want to see the children suffer. Ray Jeub, one of the members' of the grand jury, was called. He was asked about the visit of the grand jury to the poor farm to interview Arthur Covell. The prosecutor told Arthur that all previous promises were called off and that his confession might change the blame of guilty but could do no other good.

Attorneys Argue Point

The question then arose as to whether Arthur was made to give his confession for fear of Alton's fate. This brought an objection and the lawyers started to argue. Judge Kendall said that this was a very important point, and he gave the attorneys time to look up their authorities. Court took a recess until 1 o'clock when the arguments were resumed.

To Protect Nephew

Attorney Giles apparently from the course of his cross-examination today intends to attempt to show that the defendant, Arthur Covell, being in a crippled condition and not caring whether he lived or died, assumes the responsibility of the crime to protect his nephew Alton. It may be that Mr. Giles will try to show that Arthur, instead of being the murderous man he has been accused of, is sacrificing himself for the-other members of his family.

Exhibits Paper

A scrap of paper on which there was some writing was shown to Lucile Covell. She identified the writing as that of Arthur Covell. Among, other notes which referred to the children were the words; "6:20 a. m. Sept. 3, Monday. Will Al do his part."

This was introduced as evidence and as an exhibit in the case.

November 10, 1923 the *Coos Bay Times* headlined: **CRIPPLE APEARS BEFORE COURT IN LIGHT OF MARTYR** — Arthur Covell Repudiates Written Confession From Witness Stand — **MURDER TRIAL TAKES SENSATIONAL TURN** — Defendant Tells of Making Confession to Save Sixteen-Year-Old — **CHILDREN TOLD TO DO SAME** — Astrologer Charged with Murder Denies Knowledge of Planned Murder to the Jury from His Cot as Witness Stand

COQUILLE, Ore., Nov. 10. — Dramatic to the extreme and fruitful of sudden and sensational surprise was the testimony of Arthur Covell, defendant in the murder case, when he was put on the stand in his own behalf late yesterday afternoon. The crippled astrologer repudiated his former confession which he claimed was false denied that he had planned the murder or knew anything about it and claimed that he assumed the responsibility for the crime because of his love for his nephew, Alton Covell, aged 16, who indicted for actually killing Mrs. Covell.

Covell appeared before the jury in the light of a martyr who was attempting to sacrifice himself for the sake of others.

Guilty or Innocent

Apparently it will be up to the jury to decide whether Covell is guilty of first degree murder or is entirely innocent of any crime in connection with the murder.

Covell was not called to the stand until about 4 p m. His cot was moved up in front of the jury box At first he remained in a reclining position but soon raised up on his elbows and stayed in that position as long as he could and after resting on his back again rested on his elbows. Most of the time he directly faced the jury. He answered the questions clearly and distinctly.

Unusual Incident

It was a most unusual incident. The helpless man who has been painted a murderous schemer of the blackest kind faced the jury members who are to decide his fate and told the story of his claimed sacrifice for those he loved and wished to protect. It was evident that the jury must decide whether he is a fiend or a self sacrificing man who was willing to risk his life and liberty for the sake of others.

In the course of the examination by Mr. Giles, Covell said that he did not know who committed the murder or how Mrs. Covell died excepting what he had since heard. He said he did not scheme the murder and did not talk with the children regarding it. He said that the statement made by Lucile that he told Alton to go in the house and kill Mrs. Covell was untrue and that she made it because he told her to do so.

Tells Story

Describing the morning of the alleged murder. Covell told of the unusual movements about the household. He said that while he was in the yard Alton had gone for the cow and later came out of the house and said that "something was the matter with mama" and that she was on the floor of the kitchen. He told Alton and Lucile to see if she had fainted and carry her to the bed. He was brought into the house and it became evident that Mrs. Covell was dead. He wanted to call a physician at once but did not feel that he should take the responsibility until Dr. Covell returned. He called the doctor on the telephone and said something awful had happened.

The witness recited the other movements as told by other witnesses. He said he had Alton take him upstairs soon after they found Mrs. Covell because he was so excited he feared he would fall over in a faint.

Fear for "Papa"

After the arrest of the doctor the witness said Alton and Lucile talked with him a long time that night. The children asked if he thought they "might hang papa," because of the death and because he was arrested. The witness said he told the children sometimes circumstantial evidence was had against a man.

Alton said that before he would them hang his father he would take the blame for killing Mrs. Covell but the witness told him not to do anything rash but to await developments.

To Save Alton

Covell said he feared Alton would make a "mess" of things and that when Detective May called upon him at the poor farm he was shown a written confession, which was given the grand jury and was introduced as evidence. He did not give the confession to the district attorney until he asked whether Alton would be released. The attorney said that would be up to the grand jury. He also asked if Alton would be sent to a feeble-minded institution, as he did not want to see him sent there. He then took the confession out from under the bed covering and gave it to the prosecutor and grand jury.

Will Not Help

"Why did you make that false confession." asked Mr. Giles.

"Because I wanted to protect Alton," was the reply.

"Why do you now repudiate that confession and say that it is false?"

"Because I know now that it will not help anyone."

"You know it will not help Alton?"

"Yes. I know now that it will not be of any help to him."

"You know now that the false confessions would not be of any good to your brother, Dr Fred Covell?"

"Yes, I know that it would not help him either."

Cross Examined Today

With this Mr. Giles concluded his examination of the witness and turned him over to the prosecution but it was adjournment time and the cross-examination was put off until this morning.

In the course of his testimony Covell said that he did not exercise any power over Alton. He said he was very, fond of him and looked upon him as his own child. He was also fond of Lucile. He said he never exercised anything wrong in the way of influence over Alton and never asked him to do anything wrong.

Alton Cares for Cripple

The witness told about how Alton cared for him and carried him down to the yard each day so he could get as much sunlight as possible. He said he had a trapeze arrangement in his room so he could take exercise and try to help his condition some.

Covell was asked if there was any ammonia in the house. He said that Mrs. Covell had asked Alton to buy her a bottle so she would have it to clean some clothes for Lucile. Alton when they were in town bought the ammonia for five cents. Covell said it was paid for with his money as Alton carried his purse and was told to use any of what little money he had at any time he needed it.

Reads Horoscopes

He was asked about his astrology studies. He said he was an astrologer. He said he read horoscopes and made a little in that way. He studied under Lewellyn George, formerly of Portland and now of Los Angeles.

Sometimes, the witness said, it would take him ten days to complete a horoscope because he did not dare to work too hard. He went to Portland and had an operation performed on his spine and was to be operated on again as soon as there appeared enough life in his legs to feel a pin point. Lewellyn George loaned him $100 to go to Portland for the operation. Through a friend there he got the operation, hospital treatment and ambulance work free of charge so the $100 paid fare up and back and for his living while there. He came home with $4 in his pocket and a check for $5. That was all the money in the world he possessed at that time. He said he was penniless now but he hoped to read enough horoscopes to pay the $100 he had borrowed and then hoped to borrow $100 again from Mr. George to have the operation needed performed.

Tells of Accident

The witness described the manner in which he was hurt. He said he had an auto jacked up when it fell down on him and injured his spine so he was practically helpless below the waist. He said that he had constant pains and aches in his legs.

He told of coming back to Bandon in July and being taken to the Covell farm.

Mrs. Covell Cool

He was asked about his relations with Mrs. Covell. He said he could not say that he liked her and that he did not believe she liked him so they stayed away from each other. He said: "She seemed cold and aloof and did not seem real sociable like." That was all I had against her.

Mr. Giles asked the witness if he would benefit by the death of Mrs. Covell.

He said, "No, I would not benefit but would suffer. I came to the ranch because I thought I could get better care than at any institution and I could have gone no place but to some institution. I wanted to go to the ranch to get peace of mind and rest in the hopes of bettering my condition for the operation which I was to have performed."

Aspect Not Right

The witness was asked whether with his knowledge of astrology September 3 would be a good time for him to perform any act. He said: "No, it would not. On that date the moon is square to the sun, an aspect of 90 degrees, and this is a very evil aspect. Besides the moon was in its last quarter. The only time I made any astrological observances regarding myself was with the purpose of finding when would be the best time for treatment of my ailment."

The sheet of paper which contained writing identified by Lucile as being that of Arthur was shown the witness. He said it was his writing. Some of the sentences he explained were regarding matters he wanted to speak to the children about. At the top of the sheet were words which had been partially erased but which looked like: "Sept. 3, Monday. Will Al do his part." The witness said that he did not write those words before the murder. The best of his recollection was that they were written after the murder and that he probably referred to what Alton had said regarding shouldering the burden of guilt.

Sister Is Insane

Covell told about himself. He said he was 44 years of age and had lived near Bandon for 20 years. The ranch was taken up by his father as a homestead. He told of the death of his father and mother at the ranch. A sister is in the insane asylum at Salem.

Dr. Covell had four wives. The witness said the first wife was divorced. He knew her but slightly. The second wife was the mother of Alton and Lucile and she died. He had seen her once, some time before her death. The third wife the witness knew quite well. She also died, the death taking place at St. John. Ebba Covell was the fourth wife.

Written Confession

The following is the written confession given by Arthur Covell to the grand jury and district attorney and which in his testimony he repudiated and now claims is false:

"I make this as a voluntary statement. I alone was the one to plan the details and select the day. Lucille had nothing to do with the plan or its execution".

Both Under Control

"Both Alton and Lucille were at all times under control of my mind and will. My will was their will. They never resisted my influence, but done without question as I wished it done. They never argued, or thought if the action was right or wrong, but my influence over both was so complete they seemed incapable to resist or think independently beyond my wish."

"In regard to Ebba, soon after moving upstairs. I told Alton I wanted her out of the way. I told him how do it without violence or bloodshed and with ammonia. I told him I would choose the day that I would not force him to do and that if he wanted to refuse it was all right with me but as I said this, I knew in my own heart he couldn't help doing as I wanted."

Brother Innocent

"My brother Fred is entirely innocent. Lucille is innocent of any participation in the crime. Alton as an individual is innocent. I forced my will on him and made him act for me, in other words I used his body and his strength as though it were my own, he had not the power or will to resist me. I alone am guilty of the whole thing. I have kept Alton under my control for a great many years and it is this which makes him seem not bright, sometimes deficient. My last instructions to him before we were separated was, If you get in a tight pinch with this and there is no other way out, it will be all right with me if you tell how I made do it. I do not want you to suffer for my sake. Hence his and my statement."

"Alton has a very mild nature, nothing vicious in his make-up and if left to his own devices be incapable of ever taking a human life."

(Signed) "ARTHUR COVELL."

Elderly Man Weeps

There was an incident, not seen by many during a recess in the court room. An elderly man and evident friend of the defendant came up and sat down on his cot. The visitor seemed much moved when talking to Arthur and wept while he talked.

Previous to the time Covell was put on the stand several witnesses, were examined. C. B. Zeek, W. S. Brummett, W. R. Brummett all testified that they had known Covell for a long time and had always found him a man of quiet disposition and easy to get along with.

Dufree Comments on Death

H. H. Dufree of Bandon said that he was on the road the Saturday before Mrs. Covell's death and met her with the two children. She had been crying and he noticed it at the time. On Monday when he came to town with his wife he learned Mrs. Covell was dead. The witness said: "When I heard that I said Mrs. Covell had either committed suicide or been murdered and my wife slapped me on the mouth and told me to cut out that kind of talk."

Youth Is Attractive

Alton Covell when he went on the stand as a witness for the prosecution presented a neat appearance. He is somewhat deaf and this seemed to embarrass him on the stand. He was quiet and a little nervous and his answers were slow in coming and very low spoken. He said little but yes and no and did not answer the questions pertaining to the alleged murder directly having been told by the court that he need not say anything to incriminate himself. He is under indictment for murder in the first degree and is protected by constitutional rights.

Alton, when one talks to him in ordinary conversation is a pleasant person in his address. He speaks in a low tone, has a manner indicating gentleness, is rather appealing in his way and by a number who have talked with him is regarded as having a certain personal magnetism and as being a rather attractive youth.

Another Angle Presented

Another angle to the case was brought out. Through several witnesses it was shown that one could leave the house unobserved by going through the brush and striking a trail which leads to the main road.

Evidently the defense will claim that someone else committed the murder and went away from the place by that route.

The article was followed by: **STATE ASKS FOR VERDIC FIRST DEGREE MURDER** — District Attorney Fisher Concludes Remarks in Arthur Covell Trial — **CASE TO GO TO JURY TODAY, EXPECTATIONS** — Notes Written in Jail Are Intercepted and Used as Evidence for State — **ALTON TOLD WHAT TO SAY** — Trial Expected to Go to the Jury This Afternoon — Notes Were Passed to Alton in Magazines and in Other Ways

CASE GOES TO JURY AT 3:40 THIS AFTERNOON

COQUILLE, Ore., Nov. 10. — The case of Arthur Covell went to the jury at 3:40 this afternoon.

COQUILLE, Ore., Nov. 10. — At 2:30 this afternoon District Attorney Fisher started his final argument to the jury. He said that Attorney Giles had failed to put up any defense. His speech was to be followed by instructions from the court and the case was then to go to the jury.

Giles said in his defense that he was making no plea for Arthur C. Covell because of his crippled condition nor was he making a plea of insanity. He said that Dr. Fred Covell had cheerfully made an effort to testify against both his brother and his son, especially as to the latter's behavior on the day preceding the murder. He cautioned the jury that they must weigh the conduct of Dr. Covell throughout the trial in the official capacity to prevent Arthur Covell's committing legal suicide. He said further that no motive for the crime had been shown save what Arthur Covell himself had created in his effort to shield his nephew and if there was any doubt in the minds of the jury that the defendant should have the benefit of it. Giles said that he pointed the finger of suspicion toward the behavior of Dr. Covell.

COQUILLE, Ore., Nov. 10. — Murder in the first degree without recommendation and hanging as a punishment, were demanded by District Attorney Fisher of the jury in his final argument before the jury in the Arthur Covell case this morning. Both the defense and the prosecution rested at 11 a.m.

Mr. Fisher concluded his remarks shortly before noon. He said that the murder was clearly planned by Arthur Covell; that there was no doubt that Alton committed the murder and that Arthur became a principal. He said that the murder was planned and executed just as Lucile had described and that Arthur, who admitted he disregard an oath, asked the jury to believe him this time and take for the truth his statement and regard that everyone else had lied.

Asks First Degree

Mr. Fisher said that the plans were cleverly made in every way but that Arthur had overlooked the mark on the woman's face which he did not expect. The photo showing this mark the prosecutor said was the thing which would send him to the gallows.

In conclusion Fisher said; "I only ask one thing of the jury: murder in the first degree without recommendation. Hang Arthur Covell or turn him loose."

Before the arguments were called for, Judge Kendall asked if there was to be any claim for manslaughter. Mr. Giles said that there would be no claim.

Notes Intercepted

In the cross-examination of Arthur Covell the state introduced quite a number of notes which Arthur had attempted to send to Alton while the two were in jail. He had tried to send them in various ways. These notes showed directions regarding testifying and telling Alton what to do to save himself.

The following is a note which was sent in an apple by Arthur to Alton and which was intercepted:

Tell What to Say

When they ask you say: I confessed because I was afraid my father would be hanged and I wanted to do something for him. To say I done it was all I could think of to help free him. The night I heard father was arrested I told uncle and sis I would not let my father go to prison and be hanged but would say I killed her so father would go free. Uncle said he would not advise me either way only for me to wait a while and see how the evidence against daddy was. But if I was generous enough to take suspicion off papa's shoulders for me and sis to blame him and us both to say he told me to do it and he would say the same and take the blame. I was going to wait and not say a word but the detectives scared me so I was ready to say anything. I was so afraid of what might happen and of the detective that he influenced me to make my statement against my better judgment. Uncle and i never at no time planned to harm her in any way, and my old statement about killing her and about uncle telling me to do it is false. I deny the statement I made. I was in influenced to make it, but at no time has uncle influenced me against m own will. I always tried to be obedient and mind uncle and that was as far as his influence went with me. The following note from Arthur to Alton was taken from page 52 of a Western Story magazine:

Magazine Method

"Destroy this as soon as you can — I know how you feel — but be reasonable its allright — dad is now out for good. Now save yourself do as you were told — never mind your pride. You have all to gain and nothing to lose. I'm working with you, Lathera is in line O.K. we can beat the case easy but you must obey orders — the gods (aspects) only help those whom try to help themselves dangerous to do as others advise deny the confession is true here is right dope, ammonia was to clean clothes with. The night dad was arrested you and I talked about taking blame to save dad at 11 or after you went out in pasture to see about cow, if safe — then came back went in for drink and found her on kitchen floor."

"deny that you killed her or that I told you to. You only confessed to save dad and nothing more. You blamed me because I told you to, they have nothing but your story. My story and sis story to go on."

Both Done For

"No other evidence that you and I were responsible for death and if you stick to confession we are both done for. I don't care so much about myself but I do want to see you O K."

(Page 2) "Acknowledge this note. So as I say it is now up to you and if you want to go under all right but do as you are told and you are save. I cant be writing to you like this as aspects are not right after this one. You send for your lawyer very soon and tell him what you are going to say and that you will deny confession as you made it (confession) through fear at the time. There is a law which covers such a matter as this so that part is allright the detectives and others so frightened you that it seemed the only thing to do at time. Golly this is going to be an interesting case, I have a good lawyer named giles and he will fight her through so fall in line boy fall in line. Think MeH is coming to testify for us the papers think

I am crazy, and you are feeble minded, lets show them how smart we are, we can make case turn out either way, keep up your nerve and think of your 054 but you cant confess to a crime and expect jupiter to do the work of clearing you, I am going to pull right with you."

Writes on Envelope

Written on an envelope, which District Attorney Fisher said was inclosed in an apple, was the following note:

(Front of envelope) "the biggest things they have on me is my notes. So dont know anything about them or anything else on the witness stand U say what I have told U & I will back you up."

Flaps Used

"If they say anything about the bottle of ammonia remember my stepmother told me if I would get her a bottle ammonia she would freshen up my suit, so I got a small bottle at the drug store and give it to her for that purpose and I think she used it up as she cleaned up mine and sis clothes."

(On flap) "Uncle never told me to look at her — only to put her on the bed and bathe her hands and face as we that she had only fainted." (Reverse flap) "U was a fool to say anything — take back what you said your are to learn what follows let no one see this writing and destroy as soon as you can I think the trial comes off on 29th so get busy and learn this to say."

Deny Everything

On page 60, American magazine, was the following note:

"Deny that I told you to kill her"

"Deny that you did kill her"

"Deny that you would ever want to hurt her"

"Your business was to take care of me not to hurt anyone."

"Deny that you bought ammonia for any purpose, except that she asked you (correct) to get it, and she wanted to use it for cleaning some of sis skirts"

"Deny that you knew Ammonia was dangerous and would kill anyone if they smelled it"

"You mentioned ammonia in your confession because you did not know what to say."

On November 16, 1923 the *Coquille Valley Sentinel* headlined: **DEATH PENALTY** — Arthur Covell Sentenced Here Tuesday to Be Hung December 21st

Arthur Covell, convicted of first degree murder last week, was sentenced by Judge Kendall on Tuesday afternoon to be hanged at Salem on Friday, Dec. 21. There was no delay in starting him for the penitentiary and that evening Deputy Sheriff Malehorn left with his prisoner on the evening train from Marshfield.

The case was given to the jury last Saturday afternoon a little after three o'clock and by 5:30 they were ready to report - murder in the first degree, without any recommendations.

Covell took the verdict in an apparently cheerful manner, thanked the officers and others who came near him, including Luke S. May, who had so much to do with unearthing Covell's activity in the murder of his sister-in-law.

Before leaving Marshfield he gave out a statement to newspaper men in which he proclaimed his innocence, and reiterated his repudiation of his former confession.

He declared that Lucille had nothing to do with the murder, that Alton was a good boy, who had done a noble deed in trying to take the blame when Dr. Fred Covell was under arrest, and hinted that something might yet develop which would show the affair in a different aspect.

"He had no chance," he said, he had no regrets, his heart was right, and his last words before leaving Coos Bay were thanks to those who assisted him on the train which was taking him to his life's journey's end.

November 16, 1923 the *Coos Bay Times* headlined: **COVELL BELIEVES IN REINCARNATION — EXPECTS TO RETURN TO ANOTHER EARTH LIFE** — Gives His Version of Religion and Life and its Meanings to Him

SALEM, Ore., Nov. 16. — Arthur Covell, sentenced to be hanged on Friday, December 21st, for instigating the murder of Mrs. Ebba Covell soon after his arrival at the state prison here, gave out some weird statements. One was a denial of his guilt and the other of his beliefs, claiming that he was a disciple of Coue. One statement was written in large flourishing letter: but the latter was in a cramped hand, abbreviations and astrological signs being used in it. In part, it said:

"The state can have my poor bed ridden and crippled body but as a tenant of that body I will move on at the time appointed. This body has served me faithfully and well and I have been proud of the service it has rendered me."

"I do not fear to make the change and shall go out with a clear heart at peace with world and with a conscience clear of guilt for the crime charged. Somewhere there is a party or parties whom I do not envy—always as long as life shall last they will carry their guilty secure and what is a more terrible load to carry than that of a guilty conscience coupled with the fact that an innocent life is also sacrificed to help hide that guilt?"

"I have not made a material success of my life so far as wealth possessions or worldly goods art concerned but have lived an interesting life. When we depart it is what we can take with us that counts — we cannot take money, or property or a great name but it we have tried to do good, kind and true to self and others this is food upon which soul shall feed after change called death. The sole aim and purpose of this material existence which we call life is that soul is imperishable. My development to ward that perfect state which Jesus, the great master, recognized when he said: 'Be ye perfect as Father in heaven is perfect.' But perfection is not attained in one's earth life of a few short, years. The attainment toward perfection is a gradual transformation and takes a round of innumerable lives, of physical births and deaths. During the few short years of each life we learn certain things, gain certain expressions to fit us for a higher road of expression. And the expression we have acquired in our earth life form the web and garment for the beginning of an other life. I look upon the change called death as just a short period of rest in between. I am taking with me my rich truths; have proven to our satisfaction what we do aired to know upon this earth at cost of much pains, care, effort and study. I have drank deeply at the well of truth, settled my religious doubts, made positive and sure where I stood and so do not feel like a stranger going to a strange land, but more like a pilgrim who is about to arrive at a certain destination on the route of his journey."

Expects Reincarnation

"I have too much faith in the supreme power, and intelligence which for want of a better name we call God, to doubt but what this same power that placed me here to live and learn will still continue to guide my progress hereafter. And I expect soon to return to another earth life and occupy my place in world affairs. So in a sense I look upon death as a sleep of the soul and birth as the soul's awakening for another period of activity. Just as physical body needs its period of sleep and rest for relaxation so does soul require death of body for its period of rest and sleep that it may grow and develop. Sleep and rest, death and birth are natural processes and should be as welcome as any other fact in life."

"I carry with me a conscience rich in truth, a heart full of tender sympathy for those I must leave behind, a feeling of perfect peace and satisfaction in that I have tried not to shirk any duties of service which environment forced upon me. I am ready to make change willingly and with no regrets for having sworn life trying to save one who is very near to me and whom I expect to meet again in the flesh in the very near future."

On November 21, 1923 the *Coos Bay Times* headlined: **WANTS HOROSCOPE OF MURDER HOUR — ARTHUR COVELL, ASKS FOR ASTROLOGY BOOKS** — Wishes to Ascertain What the Hour Holds — Not Known Yet Whether Appeal Is Desired

COQUILLE, Ore., Nov. 21 — Arthur Covell has written from the penitentiary in Salem to his attorney, Claude Giles, asking that he be sent his astrology books. Mr. Giles said he would send the books if the court would release them. Covell wants to make a horoscope of 11 a.m., September 3, the hour of the murder, to see what it calls for.

Giles has asked Covell whether or not he wishes an appeal but has received no answer as yet.

Also headlined: **COVELL CASE COST TO COUNTY $3000 — CLOSE ESTIMATE IN CLERK'S OFFICE SETS EXPENSE** Luke S. May Gets $1406 — Attorney Giles Allowed $175 Fees to Defend Covell

COQUIILLE, Ore., Nov. 21. — The Covell murder case has already cost the county about $3000 according to the close estimate made by R. R. Watson, bookkeeper in the county clerk's office today. This figure does not include the prisoners board and keep since the arrest

It is estimated that before the case is disposed of the county will pay out another thousand dollars.

Nearly half of the $3000 goes to Luke S. May, the Seattle detective called to solve the mystery of the murder. The county was under contract of $1000 to him and his Corps of assistants, and in addition paid him $406.35 expenses, totaling $1406.35 to the detective agency.

Attorney Claude Giles, appointed by the court to defend the crippled astrologer charged with murder in the first degree, received a fee of $175 by the court and expense money amounting to $191.65. The trial of Arthur Covell continued for five days, which cost the county about $500 more for jurors and witnesses.

This estimate carries the case up to the present time, and with the trial of Alton Covell, the youth, set for December 10, there is no means of estimating what the case will cost the taxpayers of Coos county before it is completed.

December 10, 1923 the *Coos Bay Times* headlined: **EXPECTS STARS TO SAVE COVELL — COOS COUNTY MURDER HOPES TO ESCAPE HANGING** — Astrologist Who Admitted Bandon Slaying Believes He Will Be Freed of Crime

SALEM, Ore., Dec. 10. — Arthur Covell of Coos county, who is in the state penitentiary here awaiting execution for the part he played in the murder of his sister-in-law, still believes that the stars will guide his destiny.

"If the stars are right I will not hang December 21," said the crippled astrologer today. Officials, on the other hand, declared that if Covell is rescued from the gallows it probably will be through a decision of the supreme court, and not because the stars happen to be in any particular position.

Covell entertains hope that he will recover use of his legs, despite that he has not walked for three years. He is suffering from a broken back.

Although Covell has asked repeatedly for his books on astrology they have not yet arrived at the prison.

CHAPTER 15

THE EXECUTIONS OF L.W. PEARE AND ARTHUR COVELL

February 20, 1925 the *Coos Bay Harbor* headlined: **Coos County Murderers Will Be Hanged at Salem on Same Scaffold — Sentences to Be Passed About Middle of March.**

> A few weeks ago Arthur Covell's appeal to the supreme court was lost and the Coos county circuit court's findings approved. On Tuesday, L. W. Peare also lost his appeal, and so both men stand without a hope. There is, however, opportunity to appeal to the next higher court before twenty days, but this is not a contingency expected, and so it is likely the second sentences will be passed some time after March 18th.

On April 1, 1925 the *Southwestern Oregon Daily News* headlined: **COVELL, PEARE SEE OLD HOMES FOR LAST TIME – SUNSHINE AND LAUGHING CHILDREN GREET PAIR ON RETURN**

> All hope gone unless the governor acts to save them from the noose, two convicted murderers gazed to the last time today upon their home county as they rode from Marshfield to Coquille to hear themselves re-sentenced to death by the inexorable command of the state of Oregon.
>
> Tonight they will return over the same winding way and as the sun is sinking over the Pacific they will depart from Marshfield to their death cells in Salem prison to wait the fastening of the noose about their neck on Friday, May 22.
>
> These men were Arthur Covell and L.W. Peare – Covell, the cripple astrologer who cannot walk a step and who will have to be strapped to a board when justice stalks into his cell on that fatal Friday; and Peare, a man gray of hair and mustache who is already in the evening of life and only lacks two years of the allotted three score and ten.
>
> **Children Pass**
>
> Children laughed their way to school and the placid waters wound their picturesque way to the sea as these two men rode through the crisp morning to hear themselves once more condemned to a felons end. The rising sun touched eastern peaks to crimson and the world was gay with the gladness of another day while these two men rode to doom.
>
> Covell, ahead in custody of a prison guard, lay silent upon the seat of the automobile and looking into the crystal heavens – thinking, musing as in a day dream such as he might have done some thirty years ago on the plains of Kansas when his body was erect and stalwart and the world was before him.
>
> Now he lay with his useless limbs before him riding to hear death pronounced upon him – musing, and dreaming!
>
> **Peare Cheerful**
>
> Behind another car bore Peare. He appeared cheerful and talked throughout the trip, asking questions of old neighbors before the law closed its net about him. Now he gazed into the somber depths of pine forests as one who sees far away – perhaps they reminded him of the great forests in Maine in which he was reared.
>
> "My ancestors," he said reflectively, "were French pioneers in the woods of Maine, my great grandfather was a hero in the revolution, my grandfather fought in the war of 1812, my father was a soldier of the Union in '61 and I" – he paused and turned his head away as he looked into the placid river where the morning sun case the shadows of the towering pines.
>
> **Claims Innocence**
>
> "If I die," he continued later, "I die an innocent man but none the less I believe the United States is the greatest country in the world."
>
> Later in the morning when Peare had heard the fatal sentence he appeared more nervous. He revolved his hat in his hands and his lips trembled as he spoke.
>
> "Whatever happens,: he said, "I want to thank all the officials of coos county for the way they have treated me. I still hope, but —," and he turned away as he looked over the hills where he had lived so long.

Around the court house children laughed and played with the joy of youth. Inside two men prepared to return to two cells in Salem for a fatal Friday that is only a few weeks away.

April 4, 1925 the *Coos Bay Harbor* headlined: **Judge Kendall For the Second Time Passes Death Penalty Upon Murderers Convicted Two Years Ago**

Arthur Covell and L.W. Peare, on being presented in court Wednesday at Coquille for resentencing, were ordered to hang at the Salem penitentiary on the 22nd of May. The respite was made to that date to permit attorneys who represented the convicted men to prepare asking for Governor Pierce's interference, perhaps commuting the sentences to life imprisonment. Since the state supreme court had refused to grant retrial or change the findings, there was no way to save the men longer excepting to obtain a change of penalty, which only the governor can grant.

Possibly, in the case of Covell there might be a chance that the governor would take a hand. Covell being a principal in a hanging would make a spectacle not often witnessed.

He is a cripple and to be hanged would need the assistance of somebody to hold him erect when the trap is sprung.

The crime Covell was convicted of conspiracy in influencing his nephew, Alton Covell, to smother Mrs. Ebba Covell, wife of Arthur Covell's brother and step-mother of Alton. It took a long time for the scheme to be worked up and for Alton to prepare his nerve for the act. He saturated a cloth with ammonia and held to the woman's mouth and nose until she died.

L. W. Peare made moonshine liquor and in a Christmas celebration beat his wife to death and afterward went to his neighbor's, James Culver, and killed Culver.

The men were tried before Judge Kendall and were the first to come under Judge Kendall's bench as murderers after he became judge of the Coos county circuit court.

On May 22, 1925 Salem's newspaper the *Oregon Statesman* headlined: **COVELL AND PEARE WILL HANG TODAY** Executive Clemency Denied Condemned Men Who Must Pay for Crimes — **MYSTIC TO DROP FIRST** Executions Begin At 8 O'clock Warden Dalrympte Bars All Outsiders Except Newspapermen

Hopes held by Arthur Covell and L.W. Peare for a commutation of sentence or a reprieve faded late Thursday afternoon when Governor Walter M. Pierce, after careful consideration, refused to extend executive clemency to the condemned men who must die on the gallows at the state prison beginning at 8 o'clock this morning.

The announcement was made after a delegation of Portland people had spent several hours closeted with the governor in the interest of anti-capital punishment organizations. The delegation was headed by Dr. Evangeline Woods, who acted as spokesman. Dr. Woods told the governor she was the first woman to be admitted to like Oregon bar back in 1896. The governor gave his callers every opportunity to present their views, but held firm to his course as they failed to point out any reason, beyond principle, why clemency should be extended.

I have given long and conscientious study to the cases of Arthur Covell and L. W. Peare the governor's statement read. "I have read the testimony. I have studied the eases from every angle. Each of these men was tried by a jury in the county where the crimes were committed and each found guilty. An able, impartial Judge presided. Both cases were appealed to the supreme court and the decisions sustained. The mandates of our courts should not be lightly set aside. All the elements of first degree murder appear in each case. I can find nothing to justify the extension of executive clemency."

Since taking office Governor Pierce has been called upon seven times to save the life of a condemned man. Three of the men in question were hanged and two, Russell Hecker and Abe Evans, commuted to life imprisonment. The remaining two will be executed today.

Arthur Covell is paying for the murder of his sister-in-law, Mrs. Ebba Covell, near Bandon, September 3, 1923 and L. W. Peare for the murder of his wife and James R. Culver, a neighbor, near Myrtle Point, December 27, 1922. Covell, self-styled astrologer and mystic, is paralyzed from the waist down and has been a hopeless cripple for several years. Peare is nearly 70 years old and is white-headed. Both were convicted in Coos county. The men will be hanged in the order named. Warden Dalrmmple has been besieged with the request from all parts of the state from, people seeking to witness the execution. This will take place with as little of the spectacular as possible and the only outsiders present will be a few newspapermen, Dr R. L. Edwards, prison physician, his assistant and religious advisers.

May 22, 1925 the *Southwestern Oregon Daily News* headlined the following regarding the execution of Peare: **MURDER OF WIFE, NEIGHBOR BRINGS DEATH ON GALLOWS FOR PEARE IN STATE PRISON** – COOS COUNTY RANCHER REFUSES TO EAT BREAKFAST WHICH HAD BEEN PREPARED FOR HIM – BODY REMOVED AT 8:200 A.M. – **MAN DIES WITHOUT FLINCHING** – WHILE LIFELESS BODY OF ONE IS BEING REMOVED, DEPUTIES PRERPARE TO CARRY CRIPPLE TO SALEM GALLOWS

> SALEM, May 22. – The gallows trap opened here this morning and took the life of L.W. Peare, coos county rancher.
>
> He went to the scaffold without flinching and without eating a breakfast which was ready for him.
>
> While Peare's body was being removed from the scaffold at 8:20 a.m., Deputy Wardens were preparing to carry Arthur Covell, crippled astrologer, on a couch, the second to hang in today's double execution.

The *Southwestern Oregon Daily News* also printed three articles regarding the execution of Arthur Covell. The first of wich headlined: **DEATH FAILS TO FRIGHTEN COVELL** – IN THE SHADOW OF GALLOWS HE WROTE ABOUT HIS FEELINGS

> SALEM, MAY 22, — In the shadow of the gallows, Arthur Covell wrote the "feelings of a condemned man," a long statement on his philosophy of life.
>
> He pitied the hangman who would take his life. His statement said "man can kill when his blood is hot, or in fear, or self defense; but to lead a condemned man to the scaffold, place a rope around his neck and spring a trap that hurls him into eternity, takes more nerve than I am capable of."
>
> Another part of the statement declared:
>
> "We all take death too seriously and worry about it innecessarily; think of it and fear it, no children think of and fear the dark."

Laughs at Hangman

The law has exacted its due. Arthur Covell, crippled astrologist gave up his life today for his part in the "star" murder of his sister-in-law, Mrs. Ebba Covell. He smiled as the judge pronounced sentence upon him. And he is smiling here as jail attaches carried him back to his cell after the court uttered the words that sent him to the gallows today.

Figure 31: Arthur Covell – *Southwestern Oregon Daily News*, May 22, 1925

Second: **ARHTUR COVELL DIES TODAY ON STATE PRISON SCAFFOLD FOR BRUTAL BANDON MURDER** – CARRIED TO THE GALLOWS, CRIPPLED ASTROLOGER HANGS AT OREGON STATE PENITENTIARY FRO SLAYING SISTER-IN-LAW, MRS. COVELL – **SENT TO DOOM AT 8:30 A.M. TODAY** – COOS COUNTY MAN FOLLOWS L.W. PEARE TO GALLOWS IN DOUBLE EXECUTION AT STATE PRISON IN SALEM

SALEM, May 22. – carried to the gallows, Arthur Covell, crippled astrologer of coquille, was hanged here at the Oregon penitentiary today for murdering his sister-in-law.

The trap was sprung at 8:28 sending his to his doom. His hanging was the second in a double execution today, following shortly after the execution of L.W. Peare, another murderer.

Covell was rolled into the death chamber on a wheel chair and strapped to a board as the noose was placed around his neck.

"I wish everybody well," he said. "I bear no ill feelings towards anyone, good bye, everybody," he declared in his last statement.

Covell said nothing about his science of the stars that led to his doom. In a confession he made soon after the slaying he said he killed his brother's wife "because the stars directed it."

Up to last night he kept faith in his stars which told him in his horoscope that he would not die on the gallows. His faith was broken in his astral science, however, last night when Governor Pierce refused to pardon him.

Neither Covell nor Peare ate any breakfast before going to their deaths.

But they each faced their execution without faltering.

When the trap was sprung for Peare a wound in his throat, inflicted when he attempted to commit suicide in the Coos county jail, opened and created a nauseating scene.

"Don't be afraid to get the rope tight," Peare said as a deputy warden adjusted the noose. "I want to die quick."

Covell's neck was not broken when he dropped from the trap and death resulted from strangulation. He was not pronounced dead until 26 minutes after he was hanged."

Fred Covell Family

Group photo of the family of Fred Covell. Mrs. Ebba Covell for whose murder Arthur Covell paid with his life today, is shown at the left. She was slain with ammonia by her stepson at Bandon under orders from the astrologer uncle, according to his own confession. The man is Fred Covell who was cleared of suspicion by the boy's

Figure 32: The Covell Family – *Southwestern Oregon Daily News,* May 22, 1925

The third article headlined: **Niece See Innocent Covell – Lucille here to Find Father**

While attendants in Salem prison this morning were removing the crippled and lifeless body of Arthur Covell from the hangmen's noose a little girl over Coquille way cried out against both laws and stars. Her faith in the astral wisdom was shattered; her heart was broken.

Was a Pal

To the 12 men who tried him and the world that knew him Arthur Covell may have been a ruthless murderer with a mind as distorted as his body, but to Lucille Covell, his 17-year-old niece, he was a "pal" without fault or blemish who read the riddle of life in the heavens.

Perhaps, like her brother who is in a murderer's cell for life, who was under the astrologer's hypnotic influence. Perhaps that spark of good that is said to be in every man was revealed to her alone and crowded out the evil that he did.

Lucille came to Coquille last night from another uncle's home in Medford and visited Mrs. A.T. Morrison, wife of the county probation officer, who cared for her during those days when her uncle

Arthur was on trial for his life. She said she was looking for her father.

Girl Brave

She was still smiling last night bravely but a bit nervously.

"Uncle Arthur won't hang," she said. "The stars say he won't and Uncle Arthur knows all about them."

Even this morning she was hopeful. But as the fatal hour approached tears gathered in her eyes. Perhaps the stars might be wrong? No, they couldn't, Uncle Arthur said so."

But they were. Up in Salem prison a trap was sprung and Arthur Covell paid his own life for the life of Lucille's step-mother.

"The stars played Uncle Arthur false," sobbed Lucille. "They deceived me. Uncle's gone – gone," she cried as spasms of grief wracked her childish body.

No words could comfort her. She was reminded that her uncle had killed her step-mother, had caused her brother to fill a murderer's cell, and broken up the home that gave him food and comfort.

Good to Her

"He was innocent and was so good to me," she declared between her sobs as she pressed his last letters to her heart.

A score of letters were in the bundle, all from Covell as he counted off the days and hours between him and death in Salem prison. They were letters to "my dearest darling Lucille" expressing eternal regard and affection. He sent her two every week during his long "death watch" in Salem.

These letters are all Lucille treasures in the world today outside of memories of her childhood when Uncle Arthur explained the zodiac and the courses of the constellations. Perhaps the thought that such was true comforted Covell today when he faced the morning sun and felt the noose around his neck

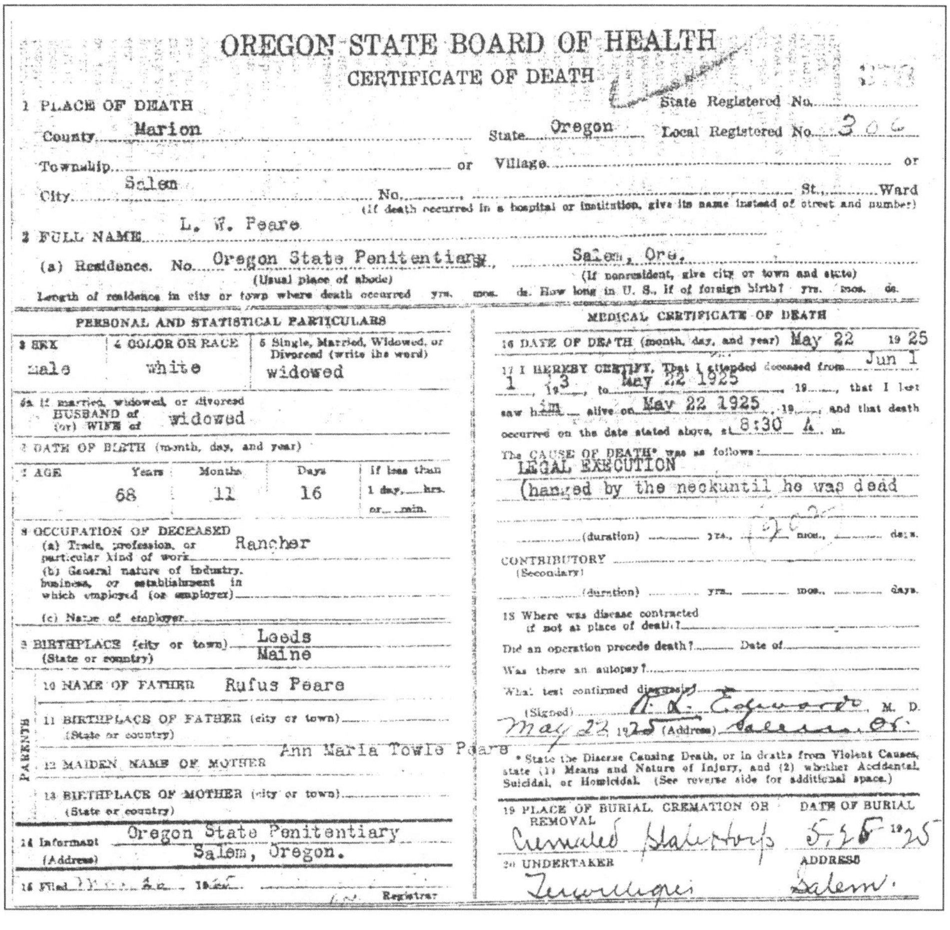

OREGON STATE BOARD OF HEALTH
CERTIFICATE OF DEATH

1 PLACE OF DEATH — State Registered No.
County Marion State Oregon Local Registered No. 306
Township or Village or
City Salem No. St. Ward
(If death occurred in a hospital or institution, give its name instead of street and number)
2 FULL NAME L. W. Peare
(a) Residence. No. Oregon State Penitentiary (Usual place of abode) Salem, Ore. (If nonresident, give city or town and state)
Length of residence in city or town where death occurred yrs. mos. ds. How long in U. S., if of foreign birth? yrs. mos. ds.

PERSONAL AND STATISTICAL PARTICULARS

3 SEX male | 4 COLOR OR RACE white | 5 Single, Married, Widowed, or Divorced (write the word) widowed
5a If married, widowed, or divorced HUSBAND of (or) WIFE of widowed
6 DATE OF BIRTH (month, day, and year)
7 AGE Years 68 Months 11 Days 16 If less than 1 day, hrs. or min.
8 OCCUPATION OF DECEASED
(a) Trade, profession, or particular kind of work Rancher
(b) General nature of industry, business, or establishment in which employed (or employer)
(c) Name of employer
9 BIRTHPLACE (city or town) Leeds (State or country) Maine
PARENTS
10 NAME OF FATHER Rufus Peare
11 BIRTHPLACE OF FATHER (city or town) (State or country)
12 MAIDEN NAME OF MOTHER Ann Maria Towle Peare
13 BIRTHPLACE OF MOTHER (city or town) (State or country)
14 Informant Oregon State Penitentiary (Address) Salem, Oregon.
15 Filed Registrar

MEDICAL CERTIFICATE OF DEATH

16 DATE OF DEATH (month, day, and year) May 22 1925
17 I HEREBY CERTIFY, That I attended deceased from Jun 1 1, 1923, to May 22 1925, 19, that I last saw him alive on May 22 1925, 19, and that death occurred on the date stated above, at 8:30 A. m.
The CAUSE OF DEATH* was as follows:
LEGAL EXECUTION
(hanged by the neckuntil he was dead
(duration) yrs. mos. days.
CONTRIBUTORY (Secondary)
(duration) yrs. mos. days.
18 Where was disease contracted if not at place of death?
Did an operation precede death? Date of
Was there an autopsy?
What test confirmed diagnosis?
(Signed) R. L. Edwards M. D.
May 22 1925 (Address) Salem, Or.
* State the Disease Causing Death, or in deaths from Violent Causes, state (1) Means and Nature of Injury, and (2) whether Accidental, Suicidal, or Homicidal. (See reverse side for additional space.)
19 PLACE OF BURIAL, CREMATION OR REMOVAL Cremated — DATE OF BURIAL 5-25 1925
20 UNDERTAKER — ADDRESS Salem.

Figure 33: L.W. Peare Certificate of Death

IN THE CIRCUIT COURT OF THE STATE OF OREGON FOR COOS COUNTY

STATE OF OREGON, Plaintiff,

vs.

L. W. PEARE Defendant.

WARRANT.

TO THE Warden of the State Penitentiary of the State of Oregon.Salem, Oregon.

The Court, having this 1st day of April, 1925, pronounced sentence upon the above named defendant in said County and State, directing and requiring that he, the said defendant be executed in the manner prescribed by law, and the Court having this day executed an Order,-

YOU ARE HEREBY directed and commanded to execute the order of said Court upon the said defendant by forthwith taking said defendant in your custody and control, and to keep him within the walls of the State Penitentiary until the date of said execution, and that thereafter, and on Friday the 22nd day of May, 1925 that you cause the said defendant L. W. Peare to be hanged by the neck until he is dead, in the manner and form as prescribed by law, and of this warrant make due and legal return to this Court.

Dated at Coquille, Coos County, this 1st day of April, 1925.

County Clerk. John C. Kendall Circuit Judge.

Figure 34: L.W. Peare Execution Warrant

State of Oregon, plaintiff)
-vs-) ss.
L. W. Peare, defendant)

I, A. M. Dalrymple, warden Oregon state penitentiary, do hereby certify that the penitentiary records show that on May 20th, 1923, a warrant was received duly signed by the Judge of the Circuit Court of the State of Oregon, for the County of Coos, wherein it appears that on the 19th day of March, 1923, the said L. W. Peare was duly convicted of the crime of murder in the first degree, being sentenced on the 20th day of April 1923, to be confined within the walls of said penitentiary of the State of Oregon and on the 2nd day of June, 1923, in the manner and under the conditions provided by law, the said defendant, L. W. Peare be hanged by the neck until he is dead, stay of execution being ordered on the 1st day of June, 1923, on a certificate of probable cause, and the judgment of the lower court being affirmed, the said L. W. Peare was sentenced on the 1st day of April, 1925, to be hanged on Friday the 22nd day of May, 1925; that said warrant of execution was duly carried out, and on Friday, May 22nd, 1925, at the hour of 8: A.M. , of said day, within the inclosure of the execution chamber of said penitentiary, he the said L. W. Peare was by me and the deputy wardens of the penitentiary hanged by the neck until he was dead;

That I was personally present at the execution, that I invited Doctors R. L. Edwards and Wm B. Mott, each being a regular licensed and practicing physician and surgeon; that I also invited Hon. I. H. Van Winkle, Attorney General, Mr. E. P. Ellingsen, sheriff of Coos County, Oregon, and twelve reputable citizens of the State of Oregon, to be present; that I did not invite any person under the age of twenty-one to be present; that said warrant, which is hereto attached and made a part hereof, was duly and fully executed in all respects in accordance with the law, and that said warrant is herewith returned duly executed.

Done and dated at Salem, Oregon, May 22nd, 1925.

A M Dalrymple
Warden Oregon State Penitentiary

Figure 35: L.W. Peare Statement of Execution

RECORD OF EXECUTIONS—OREGON STATE PENITENTIARY

Name	County	Date Received	Date of Sentence	Date Executed
L. W. Peare	Coos	May 20-1923	April 20 1923	May 22 1925

DESCRIPTION

Nativity	Age	Height	Weight	Eyes	Hair	Complexion	Religion	Occupation
Maine	67	5-9	140	[illegible]	Brown	Sallow		Rancher

Trial Judge	Physicians	Prison Officials
John C. Kendall	R. L. Edwards, Wm B. Mott	A. M. Dalrymple Warden, J. W. Lillie Deputy Warden, C. M. Charlton principal keeper

JURY — DISPOSITION — REMARKS

W. L. Lindbeck Salem
Frank E. Perry Salem
O. K. Logan Salem
H. N. Robinson Corvallis
J. W. Haynes Oak Ridge
Frank Waller Portland
E. O. Morrow Portland
Al Bizocky Myrtle point
E. Bowers Myrtle point
J. Young Portland

Figure 36: L.W. Peare Record of Execution

RECORD OF EXECUTIONS—OREGON STATE PENITENTIARY

Name	County	Date Received	Date of Sentence	Date Executed
Arthur Covell	Coos	Nov 14-1923	Nov 13-1923	May 22 1925

DESCRIPTION

Nativity	Age	Height	Weight	Eyes	Hair	Complexion	Religion	Occupation
Queda Springs Sumner Co Kansas	44	5-3	138	Brown	Brown	Dark	None	Rancher

Trial Judge	Physicians	Prison Officials
John C. Kendall	R. L. Edwards, Wm B. Mott	A. M. Dalrymple Warden, J. W. Lillie Deputy, C. M. Charlton principal keeper

JURY — DISPOSITION — REMARKS

A. L. Lindbeck Salem
F. E. Perry Salem
H. N. Robinson Corvallis
O. K. Logan Salem
J. W. Haynes Oak Ridge
Frank Waller Portland
E. O. Morrow Portland
Al Bizocky Myrtle point
J. E. Young Portland
Ambrose [illegible] Padilla Eugene
Wm. [illegible] Salem
R. E. Bowers Myrtle point

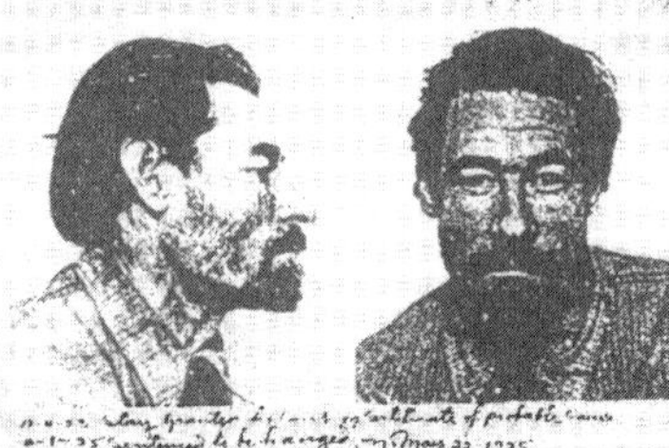

Figure 37: Arthur Covell Record of Execution

May 23, 1925 the *Oregon Statesman* headlined: **ATONE TWO CRIMES A PRISON FRIDAY** L. W. Peare and Arthur Covell Give Lives in Forfeit for Murders — HANGING IS GRUESOME Old Wound Reopened and Neck Not Broken; Thirty-three Men Have Died on Scaffold Since 1903

L.W. Peare and Arthur Covell are dead, their lives having been taken in forfeit by the state for crimes committed many months ago. The double execution in the bertillion chamber of the penitentiary Friday morning was grim in the main and grewsome in detail.

Peare, the old mountainer coming from pioneer American fighting stock, was the first to pay the penalty. Nervousness was evinced and a wispered farewell was given from the scaffold.

"I have nothing to say except goodbye to you all," he whispered. Turning to the hangman he requested that the rope be made tight so that it would not slip. A short prayer by Rev. O. H. Bryant, prison chaplain, and the trap was sprung at 7:59 o'clock. At 8:11 o'clock be was pronounced dead.

Prison Hours Calmest

While confined to the Coos county jail Peare attempted suicide by cutting his throat. While the wound had healed it was not strong enough to stand the sudden jerk and was opened, the blood coursing down his swaying body, and forming a pool at his feet.

Late Thursday night Peare told officials that the hours spent in prison were the most calm that he had ever known, he had gained weight and was ready to die. He professed belief in a Supreme Being but accepted no creed.

Peare's great grandfather, prison records show was a soldier in the Revolutionary war; his grandfather a soldier In the War of 1812 and his father a veteran at the Mexican and Civil wars. He is 69 years old himself.

Delay is Caused

Delay occurred before the execution of Covell, helpless paralytic who has spent the last few years in bed. It was discovered that he had no clothing and a pair of prison trousers, shirt and socks were brought up from the tailor shop and the condemned man dressed before placed in his wheel chair. He was carried up the steps of the scaffold and strapped to a board. Several prison officials were necessary to perform this task.

Speaking clearly and in a cultured voice, Covell said, "I wish all well. I have no ill will toward anyone. Goodbye to you all." A short prayer and then the crash of the trap at 8:32 o'clock.

Covell's light weight was insufficient to cause his neck to break and death resulted from strangulation, attending physicians said. He was unconscious and did not suffer. Death was pronounced at 8:58 o'clock, 26 minutes later. Covell was 47 years old.

Bequeaths are Made

Peare's effects, consisting of a few dollars and several cans of tobacco were bequeathed to Floyd Hall and the Goldstein brothers of Portland, with whom he had worked in the tailor shop. His body was cremated at the hospital.

Several letters were left by Covell addressed to numerous persons, including one to Alton Covell his nephew, who is serving a life sentence for the crime which resulted in the execution. None of these had any bearing upon the crime, prison officials announced. A written statement made Thursday retracted shortly before the execution was designed to aid the nephew and indicated that a third person was guilty of the crime. He requested that his remains be turned over to Mrs. M.E. Hecht, of Portland, who is belong to the same cult.

Covell studied astrology for the last 15 years and was believed to have been well-informed upon the subject.

Physicians are Present

An usually large number of physicians and surgeons were present, beside, Dr. R. L. Edwards, prison physician and Dr. William B. Mott, city health officer. These included Dr. T. T. Manzer of Seattle, representing Judge Kendall, of Coos county; Dr. Earl V. Morrow and Dr. Earl Smith both of Portland. Ben Fisher, Coos county district attorney and representatives of the sheriff's office were also present in addition to newspapermen.

Peare was hanged for the murder of his wife and a neighbor James Culver near Myrtle Point, December, 27, 1922 and Covell for inciting the death of his sister-in-law, Mrs. Ebba Covell, near Bandon, September 3, 1923.

Since capital punishment was inaugurated in l903, with a brief intermission of several years, 33 men have been handed; 14 received commuted sentences; 1 received a reversal of the case. Another man sentenced several months ago, is awaiting retrial in eastern Oregon.

May 29, 1925 the *Coos Bay Harbor* headlined: **EUGENE GUARD DEPLORES PUNISHMENT** Depicts Horribleness of Hanging a Cripple and An Old Man — Declares Hangings Do Not Prevent Crime.

The Eugene Guard prints the following ably written editorial as a comment on the hanging last Friday of Peare and Covell, two Coos county murderers.

"A poor wretch of a cripple who couldn't stand alone was strapped to, a board and placed on the trap of our official Oregon gallows. The drop when the trap was sprung failed to break his neck, and it took him practically half an hour to choke to death.

An old man of nearly 70 years was escorted to the gallows tree after the dead cripple had been taken away. He was a mere wreck of a man, suffering still from the effects of an unhealed wound in his neck; self inflicted in an attempt at suicide. At the drop the wound opened anew and blood drenched the dying man and everything near him.

A goodly though select gathering witnessed the executions. Some of those present had come considerable distances for the sake of the spectacle. All were there by hospitable invitation of the state of Oregon. If it be said that all to whom invitations were issued were legally entitled to them, let the answer be that of all those present not more than four or five could truthfully attribute their presence to any reason other than that of desire to see human beings die horribly.

Peare was guilty of murder. Covell was guilty of having instigated murder. Both of them were vicious men. Neither was of use in the world. The fact that they were cut off was not the greatest evil of their execution nor was it the unusually horrible circumstances attending the execution. The greatest evil about it all was the renewed demonstration before the world that here in Oregon men still kill other men legally and do it in a frightful manner. The evil is greatest in its debasing effect upon society."

Of the execution the Roseburg News-Review says: "The published facts will be fine morsels for the sob-sisters of this state and that as an object lesson for the criminally inclined the 'exhibition' ought to prove of some benefit." Perhaps it ought to but it will not. We have ample demonstration here in Oregon that the law for hanging does no deter murder. Hanging is an act of the law's vengeance, not a deterrent. It was so designed originally and is so today. As for the rest, we will venture the guess that the News-Review holds with Bryan for fundamentalism, the Mosaic law and the righteousness of what was done a recounted in the story of the men of Al.

CHAPTER 16

THE SPARING OF ALTON B. COVELL

Alton B. Covell, the eldest child of Fred Covell was born in California on October 13, 1907.

September 14, 1923 the *Coquille Valley Sentinel* headlined: **Young Covell Feeble Minded**

> Judge R. H. Mast received a letter yesterday from the Court of Domestic Relations at Portland informing him that the 16-year old boy, Alton Covell who is being held in jail here during the investigation of the killing of his step-mother, Mrs. Fred Covell, had been adjudged feeble-minded in that court some years ago. The family lived out from Portland on the Powell Valley road and after he had been examined but before the commitment paper had been made out for his admission to the asylum, the family left there and came down here. No further effort to have him committed was made by the Multnomah county court.
>
> There have been no new developments in the murder case the past week. Officials are working on the case and every incident and phase of the crime is being investigated. No charge has yet been preferred against Dr. Covell, nor his son.
>
> District Attorney Fisher is reported in a Bay paper as saying that Dr. Covell's hearing will be held next week.

Figure 38: Alton Covell - *The Coos Bay Times,* October 17, 1923

On October 17, 1923 the *Coos Bay Times* headlined: **ALTON COVELL IS LOW GRADE MORON** Concerning Alton Covell, confessed slayer of his stepmother, Mrs. Ebba Covell, at Bandon, a Portland paper says:

> If Oregon's school for the feeble minded had not been overcrowded in April of this year, Alton Covell might not today face charges at Coquille of murdering his stepmother.
>
> This was revealed here Tuesday when records of the juvenile court disclosed that young Covell was examined by Multnomah county authorities, found to be a "low grade moron" and ordered committed to the state school for the feeble minded.
>
> Because the school was crowded to capacity he was sent back to his family, where he was again under the influence of his uncle's superior will power.
>
> From November of 1922 until March of this year the Covell boy was a pupil at the Ainsworth School, juvenile court records show.
>
> Mrs. L. D. Thomas, principal of the school, observed that he was behind in his classes and was not responsive to the questions put to him.
>
> He associated only with children younger than himself, Mrs. Thomas told Dr. S.C. Kohs, psychologist of the court of domestic relations.
>
> In response to a request from Mrs. Thomas an intelligence test was given the boy by Dr. Kohs and Dr. S. E. Josephi, alienist.
>
> The result was a grade of 59 per cent, intelligence quotient, rating him as a "low grade moron." At that time Alton Covell was living with his uncle, Arthur Covell, also indicted for murder of Mrs. Ebba Covell at

Bandon, and the two were boarding with a woman on Portland Heights.

The remarkable influence of the uncle upon the young man was commented upon by Mrs. Thomas at the time of the examination, and the apparent weakness of the youth was brought out it is said.

December 14, 1923 the *Coos Bay Times* headlined: **RECORD MADE IN THE MURDER CASE — TRIAL DISPOSED OF WITHOUT WASTE OF TIME** — Officials Are Complimented for Disposition to Give Alton Covell a Fair Trial

COQUILLE, Ore., Dec. 14. — With the conclusion of the final arguments in the Alton Covell case yesterday afternoon a record probably for the entire state was broken in the rapidity in which the case was tried. Judge Kendall wanted to look up some points of law so let the jury go until this morning to hear the instructions and take the case.

The jury was secured in record time for a murder case, only three and one-half hours being occupied. The evidence of both sides was all put before the jury in a day and a half and the final arguments were brief.

The lawyers did not quarrel which sometimes takes a lot of time in such cases but both aides, endeavored to facilitate matters.

Presents Good Case

District Attorney Fisher presented the case clearly both in the handling of the testimony and in his arguments. He showed an entire lack of any vindictiveness in his prosecution. In fact he frequently expressed the sympathy for one of such youthfulness being in such a position but he insisted in his arguments that the boy was guilty Mr. Fisher did not ask for the death penalty when addressing the jury. Many who heard the case said that the prosecution was well presented and that the district attorney had shown a disposition for fairness.

Made Strong Plea

Grant Corby, the defense attorney, made a very strong plea to the jury in presenting his claim that the boy was subnormal and influenced and dominated by the superior mind of Arthur Covell. The attorney pictured the position of the boy who had given up much of his education in order to be the constant attendant up the crippled uncle. The attorney also blamed the state for not having given the boy the protection of the feeble minded institute to which he was committed at Portland.

Judge Kendall had some rather hard legal questions to decide and he awaited the giving of the instructions until this morning so ho could satisfy himself fully on several points of law.

Father Satisfied

That the boy had a fair trial was the general opinion of those who heard the proceedings. In fact Dr. Fred Covell, the father of the boy, said he felt that everyone wanted to be fair and complimented the judge.

December 15, 1923 the *Coos Bay Times* headlined: **SIXTEEN YEAR OLD YOUTH FOUND GUILTY OF FIRST DEGREE MURDER** — Alton Covell Jury Returns After Forty-Five Minute Deliberation — Recommendation Is Made For Life Imprisonment as Punishment for Murder of Mrs. Covell — **TRIAL OF YOUTH SPEEDILY EXECUTED; CASE STARTED LAST WEDNESDAY MORNING** — Expression on Boy's Face Does Not Change When Verdict Is Read — Eyes Are Cast Downward as They Were During Greatest Period During Trial — Silence Strains Nerves

COQUILLE, Ore., Dec. 15. — Guilty of murder in the first: degree with the recommendation of life imprisonment as the punishment, was the verdict of the jury in the trial of Alton Covell, 16-year-old youth, for the murder of his step-mother Mrs. Ebba Covell, by strangling her to death with an ammonia soaked rag, the family home near Bandon on September 3. The jury returned the verdict this morning at 10:35 after deliberating for 45 minutes.

The jurors filed into the court room and look their seats following the announcement that a verdict had been arrived at. The faces of the members of the jury indicated that they had found a verdict against the boy.

Silence Straining

Grant Corby, the defense attorney, was not present and Judge Kendall could not receive the verdict until he was sent for. During that period of five minutes a silence fell over the court room, a silence that strained the nerves of even the strongest. No word was uttered.

When the verdict was read; Alton Covell, the defendant, did not alter an expression on his face. He did not even look up, but kept his eyes on the floor, the pose he had maintained during the trial which started Wednesday morning.

Sentence Tuesday

Judge Kendall announced this afternoon that he would sentence Alton Covell at 10 o'clock Tuesday morning.

It has not been decided what will be done with Lucile Covell. According to her own testimony she knew of the murder before it occurred and is regarded as an accomplice. Her case may be handled in the juvenile court or may come before the grand jury. She is now in the custody of the juvenile officer.

The jury in arriving at the verdict first voted on sanity. They all agreed that the defendant was sane. A vote was then taken on guilt and another on the punishment. All agreed on life imprisonment.

Compliments Attorneys

Judge Kendall on the convening of the circuit court this morning gave his instructions to the jury, the final arguments having been made last night. The judge complimented the attorneys for the manner in which they had conducted the case and for avoiding delays and expediting the progress of the case.

Very few were in the court room this morning The defendant was seated with his lawyer and assumed the same attitude he had held during the trial, with his eyes cast down. Dr. Fred Covell, father of the defendant, was in the court room and Lucile, the boy's sister, arrived early and took a seat at the back of the room.

Gives Instructions

The court instructed as to murder in the second degree. The Judge said that murder in the second degree was murder purposely but without deliberation. The judge said that in murder in the first degree deliberation and premeditation must appear but in murder in the second degree they would not exist, although in each case the murder could he committed purposely.

The court said that murder due to a sudden passion without deliberation would constitute manslaughter.

Sister's Evidence Questioned

The judge said that the jury could not convict on the testimony of an accomplice unless it is corroborated. He said it was the duty of the jury to decide whether Lucile Covell was an accomplice and if such is found to be the case her testimony could not be used to convict unless it was corroborated by other testimony.

As to the confessions the jury was told that is was the duty of the state to show that any confession was voluntarily made.

Insanity Be Proven

The judge said that with the claim of insanity it was up to the to defense to prove it. The judge defines insanity legally as a condition of a dethroned mind to the extent that he did not know the extent and consequences of his crime.

The court instructed the jury that feeble mindedness was not a defense for murder in this state but that evidence of feeble mindedness could be considered as contributing to the mental condition of the defendant or as a step leading to insanity which is a defense.

Six Verdicts Possible

The jury was instructed that first degree murder was punishable by hanging unless the jury recommended life imprisonment.

The court told the jury it could find a verdict in one of six forms, as follows:

Guilty of first degree murder.
Guilty of first degree murder with recommendations for life imprisonment.
Guilty of manslaughter.
Guilty of second degree murder.
Not guilty because of insanity.
Not guilty.

Fisher's Argument

District Attorney Fisher in his argument spoke of the rapidity with which the case was tried, the evidence all being presented in a day and a half but said that this did not make the affair any less serious than if the trial had taken up a longer time. Mr. Fisher claimed that the facts he had recited in his opening statement had been proved and none had been disputed by the defense. He said when Arthur and Alton came back from Portland they planned night after night to commit a cold blooded murder of a defenseless woman. Mr. Fisher said it was a well planned murder but they were caught up on one point.

Mr. Fisher insisted that Alton was not insane and that his acts on the Sunday before the murder indicated that the boy was worried because he was to commit murder the next day. It was held that the boy got up Monday morning with the intention of killing the woman. Mr. Fisher held that because Arthur helped him did not lessen the crime of the part of Alton, and that it was Alton that did the actual killing and that instead of sympathy for Alton there should be sympathy for the three motherless children of the murdered woman.

Mr. Fisher said that the murderer did not figure that the ammonia stain could not be removed after death as it could be in life and that it was this mark on the face which led to the establishment of guilt. The prosecutor that a clever story about going for the cow and finding Mrs. Covell on the floor was cleverly managed. Alton, he said, cold bloodedly committed murder, ate lunch and went on with the washing as though nothing had happened. Mr. Fisher said that the confession was in Alton's handwriting and was not the writing of an insane person but that of a mature individual.

Mr. Fisher said that the examination made by Dr. Joseph was theoretical but that the doctors locally who made a practical examination said the boy was sane. Mr. Fisher said that different experts had arrived at various degrees of mentality but that they had all said that the boy was not insane.

Defense Argument

Attorney Grant Corby for the defenses made his argument following Mr. Fisher, he held that when the defendant was committed lo the institution for feeble minded when arraigned in the court of domestic relations in Multnomah county, it was not the fault of the defendant that he was not sent to the institution but instead was sent back home to bear the burden of nursing his uncle and going through the drudgeries of his home. The attorney quoted the report of the Multnomah court that the boy was not safe to be at large. Mr. Corny said that aside from the influence which was exercised that on account of the boy's age there would be a question as to his responsibility. The lawyer said it was possible for a persons mind to be constantly directed to one such act until it might not seem serious before it was performed but afterward would look differently.

Mr. Corby held that no motive was shown. There was no money to be gained and nothing in any way to profit by the murder and no malice shown but that the boy was subnormal, ingressive, not cruel and with nothing to gain or escape. Under such circumstances it was claimed he could not have been accountable and committed such a crime.

Mr. Fisher made his final arguments and the jury will receive the instructions tomorrow.

Upon loosing his appeal in the Supreme Court, Arthur Covell attempted to spare his nephew Alton from the fate of life imprisonment he was experiencing. On April 3, 1925 the *Coos Bay Harbor* printed the following: **ARTHUR COVELL SHIELDS ALTON** — Condemned Murderer Repudiates Confession Given Before Trial of 1923 — Says Nephew did not Kill Step-Mother.

When he was sentenced Wednesday in the circuit court for conspiring to cause the death of his sister-in-law, Mrs. Ebba Covell, Arthur Covell, when permitted to speak before sentence was passed made a long statement which he read from a text he had prepared for the occasion, the gist of which was that Alton Covell had nothing whatever to do with the murder, nor did the condemned man.

The address hinted that Fred Covell killed the woman. This was her husband. The statement, however, was not clear as to whom should be blamed for the killing, yet it leaves enough doubt to perhaps cloud Fred's life.

Very few, it is believed, will take stock in Arthur Covell's statement, simply looking upon it as a device to save the nephew from his life sentence in the penitentiary.

During Alton's incarceration there were records from various family members seeking information ranging from requesting his release to sending Christmas gifts. The records revealed the following about Alton's family members. In 1927, Alton's sister, Lucile married and resided in Portland using her married name of Hart. In 1929 his father, Fred was living in Cornell, California.[T]

Having been spared the death penalty by the jury, Alton Covell received a Governor's Pardon from Governor

Sentence

IN THE CIRCUIT COURT OF THE STATE OF OREGON,
IN AND FOR THE COUNTY OF COOS

THE STATE OF OREGON, Plaintiff, No 1863
vs.
Alton Covell Defendant 19

Now, on this day comes the State of Oregon, by Ben S. Fisher District Attorney, and the defendant above named, in person, and by Grant Corby his attorney The said Alton Covell having heretofore been duly convicted ~~xxxxxxxxxxxxxxxxxxxxxxxxxxx~~ the crime of murder in the first degree

and this being the time fixed for sentencing said defendant and no motion having been filed for a new trial or in arrest of judgment, the said defendant being informed by the Court of the verdict of the jury and asked by the Court if he had anything to say why judgment should not be pronounced against him answered, showing no good or sufficient cause.

It is, Therefore, Considered, Ordered and Adjudged, by the Court, that said Alton Covell be confined in the penitentiary of the State of Oregon a prisoner and there kept a prisoner for the period of the remainder of his natural life. ~~xandxthatxxxxxxxpay the costs and disbursements of this action to be taxed~~.

John C. Kendall
Judge

Figure 39: Sentence of Alton Covell

Julius L. Meier on October 31, 1934, having served almost eleven years for his crime. Located within a seven page document leading to Alton's parole the following was learned about his life in prison. Alton had no prison record. The warden reported; "Record of good conduct, industry and evidence of apparent reformation that in my opinion entitles him to all credits allowed by the parole law." Additionally a portion of a letter from Margaret Bondurant of Portland Oregon was included. Mrs. Bondurant stated the following; "The boy has been employed in the bakery most of the time he has been in the institution, and I sincerely believe that through my personal efforts and those of other interested persons, work of this kind can be secured for him in Portland so that he will not be idol after his release. His sister is married and living in Portland and her home is open to him, where he will have a modest but desirable place to live. I have personally inspected the residence of his sister and find the conditions there well suited to his mental and physical well being. His sister and her husband are very anxious to have him with then.

This boy has now reached an age where if he is to make anything of his life he must have the opportunity. He has been faithful and earnest while in prison and has done everything in his power to fit himself to take his place in the world. I personally am willing to take any responsibility that you or the Board care to ask of me in this matter and will extend every effort in his behalf if he is released."[48]

[T] Cornell is an unincorporated community located on Highway 139 in Modoc county California.

Figure 40: Alton Covell Booking and Release Photograph from the Oregon Sate Penitentiary

At the age of 26 Alton Covell left prison a free man. In 1997 it was reported that Alton resided in Texas and had three successful children.[6969] Alton Covell died in Palestine Texas on January 29, 2002.

CHAPTER 17

THE LYNCHING OF ALONZO TUCKER

The unfortunate lynching of Alonzo Tucker is one of most erroneously reported incidents in Oregon history. With the published facts of the Coroner's Inquest and numerous articles from various newspapers, factual history is restored. No resident of Coos Bay, Coos County, or the State want to flaunt a historical "black-eye;" however, the citizens would want the truth to be known no matter how distasteful that truth may be.

Case Synopsis: An allegation of rape was claimed by Mrs. Lizzie Dennis of Libby. The crime was claimed to have been perpetrated by Marshfield resident Alonzo Tucker. Committed outside of Marshfield on the road to Libby, Tucker was alleged to have forced Mrs. Dennis into the brush where he raped her. After reporting the crime Tucker was arrested in Marshfield by City Marshal J.W. "Jack" Carter. As evening approached an angry mob formed with the intent to forcibly take Tucker from the city jail. Their effort to seize Tucker was foiled by Marshal Carter who attempted to take Tucker to a safe location; however, Tucker escaped. Tucker was apprehended the next day after being shot and chased by the crowd. In the process of being taken to Libby to be lynched, Tucker bled to death from the gunshot wounds, and his body was hanged from the Seventh street bridge.

The Motive: Mob mentality due to the fact Tucker, an African American, was alleged to have committed an act of rape against Mrs. Lizzie Dennis, an Anglo Saxon.

The Parties: Lizzie Gertrude Tripp was born May 2, 1868 in Luzerne County. Pennsylvania. At an unknown time she married Fred Kneaper and the two had four children.[U] They resided in Acme Oregon[71] during which time, Lizzie Kneaper met Ben Dennis. The two, took the three younger Kneaper children and relocated to Coos county where Lizzie took the name of Davis. The Kneaper's did divorce at some unknown point of time. After the incident the Dennis family moved to Eureka California where the two remained together till their deaths.

Nothing beyond the newspaper reports which reveal the life of Alonzo Tucker.

The Crime and Punishment: September 19, 1902 the *Myrtle Point Enterprise* headlined: **SWIFT JUSTICE FOR FIEND** Negro Commits Outrage on White Woman — Killed by Angry Mob.

> Alonzo Tucker, a negro living at Marshfield was arrested Wednesday on a charge of having committed the crime of rape upon the person of Mrs. Ben Dennis, of Libby, and died at the hands of an angry mob Thursday morning. We have been unable to get a correct account of the killing but it seems that the negro was being pursued by the mob and ran to the second story of a building, locking himself in one of the rooms. The mob broke the door down, riddled him with bullets, and then threw him out of the window onto the street below, later taking the body to the scene where the outrage was committed and hanging it to a bridge.
>
> The story of the crime for which Tucker suffered is about as follows: Mrs. Dennis had been in Marshfield and started home about 10 a. m. When she reached a point on the wagon road not far beyond the IOOF cemetery, the negro emerged from the brush. He seized her and placed his hands over her mouth to stifle her cries. Carrying her into the bushes he choked her into submission and accomplished his purpose. He then left her and started toward Marshfield. She made her way as quickly as possible to her house at Libby where she reported what had occurred.
>
> When Tucker reached Marshfield he was arrested and placed in jail. As night approached it was reported that a crowd of armed miners were collected waiting for night to come, and Marshal Carter on hearing this, took the prisoner from the jail, expecting to take him to Empire for safe keeping. They started for the wharf, but in reaching the bay found no boat, then Tucker, who was walking behind Carter, gave him a push and sprang to the mudflat, escaping from the officer as well as the mob. The mob did not give up

[U] Acme was a small milling town located south-west of Florence in Douglas County Oregon.

the hunt and when Tucker was again located, lost no time in putting him to death.

Tucker has been on the bay for some time. He professed to be a prize fighter, and recently opened a school of physical culture at Marshfield.

Also printed: A negro fiend lynched by a mob of "civilized Christians" sounds queer doesn't it? While the law is inadequate in such cases, mob violence cannot be sanctioned by law abiding citizens.

On September 20, 1902 the *Marshfield Sun* headlined: Horrible Crime Brings Swift Punishment. — **NEGRO RAPEIST SHOT TO DEATH WHILE ATTEMPTING TO ESCAPE** — Discovered in Hiding By Two Small Boys, He Comes Out and Runs For His Life — **FATALLY WOUNDED BY A RIFLE SHOT — A PISTOL BULLET STOPS HIS COURSE** —- Body Swung From South Marshfield Bridge — Coroner's Jury Finds No Crime Has Been Committed

From Thursday's Daily

Alonzo Tucker, a negro, was arrested shortly before noon yesterday, on a charge of having committed the crime of rape upon the person of Mrs. Ben Dennis, of Libby.

The information was telephoned to Marshal Carter, with the request that he intercept Tucker, who was said to be on his way to Marshfield, and place him under arrest. The marshal had seen Tucker coming into town a few minutes before and had no trouble locating his man and landing him in jail.

Mr. and Mrs. Dennis came to the Bay the latter part of last year. They lived for a while in Marshfield, where Mr. Dennis worked as a painter. Last spring they moved to Libby, where he had obtained employment in the mine. They have two children, and those who know them speak in the highest terms of Mrs. Dennis.

Tucker has been on the Bay for some time. He worked at Libby and afterward came to Marshfield where he blacked boots in a local barbershop. He professes to be a prize-fighter and recently opened a "School of Physical Culture" in the building formerly occupied by the Y.M.C.A.

Various stories of the outrage were current on the street, but the facts stated by Deputy Prosecuting Attorney Farrin, who visited Libby in the afternoon and talked with the woman, is that Mrs. Dennis had been in Marshfield and started home about 10 a.m. When she reached a point on the wagon road not far beyond the I.O.O.F. cemetery, the Negro emerged from the brush. He seized her and placed his hands over her mouth to stifle her cries. Carrying her into the bushes he choked her into submission and accomplished his purpose.

He then left her and started toward Marshfield, she made her way as quickly as possible to her home at Libby where she reported what had occurred.

One story is that Dr. Tower overtook her on the road out and took her to Libby in his buggy.

The village was soon aroused, and P. Hennessey and Alf Nichols at once armed themselves and started out after the black fiend, arriving in Marshfield but a short time after he did. They said the lady positively recognized her assailant, and that there could be no mistake as to his identity.

There was naturally much talk on the streets of making short work of the perpetrator of this crime, and the opinion was freely expressed that a crowd would be down from Libby last night to take vengeance on the perpetrator of this dastardly outrage.

As night approached it was reported that a crowd of armed miners were collected on at the railroad depot apparently waiting for night to come.

Just at dusk they came in about one hundred strong, and a large number of them with rifles. They marched down Front street and out to the jail, which is located on the wharf back of the engine house.

The miners were evidently bent on doing business. They made no unnecessary noise but went swiftly and silently to the objective point. The floating population of Front street went with them.

Arriving at the jail, it was soon discovered to be empty, and the crowd fell into confusion. Then the word was passed that the Negro was loose in the immediate vicinity and there was a scattering of the party in search of him.

The disappearance of Tucker was accounted for by Marshal Carter and Constable Sunderland in this way: A few moments before the mob reached the jail warning was brought that they were coming. This was sooner that the officers expected any trouble, and they were not prepared. They at once took Tucker from the jail and ran him across to the boat slip back of the I.O.O.F. building, where they expected to find a boat in which to take him out on bay or "to Empire." Carter was ahead with the Negro while Sunderland brought up in the rear. Reaching the slip, they saw that no boat was there.

Then Tucker gave Carter a push and sprang to the mudflat under the wharf it being low tide.

By this time the mob was on hand, and to them Marshal Carter confided his troubles. Search under the wharf showed tracks in the mud. These were traced to a point back of the O'Connell hardware store where the trail was lost.

No further trace of the fugitive could be discovered and matters were fairly quiet until just before ten o'clock, when watchers on the wharf discovered a boat two-thirds across the bay toward the East Marshfield wharf and apparently heading in that direction. The boat could be plainly seen in the moonlight but no occupant was visible.

Repeated hails bringing no response, a fusillade of rifle shots at once commenced and was kept up for seven minutes, probably a hundred shots being fired at the boat.

Then a boat load of men put out from the dock and made its way across to where the suspected craft was still floating peacefully upward with the flood. They overhauled the stranger passed around it and then a still small voice wafted back the tidings: "He ain't here."

As this paper goes to press the wharf is guarded and the search is being prosecuted by the miners, who are determined that the black fiend shall not go unpunished.

From Friday's Daily

Within 24 hours of the time when the Negro, Alonzo Tucker, committed a criminal assault on the white woman, Mrs. Ben Dennis, his lifeless body was dangling at the end of a rope from the bridge leading out from South Marshfield.

Events had moved swiftly for the black fiend in the mean time. Had been arrested and placed in jail, made his escape from the officers with a mob at his heels, had spent the night under the wharves, had heard a couple of hundred shots fired over his head at a boat in which he was suspected to be attempting his escape, had been discovered in his hiding place, had come out and made a run for his life, had been shot down and carted to the spot where his body was left hanging.

To take up the story where yesterday's paper stopped, the night passed quietly after the incident of the empty boat. It seem that the search under the dock was discontinued at that time and the avengers devoted their attention to keeping a strict guard on all possible avenues of escape. They were confident that the negro was still in hiding under some of the buildings along the water front, and they patiently waited for daylight, confident that their prey could not elude them.

After daylight the search was resumed, but was unsuccessful until about nine o'clock. Then two small boys Shirly Prentiss and Madoc Gulovson discovered the fugitive under Dean & Cox's store, where he had crawled back on the ballast as far as he could get. When he found the boys had seen him, the Negro started for them with a threat to wring their necks. Fortunately for them he could only crawl, in the cramped space, and they were able to scramble out before he could reach them. The boys raised the alarm, and the Negro made his appearance immediately after they did.

He emerged at the south side of the warehouse and started around the south east corner. Several men were on the corner of the wharf behind him and one fired a shot which passed through the Negro's right leg about half way between the knee and the hip, severing the large artery and inflicting a wound from which, the doctors testify, death must have resulted in about ten minutes, but which did not stop the fugitive.

He ran across from the warehouse with the evident intention of going west on "A" street. Seeing guards in that direction he then turned north and started down Front street. He was running easily with his arms at his sides, as if taking his exercise.

When the fugitive was nearly in front of Dean & Cox's. store, he staggered and threw up his hands but did not fall. Turning, he ran in at the front door of the store. Seeing Eligah Lewis in store, Tucker again threw up his hands and ejaculated, "Oh lord, have mercy."

He then ran through the opening into the side wareroom and to the back door opening upon the wharf. Seeing armed men closing in from that direction, he passed through the small door into the main store and started up the stairs, leading to the second story. When half way up one of his pursuers armed with a revolver reached the foot of the stairs. He called on the fleeing man to stop but the warning was unheeded, and just as Tucker reached the head of the stairs his pursuer fired. The Negro reeled and fell headlong through a door which lead into the loft over the ware room.

This shot was from a 38 caliber revolver and took effect in the back. It lodged against and broke a rib, and while the wound in itself would not have been fatal, the shock and impact of the bullet was enough to stop the action of he heart, already about to collapse from an immense loss of blood.

Several men reached him a moment later and found him stretched upon his back, as if dead. He was not dead, however, as he had life enough to make some resistance when he was dragged to the wide back door of the loft from which he was lowered on a rope to the wharf below.

Here a rope was placed around his neck, and loading him upon a store truck the crowd started with him for the scene of his crime.

Before the outskirts of town were reached, however, he was discovered to be dead, and when the bridge leading from South Marshfield toward the cemetery was reached, the rope which was already around his neck was tied to a timber of the bridge and the body was pushed over the side and left hanging about six feet below the roadway. This was a few minutes before ten o'clock.

The crowd which witnessed the last act of the tragedy is estimated at about three hundred. They were quiet and orderly, and it is safe to say that no such lawless preceding was ever conducted with less unnecessary disturbance of the peace.

Coroner Horsfall being notified proceeded to the scene and impaneled a jury for the inquest. At 1:35 p.m. the body was cut down and brought into town, where it was taken to the room where the dead pugilist had been conducting a school of physical culture, where the inquest was held.

The coroner's jury consisted of the following well-known and responsible citizens: W.B. Curtis, foreman, R. Walter, Dr. A.B. Prentiss, Chas. Stauff, A.C. Kruse and J.W. Flanagan.

Examination of the body showed only the two wounds mentioned above. Doctors McCormac and Gross testified that the wound in the leg was sufficient to cause death in a very limited time.

Dr. McCormac had met and joined the crowd as they carted the Negro out of town and had examined him before the hanging and he stated positively that the man was unquestionably dead before he was swung off the bridge.

Some other witnesses were examined but no evidence as to the identity of the parties responsible for the death of Negro fiend was elicited. It was shown in evidence that the Negro was a fugitive from justice, and that the shooting was undoubtedly done by parties who were assisting the officers in his re-capture.

The verdict of the jury was to the effect that the deceased came to his death by a gunshot wound in the thigh, inflicted while resisting arrest for a felony; that the persons who inflicted said wound were unknown to the jury; and that no crime was committed thereby.

This seems to settle the matter officially, so far as any complications are concerned, and it is not likely that any attempt will be made to go behind the verdict of the jury.

September 20, 1902 the *Coast Mail* headlined: From Thursday's Daily **NO MOB LAW FOR MARSHFIELD**

The MAIL would suggest that there may be imminent need, even before this paper reaches its readers, for the coolheaded, law-abiding citizens of this community to exert their influence on behalf of law and order. The dastardly crime committed at Libby yesterday has naturally aroused horror and indignation, and among all classes a desire that the perpetrator may be adequately punished. It is but natural that there should be much talk of "lynch him," and even people whom we would expect to see ranged on the side of the good name of this community have been heard counseling a course which would place Coos Bay in the category of places where Judge Lynch prevails.

Against this sentiment all who regard the good name of the community should set their faces. No matter with what feelings of anger and abhorrence we may regard the monster who commits such a crime, the law should be allowed to take its course. Even though the extreme penalty of twenty year's imprisonment is not an adequate punishment for the crime, yet nothing could be gained by a course for which there is seldom any excuse where the law and the law's officers are able to cope with the situation.

There is no question but the law is inadequate for a case of this kind. a certain squeamishness and maudlin sentimentality prevents the enactment of laws which would provide punishment to fit crimes of this nature, but mob law certainly does not cover the case, and it has not been shown that any good has been accomplished by the exhibitions of unlicensed cruelty and torture to which different sections of the country have been treated in the last dozen years.

The annals of Coos Bay are remarkably free from deeds of violence and lawlessness. It would be best to keep them so.

Since the above was in type the attempt against which the MAIL protests has been made, and the negro has escaped, not only from the mob but from the officers. It should be seen to that the attempted lynching does not result in his escaping punishment altogether.

MIGHT HAVE BEEN WORSE

Now that the thing against which the MAIL protested has actually occurred, it is no use crying over spilt milk. The nigger is dead and it may be said of the manner of his death that it was at least easier than he deserved. It is a matter for congratulation that he was practically dead when he fell into the hands of the parties who had been after him, for had they captured him alive, it is hard to predict just what might have occurred, and it is nearly certain serious complications would have arisen over the affair.

As it is, the official records seem to present a remarkably smooth and finished surface, and an investigation which would have entailed endless expense does not seem to be called for.

Perhaps the worst feature of the affair is the black eye which may be given to this community in the estimation of the outside world.

This much must be said for the crowd of miners which accomplished the work: they were quiet and orderly and made as little disturbance as possible and thereby were in deadly earnest.

While the MAIL would have preferred to see the law take it course, the actual outcome was better than to let the black fiend escape, even temporarily.

September 25, 1902 the *Bandon Recorder* headlined: **The Marshfield Lynching Incident** - Marshfield was the scene of mob law last Thursday in which the life of a human being was sacrificed to satisfy the rage of an angry crowd.

The cause which led up to the killing is given below as found in the Coast Mail of September 18:

Alonzo Tucker, a negro was arrested shortly before noon yesterday, on a charge of having committed the crime of rape upon the person of Mrs. Ben Dennis, of Libby.

The information was telephoned to marshal Carter, with the request that he intercept Tucker, who was said to be on his way to Marshfield, and place him under arrest. The marshal had seen Tucker coming into town a few minutes before and had no trouble locating his man and leading him to jail.

Various stories of the outrage were current on the street , but the facts as stated by Deputy Prosecuting Attorney Farrin, who visited Libby in the afternoon and talked with the woman, is that Mrs. Dennis had been in Marshfield and started home about 10:00 am. When she reached a point on the wagon road not far from the I.O.O.F. cemetery, the Negro emerged from the brush. He seized her and placed his hands over her mouth to

stifle her cries. Carrying her into the bushes he choked her into submission and accomplished his purpose.

He then left and started toward Marshfield. She made her way as quickly as possible to her home at Libby where she reported what had occurred.

In the evening a crowd of miners from Libby about a hundred strong appeared on the scene at Marshfield, so the story goes, but they failed to find the man they were after in the jail but whose disappearance was thus accounted for according to the Mail:

A few moments before the mob reached the jail warning was brought that they were coming. This was sooner than the officers expected any trouble, and they were not prepared. They at once took Tucker from the jail and ran him across to the boat slip back of the I.O.O.F. building where they expected to find a boat in which to take him out on the bay or "to Empire." Carter was ahead with the negro while Sunderland brought up the rear. Reaching the slip they saw that no boat was there, then Tucker gave Carter a push and sprang to the mudflat under the wharf it being low tide.

By the time this the mob was on hand, and to them Marshal Carter confined his trouble. Search under the wharf showed tracks in the mud. These were traced to the point back of O'Conell hardware store, where the trail was lost.

A watch was kept up all night and next day he was discovered by some of the boys who peppered him with an air gun until driven out. The Sun gives the following account of the killing:

As he emerged from under cover a 30 30 cracked and the bullet caught him in the leg. A moment later two shots were fired and Tucker, with the blood streaming from his wounds ran into Dean & Cox's store, with the mob following at his heels. At first it was intended to string him up on the spot, but second thought was to take him to the scene of his crime. Tucker was placed into a cart and the start was made, but it was noticed on the route that life about extinct, and a rope was placed around his neck and the other fastened to a beam on the South Marshfield bridge leading to the cemetery and Libby. Tucker's remains dangled from the end of a rope here for several hours until they were cut down by the order of the coroner and an inquest held over the remains, the jury reaching a verdict that Tucker died from a gunshot wound in the thigh inflicted while attempting escape arrest for felony; that said wound was inflicted by parties unknown to this jury and that no crime was committed thereby. The jurors were W.B. Curtis, Foreman; R. Walter, A.B. Prentis, Chas. Stauff, Archie Kruse, J.W. Flanagan.

Immediately following: It is a lamentable disgrace that has overtaken Coos County and through her the State of Oregon whose name has been tarnished by the untoward conduct of some of her citizens.

If the Negro was guilty of the crime, as charged, he merited punishment adequate to his crime; he was in the hands of the law and the law should have been respected. Tucker had been arrested and held, but the public has not been apprised of a preliminary examination, nor of a single legal inquiry as to whether the man was guilty or innocent, and from the reports that come out from Marshfield there is grave doubt cast as to the guilt of the party whose life paid the penalty.

There is one thing apparent now at least and that is that a murder has been committed. There is a difference as to how a criminal may be dealt with. When he is once in the toil of the law, it acts, and if he found guilty the law condemns and punishes. But when any man presumes to take the office of the law into his hands, he has exceeded such authority, takes the life of a human being, he simply commits murder, and the same is true of any number of men so engaged.

That twenty years imprisonment is not adequate punishment for such crimes is no argument in favor of mob law. Lawyers and courts have found as a fact that out of every ten such cases that come into the courts but one is a genuine case.

September 26, 1902 the *Myrtle Point Enterprise* headlined: **An Oregon Lynching.**

It has been not long since a lynching took place in Oregon that with in recent years the assertion has been frequent that the history of the state is free from the disgrace of such episodes. While this is not strictly correct, the self respect and orderly habit of our people are such that the law has almost without an exception been permitted to take its course. Coos County, in particular, the scene of yesterday's outbreak, has punished its offenders with exemplary promptness and vigor.

The certainty that the negro wretch would have met condign punishment in due process of law is chiefly pertinent, however, in stamping the weak and foolish deed of mob law as unnecessary as well as lawless,. No such outbreak of lynch law should be suffered to pass without severest reprobation, for the eradication of the lawlessness from its life is one of the things must to be desired by any community. Especially in a new ambitious region like Coos bay, the effect of an occurrence like that reported from Marshfield can only be to militate against both capital and settlement. Who does not know that the horrors of southern lynching hang like a pall over the industrial development of "the black belt?"

We would not do injustice to any one in so serious a matter, but it seems to us that this lynching, as well as others in Northern States, may be in some measure indirectly attributed to the increase of Southern lynching and to the considerable body of public opinion that has been enlisted in their defense can breed only lawlessness. Lynchings is more certain to breed crime than order. So long as lynching is up held on any grounds, it will not only prevail, but it will increase. No crime, however revolting, justifies resort to mob law, whether in Oregon or South Carolina. There is a blot upon the history of Coos County that can never be erased and can only be dimmed by greater circumspection from now on. Oregon will be in the next year's table of lynchings, whence it has a long time been proudly absent, and from the Southern papers we shall hear is estoped from condemning Southern lynchings. — Oregonian.

September 28, 1902 the *Coquille City Herald* headlined: **Swift Justice.**

Mrs. Ben Dennis, of Libby, was waylayed on the road Tuesday forenoon as she was returning home from this city by Alonzo Tucker, colored, who dragged her into the bushes where he criminally assaulted her. Tucker is a big powerful brute and he told Mrs. Dennis that if she ever murmured he would choke her to death. When his beastly desires were gratified he turned his prey loose at the same time threatened her, if she ever divulged the proceedings.

Mrs. Dennis half prostrated from the shock and overcome with excitement managed to get home and told what had happened. Superintendent Hennessey and Al Nicholls on learning what had occurred shouldered their rifles and started in search of Tucker. They were hot on his trail and within range of the negro as he entered the town. Tucker knew they were after him but made no attempt to escape and he was finally arrested and placed in jail. There were loud mutterings of "necktie party." Little attention was paid to this, though the indignation of the miners kept growing as each man returned to his home and ascertained what had happened, and a band of two hundred men, unmasked, marched into town at 7:30 o'clock. The van of the party was heavily armed. As they proceeded up to the jail door Marshal Carter attempted to get his prisoner into a boat and get him out of the way of the mob. As he was doing this Tucker jumped into the mudflat and got under the wharf. The miners were more indignant now than ever. They stationed guards at every point of egress from the city, every nook and crevice was searched in vain. Tucker managed to elude his pursuers all night but in the morning the searchers were reinforced by the small boys of town. The lads located him under Dean & Co's wharf and fortunately enough for them Tucker did not get hold of them or he would have wrung their necks as he told them. The boys peppered Tucker with an air gun and finally drove him from his hiding place. As he emerged from under cover a 30-30 cracked and the bullet caught him in he leg. A moment later two shots were fired and Tucker, with blood streaming from his wounds ran into Dean & Co's store, with the mob following at his heals. At first it was intended to string him up on the spot, but a second thought was to take him to the scene of his crime. Tucker was placed into a cart and the start was made, but it was not iced on the route that life was about extinct, and a rope was placed around his neck and the other end fastened to a beam on the South Marshfield bridge leading to the cemetery and Libby. Tucker's remains dangled from the end of a rope for several hours until they were cut down by the orders of the coroner and an inquest held over the remains. The jury reached a verdict that Tucker died from a gunshot wound in the thigh inflicted while attempting to escape arrest for felony; that said wound was inflicted by parties unknown to the jury and that no crime was committed thereby. The jurors were W.B. Curtis, foreman; R. Walter, A.B. Prentis, Chas. Stauff, Archie Kruse, J.W. Flanagan.

The crime and the following proceedings precipitated the most intense excitement. It is without doubt one of the worst crimes ever committed in this section.

Mrs. Dennis, the outraged woman, has a husband and three small children, and is a woman whose reputation is above reproach.

Tucker is known to be a bad character and has threatened the life of more than one of our citizens.

While many of our citizens do not favor lynch law and would prefer to allow the law to take its course, in this case they say well done. — Sun.

The old E. B. Dean store as it appeared in 1907 when Ekblad & Son opened business there. Note the hitching rack in the foreground.

Figure 41: E.B. Dean Store - *Coos Bay Times,* June 28, 1944

October 10, 1902 the *Myrtle Point Enterprise* printed three more articles regarding the Tucker lynching. Headline: **More About that Marshfield Lynching.**

From the Florence West: Further information concerning the lynching of the negro Tucker at Marshfield recently, serves to emphasize the fact that many people are anxious to see others punished for wrong-doing, though they themselves may be guilty of similar or even worse crimes. Some of the parties connected with that disgraceful affair are well known in this vicinity and bear most unenviable reputations. The woman in the case, Mrs. Dennis so called, is said to be a former resident of Acme, who having become infatuated with another man, last winter deserted a respectable husband and son, and taking their three younger children, went to Marshfield to join in her paramour and assumed his name. The man, Ben Dennis a member of the mob, is the despicable wretch who broke up the family and induced the woman to leave her husband and live with him, in open violation of the law. We are informed that before he left Acme last winter, he received intimation that if he wished to avoid punishment for his misconduct he had better make himself scarce. Now he poses as the champion of the woman and incites the mob to punish the negro for conduct no worse than his own. The people of Marshfield will make grievous error if they permit this wretch to escape without severe punishment. Were it not that we are strongly opposed to mob law we would say that he deserves the same fate as the negro.

(To spare the feelings of the woman's relatives, who are highly respectable people, we refrain from mentioning her real name in the above article.)

Second: Gardiner correspondent to the West: The recent lynching of a negro at Marshfield is another proof that there is no North, no South, no East and no West. The negro charged with a certain offense must go. We wonder if many are as unjustly murdered as was this poor fellow. Something could be said that would so mitigate his alleged crime as to brand his self appointed executioner as well, we might say reckless citizens. Some of us know a thing or two that would throw a different light upon this matter, we think the sheriff of Coos county wants something to base an action for murder upon the lynchers, he can get enlightened by coming this way, unless we have been misinformed. Mob law is usually dangerous remedy for the ills of society. This case should be investigated.

Third: A mysterious visitor who is in Portland has caused considerable excitement among the colored population. It is claimed that he has for his purpose the banding of colored men, all over the United States, whose object is to declare war unless the government shall give them better protection in the South. When the war is declared, Coos bay, the scene of a recent negro lynching, will probably be swiped off the face of the earth.

The final article regarding the lynching of Tucker by the *Myrtle Point Enterprise* is, unfortunately, incomplete. The paper was torn with a good portion of the article now lost to history. Here is the portion that survived: **THE BRAYING DONKEY. Headless Editor off His Trolley Again.**

The Coast Mail has gone wild because the ENTERPRISE published an article from the Florence West, last week, regarding the recent lynching at Marshfield. We have never said the negro was innocent, certainly there is reason to doubt his guilt. Of all the asses that have ever met the Coast Mail … them ah. The idiot should keep its head shut and attend to its own business. We published the article because we are running a newspaper and knew it would be of general interest. The assertion by the Mail that it was on account of the Coquille Valley's jealousy toward the Bay is too silly for even a consideration, and tends to show what kind of stuff the headless editor is made of. The trouble is the Coast Mail didn't have the sand to criticize the mob. The Oregonian and other papers have criticized it more severely than the ENTERPRISE … but the Mail seems to be after *(missing text)* in particular. The Mail says the ENTERPRISE is a Coos county paper and should have some care for the reputation of the county — indeed we have.

This is the reason we do not endorse that lynching, and would like to see the matter investigated. If we are permitted to have such occurrences in the county, then we do not want this reputation. We are here to discourage lawlessness and…" *(This was perhaps just over half the article.)*

October 18, 1902 the *Coast Mail* headlined: **GIVE US A REST**

The *Myrtle Point Enterprise* copies from the *Florence West* abusive song and dance about the woman, for outraging whom the Negro Tucker, recently met a richly deserved fate here in Marshfield. Coupled with condemnation of the woman is a still more abusive attack on the man Dennis. The animus of the article is a desire to show that the negro was presumably innocent and that a lawless mob perpetrated in the streets of Marshfield the blood-thirsty and unprovoked murder of a defenseless human being, whose only offense was his color.

Nothing could be further from the truth. Of the negro's guilt, there was ample evidence, and not the slightest doubt exists amongst those best acquainted with the facts. All that the West has to say is entirely beside the question. Even if it all be true, which the MAIL doubt, it does not in the least effect the question of the negro's guilt, the evidence of which did not lie in the unsupported word of the woman, but in indisputable corroborative circumstances. The negro was guilty, and he got exactly what he deserved. The MAIL's protest against lynching him, at the time, was based on other grounds.

The *West* is, perhaps, excusable for slopping over, as it is some distance from the scene and is not directly interested in the good name of Coos Bay. With the *Myrtle Point Enterprise* the case is somewhat different. The *Enterprise* is a Coos county paper and one would expect it to have some care or the reputation of Coos county. It is said to be an ill bird that defiles its own nest. Perhaps, however, the senatorial journey, which is not entirely absent from the office of the Enterprise. has carried it off its feet in this case, to the extent of giving needless publicity to the senseless creed of the West, which can do no possible good and may do harm among those not acquainted with the to facts. Very likely the Enterprise itself is numbered among the last named, for we are constrained to remember that, two days after the tragedy here, a day after it had a correct and circumstantial account in the Daily, a day after the Coquille Bulletin had published one nearly as complete, the Enterprise gave to the wondering light the following account of the manner of the negro's death.

"The negro was being pursued by the mob and ran to the second story of a building locking himself in one of the rooms. The mob broke the door down, riddled him with bullets, and then threw him out of the window on to the street below, later taking the body to the scene where the outrage was committed and hanging it to a bridge."

This matter should be allowed to rest. The black beast, who met a much easier death than he deserved, was unquestionably guilty. The circumstances surrounding his death were such that endless, useless and expensive complications with the law were happily averted. Now let the matter alone.

September 21, 1974 Coos Bay newspaper *The World* published the following article regarding interviews of the last surving witnesses of the tucker lynching. Headline: **Oldtimers recall a tragic incident— Libby miners lynch Marshfield Negro in 1903** By DINAH ADKINS, Staff Writer

In 1903, Libby miners lynched a Marshfield Negro, bootblack[V] and prize-fighter known only as "Tucker." The incident, resulting in the rapid exodux of the many blacks working at that time in the Beaver Hill and Libby mines, is rarely spoken of and remembered by only a few aging residents of the Bay Area.

As told by eyewitnesses, the story of Tucker and his executioners is a tragedy that teaches well the real passions that motivated the real men who have since become faded caricatures of history.

The hands that raised the timbers that built Coos Bay and other pioneer communities were the hands of a legion of nameless and faceless men who were sometimes decent, courageous and inspired, even heroic, and were also at times ignorant and vicious. The history of Coos Bay, like the history of mankind in general, is complex and sometimes tragic.

Harry Walker looked out the window to the new buildings and highways glistening in the sun. The physical aspect of the city had been transformed almost beyond belief since Harry was a child. And Harry was a very old man. He would celebrate his 86th birthday during the year of the centennial. The history of Coos Bay was in part the personal history of Harry Walker.

Harry's friends who were sitting with him, Martin Steckel, (now dead) and Oscar Gulovsen, were equally old men — Oscar was the same age and Martin only two years younger.

Harry addressed himself to the conversation: "When that Negro was lynched up there—he was a Marshfield Negro but the Libby men was the ones that lynched him — the Negroes pulled out. They was afraid, scared, and left. And there were not very many ever came back any more."

[V] A person who cleans and polishes shoes for a living.

"I know when I was a kid in Marshfield the Negroes used to come down from Libby and play baseball with us and one thing and another. But after Tucker was lynched, why, the Negroes all left. I guess there were some Negroes in Beaver Hill, but I don't know very much about them."

Martin intervened: "There was more in Beaver Hill than to Libby." Guess so "Yeah, I guess so, yeah," said Harry. "I wasn't acquainted much with Beaver Hill because it was too far away. Beaver Hill was a long ways off in those days. Libby, we could walk up there in a couple hours, in an hour — three miles away from Marshfield."

Martin reflected on his friend's comments. The memory of Tucker was a disquieting one: "I was not over 20 feet from Tucker when they shot him. I was about seven years old," he said. "They accused him of assaulting a woman."

"Yeah," said Harry, "assaulting a woman, attacking a woman."

"But I don't believe he ever did," continued Martin.

"No," said Harry, "they claimed he was an innocent man."

Harry sensed a good story, and being a born storyteller he became expansive with the knowledge of the excellence of his story, and his voice took on the rhythm of the experienced raconteur.

"Well, I'll tell ya now," he opened his narration. "I remember that and so does Oscar. Tucker was a Negro. He was a prizefighter and a bootblack there in town, Well, he'd run every day for his exercise from Marshfield towards Libby. They lynched him. They claimed that he was a 'rapin' a woman... Well, I'll tell you what I heard, now. I think Oscar heard the same. He was an innocent man. He'd run up there and he'd meet her up there at a certain place—somewhere at the side of the old cemetery on down there somewhere."

On his back "You see," Oscar broke the fluidity of the narration. "This Tucker for exercise carried the mail on his back between Marshfield and Libby ... and he just had a packsack. It wasn't much mail. And so that's the way he got paid. He was a beautiful looking Negro, a well built man. He operated a gymnasium there."

Harry picked up his thread again: "And Dr. Tower was the a doctor at Libby, the company doctor. Well," he paused, "they'd been out in the brush and they come back onto the road, and Dr. Tower came with his horse and his buggy to go on to Libby. And she saw she was caught, so to clear her skirts, she claimed he attacked her. She was some woman lived in Libby. I've forgotten her name."

Locked him up.

"They arrested him — Tucker. Carter locked him up in jail. And that evening, I remember that well, us kids was a 'playin' downtown and I was up on Broadway right in behind the Eldorado store, that brick building there on Front Street — Wyatt's store, right there. And right down there at the corner of Central and Broadway was an arc electric light. And we heard they was agoin' to lynch 'im — the miners from Libby was agoin' to lynch 'im." "Well, I remember running up there, I was a'playin' then. And I looked down toward the electric light and here they came. They was down a little further than the arc light, a little bit... And they were marching four abreast with Winchester rifles. I don't know how many of 'em. It was like a young army. I made a run for that brick building that's down on Front Street now. Magnusen and Matsen had a store in there and Jim Hutchinson was clerkin' in there and I run down there and told Jim. I said, That mob's a'comin'.' 'Oh,' he said, 'you're crazy!' I can hear him say it as well as I'm talkin' to you. 'Well,' I says, 'I'm not crazy. There they are marching right by there now."

In a group. "No!" Oscar exclaimed, "excuse me for interruptin' ya. No, no! I happened to be right there. They came marchin', in a group. Then the first four of 'em went to the foot of Hall Avenue. That was the railroad then, and they put four of 'em there. Then, at the foot of Anderson and the foot of Curtis Avenue — they put two more men. Then they went on down the dock, all the way down to the port dock, they had these men scattered, and all of 'em with rifles."

"Well, I was there too!" Harry exclaimed and shifted angrily in his chair. "I know what happened!"

"Anyway," he continued, "Jack Carter, he heard about it and he took Tucker out of jail — with the intentions of takin' him to Eastside and gettin' him to Roseburg. And there's a slip down off 'a the jail a bit, that they called the brewery slip. And they took him down there with the intentions of puttin ' him in a boat and takin' him across the bay."

"You see," Oscar interrupted again, "there was a pier that came out from the north end of Eastside, out there. And there was a stable on the end of that pier. That was where the mail that came from Roseburg by stage came. And then, you see, they used to row — put it in a rowboat — and row it right across. And the post office was down where Fergusen Transfer Cos. is."

"So they were goin' (to go) across there. And they were goin' to take him to Eastside, and Sumner and over to Fairview and to Coquille and put him in jail. .."

"No boat"

"But they was no boat there," Harry insisted. "And Tucker was a big husky man, and they was squatted down there in the dark while this gang come in an alleyway between the city hall and another building."

"And old John Sutherland was there. And he stopped 'em — he was guard. He had a big six-shooter about that long and he stopped 'em. And the fellas in the back ranks went around the other way — come in from behind. And they come around the other way and come in around to the brewery slip and looked right down there and saw Tucker."

"And of course, Tucker then jumped away from Carter. He was a big, powerful man. And he just jumped right out of Jack Carter's arms and jumped in under the dock. There was lots of mud there and lots of rock in there in those days. . .from ships that brought in rocks from Frisco for ballast. And they couldn't track him. They tracked 'em a little ways in the mud there...." Harry paused and shifted his weight again.

Oscar looked up from his lap. "And that night was a beautiful moonlit night. And here, oh round midnight there' was a rowboat floating down on the east side of the bay. The tide was going out. And boy! That boat was just riddled. They thought Tucker was pushin' that boat."

"Under the dock 'And the next morning. Oh, along about 10 o'clock, they got these two boys, my brother Madoc and Dr. Prentiss, he was a dentist, his son. And they got I these boys to go down. And they went under the dock. And they ran into him. You see, he worked his way up two blocks and a half to Commercial Avenue. And that's where they ran into him. And he ran after 'em, of course."

"And they came back up the same place they went in. It wasn't big enough for him to follow them up. So he came out just south — oh, a hundred feet south of what would be normally the foot of Central Avenue. There was an opening there. And there were two men sittin' there with their rifles across their legs. And when he came out, they shot him just as he turned north on Front Street."

"And they got him in the hip. He ran into the mill store."

Harry broke in: "And Tucker run right down Front Street. And every step he took there was a gush of blood came out. They cut a big artery."

"And he run into Merchant's store and upstairs. And he went down. And they lowered him out and put him on one of these grocery trucks and were goin' to wheel him out to the place of the scene and hang 'em. But he died before they got there and they hung 'em on the Seventh Street bridge. But he was dead when they hung 'em."

Martin broke his long silence: "When the kid ran up the steps and shot em, he wasn't any further than across this room from me."

"Yeah," Harry said, "You was there and that's when Bill Merchant dragged you outa there."

"Yeah, he drug me into the store," explained Martin, "and I went in and went onta the stairway. And Tucker came in the little, door right up the stairway. I run up purt near the top, and he came in there. And the blood was just flyin'. And he said as he come in the door, I'll never forget him, he said, 'Lord have mercy on a colored man.'"

"And they'd shot the arteries off, and the blood was just flyin'. You know, it don't do anything to make a kid brave. And of course he run right up above me and he fell. And after he fell, some kid come up there with a damn little .22 and shot him while he was layin' there."

"I thought some fella shot him in the ribs with a pistol," said Harry.

"That's what it was... a young kid ____" Martin lapsed again into thoughtful silence.

Oscar spoke up during the pause: "They lowered him with a rope from there and put him on a handcart. And tied him fast to that. And then they took him and went up Front Street to Central Avenue, and from Central Avenue to Fourth, and then from Fourth Street on out, just about a hundred feet this side of Elrod Avenue. It was a hill up there and it was a plank street and those planks were rough. And here was this fellow... I don't remember whether his head was on the foot of it or …."

Oscar faltered. Harry recalled the sight, "His head," said Harry, "was laying across that iron bar on the front end of the truck. His head was laying on that and he was gaspin', dyin' while they went on." He stopped.

Out Elrod Avenue.

"Then they went out Elrod Avenue," said Oscar, marking the streets carefully in his — memory. "It was a rock street, The rocks for that street were from Telegraph Hill from San Francisco. The way they got here was they were used for ballast on the old sailing vessels. And there was a bridge across where Golden Field for the high school is now. Right across there was an elevated bridge. And that's where they hung him."

"But he was dead when they hung 'em," Harry insisted. "Dr. McCormac stood down below and told us. They tied a rope around his neck and kicked him off the bridge. Dr. McCormac was down on the marsh there." And he said, "That man was dead when you hung 'im," he said. And he was dead when they hung 'im. He bled to death.

The old men paused for a minute. The corners of the room filled with silence and passions aroused by vivid memories.

"About the woman, I think he was an innocent man all the way," said Martin. "I had a sister lived in Libby. Used to, to go to Libby, you had to walk those big high trestles. And mother wouldn't let us. And we were goin' up there to visit our sister in a boat. And right where he was supposed to have attacked that woman he was joggin'. I guess that's what you'd call it, you know kinda hop, skip. He was trainin' for a fight and he had one of these little Fourth of July canes."

"And we were right down in there at old Eastport. And he was supposed to have attacked her right up on top that hill there."

"Yeah," said Harry, "between Eastport and here and the old cemetery."

"Yes." Martin nodded, "and he was comin' along there and he was twirlin' this cane and a joggin' and he was trainin' fer a fight at that time. And I don't know what the score was, but I don't think that he had attacked any woman...." "No! No!" Harry exclaimed. "... And just come on," said Martin, "as nonchalant as he was. He didn't seem to have a worry in the world. He just come over the hill there and down in sight of us and they made up that mob and never asked any questions. She left the country right away afterwards."

(This story is actually an adaption of two separate tapes, one made of a conversation between Harry Walker and Martin Steckel in 1972, and the other made this year during a conversation between Oscar Gulovsen and Harry Walker.)

THE CORONER'S INQUEST

September 18, 1902 Coroner W. Horsfall empanelled a juror and conducted an inquest to the death of Alonzo Tucker. The post mortem examination was conducted by Doctor A.G. Gross, who received $50 for his services. The county file contained three documents; the hand-written inquest findings, a hand-written bill from Dr. Horsfall for the inquest and associated fees, and the typed transcript of witness statements.

First presented is the official finding of the Coroner's Jury:

IN THE MATTER OF THE INQUEST on the body of Alonzo Tucker deceased, held at Marshfield, Coos County, Oregon.

We, the undersigned jurors, sworn to inquire the death of Alonzo Tucker on oath do find that the person killed and upon whom this inquest is held one Alonzo Tucker; that he came to his death by a gun shot wound in the thigh, inflicted on the 18th day of September, A.D. 1902, at Marshfield, Coos County, Oregon, while attempting to escape arrest for a felony; that the wound was inflicted by parties unknown to this jury, and that no crime was committed thereby.

The document was then signed by the following members of the jury: W.B. Curtis, Foreman, R. Walter, Archie Kruse, John W. Flanagan, A.B. Prentis, and Chas. Stauff. Each juror was paid one dollar for their services.

Witnesses examined were Doctor J. T. McCormac, E. Henchendorff, A.G. Aiken, John Merchant, Marshal J.W. Carter, and Doctor A.G. Gross. Each witness received a one dollar and fifty cents for their testimony. The following is their typed statements:

Examination of witnesses:

Dr McCormac was then called as a witness and after being duly sworn testified as follows:

Q. 1. Doctor will you please tell the jury whether or not you examined Alonzo Tucker between the time he was shot and the time he was put down from the bridge at south Marshfield?

A. Well I arrived at the bridge about 22 minutes of ten and Tucker's body was then laying on the bridge, and I was some little distance from him, and a crowd was around the body, and in about a minute from the time arrived there a rope was about his neck, or one end was fastened around his neck, and the other around a plank, and there was about six feet of slack, and then he was pushed off and rolled over by parties standing on the bridge. He just dropped from the bridge, and I was standing right close by, and could see that he was dead. He never heaved, his muscles never moved, and his eyes were closed. He never showed any signs of life.

Q. 2 Then from your examination doctor you are confident he was dead before the time they rolled him off the bridge?

A. I am positive he was dead when he was rolled over the bridge.

Mr. A.G. Aiken was then called as a witness and after being duly sworn testified as follows:

Q. 1. Mr. Aiken you may state to the Jury whether or not you were at or near Dean & Co.'s store on Front street in this town about ten o'clock this morning when one Alonzo Tucker was shot.

A. I was standing near the post office and I heard a shot over towards the ship yard, and I looked around and this darkey was coming pretty fast, and I thought he was wounded, and I ran across to head him off, and then I thought may be they would shoot at him again. He stopped short a minute and got inside Dean & Co.'s store. I ran to the floor. I ran to the door, and he dodged to the left hand door and ran behind the first counter into the warehouse at the store, and I ran into their store in order to head him off at that end, and then he dodged into the store at the foot of the stairs and ran up the stairs.

Q. 2. You may state to the jury whether or not you saw the person or persons who shot at this Tucker?

A. I do not know. I did not see any person. I saw the person fire the first shot and there was a shot fired afterwards. I stood at the foot of the steps looking on. There was a shot fired behind me but I do not know who shot it. There was quite a crowd.

Q. 3. You may state to the jury whether or not you knew at that time that this Tucker was a fugitive from justice?

A. That is what I understood. Yes that he was a fugitive from justice at that time.

Capt. Hykendorf was then called as a witness and after being duly sworn testified as follows:

Q. 1. You may state whether or not you were at or near Dean & Company's store this morning on Front street when Alonzo Tucker was shot?

A. I did not see Tucker get shot I was over in the shipyard when I heard the shooting, and when I came over there he was lying on

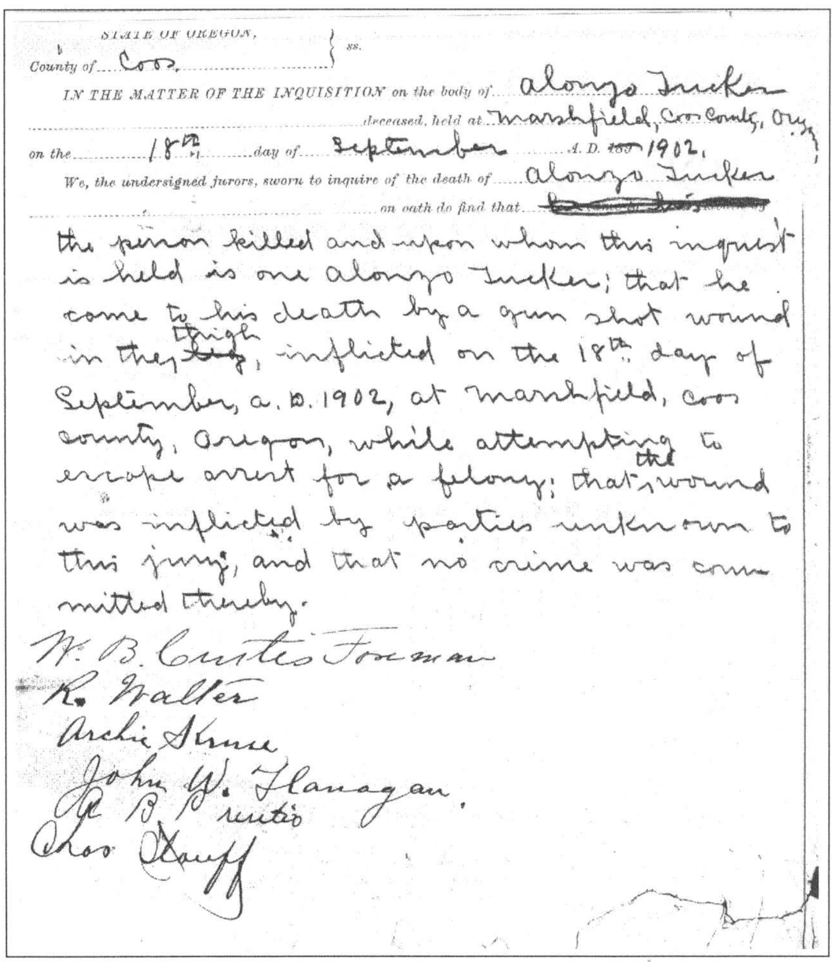

STATE OF OREGON, } ss.
County of Coos }

IN THE MATTER OF THE INQUISITION on the body of Alonzo Tucker deceased, held at Marshfield, Coos County, Org on the 18th day of September A. D. 1902,

We, the undersigned jurors, sworn to inquire of the death of Alonzo Tucker on oath do find that the person killed and upon whom this inquest is held is one Alonzo Tucker; that he came to his death by a gun shot wound in the thigh, inflicted on the 18th day of September, A. D. 1902, at Marshfield, Coos county, Oregon, while attempting to escape arrest for a felony; that the wound was inflicted by parties unknown to this jury, and that no crime was committed thereby.

W. B. Curtis Foreman
R. Walter
Archie Kruse
John W. Flanagan
R. B. Curtis
Chas Stauff

Figure 42: Coroner's Inquest Findings

the floor bleeding.

Q. 2. You did not see who shot him?

A. No. I did not see who it was I was over in the shipyard, and when I got to the store he was up-stairs bleeding from the wound.

Q. 3. Did he show any evidence of life when you saw him up there?

A. He was bleeding there when I saw him. That was about all I could see.

Q. 4. Did he appear to be alive?

A. He appeared to me to be more dead than alive.

Q. 5. I will ask you Mr. Hykendorf whether or not you helped to lower the body of this Tucker from the store window down to the ground?

A. Yes. I did.

Q. 6. What was his condition as to being alive?

A. Well I could not tell you whether he was dead or alive. It looked to me he was more dead than alive.

Q. 7. Was he breathing?

A. Yes I think he was I rather think he was.

Q. 8. Did he make any effort to help himself at all?

A. No.

J. W. Carter was then called as a witness and after being duly sworn testified as follows:

Q. 1. Mr. Carter you may state to the jury whether or not on the 17th day of September 1902 at Marshfield Coos County, Oregon, you arrested one Alonzo Tucker?

A. Yes sir.

Q. 2. You may state on what charge?

A. I arrested him on the charge of rape.

Q. 3. You may state what you did with the prisoner.

A. I locked him up in the City jail.

Q. 4. You may state whether you have him still in jail, and if not what has become of him?

A. Last night there was said to be quite a crowd coming about half past seven, I am guessing at this, there was about 150 to 200 people coming there, when they was coming it occurred to me that may be I could take him out of the jail. It was all done in less than a moment, and I calculated that I could, get him out of there on a boat so that we could take him to Coquille City or somewhere away from the mob. While we was doing this the crowd was right on hand, and we started to get into the boat, but just then he broke away from me and jumped into the bay or "rather" under the wharf and got away.

Q. 5. You may state whether, or not you made any efforts to recapture him?

A. I did.

Q. 6. You may state where you saw the prisoner next.

A. I saw him about ten o'clock this morning coming around by the shipyard near Merchant's warehouse running. I was after him trying to capture him.

Q. 7. Did you ask him to stop?

A. I hollered to him to stop, and then someone fired a shot. I did not know if he was hit. He back way, and I ran into Mr. Aiken at the door, said I asked him where he was and he said he was in here and we looked in the store room, and also in the storeage room then I thought we better step inside, and some one hollered he was up stairs Mr. Aiken stayed down stairs or outside, and I ran up stairs and found him lying on the floor. After you get up stairs there is a little over four feet space and he had fallen down there. He seemed to be dead. By this time the crowd was there and I said boys keep quiet and I will go and get the coroner and I then went down to Sengstacken's store to get the coroner but he was not there, so I telephoned to his house, and his wife answered that he was not home, but was around town somewheres, then I went to hunt for the deputy district attorney, and when I went back the nigger was disappeared from there.

Q. 9. You may state whether or not Tucker was alive when you found him lying at the head of the stairs, or in what condition was he?

A. Well he had some life in him, but he seemed to be just about gone I could see him move his hands, he was lying on his back.

Q. 10. You may state Mr. Carter when you say this Tucker running down near the shipyard whether or not you called upon any person or persons to help you?

A I hollered to some parties standing near by to be careful about shooting down Front street as you might kill some innocent man, and then some one shot and hit him. It was all done that quick.

Q. 11. Did you call upon any of the byestanders to help you arrest him?

A. Yes I did. I called upon quite a number. I called upon a good many parties to help me to hunt for him and I had men stationed down there and up there at Merchants store and all around, and I was tired and wore out, and during the excitement I was petered out, and at that time about ten or eleven o'clock. I stationed some men right back here at this wharf, and some at Christensen & Johnsons, and I cautioned them and told them not to shoot any one until they spoke to them and told them they was to hunt for Tucker and they said they would.

Q. 12. State Mr. Carter whether or not you know who the persons were who shot this man Tucker?

A. I do not know, when the first shot was fired it called my attention I was on C. street right back of the Garfield, I started to go on under there, and some parties called me away from there, and I stood out on the street and was standing there when this shot was fired, and then I seen this man Tucker turn this corner. I hollered to them to be careful about shooting on the street, he was running then towards Front Street I ran and he want into the company's store and I ran to back way and ran into Mr. Aiken, he said he was in here, then some one said he was upstairs.

Q. 13. Mr. Aiken and these other persons were trying to help you to capture this man Tucker?

A. Yes they was.

John Merchant was then called as a witness and after being duly sworn testified as follows:

Q. 1. You may state Mr. Merchant to the jury where you are employed.

A. Dean & company's store

Q. 2. In this City?

A. Yes sir.

Q. 3. You state whether or not you were in the store about ten o'clock this morning when one Alonzo Tucker ran in there.

A. I was in the warehouse.

Q. 4. Did you see this man Tucker when he came in?

A. No. I saw him as they were taking him out.

Q. 5. Did he appear to have any signs of life?

A. I did not notice I just glanced at him.

Q. 6. From what you saw did he appear to be dead?

A. I did not notice particularly. I just glanced at him.

Dr. A.G. Gross was then called as a witness and after being duly sworn testified as follows:

Q. 1. What is your occupation?

A. Physician.

Q. 2. You may state Dr. whether or not you performed, a postmortem examination upon the body of Alonzo Tucker, and doctor you may state to the jury the result of that examination?

A. We examined the body, and after taking the clothes off we noticed a great deal of effused blood, and after the body was nude we examined him, and we found a bullet one in the thigh about the middle of the upper third, also found where it got out at the posterior circuit, also found a bullet went one and a half inches along the actionary line about the 6th rib. The muscles of the neck on the right side appeared as if they were almost severed or badly mashed, no doubt due to the rope. We then cut down on the one on the thigh and followed the course of the bullet and found the large blood vessels almost severed not entirely but almost severed, and we then cut down on the one on thorax external surface and there found that the course of the bullet ran a little upward, and found the bullet embedded in the fourth rib, and that the rib was fractured. That is about all.

Q. 2. You may state doctor to the jury whether or not, the wounds inflicted upon this man Tucker were in your opinion sufficient to cause his death?

A. I do.

Q. 4. You may state Doctor how long in your opinion this man would have lived after receiving the wound?

A. Well I do not think he could possibly have lived over ten minutes, Hardly that of course it would depend whether or not the wound was blocked up by his clothing. We did not see much angulation. It seemed to have free current to come out.

Q. 5. Then you think Doctor from the examination of the wound that he could not have lived at most more than ten minutes after receiving it.

A. Not more than ten minutes hardly that.

September 20, 1902 the *Coast Mail* reported: The body of Tucker, the Negro, was buried yesterday in the old cemetery west of town.

March 16, 1920 the *Southwestern Oregon Daily News* headlined: OLD CEMETERY TO BE VACATED NEXT — SECOND STEP TOWARD OBTAINING THE $100,000 HOSPITAL WHICH SISTERS OF MERCY OFFICER TO ERECT ON HILL WAS TAKEN AT THE COUNCIL MEETING LAST EVENING

> An ordinance passed by the city council last night declared the use of the plot of ground known as the "old cemetery," be abandoned as a cemetery and ordered the removal bodies of persons interred there by relatives or by the city, and a second ordinance directed the proper officers of the city deed, in the name of the city, the old cemetery property, to the corporation of Sisters of Mercy or such other persons who will build thereon a modern fireproof hospital, costing not less than $100,000, and who will care for the city indigents at a reduced rate and provided for other terms and conditions of the transaction.

No known records exist revealing where the remains of Tucker were moved to or by whom. Even the exact location of the cemetery is unknown. Different historical sources point to different locations. It is unknown if the "old cemetery" is the one historically known as the "Chinese" or Telegraph Hill cemetery. The Telegraph Hill cemetery was used from 1875 to 1915 and located on what is now N. 5th Street off W. Commercial Street. The Chinese remains were sent to China circa 1916 and the non-Chinese were interred at the I.O.O.F. cemetery. [W] The March 1897 Sanborn Map[74] noted, "HILL to be cemetery" on the north side of "A" Street, now Commercial Street, at 6th

Figure 43: South Marshfield (7th Street) Bridge - Photo Courtesy of Alda Hofferber

[23] Founded in 1867 by D. A. Sanborn, the Sanborn Map Company was the primary American publisher of fire insurance maps.

street. The Wesley Hospital was built on the north side of Commercial Street between 7th and 8th streets. According to an exhibit at the Coos Historical & Maritime Museum, Wesley Hospital was funded from the Methodist Board of National missions. Due to the Great Depression the hospital was sold to the Catholic's who operated the hospital under the name of McAuley. The building has not housed a hospital since 1974, but still remains. Even abandoned and forgotten the building is still a key historical location.

Even with the official finding as to the cause of death regarding Alonzo Tucker there are many myths which linger to this day. The consensus of today's citizens that the whole incident was a tragedy and an unfortunate set of circumstances that anyone of any ethnicity could so brutally be treated for a crime that may have not even been committed. The whole affair is not one that the citizens are proud to have within their history books.

THE SOCIAL AFFECTS OF THE LYNCHING

On September 20, 1902 the *Coast Mail* headlined: **Run Them Out**

There was strong talk last evening of running all the Negroes out of Libby and out of the country. Against this the MAIL would have not a word to say.

An ounce of prevention is worth a pound of cure, and while the lynching of one nigger would not repair the damage that he has wrought, the removal of entire colored population would let us all rest easier when our wives are alone.

September 27, 1902 the *Coast Mail* headlined: **COLORED POPULATION QUIETY GOING AWAY**

The colored population of Marshfield and Libby is quietly disappearing. It does not seem that they have received any imperative orders to leave, though there has been much talk in that direction, and they have probably had hints that they would go. They seem to have taken the sensible view the heinous crime of Tucker and the events following had naturally aroused a great of feelings against their race, and that the best thing they could do would be to go away peaceably and quietly from the community where they are evidently not wanted.

The exodus commenced Friday and still continues, that most of the negros starting out over the Coos Bay wagon road. It is understood they will go north from Roseburg and the women and children will follow on the next Alliance. This is a satisfactory solution of the situation, and the colored people are to be commended for their good sense in accepting the inevitable without useless resistance.

It is said that a few declare their intention of remaining, but they will probably think the latter of it.

CHAPTER 18

BEYOND THE GALLOWS - EXECUTION IN OREGON

For the State of Oregon, hanging as the method of execution continued up to October 30, 1931. After which, the state began using lethal gas as the approved method for executions. There were a total of eighteen gas-chamber executions in the state with the last occurring in 1962.

On November 3, 1964, Oregon voters repealed the death penalty by 60 percent of the vote. Upon repealing the death penalty on November 5, 1964 Republican Governor Mark O. Hatfield commuted the death sentences of three people. The repeal process remained in effect until 1978, when Oregon voters once again reinstituted capital punishment with Ballot Measure 8 with 64 percent of the vote. Unlike prior death penalty laws, Measure 8 did not amend the Oregon Constitution, but rather incorporated capital punishment into the Oregon Revised Statutes, thereby amending Oregon Revised Statutes (ORS) 163.115 and creating ORS 163.116. Under the death penalty statute the sentence was determined by the trial judge, without a jury.

However, in 1981, the Oregon Supreme Court struck down the death penalty statute asserting the state law deprived the defendant of the right to trial by jury. Responding to the decision of the Supreme Court the Oregon voters once again went to the ballot. In 1984, Oregon voters approved Ballot Measure 6 creating Article I, 40 and exempted capital punishment from Article I, 15-16 of the Oregon Constitution. This measure passed with 55 percent of the vote. Additionally, Ballot Measure 7 amended ORS 163.150 to require that, following a conviction for aggravated murder, a defendant be given a separate sentencing hearing before the trial jury. This measure passed with 75 percent of the vote.

With the creation of the new law, Aggravated Murder was defined by ORS 163.095. In general, murder becomes aggravated murder if it was a murder for hire; there was more than one victim; torture was involved; the victim was a criminal justice professional, a juror or a witness; the defendant was in custody or a fugitive when the murder occurred; the defendant previously committed murder or manslaughter; the murder occurred during another felony act; the murder was committed to conceal a crime; or the murder was committed using explosives.

Pursuant to Measure 7, the jury at the sentencing hearing would determine whether:

1. The murder was deliberate;
2. Whether the defendant posed a continuing threat to society; and
3. Whether the defendant's acts were unreasonable in response to any provocation by the deceased.

The sentencing options available to the jury of an aggravated murder under ORS 163.105 were:

1. Death;
2. Life without the possibility of parole; and
3. Life imprisonment with a 30-year minimum.

Even though Oregon reinstated capital punishment in 1984, the state's first execution occurred 34 years later on September 6, 1996. The execution established the current method of execution by lethal injection occurring in the execution room at Oregon State Penitentiary in Salem.75

As of October 2007 two Coos county convicted murders sit on death row awaiting execution. David L. Simonsen, born January 27, 1968, convicted on two counts of Aggravated Murder, was sentenced February 27, 1989. Jeffrey R. Williams, born June 30, 1961, also convicted on two counts of aggravated murder was sentenced August 23, 1993. Both men, in 1988, murdered two German tourists; Kathrin Reith, age 22 and Unna Tuxen, age 24.

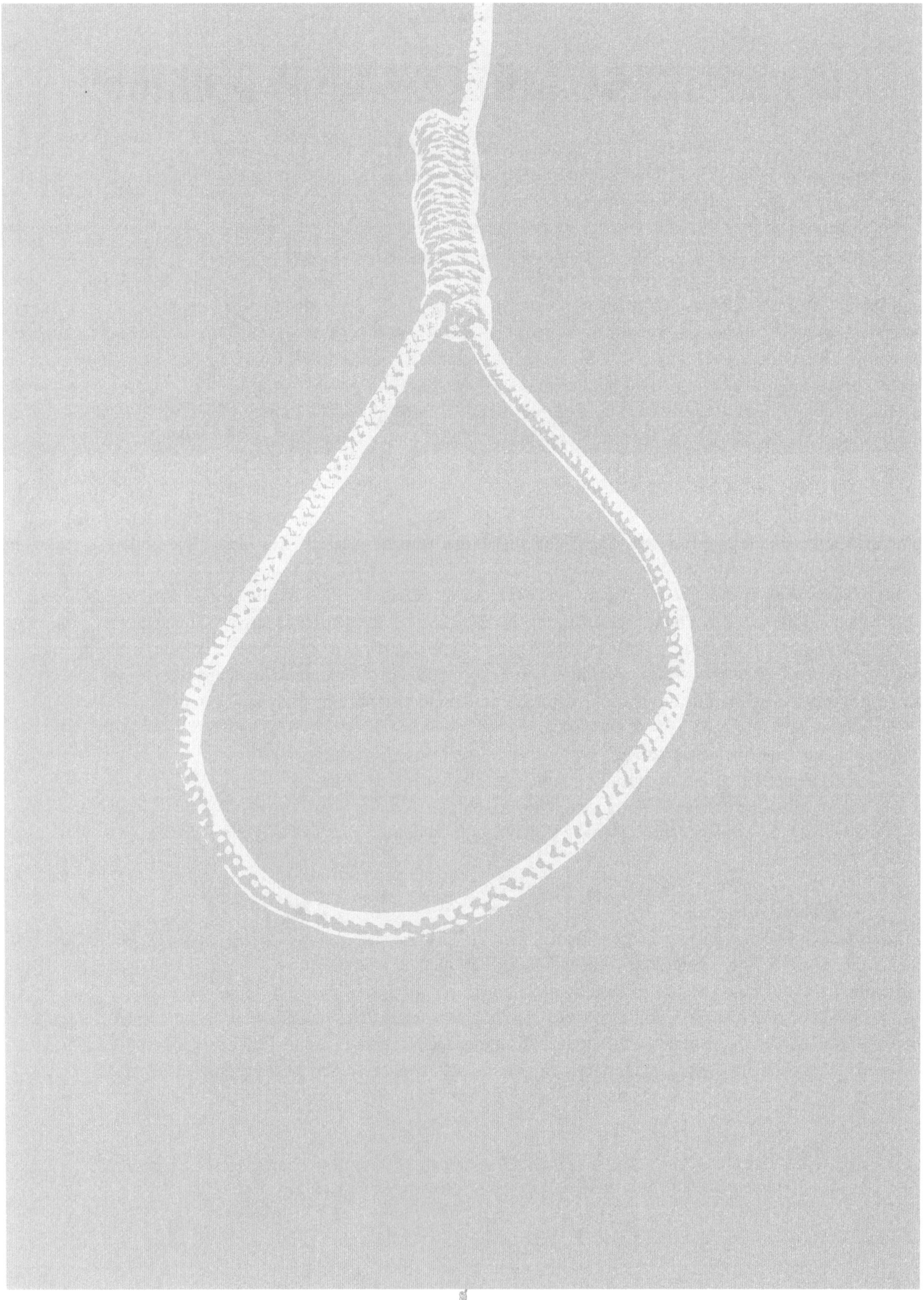

ENDNOTES

1 Oregon State Archives, "Oregon Messages and Documents, 1909-1910, Inaugural Message, Salem, Oregon, Willis S. Duniway, State Printer, 1911." http://arcweb.sos.state.or.us/governors/west/inaugural1911.html (accessed January 20, 2008).

2 Oregon Department of Corrections Public Affairs, "History of Capital Punishment in Oregon," http://www.oregon.gov /DOC/PUBAFF/cap_punishment/history.shtml (accessed March 14, 2008).

3 Before the Needles, "State Execution Totals," http://users.bestweb.net/~rg/execution/OREGON.htm (accessed March 14, 2008).

4 Long, William R., *A Tortured History: The Story of Capital Punishment in Oregon.* (Eugene: The Oregon Criminal Defense Lawyers Association, 2001), 24.

5 Wikipedia, the free encyclopedia, "Vigilance committee," http://en.wikipedia.org/wiki/Vigilance_committee (accessed March 8, 2008).

6 History is a Weapon, "Lynch Law," http://www.historyisaweapon.com/defcon1/wellslynchlaw.html(accessed March 8, 2008).

7 Wikipedia, the free encyclopedia, "Lynching," http://en.wikipedia.org/wiki/Lynching (accesssed March 8, 2008).

8 The Charles Chesnutt Digital Archive, "Lynchings, By State and Race, 1882-1968," http://faculty.berea.edu/browners/chesnutt/classroom/lynchings_table_state.html (accessed March 13, 2008).

9 *Coos County Courthouse 100 Years1896 – 1996* (Coquille: *Coquille Valley Sentinel*, 1996), 11.

10 Ibid., 11.

11 Dodge, Orvil, *Pioneer History of Coos and Curry Counties, Or.*, (Salem, Oregon: Capitol Printing Company,1898) ii.

12 Ross, Gordon, interviewed by author, Coos Bay, OR, January 28, 2008.

13 Dodge, *Pioneer History*,136

14 Peterson, Emil R. and Alfred Powers, *A Century of Coos and Curry*, (Coquille, Oregon: Coos-Curry Pioneer and Historical Association, 1952) 237.

15 Mark A. Tveskov, "A Most Horrid Massacre," in Jason Younker, Mark A. Tveskov and David G. Lewis, eds., *Changing Landscapes; "Telling Our Stories," Proceedings of the Fourth Annual Coquille Cultural Preservation Conference, 2000* (North Bend, Ore.: Coquille Indian Tribe, 2001), 63.

16 Ibid., 55.

17 Youst, Lionel and William R. Seaburg, *Coquelle Thompson, Athabaskan Witness: A Cultural Biography,* (Norman, Oklamoha: University Oklahoma Press, 2002) 31-32.

18 Sengstacken, Agnes, *Destination, West!*, (Portland, Oregon: Binfords & Mort Publishing, 1942) 152-155.

19 Youst and Seaburg, *Coquelle Thompson,* 33.

20 Ibid., 32.

21 Ibid., 33.

22 Rootsweb, "Hiram Hamilton LEWIS," *ID:* I9389, *Ancestral File #:* S7WC-V3, http://worldconnect.rootsweb.com/cgi-bin/igm.cgi?op=GET&db=wbh1963&id=I9389 (accessed January 18, 2008).

23 Rootsweb, "Sevier LEWIS," *ID:* I11685, *Ancestral File #:* 1477-JRH, http://worldconnect.rootsweb.com/cgi-bin/igm.cgi?op=GET&db=wbh1963&id=I11685 (accessed January 18, 2008).

[24] Rootsweb, "Sylvia Jane LEWIS," *ID:* I13920, http://worldconnect.rootsweb.com/cgi-in/igm.cgi?op =GET &db = wbh1963&id=I13920 (accessed January 18, 2008).

[25] Rootsweb, "Zachariah LEWIS," *ID:* I36031, http://worldconnect.rootsweb.com/cgi-in/igm.cgi?op =GET& db= w bh1963&id=I36031 (accessed January 18, 2008).

[26] Dodge, *Pioneer History,* 404-405.

[27] Rootsweb, "Lucy LEWIS," *ID:* I38712, http://worldconnect.rootsweb.com/cgi-bin/igm.cgi?op= GET&db= cvtre & id=I38712 (accessed January 19, 2008)

[28] Welch, George C., *Early Bandon and the Lower Coquille River,* (Glancing Back (Pioneer Lore): Coos-Curry Pioneer and Historical Association, June 1972) 8.

[29] Stone, Boyd, *Living in the Past Lane,* (Coquille, Oregon: The *Coquille Valley Sentinel*, 1993) 5.

[30] The Church of Jesus Christ of Latter Day Saints, "Individual Record, 1880 United States Census,Chris EATIONHOVER," http://www.familysearch.org/Eng/Search/census/individual_record.asp?INDI_CODE= 1880US _4409486_2&frompage=5 (accessed March 27, 2008).

[31] Stone, *Living in the Past Lane*, 5.

[32] Stone, Boyd, *Memories From Out Of The Past*, (Coquille, Oregon: The Coquille Valley Sentinel, 1999) 24.

[33] Ibid., 24.

[34] Ibid., 24.

[35] Hinch Family History, "Asaph H. HINCH," http://www.theladonnaproject.com/SamuelUrialAsaph.html (accessed January 19, 2008).

[36] Ibid., (accessed December 30, 2007)

[37] Dodge, *Pioneer History,* 433.

[38] Peterson and Powers, *A Century of Coos and Curry*, 510.

[39] Rootsweb, "Llewellyn Wilson (L.W.) PEARE ," http://worldconnect.rootsweb.com/cgi-bin/igm.cgi?op =GET &db=:438465&id=I22544066 *ID:* I22544066 (accessed February 2, 2008).

[40] Bandon Historical Society Museum archives, "The Astrologers Murder Mystery." *Oregonian*, October 20, 1935.

[41] Genealogical Forum of Oregon, "Draft Registration Lookup, WWI Registrations (1918)," Coos County reel 6, sequence 990 and 991.

[42] Bandon Historical Society Museum archives.

[43] Bandon Historical Society Museum Obituary File, "Mrs. Covell," *Western World*, September 6, 1923.

[44] Bandon Historical Society Museum archives *Western World*, December 18, 1996 page 14.

[45] Bandon Historical Society Museum Obituary File, *Western World* September 6, 1923.

[46] Ibid.

[47] Bandon Historical Society Museum Archives.

[48] Oregon State Penitentiary, Inmate Number 8861, Oregon Department of Corrections, Salem, Oregon.

[49] Bandon Historical Society Museum archives, Letter from Coos County Historian Boyd Stone, January 30,1997 with handwritten notes.

[50] Rootsweb, "Lizzie Gertrude TRIPP," ID: I6805 http://wc.rootsweb.ancestry.com/cgi-bin/igm.cgi ?op=GET&db = billbar&id=I6805 (accessed February 2, 2008).

[51] Byrd, Dean H. and Stanley R. Clark and Janice M. Healy, *Oregon Burial Site Guide,* (Portland, Oregon: Binfords & Mort Publishing, 2001)

BIBLIOGRAPHY

Byrd, Dean H. and Stanley R. Clark and Janice M. Healy, *Oregon Burial Site Guide,* Portland, Oregon: Binford & Mort Publishing, 2001.

Dodge, Orvil, *Pioneer History of Coos and Curry Counties,* ***Or.,*** Salem, Oregon: Capitol Printing Company, 1898.

Goeres-Gardner, Diane L., *Necktie Parties: A History of Legal Executions in Oregon, 1851-1905*, Caldwell, Idaho: Caxton Press, 2005.

Long, William R., *A Tortured History: The Story of Capital Punishment in Oregon,* Eugene, Oregon: The Oregon Criminal Defense Lawyers Association, 2001.

Peterson, Emil R. and Alfred Powers, *A Century of Coos and Curry*, Coquille, Oregon: Coos-Curry Pioneer and Historical Association, 1952.

Stone, Boyd, *Living in the Past Lane,* Coquille, Oregon: The Coquille Valley Sentinel, 1993.

__________, *Memories From Out Of The Past*, Coquille, Oregon: The Coquille Valley Sentinel, 1999.

Youst, Lionel and William R. Seaburg, *Coquelle Thompson , Athabaskan Witness: A Cultural Biography*, Norman, Oklahoma: University Oklahoma Press, 2002.

INDEX

D

E

T

U

V

W

Y

Z